HTML

in 10 Simple Steps or Less

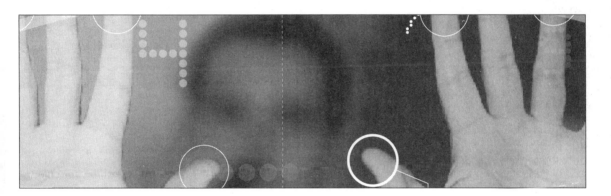

HTML
in 10 Simple Steps or Less

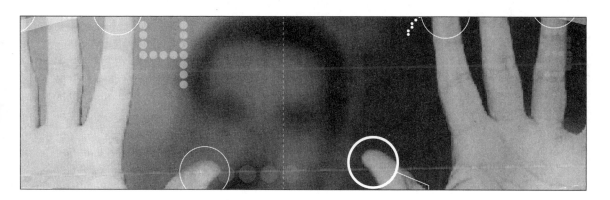

Robert G. Fuller and Laurie Ann Ulrich

WILEY

Wiley Publishing, Inc.

HTML in 10 Simple Steps or Less

Published by
Wiley Publishing, Inc.
10475 Crosspoint Boulevard
Indianapolis, IN 46256
www.wiley.com

Library of Congress Cataloging-in-Publication Data

Fuller, Robert, 1966-
  HTML in 10 simple steps or less / Robert Fuller and Laurie Ulrich.
    p. cm.
Includes index.
  ISBN 0-7645-4123-4
  1. HTML (Document markup language) I. Title: HTML in ten simple steps or
less. II. Ulrich, Laurie Ann. III. Title.
QA76.76.H94 F84 2003
006.7'4--dc22

                    2003020606

This book is dedicated to Mickey Kaigler.

He knows why . . .

Credits

Acquisitions Editor
Jim Minatel

Development Editor
Adaobi Obi Tulton

Technical Editor
Will Kelly

Copy Editor
Stefan Gruenwedel

Editorial Manager
Kathryn Malm

Vice President & Executive Group Publisher
Richard Swadley

Vice President and Executive Publisher
Robert Ipsen

Vice President and Publisher
Joseph B. Wikert

Executive Editorial Director
Mary Bednarek

Project Coordinator
April Farling

Graphics and Production Specialists
Joyce Haughey, Jennifer Heleine, LeAndra Hosier,
Lynsey Osborn, Heather Pope

Quality Control Technicians
John Greenough, Susan Moritz, Charles Spencer

Book Designer
Kathie S. Schnorr

Proofreader
Christine Pingleton

Indexer
Johnna VanHoose

About the Authors

Robert G. Fuller used to work in the Tech Sector of Corporate America. Realizing this was a big mistake, he left and began sharing what he knew with anyone who'd listen. He writes when the mood suits him, teaches wherever he can find students who are interested, and every now and again offers his skills to worthy causes. You can reach him at robert@highstrungproductions.com.

Laurie Ulrich is the author and coauthor of more than 25 books on computer software, with specific topics ranging from Office to Photoshop to Web Design. Teaching people to use computers since the 1980s, Laurie has taught more than 10,000 people to use their computers more creatively and with greater confidence. She also runs her own firm, Limehat & Company, Inc., offering general computer consulting and Web design services to growing companies and non-profit organizations. You can find out more about Laurie's books and other interests at www.planetlaurie.com.

Introduction

Welcome to *HTML in 10 Simple Steps or Less*. Our mission in writing this book is to provide a quick and accessible way for you to learn Hypertext Markup Language — the *lingua franca* of the World Wide Web. We hope this book provides a resource that beginning and intermediate HTML coders can use to improve their Web development skills. It is also our hope that it fills multiple roles as both a teaching tool and a reference once you expand your skills.

What This Book Is

Each part in this book pertains to a different aspect of HTML and Web production, and we devote each task within the parts to building a specific piece of Web page content. We've laid out these tasks in 10 steps or less so they're easy to internalize and become part of your personal skill set.

Who We Are and What We Know

Robert Fuller has an extensive background in Web development and design. He served as senior developer for Travelocity's Site59.com and takes his experience into the classroom — both live and online — every day. He believes that in order for new Web developers truly to flourish, they must gain a solid understanding of the Web's underlying language, HTML.

He has authored, coauthored, and contributed to several books about HTML, Web design, graphic software applications, and general computing. His online courses are currently available in college curricula throughout the United States, Europe, and Australia.

Laurie Ulrich has used, written about, and helped others use computers since the early 1980s. She ran two large training centers for computer resellers in Philadelphia and New York, and she served as an IT manager specializing in the proprietary software needs of midsize distributors. In 1992 she founded Limehat & Company, Inc., a firm providing Web hosting, design, and Webmaster services to growing businesses and nonprofit organizations. She has taught more than 10,000 students to make more effective and creative use of their computers and software.

Laurie has also authored, coauthored, and contributed to more than 25 nationally published books on desktop applications, graphics and illustration, and Web design.

How to Use This Book

We think of this book as a multipurpose tool — perhaps the Swiss Army knife of HTML coding. Not only can you employ it as a guide to creating individual pieces of Web page content, but you can also use this book as a valuable teaching tool. By working through the book's tasks in sequence, you will learn the basics of Web page development — from constructing tags (the core components of Hypertext Markup Language) to publishing complete sites to a Web server.

In addition to the material found in this book, the publisher maintains a companion Web site where you'll find information that doesn't lend itself to a task-oriented approach. We point you to the Web site (www.wiley.com/compbooks/10simplestepsorless) at various points throughout the book to give you detailed information about particular concepts, help you learn about other Web-based resources, and provide samples of some of the content you create.

What You Need to Get Started

As long as you have a computer, the list of requirements is quite short. To create Web page content you need only two things: a program for writing code (a text editor) and another program for viewing the finished product (a Web browser).

Text Editors

In nearly every case, a computer's operating system (OS) comes with a text editor. For example, Microsoft Windows provides its users with the program called Notepad. It is a very simple, bare-bones application that allows you to write simple text files — which is all that an HTML document is. Mac OS 9 (and earlier versions) contains a native text editor, called SimpleText. Apple refers to it as "the utility-knife of software." This simple application is designed for simple tasks. Mac OS X provides a new program, called TextEdit, that replaces SimpleText. Both of these applications are more than sufficient for writing HTML documents. Having written a vast quantity of HTML over the years, however, we're sure you'll ultimately want to work with a text editor that offers more functionality than these limited-range word processors do. Like anything else, you want the right tool for the job.

More robust programs offer advantages that make learning HTML easy. Just as a full-featured word processor makes it easy to write letters, term papers, and books — compared with using Notepad or SimpleText — an HTML code editor makes it easy to generate code properly and build robust Web pages. For example, most HTML editors feature syntax-checking and code-coloring. Because they understand the code you write, these programs assign colors to different functional parts of the code so that you can easily spot errors (mostly caused by typos) and fix them.

Each major operating system — Windows, Macintosh, and UNIX/Linux — offers a number of HTML editors that cost anywhere from nothing to over $100. (But as we said earlier, you get what you pay for.) We review here some of the more popular editors available on each platform. Later on in the book, we discuss these products and others in greater detail.

TextPad from Helios Software Solutions (Windows)

TextPad is shareware, which means you can download it for free and generally use it indefinitely. However, if you intend to use the program for an extended period, and derive much productive use from it, you should register and pay for the program — if at least to get technical support and notifications of upgrades or improvements (bug fixes). TextPad currently runs about US $26.

The creators of TextPad feel there shouldn't be a steep learning curve when picking up a new application. Your familiarity with other Windows programs should be sufficient experience. TextPad therefore provides the kinds of tools you expect from other applications, including keyboard shortcuts, spell-checking (in 10 languages), the ability to open and edit multiple files simultaneously, drag and drop, undo and redo, and the ability to create macros. TextPad also provides many code-specific tools, such as syntax-checking, code-coloring, and libraries for storing reusable code snippets.

BBEdit from Bare Bones Software (Macintosh)

BBEdit, whose marketing slogan is "It Doesn't Suck," emphasizes its HTML editing capabilities, although it certainly isn't limited to HTML. BBEdit functions similarly to TextPad and includes color syntax-checking, spell-checking, and multiple undo and redo, just to name the basics. The only drawback to BBEdit is its US $179 price tag. However, Bare Bones Software makes a free version called BBEdit Lite. Although they don't target it as keenly at the HTML coder, it is still a powerful, all-purpose text editor.

Web Browsers

We suspect you already have a favorite Web browser, but if you're serious about developing Web sites, one browser isn't enough. At the very least you should install the most current releases of both Netscape and Microsoft Internet Explorer. As of this writing, here are the most current versions of these browsers (version numbers may vary by the time you check these sites):

- Netscape 7.1 for Mac OS and Windows: http://channels.netscape.com/ns/browsers/

- Internet Explorer 6 Service Pack 1 for Windows, Internet Explorer 5.1.7 for Mac OS 8.1 to 9.x, and Internet Explorer 5.2.3 for Mac OS X: www.microsoft.com/downloads/search.aspx

Professional Web development environments test their Web sites with more browsers than these. They test with computers running different operating systems using different monitor configurations and both current and older versions of the most commonly — and sometimes not so commonly — used browsers. They do this so that their site looks as good as possible for as many visitors as possible.

Don't feel you need to strap yourself financially in the name of good Web design. Neither of us maintains the ultimate testing suite at home (the office is a different story, but those costs are a business expense). Although hardware costs money, browsers are typically free, so you should be able to round out your browser-testing suite without spending a dime.

In addition to the current releases of Netscape and Internet Explorer, test your sites with a few older versions of the big-name browsers. For example, get copies of Netscape 6.x and 4.x. There's still value in having old versions of browser software. Netscape made significant changes to their support for Cascading Style Sheets and JavaScript when they released version 6.x, and it's valuable to know the differences. You may be asked to develop a Web site that's compatible with Netscape Navigator 4.7 — we've had stranger requests.

Unfortunately, running multiple versions of browsers requires significant planning. For instance, you can't run two versions of Netscape at the same time, and you can't even install two versions of Internet Explorer on the same Windows machine (the later version overrides the earlier one). That's one reason why professional Web developers test their sites on more than one machine.

Stick with the Internet Explorer version you already have, or upgrade to the latest version and leave it at that. Don't downgrade your home machine; your operating system may be adversely affected. Macintosh users seem to be able to install more than one version of Internet Explorer without incident but Microsoft doesn't recommend doing this.

The world of browsers extends beyond that of Netscape and Internet Explorer. Opera 7 (`www.opera.com`) is a favorite among those who are fed up with Microsoft and Netscape. You can find current versions of many alternate browsers on CNET (`www.browsers.com`). It is also important to realize that there are Web surfers who do not see the Web but who listen to it instead. They use text-to-speech browsers, of which WeMedia Talking Browser (`www.wemedia.com`) is perhaps the best known.

If you ever need to test your work on any flavor of practically any browser ever made, you'll find a comprehensive archive of browsers at Evolt.org (`http://browsers.evolt.org`). It contains not only previous versions of Netscape Navigator or Internet Explorer but also some of the earliest browsers ever made — including the world's first Web browser, Nexus, created by the inventor of HTML, Tim Berners-Lee.

Are you ready to start coding? Let's go.

Acknowledgments

The authors would like to thank Jim Minatel for thinking of them, Adaobi Obi Tulton for putting up with them, and Stefan Gruenwedel for correcting them.

Contents

Part 1: HTML Document Structure

How to Write a Tag

Prior to computer-assisted publishing, you wrote notes to the manuscript's typesetter directly in the document — hence the phrase *to mark up*. In an electronic text document, like a Web page, you can't scribble in the margins; you need another mechanism. That mechanism is the *tag*. Hypertext Markup Language is based on tags that mark up text-based documents. They instruct Web browsers how to display content. What we'll look at in this task is the basic *syntax* (grammatical rules) for writing HTML tags.

1. To indicate where a given element begins, place the appropriate tag before it. This consists of a certain abbreviation sandwiched by the less-than (<) and greater-than (>) symbols. For example, to mark up a paragraph, precede the text with the opening-paragraph tag (<p>), as shown in Listing 1-1.

```
<p>She stretched herself up on tiptoe, and peeped over the
edge of the mushroom, and her eyes immediately met those of
a large blue caterpillar, that was sitting on the top, with
its arms folded, quietly smoking a long hookah, and taking
not the smallest notice of her or of anything else.
```

Listing 1-1: Placement of the opening-paragraph tag

2. To indicate where an element ends, place the corresponding closing tag at the end. This looks the same as the opening tag, except for the addition of the forward slash, as shown in Listing 1-2.

```
<p>She stretched herself up on tiptoe, and peeped over the
edge of the mushroom, and her eyes immediately met those of
a large blue caterpillar , that was sitting on the top, with
its arms folded, quietly smoking a long hookah, and taking
not the smallest notice of her or of anything else.</p>
```

Listing 1-2: Placement of the closing-paragraph tag

notes

- When HTML was first created, the standard practice was to write tags in uppercase. Over time, this standard changed to lowercase to mimic the syntax of programming languages. Browsers currently treat uppercase and lowercase code identically. However, Extensible Hypertext Markup Language (XHTML), which is destined to replace HTML, is case-sensitive, so XHTML-compliant browsers will see <P> and <p> as different tags. To make sure your code is always XHTML-compliant, write your code in lowercase.

- The majority of tags in HTML come in pairs: the opening and closing tags. Together, these tags form a container around the page content they define, indicating to your Web browser the beginning and end of a particular element.

- Not all HTML tags have a corresponding closing tag. Some tags only have an opening one. These *empty tags* are used to define elements that don't have logical beginnings and endings. For instance, the line-break tag is written as just
 (there is no closing </br> tag).

3. When you define a tag's *attributes*, which are its individual properties, enter them inside the opening tag and separate them by spaces. The closing tag doesn't get any attributes. For instance, the attribute for aligning a paragraph is written, simply enough, as align. Add it to the opening tag as shown in Listing 1-3.

```
<p align>She stretched herself up on tiptoe, and peeped
over the edge of the mushroom, and her eyes immediately
met those of a large blue caterpillar , that was sitting
on the top, with its arms folded, quietly smoking a long
hookah, and taking not the smallest notice of her or of
anything else.</p>
```

Listing 1-3: The opening paragraph tag and its align attribute.

4. To set the attribute equal to an appropriate value, define that value by using an equal sign and quotation marks, as shown in Listing 1-4.

```
<p align="right">She stretched herself up on tiptoe,
and peeped over the edge of the mushroom, and her eyes
immediately met those of a large blue caterpillar , that
was sitting on the top, with its arms folded, quietly
smoking a long hookah, and taking not the smallest notice
of her or of anything else.</p>
```

Listing 1-4: A properly defined attribute that right-aligns the paragraph text

Figure 1-1 shows how this paragraph appears in the browser.

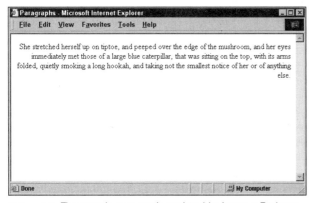

Figure 1-1: The sample paragraph rendered by Internet Explorer

tip

• If what you see when you test your work in a browser doesn't correspond to the code you thought you wrote, chances are you just missed a space between a tag character and its attribute, forgot an equal sign, or omitted a quotation mark.

cross-reference

• To learn more about XHTML, the next generation of HTML, visit our Web site at www.wiley .com/compbooks/ 10simplestepsorless.

Structuring an HTML Document

The simple document template that you are about to build can be used again and again as the starting point for every page you create. All HTML documents share this identical underlying structure — a kind of backbone onto which you build your unique page content. As you learned in the previous task, most HTML tags come in pairs which define the content within them. HTML refers to these as *container tags*. An HTML document's basic structure is really just a series of large containers, inside of which you define the two main sections of your page: the document head and the document body.

1. Open your text editor and begin a new blank document.

2. Type the tag `<html>` at the top of the document. This tag begins the document's primary container. It defines the type of document you're creating: an HTML document.

3. This opening `<html>` tag requires a closing tag, so hit Enter (or Return) twice to move down a few lines and then enter the closing tag, `</html>`. Your document should appear like this:

```
<html>

</html>
```

4. Place your cursor on the line between the opening and closing tags. Type the tag `<head>`, which defines the head section of the document.

5. Hit Enter (Return) twice and then type `</head>`. Your document should now resemble Listing 2-1.

```
<html>
<head>

</head>
</html>
```

Listing 2-1: The head section of your HTML document

notes

- Indenting the tags for the document title, as we've done in Listing 2-2, has no impact on the way the code is rendered by a browser. However, it greatly improves the readability of your code by others, including yourself.

- The head section defines information about the document that doesn't get displayed in the browser window. You'll learn how to define much of this type of content in Tasks 3–8.

6. To create the document title, which appears in the title bar of the browser window, enter `<title>` and `</title>` between the head tags of your document, as shown in Listing 2-2. For example, entering `<title>HTML in 10 Simple Steps or Less</title>` produces what you see in Figure 2-1.

```
<html>
<head>

   <title>HTML in 10 Simple Steps or Less</title>

</head>
</html>
```

Listing 2-2: Defining the document title

Figure 2-1: The document title displayed on the title bar of the browser

7. The last element to add to your document template is the body section. Between the closing `</head>` and the closing `</html>` tags, enter opening and closing body tags, as shown in Listing 2-3.

```
<html>
<head>
   <title> HTML in 10 Simple Steps or Less </title>
</head>

<body>

</body>
</html>
```

Listing 2-3: An HTML document with head and body sections defined.

8. Save your document. You can give it a name like `blank.html` and then use it each time you want to start a new document by opening it, making changes, and resaving the file with a different name.

cross-reference

■ Many text editors have features that write these initial document tags for you. See Part 12: TextPad; Part 13: Working with BBEdit; and Part 14: Working with HomeSite.

Defining Meta Tag Keywords

A document's head section often contains descriptive information about the document, referred to as metadata. Using the `<meta>` tag and its various attributes, you can define such document properties as the author, the expiration date, document key words, and descriptions. When search engines that support metadata read your document, they can use this information to index it in order to return your page when someone does a search on subjects matching the keywords you have defined.

1. In the head section of your document, below the document title, enter the `<meta>` tag, as shown in Listing 3-1.

```
<html>
<head>
    <title>HTML in 10 Simple Steps or Less</title>
    <meta>
</head>
```

Listing 3-1: Inserting the <meta> tag

2. Add the `name` attribute to the `<meta>` tag and set it equal to `"keywords"`, as shown in Listing 3-2.

```
<html>
<head>
    <title>HTML in 10 Simple Steps or Less</title>
    <meta name="keywords">

</head>

<body>

</body>
</html>
```

Listing 3-2: The name attribute set equal to "keywords"

caution

- If you repeat yourself by using the same or similar keywords, for example "stamp, stamps, stamp collecting," some search engines may view this as a spamming tactic and rank your page low, or not at all.

3. Insert a space and add the `content` attribute, as shown in Listing 3-3.

```
<html>
<head>
    <title>HTML in 10 Simple Steps or Less</title>
    <meta name="keywords" content>

</head>

<body>

</body>
</html>
```

Listing 3-3: Adding the content attribute

tips

• The object is not to supply every conceivable keyword you can think of but to tailor your keywords to the specific information contained in the document. Keywords can be single words as well as two- or three-word phrases.

• Work your keywords into your document titles and body text. The first word in your document title should be referenced early in your list of keywords, too, so you probably shouldn't start page titles with words like "The." Any keyword that appears in the text of your document shouldn't be repeated more than seven times in that page.

4. Set the `content` attribute equal to a comma-separated list of keywords pertinent to your page's subject matter, as shown in Listing 3-4.

```
<html>
<head>
    <title>HTML in 10 Simple Steps or Less</title>
    <meta name="keywords" content="HTML, Hypertext Markup
Language, 10 Simple Steps or Less">

</head>

<body>

</body>
</html>
```

Listing 3-4: Defining keywords for the <meta> tag

5. Because the `<meta>` tag is an empty tag, you want to make sure that the code is both XHTML-compliant and still recognizable to browsers that don't yet support XHTML. To do that, conclude the tag with a forward slash (/), placing a space between the last entry in the tag and the forward slash:

```
<meta name="keywords" content="HTML, Hypertext Markup
Language, 10 Simple Steps or Less" />
```

Defining Meta Tag Descriptions

Search engines use the `<meta>` tag's description of the document for indexing and ranking purposes. Some search engines also display the description entries underneath the links on results pages. Because this text is meant for both human and search engine readability, be sure to write it in a way that entices people to click to your site.

note
- What you enter for the `name` and `content` attributes defines something called a *property/value pair*. The `name` attribute defines what the property is, and the `content` attribute defines the value of that property.

1. In the head section of your document, below the document title, insert another `<meta>` tag.

2. Add the `name` attribute to your `<meta>` tag and set it equal to `"description"`, as shown in Listing 4-1.

```
<html>
<head>
    <title>HTML in 10 Simple Steps or Less</title>
    <meta name="keywords" content="HTML, Hypertext Markup
Language, 10 Simple Steps or Less" />
    <meta name="description">
</head>

<body>

</body>
</html>
```

Listing 4-1: Specifying that this <meta> tag contains a document description

3. Press the Spacebar and add the `content` attribute, which accepts your description, as shown in Listing 4-2.

```
<html>
<head>
    <title>HTML in 10 Simple Steps or Less</title>
    <meta name="keywords" content="HTML, Hypertext Markup
Language, 10 Simple Steps or Less" />
    <meta name="description" content>
</head>

<body>

</body>
</html>
```

Listing 4-2: Adding the content attribute

4. Set the content attribute equal to a short piece of descriptive text, as shown in Listing 4-3.

```
<html>
<head>
    <title>HTML in 10 Simple Steps or Less</title>
    <meta name="keywords" content="HTML, Hypertext Markup
Language, 10 Simple Steps or Less" />
    <meta name="description" content="HTML in 10 simple steps
or less.  An introductory guide for the beginning coder." >
</head>

<body>

</body>
</html>
```

Listing 4-3: Completing the property/value pair of a <meta> tag description

5. To make the <meta> tag both XHTML-compliant and still recognizable to browsers that don't yet support XHTML, insert a space and forward slash at the end of the tag, as shown:

```
<meta name="description" content="HTML in 10 simple steps
or less.  An introductory guide for the beginning coder"
/>
```

tip

- In search engines that make use of <meta> tags, it is this descriptive text, combined with the text you place between your title tags, that potential site visitors see in their search results. Your primary keyword or keyword phrase for this document should be part of your description text. You don't want to pack the description with keywords, or be heavy-handed with text that reads like a late-night infomercial. Remember that this text is for human consumption; there's a reason why infomercials aren't regarded positively as sources of objective information.

cross-reference

- You can use <meta> tags to instruct a search engine how or even if you want a document to be read by its search engine-updating robots. See Task 8 for more information.

Task 5

Defining the Author of a Document Using Meta Tags

If you want to put your John Hancock on your document, <meta> tags allow you to do this quite simply. To date, none of the search engines that take advantage of metadata specifically target author information, but supplying it does clearly mark who the content author is and who is responsible for updating the page.

1. Enter a <meta> tag into the head section of your document, setting the name attribute equal to author, as shown in Listing 5-1.

```html
<html>
<head>
    <title>HTML in 10 Simple Steps or Less</title>
    <meta name="keywords" content="HTML, Hypertext Markup
Language, 10 Simple Steps or Less" />
    <meta name="description" content="HTML in 10 simple steps
or less. An introductory guide for the beginning coder" />
    <meta name="author">
</head>

<body>

</body>
</html>
```

Listing 5-1: Set the name attribute equal to "author".

2. Follow the name attribute and author value with the content attribute:

```html
<meta name="author" content>
```

3. Set the content attribute equal to the name of the author, as seen in Listing 5-2.

```
<html>
<head>
    <title>HTML in 10 Simple Steps or Less</title>
    <meta name="keywords" content="HTML, Hypertext Markup
Language, 10 Simple Steps or Less" />
    <meta name="description" content="HTML in 10 simple steps
or less.  An introductory guide for the beginning coder" />
    <meta name="author" content="Robert Fuller and Laurie
Ulrich">
</head>

<body>

</body>
</html>
```

Listing 5-2: The content attribute set to the author's name

4. To make the `<meta>` tag both XHTML-compliant and still recognizable to browsers that don't yet support XHTML, insert a space and forward slash at the end of the tag, as shown:

```
<meta name="author" content="Robert Fuller and Laurie
Ulrich" />
```

tip

- You can also include an e-mail address for the content value.

cross-reference

- Metadata isn't the only thing that appears in the head section of HTML documents. Cascading Style Sheets and JavaScript code goes there too. To learn more, see Parts 9 and 10.

Defining Meta Tag Expiration Dates

The default behavior of most browsers is to *cache* (a fancy word for save) the pages it visits so that if you request the page again, it can pull it quickly from your computer's hard drive instead of pulling it off the Internet, which might take more time. Although most browsers allow users to control this behavior, as a developer you can specify the date on which the current content of your page expires. From that point on, browsers visiting the site will have to connect to your server to get the latest version. You can also instruct browsers not to cache your Web pages at all.

1. Insert a `<meta>` tag in the head section, setting the `name` attribute equal to `expires`, as shown in Listing 6-1.

```
<html>
<head>
    <title>HTML in 10 Simple Steps or Less</title>
    <meta name="keywords" content="HTML, Hypertext Markup
Language, 10 Simple Steps or Less" />
    <meta name="description" content="HTML in 10 simple steps
or less.  An introductory guide for the beginning coder" />
    <meta name="author" content="Robert Fuller and Laurie
Ulrich" />
    <meta name="expires">
</head>

<body>

</body>
</html>
```

Listing 6-1: Setting the name attribute equal to expires

2. Insert the `content` attribute as shown:

```
<meta name="expires" content>
```

3. Set the `content` attribute equal to the expiration date, in Greenwich Mean Time (GMT), as shown in Listing 6-2.

4. To prevent browsers from caching your documents at all, enter a `<meta>` tag with the `name` attribute set equal to `pragma` and the `content` attribute set equal to `no-cache`, as shown in Listing 6-3.

Task 6

```
<html>
<head>
    <title>HTML in 10 Simple Steps or Less</title>
    <meta name="keywords" content="HTML, Hypertext Markup
Language, 10 Simple Steps or Less" />
    <meta name="description" content="HTML in 10 simple steps
or less.  An introductory guide for the beginning coder" />
    <meta name="author" content="Robert Fuller and Laurie
Ulrich" />
    <meta name="expires" content="Mon, 17 February 2003
02:00:00 GMT">
</head>

<body>

</body>
</html>
```

Listing 6-2: Expressing the expiration date in GMT

```
<html>
<head>
    <title>HTML in 10 Simple Steps or Less</title>
    <meta name="keywords" content="HTML, Hypertext Markup
Language, 10 Simple Steps or Less" />
    <meta name="description" content="HTML in 10 simple steps
or less.  An introductory guide for the beginning coder" />
    <meta name="author" content="Robert Fuller and Laurie
Ulrich" />
    <meta name="expires" content="Mon, 17 February 2003
02:00:00 GMT">
    <meta name="pragma" content="no-cache">
</head>

<body>

</body>
</html>
```

Listing 6-3: Preventing a browser from caching your page with a special <meta> tag

5. To make these <meta> tags both XHTML-compliant and still recognizable to browsers that don't yet support XHTML, insert a space
   and forward slash at the end of each tag:

```
<meta name="expires" content="Mon, 17 February 2003
02:00:00 GMT" />
   <meta name="pragma" content="no-cache" />
```

cross-reference

* See Task 7 to learn how to
  use meta tags to refresh
  page content.

Refreshing Page Content Using Meta Tags

It's possible to modify a browser's behavior using <meta> tags. In this task, you're going to generate code that has the same effect as hitting the browser's refresh button. You'll also see how this same code can force the browser to load another document.

note

- Use the http-equiv attribute in place of the name attribute when the action being taken retrieves data using the Hypertext Transfer Protocol (http://).

1. In the head section of your document, below the document title, enter a new <meta> tag.

2. Add the http-equiv attribute and set it equal to refresh, as shown in Listing 7-1.

```
<html>
<head>
    <title>HTML in 10 Simple Steps or Less</title>
    <meta name="keywords" content="HTML, Hypertext Markup
Language, 10 Simple Steps or Less" />
    <meta name="description" content="HTML in 10 simple steps
or less.  An introductory guide for the beginning coder" />
    <meta name="author" content="Robert Fuller and Laurie
Ulrich" />
    <meta name="expires" content="Mon, 17 February 2003
02:00:00 GMT" />
    <meta http-equiv="refresh">
</head>

<body>

</body>
</html>
```

Listing 7-1: Inserting the http-equiv attribute

3. Follow the http-equiv attribute and refresh value with the content attribute and set it equal to the number of seconds you want the page to remain static before refreshing, as shown in Listing 7-2. In this example, the page will refresh every five seconds.

```
<html>
<head>
    <title>HTML in 10 Simple Steps or Less</title>
    <meta name="keywords" content="HTML, Hypertext Markup
Language, 10 Simple Steps or Less" />
    <meta name="description" content="HTML in 10 simple steps
or less.  An introductory guide for the beginning coder" />
                                                    (continued)
```

```
    <meta name="author" content="Robert Fuller and Laurie
Ulrich" />
    <meta name="expires" content="Mon, 17 February 2003
02:00:00 GMT" />
    <meta http-equiv="refresh" content="5">
</head>

<body>

</body>
</html>
```

Listing 7-2: Setting the number of seconds to wait before a forced refresh

4. To force the browser to load another document after the refresh time elapses, follow the refresh rate value with a semicolon and enter url=pathname, where pathname equals the file path to a document on your Web server or a complete URL to a document on another site, as shown in Listing 7-3.

```
<html>
<head>
    <title>HTML in 10 Simple Steps or Less</title>
    <meta name="keywords" content="HTML, Hypertext Markup
Language, 10 Simple Steps or Less" />
    <meta name="description" content="HTML in 10 simple steps
or less.  An introductory guide for the beginning coder" />
    <meta name="author" content="Robert Fuller and Laurie
Ulrich" />
    <meta name="expires" content="Mon, 17 February 2003
02:00:00 GMT" />
    <meta http-equiv="refresh" content="5;
url=http://www.w3c.org">
</head>

<body>

</body>
</html>
```

Listing 7-3: Supplying the URL of another document you want the browser to load after the forced refresh

5. To make your code both XHTML-compliant and still recognizable to browsers that don't yet support XHTML, insert a space and forward slash at the end of the <meta> tag:

```
    <meta http-equiv="refresh" content="5;
url=http://www.w3c.org" />
```

Defining Meta Tag Robot Values

A *robot* is a type of program that search engines use to browse Web site documents and update their databases. Robots that make use of `<meta>` tag information read the metadata and index it for the search engine. You can control how much or how little of your site a robot reads using the following attributes and values for the `<meta>` tag.

1. Enter a `<meta>` tag in the head section of your document, below the document title.

2. Define the `name` attribute and set it equal to `robots`, as shown in Listing 8-1.

```
<html>
<head>
    <title>HTML in 10 Simple Steps or Less</title>
    <meta name="keywords" content="HTML, Hypertext Markup
Language, 10 Simple Steps or Less" />
    <meta name="description" content="HTML in 10 simple steps
or less.  An introductory guide for the beginning coder" />
    <meta name="author" content="Robert Fuller and Laurie
Ulrich" />
    <meta name="expires" content="Mon, 17 February 2003
02:00:00 GMT" />
    <meta http-equiv="refresh" content="5;
url=http://www.w3c.org" />
  <meta name="robots">
</head>

<body>

</body>
</html>
```

Listing 8-1: Setting the name attribute equal to robots

note

• The reasons for allowing a robot to crawl your site are obvious. You want the search engine to explore your site fully in order to index everything, baring it all for public consumption. However, there are times when you don't want this to happen; for example, if you have pages you don't want the world knowing about yet, like ones you're in the process of testing, or pages that contain information you only want a limited audience to know about.

3. To instruct robots to read your entire page and follow all the links within it, follow the `name` attribute and `robots` value with the `content` attribute and set it equal to `all`, `follow`, as shown in Listing 8-2.

```
<head>
    <title>HTML in 10 Simple Steps or Less</title>
    <meta name="keywords" content="HTML, Hypertext Markup
Language, 10 Simple Steps or Less" />
    <meta name="description" content="HTML in 10 simple steps
or less.  An introductory guide for the beginning coder" />
    <meta name="author" content="Robert Fuller and Laurie
Ulrich" />
    <meta name="expires" content="Mon, 17 February 2003
02:00:00 GMT" />
    <meta http-equiv="refresh" content="5;
url=http://www.w3c.org" />
  <meta name="robots">
<meta name="robots" content="all, follow">
</head>
```

Listing 8-2: Code allowing robots to read the entire page and follow all links

4. To instruct robots to read your page, but refrain from following the links within it, set the `content` attribute equal to `all, nofollow`:

```
<meta name="robots" content="all, nofollow">
```

5. To prevent robots from reading your page at all, set the `content` attribute equal to none:

```
<meta name="robots" content="none">
```

6. Insert a space and forward slash at the end of the `<meta>` tag to make sure your code is both XHTML-compliant and still recognizable to browsers that don't yet support XHTML:

```
<meta name="robots" content="none" />
```

Controlling the Document Background

You can specify a document's background color or background image using two different attributes of the <body> tag. Background colors simply fill the entire document. Background images are *tiled* by the browser, meaning they are repeated left to right, top to bottom, filling up the visible space of the browser window.

note

- The default body text color is controlled with the text attribute of the <body> tag. To learn more, see Task 15.

1. To define a background color for a document, add the bgcolor attribute to the <body> tag, as shown here:

   ```
   <body bgcolor
   ```

2. Set the bgcolor attribute equal to a hexadecimal color value or pre-defined color name. Listing 9-1 shows a document with a black background color defined in hexadecimal notation. Figure 9-1 shows the result in a browser.

   ```
   <html>
   <head>
       <title>Background Color</title>
   </head>

   <body bgcolor="#000000" text="white">
   <h1>Here we have a black background with white text...</h1>

   </body>
   </html>
   ```

   Listing 9-1: Setting the bgcolor attribute (and text color)

3. To specify a background image, add the background attribute to the <body> tag, as shown here:

   ```
   <body background
   ```

4. Set the background attribute equal to the pathname of the image file on your Web server. Listing 9-2 provides a code sample of a document that makes use of a tiling background texture graphic. Figure 9-2 displays the result in a browser.

```
<html>
<head>
    <title>Background Images</title>
</head>

<body background="images/bg_stone.jpg">
<h1>Isn't this a nice stone background?</h1>
</body>
</html>
```

Listing 9-2: The background attribute

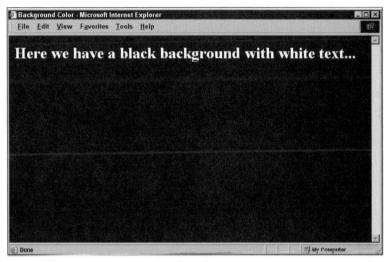

Figure 9-1: White text on a black background

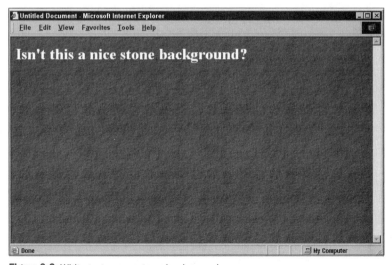

Figure 9-2: White text over a stone background

cross-references

- To see a hexadecimal color chart and learn more about hexadecimal notation, see our Web site at www.wiley .com/compbooks/ 10simplestepsorless.

- Each listing here shows an example of a heading tag. To learn more, see Task 11.

Working with Source Code in the Browser

All major Web browsers allow you to view the source code of documents you view — an extremely useful feature. For example, imagine you're surfing the Internet and you come across a page you're really impressed with. To see how it was built, just view the source HTML code. Granted, if this book is your first foray into HTML you may not understand what you're looking at, but you will in time. Each browser has slightly different commands and it supplies slightly different options. Here's how you can view source code using Netscape Navigator and Microsoft Internet Explorer.

1. While viewing a page in Netscape Navigator, go to the View menu and select Page Source. This opens the Source window, as shown in Figure 10-1. From here you can examine the source code, copying and pasting the code into a text editor if you wish.

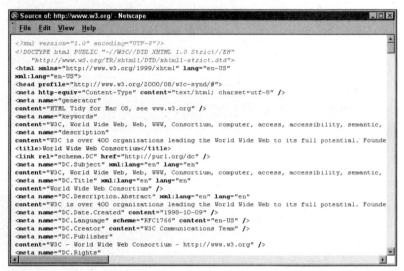

Figure 10-1: The Source window in Netscape Navigator

2. To save the source code from the Source window, select File ⇨ Save Page As and enter a filename.

3. In Microsoft Internet Explorer, select View ⇨ Source. This opens the source code of the document in Notepad, as shown in Figure 10-2.

4. To save the source code, choose File ⇨ Save As from the Internet Explorer window. This opens the Save Web Page dialog box shown in Figure 10-3.

5. In the Save Web Page dialog box, set the Save As Type pop-up menu to Web Page Complete, as shown in Figure 10-4.

notes

- While it's fine to copy source code to examine and learn from, do not plagiarize another developer's HTML. You could run into potential legal issues with the site's owner.

- Because Notepad is a text editor, you can make changes to the code right there. Of course, if you're viewing a Web page on the Internet, changes you make to the code won't have an effect on the actual Web site.

6. Choose a location on your hard drive to save the file and click Save. A copy of the HTML document and a folder containing all the associated images and media are saved to the location you chose.

Task 10

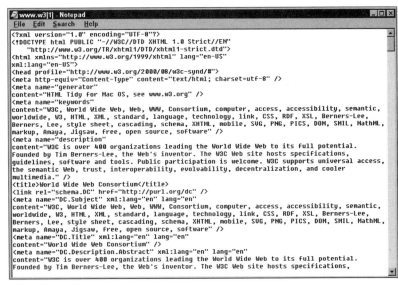

Figure 10-2: Source code in Notepad

Figure 10-3: The Save Web Page dialog box in Internet Explorer

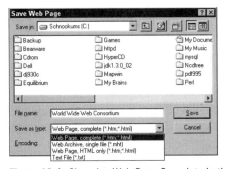

Figure 10-4: Choosing Web Page Complete in the Save As Type menu

tips

- If you are viewing a page in Internet Explorer that's located on your computer, you can open the HTML document in Notepad, make edits, and choose Save As from Notepad's File menu, and add a .htm or .html extension to the file. By clicking the browser's refresh button, you'll see your changes take effect.

- Internet Explorer offers an extremely useful feature for copying an entire Web page to your computer that not only saves a copy of the HTML document but also saves all the images and other media into a folder beside the document. This allows you to later open the file locally and see the document in its entirety. If you then make changes, you can see how they affect all the content. Simply choose Save As, and select Web Page, Complete from the Save As Type menu in the dialog box.

Part 2: Working with Text

Task

Working with Headings

The following series of tags create document headings akin to those in newspapers and magazines, or the task headings you see in this book. There are six levels of headings, ranging from a heading 1 (the largest) to a heading 6 (the smallest).

1. To format a word or phrase as a heading, place an opening heading tag in front of it, as shown in Listing 11-1.

```
<h1>This is a Heading 1
<h2>This is a Heading 2
<h3>This is a Heading 3
<h4>This is a Heading 4
<h5>This is a Heading 5
<h6>This is a Heading 6
```

Listing 11-1: A series of opening heading tags

2. Place a corresponding closing heading tag after the word or phrase, as shown in Listing 11-2. Figure 11-1 shows how these six headings appear in the browser.

```
<h1>This is a Heading 1</h1>
<h2>This is a Heading 2</h2>
<h3>This is a Heading 3</h3>
<h4>This is a Heading 4</h4>
<h5>This is a Heading 5</h5>
<h6>This is a Heading 6</h6>
```

Listing 11-2: A series of corresponding closing heading tags

3. The heading tag's only allowable attribute is `align`. Its possible values are `left`, `right`, and `center`. To align a heading, insert the alignment attribute within the heading tag, as shown here:

```
<h1 align>
```

4. Set your `align` attribute equal to the desired alignment. Here we use the `center` alignment. The result appears in Figure 11-2.

```
<h1 align="center">Heading 1 - Centered</h1>
```

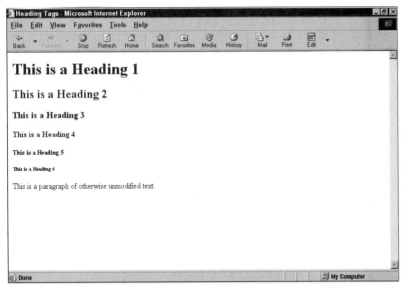

Figure 11-1: Six levels of HTML headings

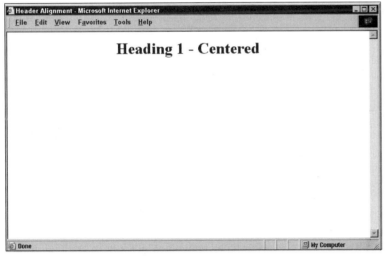

Figure 11-2: A center-aligned heading

tip

- These heading tags indicate a subject's level of importance. For example, if a heading 1 marks the introduction to a main topic, then a subtopic would be indicated with a heading 2. A subtopic of a heading 2 topic would be a heading 3, and so on.

cross-reference

- To learn how to control fonts, see Task 13.

12

Working with Paragraphs

HTML only recognizes single spaces between characters. Other than a single tap on the Spacebar, HTML has little regard for how you physically type your paragraphs. What HTML does recognize is tags to format paragraphs. This task shows you how to format basic paragraph text.

notes

- Enclosing text in paragraph tags does not produce any eye-catching effects in your browser. Embellishments come from style sheets or other tags. Browsers have traditionally rendered paragraphs with white space before and after.

- The `align` attribute is the `<p>` tag's only attribute. By default, a paragraph (and just about everything else in HTML) appears left-aligned. However, paragraphs sometimes fall inside other elements that include their own alignment settings. For example, table cells (covered in Part 6) specify horizontal alignment with `align` too. Therefore, to force left-alignment of a given paragraph, set its `align` attribute to `left`.

1. To indicate the beginning of a paragraph, enter an opening `<p>` tag in the `<body>` section of your code, as shown in Listing 12-1.

```
<body>

<p>

</body>
</html>
```

Listing 12-1: Starting a paragraph in the body of the document

2. To mark the end of a paragraph, place the closing `</p>` tag at the end of your paragraph, as shown in Listing 12-2.

```
<html>
<head>
<title>Defining and Aligning Paragraphs</title>
</head>

<body>

<p>HTML only recognizes single spaces between characters.
Other than a single tap on the space bar, HTML has little
regard for how you type things.  What it does have regard
for is tags.</p>

</body>
</html>
```

Listing 12-2: Inserting text between the opening and closing paragraph tags

caution

- Never omit the closing tags! Although many browsers do allow you to omit them, XHTML requires them. In time, XHTML-compliant browsers will penalize you for failing to include them.

3. To align a paragraph, add the `align` attribute to the paragraph tag:

```
<p align>
```

4. Set the `align` attribute equal to `left`, `right`, `center`, or `justified`, as shown in Listing 12-3. The effect, when previewed in a browser, appears in Figure 12-1.

```
<p align="right">HTML only recognizes single spaces between
characters.  Other than a single tap on the space bar, HTML
has little regard for how you type things.  What it does
have regard for is tags.</p>
```

Listing 12-3: Defining the align attribute

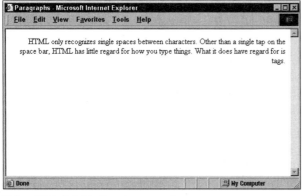

Figure 12-1: A right-aligned paragraph

cross-reference

▪ In XHTML, alignment is a style consideration; therefore Cascading Style Sheets (CSS) controls it, which we cover in Part 9. CSS makes the `align` attribute obsolete. The Word Wide Web Consortium (W3C) uses the term *deprecated* to describe obsolete elements and attributes, meaning their use is disapproved of. To learn more about XHTML, see www.wiley .com/compbooks/ 10simplestepsorless/.

Applying Fonts

The `<font>` tag determines which font is applied to your text. By itself, this tag has no effect on text. You specify the fonts as a value of the `face` attribute. The most important thing you need to understand about specifying fonts in HTML is that you don't really determine the font that visitors see — the browsers do. The best you can achieve is specifying the font you want them to use. If people don't have the proper fonts installed on their computers, the browsers will use whatever font is installed as the default. Because you're at the mercy of visitors' font collections, you can define a list of fonts, giving them a choice of three or four similar fonts. If they don't have your first choice, perhaps they have your second choice or, failing that, your third.

1. To specify the font for a range of text, type an opening `<font>` tag and add a `face` attribute to it as shown in Listing 13-1.

```
<body>

<p> <font face=" >

</body>
</html>
```

Listing 13-1: Beginning the <font> tag

2. Set the `face` attribute equal to your first font choice, as shown here:

```
<p> <font face="Arial >
```

3. Type a comma and follow your first font choice with your second, third, and fourth (if necessary):

```
<p> <font face="Arial, Helvetica, sans-serif">
```

4. Directly following the `<font>` tag, enter the text you want it to affect:

```
<p> <font face="Arial, Helvetica, sans-serif">By itself,
this tag has no effect on the text you apply it to. You
actually specify your chosen fonts as a value of the face
attribute. The most important thing to understand about
specifying fonts in HTML is that you don't really
determine the font the visitor sees - their computer does.
```

5. At the end of this range of text, place a closing `</font>` tag:

```
<p> <font face="Arial, Helvetica, sans-serif">By itself,
this tag has no effect on the text you apply it to. You
actually specify your chosen fonts as a value of the face
attribute. The most important thing to understand about
specifying fonts in HTML is that you don't really
determine the font the visitor sees - their computer
does.</font> </p>
```

The effect of this is to display the text in this paragraph in Arial, as shown in Figure 13-1.

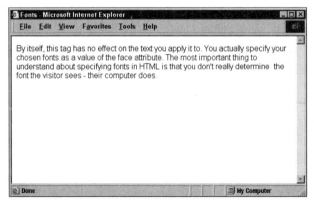

Figure 13-1: A paragraph set in Arial

Setting the Font Size

To specify the font size, use the `size` attribute of the `<font>` tag. The `size` attribute accepts a numeric value from one of two scales: the absolute or relative scale.

notes

- The absolute scale ranges from 1 (the smallest) to 7 (the largest). A size value of 3 is the same as the browser's current default font size (also called the *base* font size). Provided the user hasn't modified the default browser settings, this makes a size 3 equal to 12-point text. The rest of the scale converts as follows: 1 = 7.5pt., 2 = 10pt., 4 = 13.5pt., 5 = 18pt., 6 = 24pt., and 7 = 36pt.

- The *relative* scale runs from –7 to +7 and sets the font size in relation to the base font of the browser. So setting the font size to +1 makes the text appear one size larger than the base font size. This is why you use a relative font size value in conjunction with an absolute base font value. Otherwise, you have no idea what the browser is using for the base font size.

caution

- The relative scale doesn't allow you to display a font size outside of the absolute scale of 1 through 7. The browser's base font size always equals a font size of 3, regardless how the user sets the point value. Therefore, you cannot apply a relative size value that adds to more than 7 or subtracts to less than 1 from the current font size you've set. The relative scale is best used in conjunction with the `<basefont>` tag, with which you can force a font size for an entire document.

1. To define the font size for a preexisting `<font>` tag, simply add a size attribute set equal to your chosen value. Figure 14-1 shows what the following code looks like in your browser.

```
<p> <font face="Arial, Helvetica, sans-serif" size="2">All
text affected by this font tag is now set to size
2.</font> </p>
<p> <font face="Arial, Helvetica, sans-serif">All text
affected by this font tag is defaulting to the browser's
base font size, because no size attribute is
defined.</font> </p>
```

Figure 14-1: A font size of 2, in contrast to undefined font size

2. You can control the font size by simply adding a `<font>` tag with just the `size` attribute defined. The following code changes the font size of the word *here* to 5. Figure 14-2 shows what it looks like in your browser.

```
<p> <font face="Arial, Helvetica, sans-serif" size="2">All
text affected by this font tag is now set to size 2.
Except this word <font size="5">here</font>, around which
I've nested a second font tag with a different size
setting.</font> </p>
<p> <font face="Arial, Helvetica, sans-serif">All text
affected by this font tag is defaulting to the browser's
base font size, because no size attribute is
defined.</font> </p>
```

3. To define the base font size for your entire document, enter the `<basefont>` tag just below the opening `<body>` tag and set its `size` attribute to a value from 1 to 7:

```
<basefont size="2">
```

Figure 14-2: The word *here* augmented by a second font size value

4. With the `<basefont>` tag and `size` attribute defined, use the relative scale to increase or decrease individual regions of text. Figure 14-3 shows what this code looks like in your browser.

```
<basefont size="2">

<p>All text in this document will default to size 2.
<font size="+3">T</font>he first letter in this sentence
has now been punched up to a size 5 using a +3 size value.
</p>
```

Figure 14-3: The *T* increased to a font size of 5 using a relative +3 value

5. To make a region of text one size larger than the surrounding text, wrap it inside the `<big>` and `</big>` tags. You can make this additive by using multiple `<big>` tags. To make the text smaller, use `<small>` and `</small>` tags. Figure 14-4 shows what the code looks like in your browser.

```
<p> We've made this word three times
<big><big><big>bigger</big></big></big> by nesting it
inside three sets of big tags.</p>

<p> <font size="5">We've made this word three times
<small><small><small>smaller</small></small></small> by
nesting it inside three sets of small tags.</font></p>
```

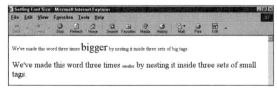

Figure 14-4: Multiple `<big>` and `<small>` tags with their cumulative effects

tips

▪ Because a user can change the default font size setting, the absolute scale isn't exactly "absolute"; any font size value you define with it will still be relative to the user's base font size. If this seems like too much to worry about, just remember that size 1 is really tiny and size 7 is really big. Size 2 is the most common because it's small enough to allow you to fit plenty of text into a page, while being large enough so that most folks don't have to squint to read it.

▪ Remember that the browser's default font size is equal to a base font value of 3. So entering `<basefont size="3">` is the same as entering nothing at all. Just like the `<font>` tag, the `<basefont>` tag is deprecated in HTML 4.0 through the current XHTML standard, in favor of CSS (see Part 9).

cross-reference

▪ Use of the `<font>` tag is deprecated in favor of Cascading Style Sheets. See Part 9.

Setting the Font Color

In the `<font>` tag, the `face` attribute sets the typeface and the `size` attribute sets the text size. It shouldn't come as a big surprise then that the `color` attribute sets the text color. In HTML, colors can be defined using *hexadecimal notation* (a six-character code for expressing the combined red, green, and blue values of affected pixels) or a number of predefined English equivalents. There are different methods for defining font color, with or without using the `<font>` tag's `color` attribute.

note

▪ Although the HTML standard only recognizes 16 predefined color words (Black, Green, Silver, Lime, Gray, Olive, White, Yellow, Maroon, Navy, Red, Blue, Purple, Teal, Fuchsia, Aqua), browsers like Internet Explorer (http://msdn.microsoft.com/workshop/author/dhtml/reference/colors/colors.asp) and Netscape (http://devedge.netscape.com/library/manuals/1998/htmlguide/colortab.html) can support a much broader list.

1. To define the font color for a preexisting `<font>` tag, simply insert the `color` attribute and set it equal to your chosen color value, as shown in Listing 15-1.

```
<body>

<p> <font face="Arial, Helvetica, sans-serif" size="2"
color="#0000FF">This text has been turned blue using
hexadecimal notation, which uses six characters preceded by
a pound sign (#). </font> </p>

</body>
</html>
```

Listing 15-1: Use of hexadecimal value #0000FF to turn a paragraph blue

2. You can also control the font color by simply adding a `<font>` tag with only a `color` attribute defined, as shown in Listing 15-2.

```
<html>
<head>
<title>Setting Font Color</title>
</head>

<body>

<p> <font face="Arial, Helvetica, sans-serif" size="2"
color="#0000FF">All text affected by this font tag is blue.
Except this word <font color="#00FF00">here</font>, around
which I've nested a second font tag turning the word
green.</font> </p>

</body>
</html>
```

Listing 15-2: Use of hexadecimal value #00FF00 to turn a word green

3. To use predefined color names instead of hexadecimal values, set the `color` attribute to equal the word color of your choice, as shown in Listing 15-3.

```html
<html>
<head>
<title>Setting Font Color</title>
</head>

<body>

<p> <font face="Arial, Helvetica, sans-serif" size="2"
color="Purple">This text is making use of the word "Purple"
- one of the 16 recognized colors in the HTML
standard.</font></p>

<p> <font face="Arial, Helvetica, sans-serif" size="2"
color="DarkOliveGreen">This text is making use of the word
"DarkOliveGreen" (no spaces) - one of the many colors
browsers like Internet Explorer and Netscape Navigator
recognize. So much for standards compliance, huh?</font></p>

</body>
</html>
```

Listing 15-3: Use of the color names Purple and DarkOliveGreen

4. To define the default text color for your entire document, instead of relying on the `<font>` tag, use the `text` attribute of the `<body>` tag, as shown in Listing 15-4.

```html
<html>
<head>
<title>Setting Font Color</title>
</head>

<body text="#8B0000">

<p> All text in this document defaults to dark red. If you
prefer words over hexadecimal notation, the value would
coincidentally be "DarkRed".</p>

</body>
</html>
```

Listing 15-4: Body text set to hexadecimal color #8B0000, which means dark red

cross-references

▪ You can find a hexadecimal color chart at www.wiley .com/compbooks/ 10simplestepsorless.

▪ To learn more about hexadecimal notation and supported English equivalents, go to www .wiley.com/compbooks/ 10simplestepsorless.

Applying Physical Styles

Your typical word processor has buttons for bolding, italicizing, and underlining text — and probably some other stylistic options hiding in a menu somewhere. In HTML, these are called *physical styles* because the tags used to create them imply specific rendering by the browser.

1. To create bold text, wrap the chosen word or phrase with `<b>` and `</b>` tags:

    ```
    <b>Bold</b>
    ```

2. To italicize text, place the text between `<i>` and `</i>` tags:

    ```
    <i>Italic</i>
    ```

3. To underline text, place the text between `<u>` and `</u>` tags:

    ```
    <u>Underline</u>
    ```

4. To strike through text, use the `<s>` and `</s>` tags:

    ```
    <s>Strikethrough </s>
    ```

5. To produce a monospace (code-like) formatting, place the text between `<tt>` and `</tt>` tags (stands for "teletype"):

    ```
    <tt>Teletype</tt>
    ```

6. Although not technically considered physical styles in HTML, the ability to superscript and subscript text also exists. To use these styles, insert text between the following tag pairs: `<sup></sup>` for superscript and `<sub></sub>` for subscript:

    ```
    <p>Superscript: a<sup>2</sup> x b<sup>2</sup> =
    c<sup>2</sup></p>
    <p>Subscript: H<sub>2</sub>O</p>
    ```

    Listing 16-1 shows all these formatting codes and Figure 16-1 shows what the results should look like in a browser.

caution

■ Because most browsers format text-based hyperlinks with an underline, most site visitors instinctively consider underlined text as hyperlinks. Avoid underlining text to emphasize it. Use italics instead.

```
<html>
<head>
    <title>Physical Styles</title>
</head>
<body>
<p><b>Bold</b> <br>
<i>Italic</i> <br>
<u>Underline</u> <br>
<s>Strikethrough</s> <br>
<tt>Teletype</tt>
</p>
<p>Superscript: a<sup>2</sup> x b<sup>2</sup> = c<sup>2</sup></
sup></p>
<p>Subscript: H<sub>2</sub>O</p>
</body>
</html>
```

Listing 16-1: Physical styles set in HTML

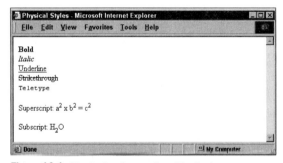

Figure 16-1: Physical styles rendered in the browser

7. You can combine these tags to double their effect. For example, if
   you want to make text both bold *and* italic, simply surround your
   chosen text with the bold and italic opening and closing tags. Figure
   16-2 shows the resulting effect in your browser.

```
<p><b><i>Bold and italicized</i></b></p>
<p><i><b>The order of tags makes no difference</b></i></p>
```

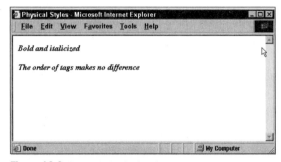

Figure 16-2: Nested physical styles

cross-references

▪ In XHTML, styles are taken
  care of by Cascading Style
  Sheets (see Part 9).
  Consequently, physical
  style tags have been
  deprecated in favor of
  logical styles (see Task 17).

▪ You guessed it – this type
  of formatting is deprecated
  in HTML. To learn how to
  accomplish this sort of
  thing in CSS, see Part 9.

Applying Logical Styles

The physical styles you learned about in Task 16 apply a specific appearance to text. *Logical style* tags format text according to the text's meaning without implying a specific appearance. This sounds like two different things, but because the HTML standard leaves the rendering of logical styles up to the browser, logical styles, to date, produce the same effect on text as physical styles.

note

- Logical styles are favored over the deprecated physical styles not only in XHTML but also in HTML 4 and 4.01.

1. To place emphasis on a chosen word, place the text between `<em>` and `</em>` tags:

   ```
   <em>Emphasis</em> looks <i>italic</i>
   ```

2. To place stronger emphasis on a chosen word, use the `<strong>` and `</strong>` tags:

   ```
   <strong>Strong</strong> looks <b>bold</b>
   ```

3. To define a section of text as a code sample, use the `<code>` and `</code>` tags:

   ```
   <code>Code</code> looks like <tt>teletype</tt>
   ```

4. To define a sample of literal characters, use the `<samp>` and `</samp>` tags:

   ```
   <samp>Sample</samp> looks like <tt>teletype</tt> too.
   ```

5. To define text as it should be typed by a user, for example in an instructional manual, use the `<kbd>` and `</kbd>` tags (short for "keyboard"):

   ```
   <kbd>Keyboard</kbd> also looks like <tt>teletype</tt>.
   ```

6. To define text as a variable name, for example in a programming language, use the `<var>` and `</var>` tags:

   ```
   <var>Variable</var> looks <i>italic</i>.
   ```

7. To format text as a term definition, use the `<dfn>` and `</dfn>` tags:

   ```
   <dfn>Definition</dfn> also looks <i>italic</i>.
   ```

8. To define a citation, as out of a book, use the `<cite>` and `</cite>` tags:

   ```
   <cite>Cite</cite> is another logical style that looks
   <i>italic</i>.
   ```

   Figure 17-1 shows the results of the code listed in Listing 17-1.

```
<html>
<head>
    <title>Logical Styles</title>
</head>
<body>

<p>
<em>Emphasis</em> looks <i>italic</i>. <br>
<strong>Strong</strong> looks <b>bold</b>. <br>
<code>Code</code> looks like <tt>teletype</tt>. <br>
<samp>Sample</samp> looks like <tt>teletype</tt> too. <br>
<kbd>Keyboard</kbd> also looks like <tt>teletype</tt>. <br>
<var>Variable</var> looks <i>italic</i>. <br>
<dfn>Definition</dfn> also looks <i>italic</i>. <br>
<cite>Cite</cite> is another logical style that looks
<i>italic</i>.
</p>

</body>
<html>
```

Listing 17-1: Logical styles set in HTML

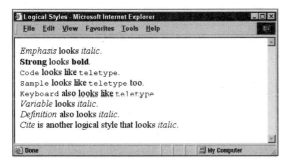

Figure 17-1: Logical styles rendered in the browser

cross-references

- To learn more about the HTML and CSS standards, visit the World Wide Web Consortium at www.w3.org.

- To control how the browser displays text formatted with a specific tag, learn about Cascading Style Sheets (see Part 9).

Inserting Character Entities

There are about 100 keys on your keyboard, but with all those choices, how do you type something obscure like the copyright symbol (©)? In a word processor, you insert a symbol from some menu or dialog box. In HTML, these symbols are referred to as *character entities* or *special characters*. Instead of tags, character entities are rendered numerically, beginning with an ampersand (&) and pound sign (#) and ending with a semicolon. This task shows you how to render a number of the more common character entities.

1. Type © to display the copyright symbol:

   ```
   <p> Copyright &#169; 2003 </p>
   ```

2. Type ® to produce the registered symbol:

   ```
   <p>W3C &#174;</p>
   ```

3. Type ™ to produce the trademark symbol:

   ```
   <p>Alpha-Gizmo&#153;</p>
   ```

4. Enter ¼ to produce the fraction one-quarter:

   ```
   <p>&#188; teaspoon salt</p>
   ```

5. Enter ½ to produce the fraction one-half:

   ```
   <p>&#189; teaspoon sugar</p>
   ```

6. Enter ¾ to produce the fraction three-quarters:

   ```
   <p>&#190; cup of honey</p>
   ```

7. Enter ¢ to produce the cent symbol:

   ```
   <p>10&#162;</p>
   ```

8. Enter £ to produce the British Pound symbol:

   ```
   <p>&#163;125,000</p>
   ```

9. Enter ¥ to produce the Japanese Yen symbol:

   ```
   <p>&#165;500,000</p>
   ```

10. Enter € to produce the European Union's Euro symbol:

    ```
    <p>&#8364;700</p>
    ```

    Listing 18-1 provides examples of these symbols and Figure 18-1 displays the results in a browser.

```
<html>
<head>
<title>Character Entities</title>
</head>
<body>
<p>This book is copyrighted &#169;2003</p>
<p>My Favorite cola is Pepsi&#174;</p>
<p>My company name: Alpha-Gizmo&#153;</p>
<p>&#188; teaspoon salt in my soup.</p>
<p>&#189; teaspoon sugar in my tea.</p>
<p>&#190; cup of honey is way too much!</p>
<p>I remember when a pay phone cost 10&#162;</p>
<p>A $500,000 house only costs &#163;300,084.44 </p>
<p>Which is an astronomical &#165;59,037,844.65 </p>
<p>But a moderate &#8364;436,305.17 </p></body>
</html>
```

Listing 18-1: Character entities in HTML

Figure 18-1: Character entities rendered in the browser

tip

- Most character entities have an English-language equivalent. For example, the copyright symbol can also be written as © and the registered sign as ®.

cross-reference

- For a full list of standard character entities, see our Web site at www.wiley .com/compbooks/ 10simplestepsorless.

Using the Preformatted Text Element

There is a way to make a browser display text almost exactly as you type it in your HTML document. The `<pre>` tag tells the browser that text is *preformatted*, which means it should leave all white space as entered. In other words, if you hit the Spacebar seven times, the browser will respect those seven spaces. Typically, browsers display any text written between `<pre>` tags with a monospaced font.

1. Begin the region of your document to preformat with an opening `<pre>` tag.

2. Enter the text you want preformatted into the document.

3. Close the preformatted region with a closing `</pre>` tag, as in the following code. Figure 19-1 shows how it looks in your browser.

```
<pre>
            |  Mon  |  Tues  |  Wed  |  Thurs  |  Fri
            |       |        |       |         |
Calculus    |   X   |        |   X   |         |
----------------------------------------------------------
English     |       |   X    |       |    X    |
----------------------------------------------------------
Latin       |   X   |        |   X   |         |
</pre>
```

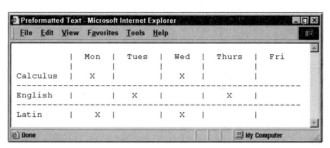

Figure 19-1: Code inside the `<pre>` tag rendered in the browser

4. If you choose, you can include `<font>` tags to control the size and color, as shown in the following code. Figure 19-2 shows how the modified code appears in the browser (except for the color, of course).

```
<pre><font size="4" color="red">
            |  Mon  |  Tues  |  Wed  |  Thurs  |  Fri
            |       |        |       |         |
Calculus    |   X   |        |   X   |         |
----------------------------------------------------------
English     |       |   X    |       |    X    |
----------------------------------------------------------
Latin       |   X   |        |   X   |
</font>
</pre>
```

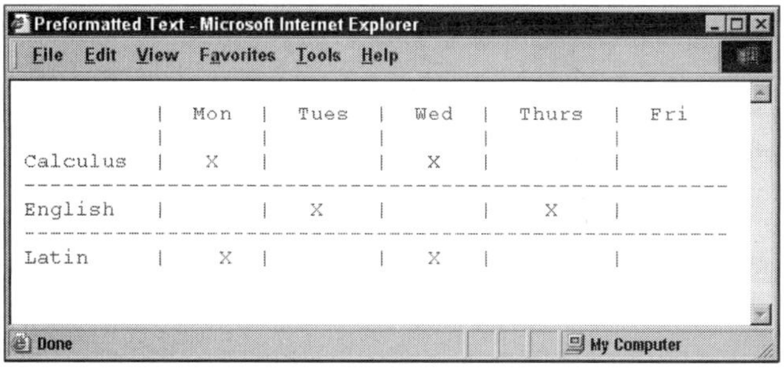

Figure 19-2: Nesting <font> tags within preformatted text to enlarge the point size

5. To include logical or physical style tags inside `<pre>` tags, first enter your text and test it in a browser to check your alignments. Then go back to the code and insert the tags around your text choices, as shown in the following code. Figure 19-3 shows how it looks in the browser.

```
<pre><font size="4" color="red">
          |  <b>Mon</b>  |  <b>Tues</b>  |  <b>Wed</b>  |
<b>Thurs</b>  |  <b>Fri</b>
          |         |         |         |         |
<b>Calculus</b>  |   X   |        |   X   |         |
-----------------------------------------------------
<b>English</b>  |        |   X   |        |   X   |
-----------------------------------------------------
<b>Latin</b>         |   X   |        |   X   |         |
</font></pre>
```

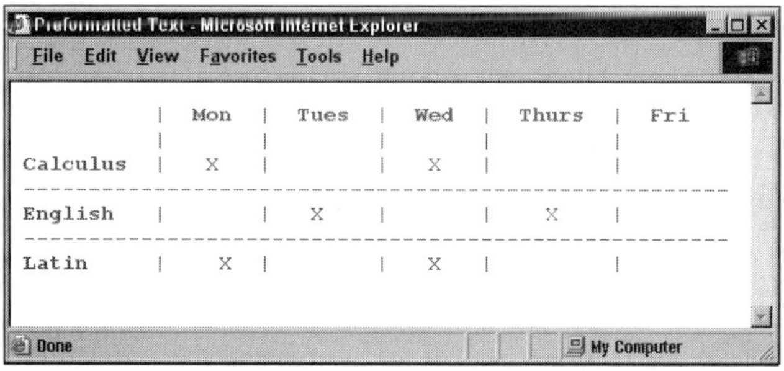

Figure 19-3: Physical styles (bolding) applied to preformatted text

tip

- Monospaced fonts give each character identical spacing, which allows you to line up text evenly. If you include a `face` attribute in your `<font>` tag and don't specify a monospaced font, the alignment of preformatted elements may be off.

cross-reference

- The `<pre>` element is ideal for displaying programming examples on a Web page. Coincidently, even though this is an HTML book, we do have a short section on JavaScript programming (see Part 10).

Using the Blockquote Element

The `<blockquote>` tag designates quoted text, specifically long quotations of paragraph length or more. Browsers typically render text wrapped in `<blockquote>` tags as an indented paragraph.

1. To designate a block of quoted text, place an opening `<blockquote>` tag at the beginning of the text to be quoted.

2. To conclude the block of quoted text, place a closing `</blockquote>` tag at the end of the text to be quoted. A completed example is shown in Listing 20-1. Figure 20-1 shows the results in the browser.

```
<html>
<head>
<title>The Blockquote Element</title>
</head>
<body text="#000000" bgcolor="#FFFFFF">

<h1>Edgar Allan Poe</h1>

<p>The following is a quote from www.poets.org:</p>

<blockquote><p>Edgar Allan Poe was born in Boston,
Massachusetts, on January 19, 1809. Poe's father and mother,
both professional actors, died before the poet was three and
John and Frances Allan raised him as a foster child in
Richmond, Virginia. John Allan, a prosperous tobacco
exporter, sent Poe to the best boarding schools and later to
the University of Virginia, where Poe excelled academically.
After less than one year of school, however, he was forced
to leave the University when Allan refused to pay his
gambling debts.</p></blockquote>

</body>
</html>
```

Listing 20-1: Code example of a block of quoted text

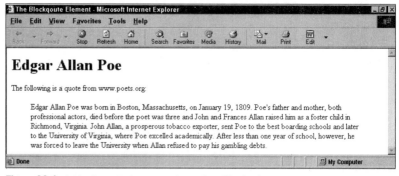

Figure 20-1: A block-quoted paragraph rendered in the browser

3. You can increase the amount of indentation using multiple
   `<blockquote>` tags, as shown in Listing 20-2. Figure 20-2 shows
   the results in the browser.

```html
<html>
<head>
<title>the Blockquote Element</title>
</head>
<body text="#000000" bgcolor="#FFFFFF">

<h1>Edgar Allan Poe</h1>

<p>The following is a quote from www.poets.org:</p>

<blockquote><blockquote><p>Edgar Allan Poe was born in
Boston, Massachusetts, on January 19, 1809. Poe's father and
mother, both professional actors, died before the poet was
three and John and Frances Allan raised him as a foster
child in Richmond, Virginia. John Allan, a prosperous
tobacco exporter, sent Poe to the best boarding schools and
later to the University of Virginia, where Poe excelled
academically. After less than one year of school, however,
he was forced to leave the University when Allan refused to
pay his gambling debts.</p></blockquote></blockquote>

</body>
</html>
```

Listing 20-2: Using multiple <blockquote> tags to increase the indentation of a quoted paragraph

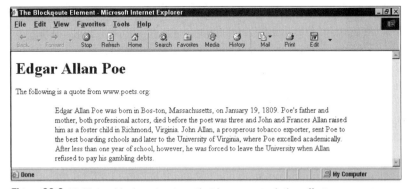

Figure 20-2: Multiple <blockquote> tags that have a cumulative effect

tips

- A quick and easy way to ensure a printable margin for a Web page is to block-quote the entire HTML document by placing opening and closing `<blockquote>` tags just inside the opening and closing `<body>` tags.

- Using multiple `<blockquote>` tags to indent text is deprecated by the W3C in favor of Cascading Style Sheets (see Part 9).

cross-reference

- To learn how to control indentation and margins using CSS, see Tasks 87 and 94.

Task **21**

Setting Document Margins

Y ou can control the document margin with four nonstandard attributes of the `<body>` tag. Two of the attributes were introduced by Microsoft Internet Explorer; the other two by Netscape Navigator. When defined together, you're guaranteed margin control, not only in these two major browsers but also in their competitors.

1. In your text editor, open an existing document whose margins you want to modify or just begin a new document.

2. To define the margins of your document, first enter Internet Explorer's two margin attributes `leftmargin` and `topmargin` in your `<body>` tag:

```
<html>
<head>
    <title>Non-standard Margin Attributes</title>
</head>

<body leftmargin= topmargin= >

</body>
</html>
```

3. Follow these two attributes with Netscape Navigator's two attributes, `marginwidth` and `marginheight`:

```
<body leftmargin= topmargin= marginwidth=  marginheight=>
```

4. Set each attribute equal to a numeric value (representing pixels), as shown in Listing 21-1. The value you specify for `leftmargin` and `marginwidth` set the width of both your left and right margins. Your `topmargin` and `marginheight` values set the width of both the top and bottom margins. Figure 21-1 shows the result of this code in your browser.

```
<html>
<head>
    <title>Non-standard Margin Attributes</title>
</head>

<body leftmargin="100" topmargin="50" marginwidth="100"
marginheight="50">

<p>The values we've set for the four margin attributes
result in left and right margins that are 100 pixels wide,
and top and bottom margins that are 50 pixels high.</p>

</body>
</html>
```

Listing 21-1: A document with 50-pixel margins set for top and bottom, and 100-pixel margins set for the left and right sides.

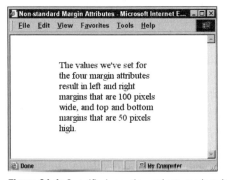

Figure 21-1: Specified margin settings rendered in the browser

tips

- Setting your margins to zero allows your design to run to the edges of the browser window.

- If being printer-friendly is an issue for your document, understand that the reason some Web pages don't print nicely is because there's content running out to the edges of the screen, which corresponds to where the printer rollers grab the paper. If you define sufficiently wide margins, there will be plenty of room for the rollers to grab without interfering with your page content.

cross-reference

- Cascading Style Sheets margin properties are covered in Part 9.

Creating an Ordered List

If you use a word processor to make a numbered list of items, all you have to do is click a button and start typing. Creating them in HTML is almost as easy: Use the `<ol>` (*ordered list*) and `<li>` (*list item*) tags. Both are container tags with opening and closing forms. As the name implies, you use ordered lists to render information of a procedural nature — for example, the items in this task.

1. In the body of your HTML document, enter an opening `<ol>` tag to mark where the list begins.

2. Proceed to the next line, indent and enter an opening `<li>` tag to mark the start of the first list item.

3. Follow the opening `<li>` tag with the text for your list item.

4. Finish the list item with a closing `</li>` tag.

5. Continue this process, entering as many list items as required to complete your ordered list. There is no limit to the number of items a list can have.

6. To conclude your ordered list, enter a closing `</ol>` tag after the last list item.

7. To format the text of your list, place an opening `<font>` tag above the list and a closing `</font>` tag after the list. This way the entire list — numbers and all — receives your formatting.

An example of an ordered list is shown in Listing 22-1. The page this code produces appears in Figure 22-1.

note

* Browsers indent list items by default, not because we've done so in the code. Indenting your code just makes it easier to read.

caution

* Even though browsers allow you to omit them, always use closing `</li>` tags. They produce cleaner, more readable code. And, of course, XHTML requires them.

```
<html>
<head>
 <title>Ordered Lists</title>
</head>
<body>
<h1>Honest Shampoo Instructions</h1>

<font face="Verdana, Arial, Helvetica, sans-serif" size="2">
<ol>
   <li>Apply to wet hair</li>
   <li>Massage gently into hair and scalp</li>
   <li>Rinse thoroughly</li>
   <li>Repeat steps 1 - 3 to ensure you burn through
       a bottle of this stuff a week.</li>
</ol>
</font>
</body>
</html>
```

Listing 22-1: An ordered list

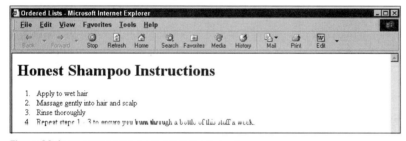

Figure 22-1: An ordered list rendered in the browser

cross-reference

- Bulleted lists (also called unordered lists) aren't radically different from ordered lists in their construction. To construct an unordered list, see Task 25.

Modifying Ordered List Styles

By default, an ordered list renders items with Arabic numerals: 1, 2, 3, and so on. You can modify the style of list items by defining the type attribute of the `<ol>` tag. The `type` attribute for the `<ol>` tag accepts five possible values.

notes

▪ Lists force a blank line after them, just like paragraphs and headings do.

▪ In theory, you shouldn't apply the `type` attribute to the `<li>` tag. However, browsers allow you to get away with using it, not that you'd ever have a reason to do so.

1. To create an uppercase alphabetical list, set the `type` attribute equal to "A":

   ```
   <ol type="A">
   ```

2. To create a lowercase alphabetical list, set the `type` attribute equal to "a":

   ```
   <ol type="a">
   ```

3. To create an uppercase Roman numeral list, set the `type` attribute equal to "I":

   ```
   <ol type="I">
   ```

4. To create a lowercase Roman numeral list, set the `type` attribute equal to "i":

   ```
   <ol type="i">
   ```

5. To create an Arabic numeral list, set the `type` attribute equal to "1":

   ```
   <ol type="1">
   ```

6. To see how each of these styles appears in a browser, enter the code shown in Listing 23-1 into your text editor and test it in a browser. Your results should look similar to Figure 23-1.

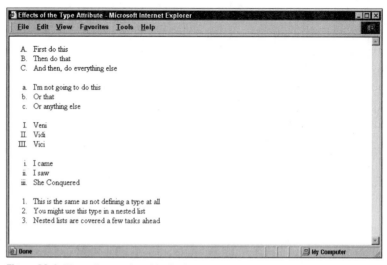

Figure 23-1: List styles rendered in the browser

```
<html>
<head>
   <title>Effects of the Type Attribute</title>
</head>

<body>

<ol type="A">
   <li>First do this</li>
   <li>Then do that</li>
   <li>And then, do everything else</li>
</ol>

<ol type="a">
   <li>I'm not going to do this</li>
   <li>Or that</li>
   <li>Or anything else</li>
</ol>

<ol type="I">
   <li>Veni</li>
   <li>Vidi</li>
   <li>Vici</li>
</ol>

<ol type="i">
   <li>I came</li>
   <li>I saw</li>
   <li>She Conquered</li>
</ol>

<ol type="1">
   <li>This is the same as not defining a type at all</li>
   <li>You might use this type in a nested list</li>
   <li>Nested lists are covered a few tasks ahead</li>
</ol>

</body>
</html>
```

Listing 23-1: Different ordered list styles

cross-references

- By nesting a series of ordered lists with different styles, you can create highly detailed formal outlines. To learn more about nested lists, see Task 27.

- Ordered list styles can also be controlled via Cascading Style Sheets. To learn more about CSS, see Part 9.

Modifying an Ordered List's Starting Character

note

- While the values of the `start` and `value` attributes are always defined with an integer, the corresponding list item character may not be numerical. For example, if the ordered list's `type` attribute equals A (creating an uppercase A, B, C list), setting the `start` or `value` attribute equal to 3 begins the list with "C." In an uppercase Roman numeral list (`type="I"`), the list would begin with III, etc.

HTML tries to be logical. Consequently, the attribute you define to specify the starting number or character in an ordered list is named `start`. This attribute allows you to maintain an unbroken ordering sequence even if you have to separate lists with paragraph text. You specify the value of an individual list item using the `value` attribute.

1. Enter an ordered list as discussed in Tasks 22 and 23.

2. Follow the list with paragraph text.

3. Create a second ordered list, defining the `start` attribute and setting it equal to the number you want the second list to begin with. Listing 24-1 shows a complete document sample, and Figure 24-1 shows the sample code displayed in the browser. In this example, the `start` attribute equals 4, which forces the second list to begin with 4.

```
<html>
<head>
<title>Ordered Lists</title>
</head>
<body>
<p>To shampoo, follow these steps:</p>
<ol>
    <li>Apply to wet hair</li>
    <li>Massage gently into hair and scalp</li>
    <li>Rinse thoroughly</li>
</ol>

<p>Then, to condition proceed by:</p>

<ol start="4">
    <li>Wringing excess water from hair</li>
    <li>Apply conditioner and massage gently into hair from
roots to ends</li>
    <li>Rinse thoroughly with warm water</li>
</ol>

</body>
</html>
```

Listing 24-1: Specifying an ordered list's starting number

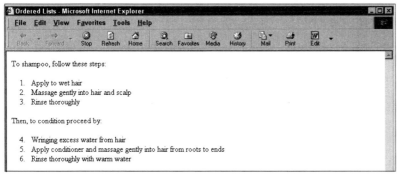

Figure 24-1: A continuous ordered list, separated by text, rendered in the browser

4. You can achieve the same effect using the `value` attribute of the first `<li>` tag, as shown here. Subsequent `<li>` tags follow in order.

```
<ol>
    <li value="4">Wringing excess water from hair</li>
    <li>Apply conditioner and massage gently into hair from
roots to ends</li>
    <li>Rinse thoroughly with warm water</li>
</ol>
```

Creating an Unordered List

What word processing calls a bulleted list, HTML refers to as an *unordered list*. You create these using the `<ul>` tag and the same `<li>` tag that ordered lists use.

1. In the body of your HTML document, enter a `<ul>` tag.

2. Begin your list items by proceeding to the next line, indenting, and entering an `<li>` tag.

3. Follow the opening `<li>` tag with the text for your list item and end it with a closing `</li>` tag.

4. Continue this process, entering list items to complete your unordered list.

5. End the unordered list with a closing `</ul>` tag. An example of an unordered list appears in Listing 25-1. The page this code produces appears in Figure 25-1.

notes

- Just like ordered lists, there's no limit to the number of list items you can have.

- As with the ordered lists, browsers indent list items by default, not because we've done so in the code. Indenting your code makes it easier to read.

- The HTML standard contains a directory and menu list, created with `<dir>` and `<menu>` tags. Like ordered and unordered lists, they used `<li>` tags for their list items. The directory list was supposed to create multicolumn lists, and the menu list was meant for single columns. Unfortunately, no browser ever attempted to render these lists. Using these tags simply creates an unordered list.

caution

- Always use closing `</li>` tags. They make for cleaner, more readable code, and XHTML requires them.

```
<html>
<head>
    <title>Unordered Lists</title>
</head>
<body>
<h1>Points to Remember</h1>

<ul>
    <li>Don't run with scissors</li>
    <li>Don't play with your food</li>
    <li>Don't forget to wash your hands</li>
</ul>

</body>
</html>
```

Listing 25-1: An unordered list

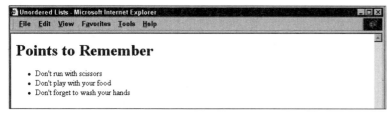

Figure 25-1: An unordered list rendered in the browser

cross-reference

- The default bullet style for unordered lists is typically a small filled-in disc. To see how to modify bullet styles, see Task 26.

Modifying Bullet Styles

Just like the `<ol>` tag, the `<ul>` tag accepts the `type` attribute. In this case, the `type` attribute governs the style of the bullet that precedes each list item. The possible values for the `type` attribute are `disc`, `square`, and `circle`.

1. Create an unordered list as described in Task 25.

2. To create square bullets, set the `type` attribute equal to `square`:

   ```
   <ul type="square">
   ```

3. To create circular bullets, set the `type` attribute equal to `circle`:

   ```
   <ul type="circle">
   ```

4. To create disc bullets, set the `type` attribute equal to `disc`:

   ```
   <ul type="disc">
   ```

5. To see how each of these styles appears in a browser, enter the code shown in Listing 26-1 into your text editor and test it in a browser. Your results should look similar to Figure 26-1.

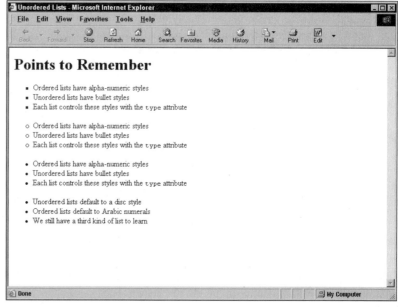

Figure 26-1: Different bullet styles rendered in the browser

```
<html>
<head>
    <title>Unordered Lists</title>
</head>
<body>
<h1>Points to Remember</h1>

<ul type="square">
    <li>Ordered lists have alpha-numeric styles</li>
    <li>Unordered lists have bullet styles</li>
    <li>Each list controls these styles with the
        <tt>type</tt> attribute</li>
</ul>

<ul type="circle">
    <li>Ordered lists have alpha-numeric styles</li>
    <li>Unordered lists have bullet styles</li>
    <li>Each list controls these styles with the
        <tt>type</tt> attribute</li>
</ul>

<ul type="disc">
    <li>Ordered lists have alpha-numeric styles</li>
    <li>Unordered lists have bullet styles</li>
    <li>Each list controls these styles with the
        <tt>type</tt> attribute</li>
</ul>

<ul>
    <li>Unordered lists default to a disc style</li>
    <li>Ordered lists default to Arabic numerals</li>
    <li>We still have a third kind of list to learn</li>
</ul>

</body>
</html>
```

Listing 26-1: Code showing different bulleted list styles

tip
- Although the HTML and XHTML standards don't recognize this practice, most browsers allow you to define the `type` attribute for the individual `<li>` tags as well.

cross-reference
- The default bullet style is also influenced by nesting. To learn how to nest lists, see Task 27.

Nesting Lists

Nesting simply means to place elements inside other elements. When you nest lists, you insert a new ordered or unordered list between list items in an existing list. The existing list is called the *parent* list and the second, nested list is called the *child* list. You can, in turn, nest a third list within the second, a fourth within the third, and so on. By nesting lists in this fashion, each list becomes a sublist of the parent list item above it. This technique is ideal for creating formal outlines.

1. In the body of an HTML document, begin the parent list by entering an `<ol>` or `<ul>` tag.

2. Define an appropriate `type` attribute.

3. Move to the next line, indent, and insert list items for your primary topics using `<li>` and `</li>` tags.

4. End the parent list with a closing `</ol>` or `</ul>` tag.

5. Beneath a list item, nest a child list whose items represent subcategories of the parent list item above it. Set an appropriate `type` attribute for this list's `<ol>` or `<ul>` tag also.

6. Nest subsequent lists for each new subcategory level you require. A full code example appears in Listing 27-1. Figure 27-1 shows how the document appears in the browser.

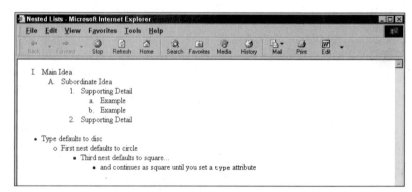

Figure 27-1 Nested lists rendered in the browser

```
<html>
<head>
    <title>Nested Lists</title>
</head>
<body>

<ol type="I">
    <li>Main Idea</li>
    <ol type="A">
        <li>Subordinate Idea</li>
        <ol type="1">
            <li>Supporting Detail</li>
            <ol type="a">
                <li>Example</li>
                <li>Example</li>
            </ol>
            <li>Supporting Detail</li>
        </ol>
    </ol>
</ol>
<ul>
    <li>Type defaults to disc</li>
    <ul>
        <li>First nest defaults to circle</li>
        <ul>
            <li>Third nest defaults to square...</li>
            <ul>
                <li>and continues as square until you
set a
                <tt>type</tt> attribute</li>
            </ul>
        </ul>
    </ul>
</ul>

</body>
</html>
```

Listing 27-1: Example of nested lists

tip

- By indenting your code, and even adding blank lines before and after nested lists, you can easily locate where each new list begins and ends.

cross-reference

- You can modify list styles using Cascading Style Sheets (see Part 9).

Creating Definition Lists

Definition lists are slightly different than the previous list types you've encountered. The list items in a definition list consist of two parts: a term and a description. Browsers render definition lists by placing the term on one line and indenting the definition underneath it, creating what's called a *hanging indent*. You use three pairs of tags to create a definition list: <dl> and </dl> tags define where the list begins and ends, <dt> and </dt> tags define the term, and <dd> and </dd> tags define the term's definition.

1. In the body of your HTML document, enter a <dl> tag to begin your list.

2. Begin your term by proceeding to the next line, indenting, and entering a <dt> tag. Follow this opening <dt> tag with the first term you intend to define and finish it with a closing </dt> tag.

3. Begin the term's definition by proceeding to the next line, indenting to be directly under the term, and then entering a <dd> tag.

4. Follow this tag with the text that defines the term and close this with a </dd> tag.

5. Continue this process, entering as many terms and definitions as you require, as shown in Listing 28-1.

```
<dl>
<dt>The Ordered List</dt>

    <dd>Created using the OL element. This list should
contain information where order should be emphasized.</dd>

<dt>The Unordered List</dt>

    <dd>Created using the UL element.
```

Listing 28-1: Example of a definition list

6. End the definition list with a closing </dl> tag. An example of a completed definition list is shown in Listing 28-2. The page this code produces appears in Figure 28-1.

```
<html>
<head>
   <title>Definition Lists</title>
</head>
<body>
<h1>Lists in HTML</h1>

<dl>
<dt>The Ordered List</dt>
   <dd>Created using the OL element. This list should
      contain information where order should be
      emphasized.</dd>
<dt>The Unordered List</dt>
<dd>Created using the UL element. This list should be
   used to express a series of significant points
</dd>
<dt>The Definition List</dt>
<dd>Create using the DL element. This list should be
   used to define a list of terms.</dd>
</dl>

</body>
</html>
```

Listing 28-2: A definition list

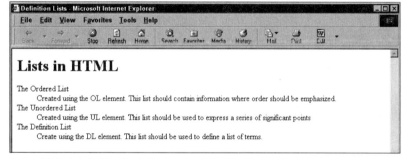

Figure 28-1: A definition list indenting the definitions beneath each term, thereby creating a hanging indent

tip
- Definition lists can be used to create written dialog. For the term, enter the speaker's name; for the definition, enter the speaker's lines.

cross-reference
- Indenting is a stylistic concern, and therefore better left to Cascading Style Sheets (see Part 9).

Part 3: Working with Images

Inserting Images

When you place the `<img>` tag in your document's code, the browser embeds the image file you reference in the document. Referencing a specific image file in the `<img>` tag requires an attribute; the `<img>` tag — just like the `<font>` tag you saw in Part 2 — doesn't really do anything by itself.

1. To embed an image, place an `<img>` tag within the body of your document, as shown here:

   ```
   <img>
   ```

2. To specify the image you want displayed, add a `src` attribute, setting it equal to the pathname of the image on the server, as shown here:

   ```
   <img src="images/daisy_calvin.jpg">
   ```

3. To specify the image's dimensions, include `width` and `height` attributes and set them equal to the pixel dimensions of the image:

   ```
   <img src="daisy_calvin.jpg" width="200" height="100">
   ```

4. To specify alternative text to be used in place of the image for users with nonvisual browsers, include an `alt` attribute:

   ```
   <img src="daisy_calvin.jpg" width="200" height="100"
   alt="Our cats, Daisy and Calvin.">
   ```

5. To place a border around an image, include a `border` attribute, setting it equal to the border's thickness in pixels:

   ```
   <img src="daisy_calvin.jpg" width="200" height="100"
   alt="Our cats, Daisy and Calvin." border="5">
   ```

6. To render your `<img>` tag XHTML-compliant, include a space after your last attribute and enter a forward slash, as shown here:

   ```
   <img src="daisy_calvin.jpg" width="200" height="100"
   alt="Our cats, Daisy and Calvin." border="5" />
   ```

Listing 29-1 shows how each attribute is used. Figure 29-1 displays the code in a browser.

note

- In the past, when connection speeds were so slow that downloading images was time-consuming, the `alt` attribute allowed you to give visitors a hint of what the picture was about. Today, alternate text is useful for visually impaired visitors who use speaking browsers to experience the Web. The inclusion of the `alt` attribute is also a federal requirement for making a site compliant with Section 508 (www.section508.gov), which states that all government sites must be handicap-accessible.

caution

- Don't simply change an `<img>` tag's `width` and `height` attribute values to resize an image that you decide is too large or small for your document. A large file resized smaller takes just as long to download; a small file resized typically becomes distorted. Instead, resize the image in an image editor like Adobe Photoshop or Macromedia Fireworks and use the new, smaller file in the `<img>` tag.

```html
<html>
<head>
   <title>Inserting Images</title>
</head>
<body>

<img src="daisy_calvin.jpg" width="200" height="100"
alt="Our cats, Daisy and Calvin." border="5" />
<p>
<font face="Arial, Helvetica, sans-serif" size="2">
<b>Daisy and Calvin - the gruesome twosome.</b>
</font>
</p>
</body>
</html>
```

Listing 29-1: An image with text below it

Figure 29-1: An image with text below it, rendered in the browser

tips

- An `<img>` tag with a defined `src` attribute is sufficient for embedding an image in your document. However, Web browsers that encounter an `<img>` tag stop rendering any code that follows it until they've downloaded the image. If the connection is poor, the rest of the page sits blank until the image loads, then continues. You can mitigate this by defining the image's dimensions using the `width` and `height` attributes. These tell the browser how much space to reserve for the image and allow it to continue rendering the rest of the document while the images download.

- Because Alt text appears in browsers when images fail to load (for whatever reason), by including the filename of the image in your Alt text, it helps you troubleshoot where missing images are on the Web server. Simply make note of the filename, and then make sure you upload that missing file to the server. If it's already present on the server, you can then check to see if it's become corrupted.

cross-reference

- Pathnames are integral to defining hyperlinks, and the same rules apply for each. To learn more, see Task 39.

Controlling Image Alignment and Spacing

notes

- Images floated to the left are pinned to the left margin; text wraps around them down the right side. When floated to the right, the image is pinned to the right margin and text starts on the left margin, wrapping down the left side of the image.

- The hspace attribute affects the spacing on the left and right side of an image; the vspace attribute affects the spacing above and below the image.

- The align attribute is deprecated in favor of Cascading Style Sheets (see Part 9).

Image alignment is controlled with the align attribute. The values top, middle, and bottom relate to the image's position relative to the surrounding text. The values left and right cause the image to float to the left or right margin, wrapping text down the image's opposite side. White space surrounding an image is controlled with the hspace and vspace attributes.

1. To align an image element, add an align attribute to the <img> tag as shown here:

    ```
    <img align="" src="images/daisy_calvin-2.jpg" width="50"
    height="50" alt="Our cats, Daisy and Calvin." />
    ```

2. To vertically align the top of the image with the top, middle, or bottom of the preceding line of text, set the align attribute equal to top, middle, or bottom. Figure 30-1 shows the results created by each value.

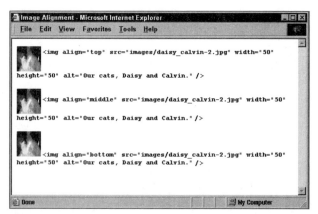

Figure 30-1: The effects of the align attribute set to top, middle, and bottom, respectively

3. To float an image element to the left or right margin, set the align attribute equal to either left or right. Figure 30-2 illustrates both alignments.

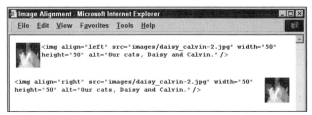

Figure 30-2: Two paragraphs with images floated to the left and right

4. To center an image, wrap the `<img>` tag inside opening and closing `<div>` tags and add an `align` attribute to it instead, setting it equal to `"center"`. Figure 30-3 shows the results of centering an image.

Figure 30-3: A centered image

5. To increase the amount of white space around an image, add the `hspace` and `vspace` attributes and set them equal to a pixel value, as shown in Figure 30-4.

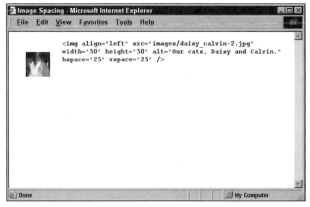

Figure 30-4: An image with 25 pixels of horizontal and vertical space added with the hspace and vspace attributes

Resizing Images Using Photoshop Elements

Image editing is not exactly specific to HTML, but it is important to understand whenever you work with images.

Changing an image's pixel dimensions in an image editor is called *resampling*. As you might guess, decreasing the image's dimensions — also called *downsampling* — deletes data from your image. Increasing the dimensions (*resampling up*) adds new pixels through a process called *interpolation* — which looks at existing pixels in the image and determines what the best color values of the added pixels should be. In general, resampling up results in a loss of detail.

1. To resample an image using Photoshop Elements, first open the file you want to resample by choosing File ⇨ Open from the menu.

2. Choose Image ⇨ Resize ⇨ Image Size from the menu. This opens the Image Size dialog box (see Figure 31-1).

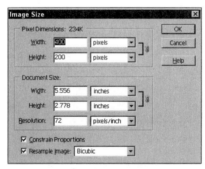

Figure 31-1: The Image Size dialog box in Adobe Photoshop Elements

3. At the bottom of the dialog box, select the Resample Image option and choose an interpolation method from the pop-up menu (see Figure 31-2).

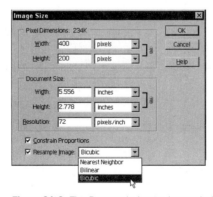

Figure 31-2: The Resample Image interpolation pop-up menu

notes

- For Tasks 31–34, we chose to use Adobe Photoshop Elements 2.0 because it's based on Adobe Photoshop — the most widely used professional image-editing application on the market. Currently list-priced at USD $99, it can be found at retailers (educational and otherwise) where discounts and manufacturer's rebates reduce the price to less than USD $50. Download a 30-day free trial version from www.adobe.com/products/tryadobe/main.jhtml#product=40. If you own a scanner, chances are it came bundled with image editing software which should also be able to handle these tasks.

- Bicubic is the most precise interpolation method in Photoshop Element. It takes longer to process but it produces the best results. Nearest Neighbor is the fastest and, consequently, least precise interpolation method. Bilinear falls between Bicubic and Nearest Neighbor, as a medium-quality interpolation method.

4. Click the Constrain Proportions option if it isn't already checked. Doing so maintains the image's proportions by automatically updating the width or height when you alter one of the dimensions.

5. Enter Width and Height values in the Pixel Dimensions fields. If you want to use percentages of the current dimensions instead, click the pop-up menus to the right of the Width and Height fields to switch from Pixels to Percent (see Figure 31-3).

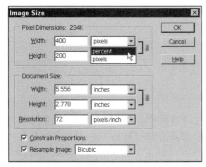

Figure 31-3: Choose a unit of measure: pixels or percentage

6. The image's resulting file size appears at the top of the Image Size dialog box, with the old file size in parentheses. Click OK to process your resampling choices and close the dialog box.

cross-reference

- Manually resizing an image in this fashion is preferred to simply changing the values of an `<img>` tag's `width` and `height` attributes. See Task 29.

Optimizing GIF Images
Using Photoshop Elements

Optimizing images results in a tradeoff between achieving the highest quality image with the smallest possible file size. In this task, you'll learn how to optimize images and save them in the Graphic Interchange Format (GIF). This file format is designed to create relatively detailed image files while retaining a small file size, so you can transfer images quickly across the Web.

1. To optimize and save an image as a GIF file, open your selected image by choosing File ➪ Open from the Photoshop Elements menu. This displays the Open dialog box. From here, locate your image and click the Open button.

2. Choose Save for Web from the File menu. This opens the Save for Web dialog box (shown in Figure 32-1). The interface displays the original image in one pane and the optimized image in the other. Make your optimization adjustments using the tools in the Settings area on the right side of the dialog box.

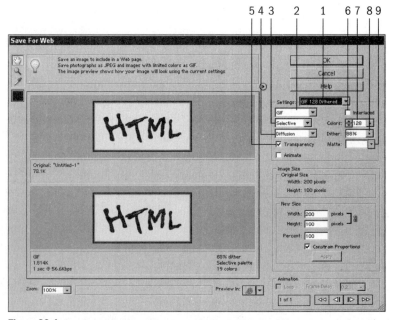

Figure 32-1: The Save for Web dialog box's Settings tools for GIFs include: 1. Optimization preset menu, 2. File Format menu, 3. Color Reduction Algorithm menu, 4. Dithering Algorithm menu, 5. Transparency check box, 6. Interlaced check box, 7. Colors menu, 8. Dither percentage, and 9. Matte Color

3. If you want to use one of the optimization presets in Photoshop Elements, make a selection from the presets menu. The choices on this menu modify all the tools in the Settings area; they have names like GIF 128 Dithered.

4. To choose custom settings, simply use the rest of the tools in the Settings area:

   a. Choose GIF from the file format menu.

   b. Select a *color reduction algorithm*, a mathematical formula for deciding where and how to remove colors from an image without making it look terrible. Choose from among Perceptual, Selective, Adaptive, Web, or Custom. For most purposes, Selective is the best choice.

   c. To specify manually the maximum number of colors in the image, select a number from the Colors pop-up menu. You can enter the value manually or click the arrows to increase or decrease the value one number at a time.

   d. Use the Dithering Algorithm pop-up menu if you choose to set a dithering algorithm. Choose No Dither, Diffusion, Pattern, or Noise. Use the Dithering Percentage pop-up menu to specify the amount of dithering.

5. Look at the lower-left corner of the optimized image to see what your optimization settings have done to the file size and download time (see Figure 32-2).

Figure 32-2: The optimized file size and download time determined by the Settings area

6. To save your optimized image, click OK. In the Save Optimized As dialog box, type a filename and click Save.

tips

- One reason why GIF files (GIFs) are small is because they contain no more than 256 colors. Consequently, some pictures are better suited as GIFs than others. Color photographs make bad GIFs because they typically contain millions of colors. Converting them to GIFs removes most of the colors, making them look like a paint-by-numbers project. The best images for converting into GIFs contain a limited number of colors that meet at discreet edges (like logos). GIFs sometimes yield high-quality, black-and-white photos, provided they aren't too detailed to begin with.

- Control-click (Mac) or right-click (Windows) next to the download information to access a menu where you can specify a connection speed to calculate the download time.

cross-reference

- If you're wondering about JPEG files, check out Task 33.

Optimizing JPEG Images Using Photoshop Elements

JPEG stands for Joint Photographic Experts Group, which is responsible for creating standards for "continuous tone image coding." An image with continuous tone has a virtually unlimited range of colors or shades of gray. Whereas GIFs can only handle 256 colors or shades of gray, JPEG images (also called just JPEGs) can display 16,777,215. JPEGs are best suited for color photographs and photorealistic images.

note

- When you choose a JPEG preset or choose JPEG from the File Format menu in Photoshop Elements, the Settings tools in the Save for Web dialog box change. JPEG quality is a function of choosing a value between 0 and 100: the higher the number, the better the final image quality, and the higher the file size. The Optimization preset menu has three choices for JPEG images: JPEG High, JPEG Medium, and JPEG Low, which correspond to values of 60, 30, and 10, respectively. (Find out more about the JPEG format at www.jpeg.org.)

1. Open your image in Photoshop Elements and choose File ⇨ Save for Web from the menu to open the Save for Web dialog box.

2. Choose a JPEG preset or choose JPEG from the File Format menu (see Figure 33-1).

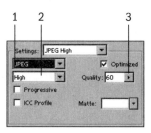

Figure 33-1: The Save for Web dialog box's Settings tools for JPEGs include: 1. File format menu, 2. Quality Level menu, and 3. Quality slider

3. If you prefer a custom setting, you can set the Quality Level menu to Low, High, Medium, or Maximum (see Figure 33-2). A Maximum option equals a value of 80.

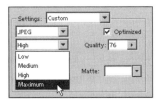

Figure 33-2: The Quality Level menu

4. If you want to manually set the value, use the Quality slider (see Figure 33-3). A value of 0 gives you the lowest possble image quality with the smallest possible file size. A value of 100 gives you the highest quality image but the largest possible file size.

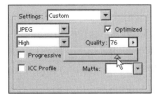

Figure 33-3: The Quality slider

5. To save your optimized image, click OK.

6. In the Save Optimized As dialog box, type a filename and click Save.

tip

▪ Just above the Quality slider sits the Optimized check box. The Optimized check box is always selected if you choose an optimization preset. Don't turn it off. The option provides enhanced color optimization, resulting in a smaller overall file size. Although this enhancement is not supported by older browsers (prior to the 4.0 versions of Netscape Navigator and Internet Explorer), they don't react adversely to you using it.

cross-reference

▪ What about PNG files? They're covered in Task 34.

Optimizing PNG Images Using Photoshop Elements

The Portable Network Graphics (PNG) format was created as a free and more robust alternative to GIF after Unisys, the patent owner of the GIF compression method (called Lempel-Ziv-Welch or LZW), sought royalties from software developers whose programs used it. PNG uses a lossless compression algorithm, just like GIF, and supports images with 8- and 24-bit color depths. At an 8-bit color depth, PNG and GIF are equal in image quality, although PNG generally results in infinitesimally larger file sizes. One reason not to use PNG in place of GIF is if a large proportion of your audience uses browsers prior to version 4.0 of Internet Explorer and Netscape Navigator, which don't support it.

1. Open your image in Photoshop Elements and choose File ⇨ Save for Web from the menu to open the Save for Web dialog box.

2. To optimize an image as PNG-8, choose PNG-8 from the File Format menu.

3. The PNG-8 Settings options are identical to those for GIF, as you can see from Figure 34-1. To select a color reduction algorithm, choose Perceptual, Selective, Adaptive, Web, or Custom from the Color Reduction Algorithm menu.

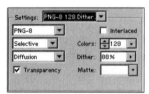

Figure 34-1: The PNG-8 optimization settings

note

* JPEG throws away image data to compress files, making it "lossy" (data is lost in the compression process). Because PNG-24 supports 16.7 million colors but doesn't throw any data away, it cannot compress a file as well as JPEG can.

4. To set a dithering algorithm, choose No Dither, Diffusion, Pattern, or Noise from the Dithering Algorithm menu. Use the Dithering Percentage menu to specify the amount of dithering you want.

5. Use the Colors menu to set the number of colors in your image.

6. If you save an image as PNG-24, the Settings tools display only the File Format menu (see Figure 34-2). Simply select PNG-24.

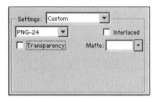

Figure 34-2: The PNG-24 settings

7. To save your optimized image, click OK.

8. In the Save Optimized As dialog box, type a filename and click Save.

tip

▪ Like GIF, PNG-8 supports a maximum of 256 colors; like JPEG, PNG-24 supports 16.7 million colors. (Find out more about the PNG format at www.libpng.org/ pub/png/.) You can use PNG-8 in place of GIF if you like, but PNG-24 generally results in larger file sizes than JPEG does. This has to do with file compression: GIF and PNG compress files by capitalizing on the inefficient method by which image files store their data. There's often unused space inside a file and GIF and PNG formats remove the empty space without deleting information from the file — making their compression methods "lossless" (no data is lost in the compression process).

cross-reference

▪ If you're interested in audio and video, read Part 4.

Part 4: Audio and Video

Task

35

Embedding Audio Files

Browsers can't play audio files without help from other applications. Enter the *plug-in*, a piece of software that runs within the browser to expand its functionality. Plug-ins are a Netscape creation, but when you have the Netscape browser installed, Microsoft Internet Explorer makes use of them as well. As of this writing, the Apple QuickTime plug-in comes installed with Netscape Navigator 7.02, so both Netscape and Internet Explorer, if installed, make use of it when playing embedded sound files.

1. In the body of your document, enter an `<embed>` tag.

2. Define a `src` attribute and set it equal to the location of the sound file on the Web server. For example:

```
<embed src="backbeat.mid">
```

3. Define `width` and `height` attributes to display a control panel in the browser window. For example:

```
<embed src="backbeat.mid" width="100" height="15">
```

This creates a control panel 100 pixels wide by 15 pixels high, as shown in Figure 35-1.

Figure 35-1: A QuickTime audio control panel

4. To prevent the sound file from playing the very moment the page loads, define an autostart attribute and set it equal to `false`:

```
<embed src="backbeat.mid" width="100" height="15"
autostart="false">
```

5. To float the control panel amongst text, similarly to an image, define an `align` attribute:

- `left` floats the control panel to the left margin and wraps text around it to the right.

- `right` floats the control panel to the right margin and wraps text around it to the left.

Listing 35-1 shows two embedded sound files, one aligned left and one aligned right. Figure 35-2 shows how a browser treats the control panels.

notes

- There are a number of different audio file types, some of which are proprietary and require specific plug-ins. The .wav format is Microsoft's proprietary file type and the .ra format is RealAudio's proprietary format (which requires RealPlayer). Only the .mid and .mp3 formats are non-proprietary; you can play them in numerous media players.

- The control panel's physical appearance varies depending on the plug-in, browser, and operating system.

```
<html>
<head>
    <title>Embedding Audio Files</title>
</head>

<body>

<p><embed src="backbeat.mid "height="35" width="150"
controller="true" align="left">To float the control panel
amongst text, similarly to an image, define an align
attribute. Setting the align attribute equal to left floats
the control panel to the left margin and wraps text around
it to the right. Setting the align attribute to right floats
the control panel to the right margin, and text begins on
the left margin, wrapping down the left side of the control
panel. </p>

<p><embed src="backbeat.mid "height="35" width="150"
controller="true" align="right">To float the control panel
amongst text, similarly to an image, define an align
attribute. Setting the align attribute equal to left floats
the control panel to the left margin and wraps text around
it to the right. Setting the align attribute to right floats
the control panel to the right margin, and text begins on
the left margin, wrapping down the left side of the control
panel.</p>


</body>
</html>
```

Listing 35-1: Using the align attribute of the <embed> tag

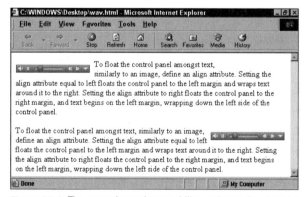

Figure 35-2: The control panel treated like an image by most browsers

tips

- If the autostart attribute is left undefined or set equal to true, the sound file begins playing the moment the page finishes loading in the browser.

- You can find several places to download sound files:
  www.findsounds.com
  www.mididb.com
  www.midifarm.com

cross-reference

- Macromedia Flash content is made possible using a plug-in. To learn about inserting Flash content, see Part 15.

Adding Background Sounds

There are two ways to define sounds meant to play in the background while visitors browse your site. One is a variation on Task 35 and another makes use of Microsoft's proprietary `<bgsound>` tag, which only works for Internet Explorer.

1. In the body of your document, enter an `<embed>` tag.

2. Define a `src` attribute and set it equal to the pathname of the sound file on the Web server.

3. Define `width` and `height` attributes, setting them equal to 1. This constrains the control panel to a single pixel that can be hidden anywhere on the page.

4. Set the `autostart` attribute equal to `true` so that the sound begins once the page has successfully loaded.

5. Define a `loop` attribute, setting it equal to the number of times you want the sound file to play. To make the sound play continuously while the page is viewed, set the attribute equal to `-1`. Listing 36-1 shows a completed `<embed>` tag.

```
<html>
<head>
   <title>Background Sounds</title>
</head>

<body>
<embed src=" bandmarch.mid" width="1" height="1"
autostart="true" loop="-1">

</body>
</html>
```

Listing 36-1: The <embed> tag formatted for use as a background sound.

cautions

- Before adding background sounds to a document, consider whether the effect is truly necessary. Many users find such sounds — and the fact that they can't disable them — extremely annoying.

- We recommend that if you must use sound, make it user-selectable. Provide a control panel at the very least, as shown in Task 37, and preferably set the `autostart` attribute to "false" so the user isn't hit unexpectedly with a sound.

6. To use Microsoft's proprietary <bgsound> tag, place the tag inside the <head> section of your document because it references something not specifically displayed in the browser window.

7. Define a src attribute and set it equal to the pathname of the sound file on the Web server.

8. Define a loop attribute and set it equal to the number of times you want the sound file to play. To have the sound play continuously while the page is viewed, set the attribute equal to -1. Listing 36-2 shows a completed <bgsound> tag.

```
<html>
<head>
    <title>Background Sounds</title>
<bgsound src="bandmarch.mid" loop="-1">
</head>

<body>

</body>
</html>
```

Listing 36-2: Using the <bgsound> tag to play a background sound

tip

- Generally avoid using proprietary elements like the <bgsound> tag. However, if you're creating an intranet site — a self-contained site that's part of an internal network, not the public Web — you can make use of proprietary elements as long as you know that your audience will only be using the one browser that supports it.

cross-reference

- Macromedia Flash content is made possible using a plug-in. To learn about inserting Flash content, see Part 15.

Embedding Video

You can use the <embed> tag to embed video files in a document. Just as with sound files, the physical appearance of control panels varies depending on the plug-in required to display the video file, user's browser, and operating system.

1. In the body of your document, enter an <embed> tag where you want the video file to be displayed.

2. Define a src attribute to specify the location of the source file on the Web server.

3. Define width and height attributes to specify the displayed video's dimensions.

4. Define an autoplay attribute and set it equal to true to make the video play as soon as the page loads. Set it equal to false to have the user click a play button to start the video clip.

5. Define a controller attribute, setting it equal to true to display a control panel. A setting of false hides the control panel. Listing 37-1 shows a completed <embed> tag. Figure 37-1 displays the results in a browser.

notes

- There are a number of different video file types, all of which require different plug-ins: the .mov format is Apple QuickTime, the .wmv format is Windows Media Viewer, the .avi format is native Windows video, and .mpeg and .mpg are non-proprietary formats that can typically be played by a number of plug-ins.

- The control panels of different plug-ins vary greatly and affect the physical size of the clip onscreen.

```html
<html>
<head>
    <title>Embedding Video</title>
</head>
<body>

<embed src="laurie.mov" width="177" height="144"
autoplay="false" controller="true">
<br>
<embed src="laurie.wmv" width="177" height="144"
autoplay="false" controller="true">

</body>
</html>
```

Listing 37-1: Using the <embed> tag

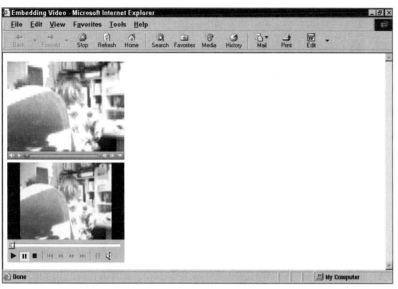

Figure 37-1: A QuickTime clip (top) versus a Windows Media Viewer clip (bottom)

6. Define a `loop` attribute as follows:

   - `true` makes the clip play continuously.

   - `false` makes the clip play only once.

   - `palindrome` makes the clip play normally and then play backwards, looping continuously.

tip

- If users come to your site and don't have the necessary plug-in, specify the Web site where they can download it (if you know it) using the `pluginspace` attribute. For example, `pluginspace=" http://www.apple.com/quicktime/"`.

cross-reference

- If you're interested in creating your own digital video (DV) for the Web, after getting your hands on a digital video camera, check out Sonic Foundry's DV editing software, called Vegas, at www.sonicfoundry.com/products/vegasfamily.asp.

Embedding Java Applets

The scope of this book is not broad enough to teach you how to write your own Java applets. Java is a complex programming language that you can use to develop entire applications. You can also use it to write small applets embedded in Web documents. There are all kinds of different applets available free for download on the Internet. They include graphics, games, and navigational elements, to name only a few. An example of a simple animated graphic is shown in this task. The two tags used to embed applets are `<applet>` and `<object>`. First you need to download an applet.

note

- Applets are like little programs; they can take a few seconds to download and run once the page is loaded in the browser.

1. Use your favorite search engine to browse for free Java applets until you come across one you're interested in downloading. They are typically packaged in "zipped" archives that you can open with applications like WinZip for Windows and StuffIt for Macintosh.

2. Enter an `<applet>` tag into the body of your document at the point in the code where you want the applet to appear in the browser window.

3. Define a `code` attribute and set it equal to the location of the Java source file:

   ```
   <applet code="Kubik.class">
   ```

4. Define appropriate `width` and `height` attributes. Exact dimensions may be specified with the applet instruction you download, or you may specify your own:

   ```
   <applet code="kubik.class" width="222" height="77">
   ```

5. Using `<param>` tags, specify parameters supplied by the programmer. Your ability to do this depends on the applet you are using. Typically, parameters and definitions appear in the sample you download. Parameters are controlled with `name` and `value` attributes, as shown here:

   ```
   <applet code="kubik.class" width="222" height="77">
   <param name="text" value="HELLO!">
   <param name="foreground" value="green">
   <param name="background" value="black">
   ```

6. Conclude your parameters with a closing `</applet>` tag, as shown here:

   ```
   <applet code="kubik.class" width="222" height="77">
   <param name="text" value="HELLO!">
   <param name="foreground" value="green">
   <param name="background" value="black">
   </applet>
   ```

cautions

- The `<applet>` tag is backwards-compatible with older browsers but is also deprecated in favor of the `<object>` tag. Use whichever tag is best for your circumstances: backwards-compatibility or standards-compliance.

- Because Java applets are programs, less than honorable programmers sometimes create applets that damage systems. Consequently, some companies and the U.S. government institute security measures that prevent applets from being viewable within their offices.

7. To use the `<object>` tag, insert the opening tag into the body of your document at the point in the code where you want the applet to appear in the browser window.

8. In place of the `code` attribute, enter a `codetype` attribute and set it equal to `application/java`. Enter a `classid` attribute and set it equal to `java:` and the source filename (no spaces); include your dimensions, as shown here:

```
<object codetype="application/java"
classid="java:kubik.class" width="222" height="77">
```

9. Include any parameters just as you would with the `<applet>` tag and finish with a closing `</object>` tag. Listing 38-1 shows a completed `<object>` tag in a document. Figure 38-1 displays the results in a Web browser.

```
<html>
<head>
   <title>Java Applets</title>
</head>

<body>

<object codetype="application/java"
classid="java:kubik.class" width="222" height="77">
<param name="text" value="HELLO!">
<param name="foreground" value="green">
<param name="background" value="black">
</object>
</body>
</html>
```

tips

• In a compressed archive, you typically get one or more Java source files and a sample HTML document with instructions.

• If your applet has no parameters to define, simply place the closing `</applet>` tag right after the opening tag.

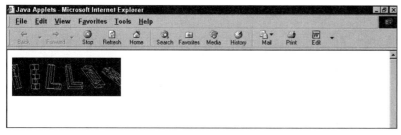

Figure 38-1: Example of a Java applet on a Web page

Part 5: Hyperlinks

Defining Hyperlinks

Hyperlinks are essential for the Web. You create them with the anchor tag, `<a>`, yet another tag that requires attributes. The attribute that transforms the little `<a>` tag into the linking powerhouse that puts the "hyper" in hypertext is `href`, which stand for *hypertext reference*. The closing anchor tag, as you can probably guess, is written `</a>`. The opening and closing anchor tags transform the text or images they surround into a region that, when clicked, loads whatever document you specify into the browser window. The `href` attribute points to the document you want to load when the link is clicked.

note

- By default, browsers under-line text links and place a border around image links.

1. In the body of an HTML document, locate the text or image tag you want to convert into a link.

2. Place an opening anchor tag in front of that text or image tag and define an `href` attribute, setting it equal to the pathname of the file you want to open when the link is clicked, as shown in Listing 39-1.

```
<a href="bingo.html">text-link

<a href="http://www.dingo.com">
<img src="dingo.gif" width="100" height="25" border="0"
alt="My dingo, Spiff.">
```

Listing 39-1: Examples of opening anchor tags

3. Place a closing anchor tag at the end of the text or directly after the image tag you're turning into a link, as shown in Listing 39-2.

```
<a href="bingo.html">text-link</a>

<a href="http://www.dingo.com">
<img src="dingo.gif" width="160" height="198" border="0"
alt="My dingo, Spiff." />
</a>
```

Listing 39-2: Examples of complete anchor tags

4. To format a link so that the document it points to opens in a new browser window, define a target attribute and set it equal to "_blank":

```
<a href="bingo.html" target="_blank">text link</a>
```

5. To control the color of text links, define the three following attributes for the `<body>` tag, setting them equal to hexadecimal or predefined color name values:

- `link` specifies the color of links that haven't been visited.

- `vlink` specifies the color of links that have been visited.

- `alink` specifies the color of links that are currently active.

Listing 39-3 shows a sample document. Figure 39-1 displays the document in a browser.

```
<html>
<head>
  <title>Hyperlinks</title>
</head>

<body link="#0000FF" vlink="#990099" alink="#FF0000">

<a href="bingo.html">text-link</a>
<br />
<br />
<a href="http://www.dingo.com" target="_blank">
<img src="dingo.gif" width="160" height="198" border="1"
alt="My dingo, Spiff." />
</a>

</body>
</html>
```

Listing 39-3: Text and image-based hyperlinks

Figure 39-1: Text and image hyperlinks rendered in the browser

tips

- Never omit the closing anchor tag. Otherwise, the browser has no idea where the linked content ends.

- To prevent an image link from displaying a border, set the image tag's `border` attribute equal to 0.

cross-references

- Task 40 covers absolute and relative pathnames.

- Targeting links is also integral to frames-based sites (see Part 8).

Task 40

Defining Pathnames

Whether you're defining the `href` attribute of the anchor tag, the `src` attribute of the image tag, or in any way referencing files within your Web site, you're working with *pathnames*. A pathname is simply a way to describe the *file structure* of your site — how files and folders (also called *directories*) are laid out on your computer, and ultimately the Web server. Figure 40-1 diagrams a simple structure of files and directories, which the following steps refer to.

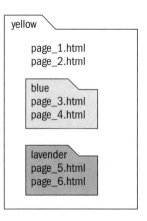

Figure 40-1: The Yellow directory containing two files (page_1.html and page_2.html) plus two additional subdirectories (Blue and Lavender), each of which contain two files

1. To reference a document in the same directory as the current file, set the `href` attribute equal to the document's filename. For example, to create a link in page_1.html that opens page_2.html, write the anchor tag as follows:

    ```
    <a href="page_2.html"> </a>
    ```

2. To reference a document inside a directory that's next to the current file, set the `href` attribute equal to the directory's name, add a forward slash, and follow it with the filename. For example, to create a link in page_1.html that opens page_3.html, write the anchor tag as follows:

    ```
    <a href="blue/page_3.html"> text or image </a>
    ```

3. To move up one directory in the file structure, referencing a document outside the directory of the current file, precede the filename with two periods and a forward slash. For example, to create a link in page_3.html that opens page_1.html, write the anchor tag as follows:

```
<a href="../page_1.html"> text or image </a>
```

4. To reference a document inside a directory that is outside the current file's directory, precede the filename with two periods and a forward slash, and follow it with the directory name and filename. For example, to create a link in page_5.html that opens page_3.html, write the anchor tag as follows:

```
<a href="../blue/page_3.html"> text or image </a>
```

5. Always use *absolute pathnames* to link to documents found on someone else's Web server. The easiest way to gather that information is to open the Web site in a browser, navigate to the exact page you want to link to, copy the URL in your browser's address bar (see Figure 40-2), and paste it directly into the HTML file, as shown here:

```
<a href="http://www.domainname.com/directoryname/
filename.html"> text or image </a>
```

Figure 40-2: Copying a URL in the browser's address bar

tips

- Each set of periods and a forward slash takes you up one directory higher in the file structure. This means that ../../filename takes you up two directories, ../../../ filename takes you up three directories, and so on.

- The keyboard shortcuts for copying are Ctrl+C (Windows) and Command+C (Macintosh). Pasting is Ctrl+V (Win) and Command+V (Mac).

cross-reference

- Pathname values are also used to define the src attribute of the <img> tag. See Task 29.

Task

Creating mailto Links

At some point, you've probably clicked a link to send an e-mail. Doing so opens your e-mail application with a new, properly addressed message window waiting for you to start typing. Creating this type of link varies only slightly from what we covered in Task 40.

note
- You are not required to define `subject` and `body` text in a `mailto` link.

1. In the body of an HTML document, locate the text or image tag you want to make into a link.

2. Place an opening anchor tag in front of that text or image tag.

3. Define an `href` attribute and set it equal to the `mailto:` protocol, including the e-mail address the message should go to, as shown here:

   ```
   <a href="mailto:robert@limehat.com">
   ```

4. To predefine the contents of the e-mail's "Subject" line, follow the e-mail address with a question mark (?), enter the word `subject`, and set it equal to the text you want displayed, as shown here:

   ```
   <a href="mailto:robert@limehat.com?subject=Party! RSVP">
   ```

5. To predefine the body text of the message, follow the subject value with an ampersand (&), enter the word `body`, and set it equal to the text you want displayed, as shown in Listing 41-1.

```
<html>
<head>
<title>Mailto: Links</title>
</head>

<body>
<a href="mailto:robert@limehat.com?subject=Party!
RSVP&body=I'll be there">Coming to our party?</a>

</body>
</html>
```

Listing 41-1: E-mail link with subject and body predefined

6. Place a closing anchor tag (</a>) at the end of the text or directly after the image tag you're turning into a link. When the link is clicked, the user's e-mail application will open with the address, subject, and body text already filled in, as shown in Figure 41-1.

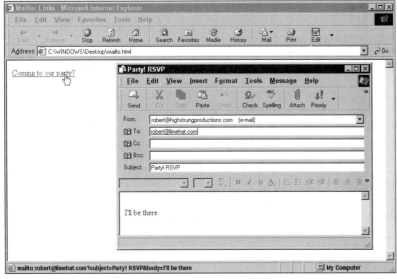

Figure 41-1: The new message window with address, subject line, and body already filled in

tips

▪ Don't include a space between the `mailto` protocol and the e-mail address.

▪ You can include spaces in the values you enter for `subject` and `body`.

Task 42

Linking to Named Anchors

You can do more than just link to documents and images. If you name an anchor tag at a specific place within a document (at the start of a section, for instance) you can specify that exact location in a hyperlink. This named anchor effectively becomes a subaddress within the document. You name an anchor tag by assigning a value to the name attribute of the <a> tag.

1. Enter an anchor tag at a specific line within a document to which you want to link.

2. Define a name attribute for the anchor tag, setting it equal to a descriptive term. For example:

   ```
   <a name="answer_2"><p>A: Push the green Power button on
   the remote. If that fails, check the surge strip.</p></a>
   ```

3. To link to this named anchor from within the same document, create an <a> tag and set its href attribute equal to the value of the named anchor. Precede the name with a pound sign, as shown here:

   ```
   <a href="#answer_2"> Q: How do I turn on the TV? </a>
   ```

4. You can achieve the same effect using the id attribute, which all tags accept. For example, in this code sample an id attribute could be applied to the <p> tag, as shown here:

   ```
   <p id="answer_2">A: Push the green Power button on the
   remote. If that fails, check the surge strip.</p>
   ```

   The hyperlink would still be defined:

   ```
   <a href="#answer_2"> text or image </a>
   ```

5. To link to the named anchor or `id` element from a document outside the current document, simply append the value to the end of the regular pathname. For example, if the named anchor were in a document named `faq.html`, the correct pathname value for a link in another document to `#answer_2` might be written as follows:

```
<a href="faq.html#answer_2"> text or image </a>
```

Figure 42-1 shows an example of named anchor links helping users navigate a long text document.

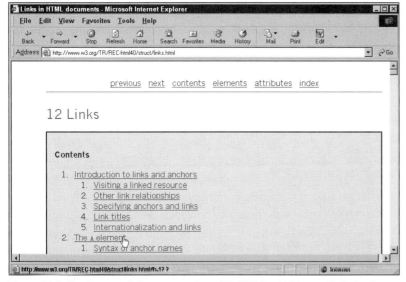

Figure 42-1: The Contents links at www.w3.org/TR/REC-html40/struct/links.html pointing to corresponding paragraphs further down the page (links.html#h-12.2 in this case)

tips

- You can insert the closing `</a>` tag right after the opening tag, or you can wrap both tags around an entire heading, paragraph, or image. Regardless of the option you choose, the line that the opening `<a>` tag sits on — the first line of a paragraph or the top of the image — determines where the document loads in the browser window.

- Frequently Asked Questions (FAQ) pages traditionally use named anchors to link each question within the Table of Contents list to the corresponding answer below. Because these documents tend to run very long, designers also place a named anchor at the top of the page and end each answer with a link back to the top anchor so that readers can easily return to the question list without having to scroll all the way back up. Figure 42-1 shows this technique used at the World Wide Web Consortium's site.

cross-reference

- See Task 40 about defining pathnames.

Part 6: Building Tables

Task 43

Defining Tables

A table is a structured element that consists of rows and columns of cells. You can place any kind of content you like in these cells: text, images, and even other tables. If you can define it in HTML, you can place it inside a table cell. There are three sets of container tags required to build any table. The `<table>` and `</table>` tags define where the table begins and ends, the `<tr>` and `</tr>` tags define where each row begins and ends, and the `<td>` and `</td>` tags define the individual cells within each row. There are no tags specifically defining columns; they result when multiple rows of cells are stacked on top of each other.

1. Within the body section of your document, enter an opening `<table>` tag.

2. Move to the next line by hitting the Enter (or Return) key, indent your cursor and enter an opening `<tr>` tag to define the start of the first row.

3. Hit Enter again to move to the next line, indent your cursor again, and enter an opening `<td>` tag to indicate the start of a new cell.

4. Follow the opening `<td>` tag with the specific content you want placed in this cell.

5. Complete the cell by entering a closing `</td>` tag.

6. Repeat Steps 3 through 5 for each cell you want to add to the row. When your row is finished, move to the next line and enter a closing `</tr>` tag vertically aligned beneath the opening `<tr>` tag to aid readability.

```
<table>
   <tr>
     <td> 1 </td>
     <td> 2 </td>
     <td> 3 </td>
   </tr>
```

7. Repeat Steps 2 through 6 to add subsequent rows to the table.

8. After completing the desired number of rows, move to the next line and finish the table with a closing `</table>` tag, vertically aligned with the opening `<table>` tag. Listing 43-1 shows the code required to produce a table with three rows and three columns. Figure 43-1 shows the results displayed in a browser.

Task **43**

```
<html>
<head>
<title>Tables</title>
</head>
<body>

<table>
   <tr>
    <td> 1 </td>
    <td> 2 </td>
    <td> 3 </td>
   </tr>
   <tr>
    <td> 4 </td>
    <td> 5 </td>
    <td> 6 </td>
   </tr>
   <tr>
    <td> 7 </td>
    <td> 8 </td>
    <td> 9 </td>
   </tr>
</table>

</body>
</html>
```

Listing 43-1: Code for a borderless table with three rows and three columns

Figure 43-1: The rather minimal table displayed in a browser

tips

- To make all text in a given cell bold and center-aligned, use `<th></th>` tags instead of `<td></td>` tags. TH stands for *table header*.

- In this example, each cell is defined on its own line. Some authors prefer to define all cells in a given row on the same line to mimic better how the table appears in the browser. It's up to you; it doesn't matter how much white space you add in HTML to aid code readability.

cross-references

- Each row must contain the same number of cells to render properly in a browser. You can merge cells, however, using the `colspan` and `rowspan` attributes discussed in Task 45.

- The `border` attribute is needed to help distinguish the cells of a table. To learn how to use this attribute, see Task 44.

Working with Table Borders

In Task 43, you created a simple table that organizes content into rows and columns. To make the individual cells more distinct, define borders for your table. Table borders are influenced by the following four attributes: `border`, `cellpadding`, `cellspacing`, and `bordercolor`.

1. To render a visible border around the table perimeter and interior cells, add the border attribute to the `<table>` tag and set it equal to a numeric value, such as:

   ```
   <table border="2">
   ```

   Figure 44-1 shows the simple table from Task 43 with this border attribute defined.

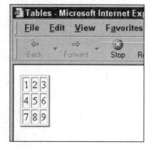

Figure 44-1: A table with a border one pixel thick

2. To control the thickness of internal borders between cells, define a `cellspacing` attribute and set it equal to a numeric value, such as:

   ```
   <table border="2" cellspacing="10">
   ```

   Figure 44-2 shows the result of adding this attribute value.

Figure 44-2: The same table in Figure 44-1 with cellspacing increased to 10 pixels

3. To control the amount of empty space between the border of a cell and the content inside it, define a `cellpadding` attribute. Set it equal to a numeric value, such as:

```
<table border="2" cellspacing="10" cellpadding="10">
```

Figure 44-3 shows the results in a browser.

Figure 44-3: The same table in Figure 44-2 with cellpadding increased to 10 pixels

4. To specify a border color, define a `bordercolor` attribute. Set this equal to a hexadecimal value or predefined color name, for example:

```
<table border="2" cellspacing="10" cellpadding="10"
bordercolor="#FF0000">
```

Figure 44-4 shows the results rendered in the browser.

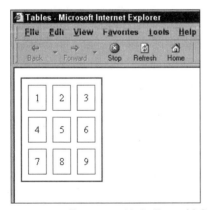

Figure 44-4: The same table in Figure 44-3 with a border color applied

tip

- When you specify no border color, both Internet Explorer and Netscape use a light gray highlight color and a darker shadow color to produce a 3-D beveled effect. Once you define the `bordercolor` attribute, Internet Explorer loses the 3-D effect (see Figure 44-4) and renders the borders in a solid color. Netscape takes the border color you specify and lightens it by 20% for the highlight color and darkens it by 20% for the shadow. To get Internet Explorer to mimic the Netscape border color effect, you must define `bordercolorlight` and `bordercolordark` attributes in addition to the `bordercolor` attribute, setting them equal to lighter and darker shades of the `bordercolor` attribute.

cross-reference

- Tables divide a page into distinct regions. In HTML you can also divide the entire browser window into distinct regions, where each region displays a separate document (called *frames*). To learn more about frames, see Part 8.

Spanning Cells

A single cell can span multiple columns or rows. The number of columns or rows a cell spans is defined using the colspan and rowspan attributes. To demonstrate how these attributes function, we'll build a small table and apply the attributes individually.

1. In the body section of your document, enter the table code shown in Listing 45-1. Figure 45-1 shows the results in a browser.

```
<table border="1" cellspacing="0" cellpadding="10">
   <tr>
      <td> 1 </td> <td> 2 </td> <td> 3 </td>
   </tr>
   <tr>
      <td> 4 </td> <td> 5 </td> <td> 6 </td>
   </tr>
   <tr>
      <td> 7 </td> <td> 8 </td> <td> 9 </td>
   </tr>
</table>
```

Listing 45-1: Simple table code

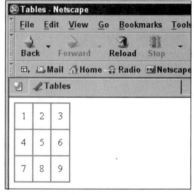

Figure 45-1: A simple nine-celled table, with three rows and three columns

2. To span a cell across a number of columns, add the colspan attribute to the <td> tag and set it equal to the number of columns you want to span. For example, to make the number 1 cell span across the other cells in the same row, add a colspan attribute equal to 3, as shown here:

```
<td colspan="3"> 1 </td>
```

3. Remove the code representing the two cells being spanned. In this example, delete `<td> 2 </td>` and `<td> 3 </td>` from the first row, save the document, and preview it in a browser. Figure 45-2 shows the result.

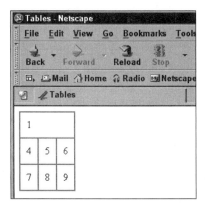

Figure 45-2: Cell 1 spanned across three columns

4. To span a cell across a number of rows, add the `rowspan` attribute to the `<td>` tag and set it equal to the number of rows you want to span. For example, to make the number 3 cell span the other cells in the same column, add a `rowspan` attribute equal to 3, as shown here:

```
<td rowspan="3"> 3 </td>
```

5. Remove the code representing the two cells being spanned. In this example, delete `<td> 6 </td>` in the second row and `<td> 9 </td>` in the third row, and then save your document and preview it in a browser. Figure 45-3 shows the result.

Figure 45-3: Cell 3 spanned across three rows

tip

- Spanning rows and columns can be useful when creating a single table heading (`<th> </th>`) across the top of a table or down its side.

cross-reference

- Tables can also include captions and summaries (see Task 50).

Aligning Table Elements

notes

- The default value for the align attribute is left.

- The default value for the valign attribute is middle. Vertical alignment, as shown in Figure 46-3, is not only relative to the cell but, in the case of baseline, relative to content in adjacent cells. In Figure 46-3, the baseline of the image is at the bottom of the cell so that's where the first cell aligns its text.

Just like many other elements we've examined, the align attribute can be used to influence a table's position as well as the content of individual table cells. When you apply the align attribute to the <table> tag, it affects the table the same way as it does an image: It positions the table relative to the other text inside the document. When you apply the align attribute to the <td> tag, it aligns the cell's content. Because cells also possess height — whether specifically defined by the height attribute or forced by the cell's content — you can vertically align content within cells using the valign attribute.

1. To specify a table's alignment, define an align attribute of the <table> tag and set it equal to left, right, or center. Figure 46-1 shows the possible results.

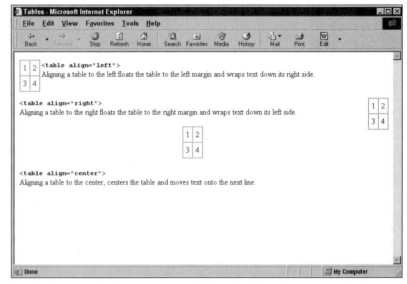

Figure 46-1: Three tables aligned around text: left, right, and center (from top to bottom)

caution

- Older browsers do not support align and valign attributes defined for the <tr> tag. Consequently, it is always best to apply them to <td> tags instead.

2. To align the content within a cell horizontally, define an `align` attribute for the `<td>` tag and set it equal to `left`, `right`, or `center`. Figure 46-2 shows the result of each value.

Figure 46-2: Cells aligned to the left, center, and right

3. To align the content within a cell vertically, define a `valign` attribute for the `<td>` tag and set it equal to `top`, `middle`, `bottom`, or `baseline`. Figure 46-3 shows the result of each value.

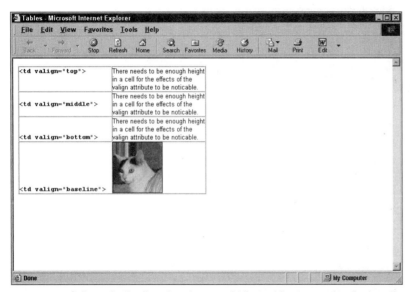

Figure 46-3: Cells vertically aligned to the top, middle, and bottom, and at the baseline

4. To set the horizontal or vertical alignment for an entire row, define the `align` or `valign` attributes of the `<tr>` tag.

cross-reference

• Tables and images respond similarly to the `align` attribute. To learn more about aligning images, see Task 30.

Defining Dimensions for Table Elements

L eft to its own devices, the dimensions of the overall table or individual cell is governed by the content placed within it. Like some other elements you've seen, the dimensional attributes `width` and `height` can also be applied to the `<table>`, `<tr>`, and `<td>` or `<th>` tags with more or less similar results.

1. To specify the width of a table, add the `width` attribute to the opening `<table>` tag and set it equal to a pixel value or a percentage. For example:

   ```
   <table width="200">
   ```

   or:

   ```
   <table width="80%">
   ```

   Figure 47-1 shows examples of different table widths.

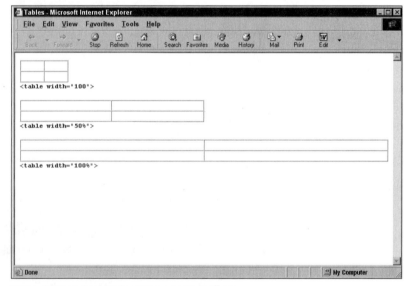

Figure 47-1: Various table widths and their effects

2. To specify the width of an individual cell, add the `width` attribute to the `<td>` tag and set it equal to a pixel value or a percentage. Figure 47-2 shows examples of cell widths.

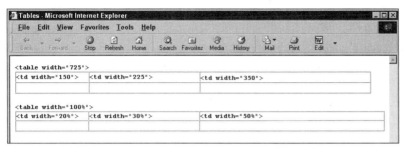

Figure 47-2: Different cell and table widths

3. To define the height of a cell, add a `height` attribute to the `<td>` tag and set it equal to a pixel value or percentage. Figure 47-3 shows the effect of different height values.

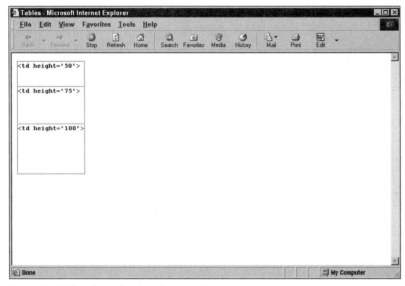

Figure 47-3: The effect of various height values

4. To set the width or height of an entire row, add `width` and `height` attributes to the `<tr>` tag, setting them equal to pixel values or percentages.

tips

- It's possible to combine percentage and pixel values across table and cell widths. For example, in a two-column table you can set the entire table to a width of 100%, yet set the first column to a width of 150 pixels. Make sure the content inside the first column is also 150 pixels wide and then set the second column equal to 100%. The second column will try to take over the screen while the first column holds its ground. Newer browsers don't necessarily require the second column value but many older browsers do, making this a good backward-compatible practice.

- Older browsers do not accept `width` and `height` attributes defined for the `<tr>` tag. Consequently, it is always best to apply them to the `<td>` tags instead.

cross-reference

- The width and height attributes are deprecated for `<tr>`, `<td>`, and `<th>` tags in favor of Cascading Style Sheets (see Part 9).

Working with Table Background Properties

All four tag pairs used in creating tables support the attributes bgcolor and background. The bgcolor attribute specifies the background color and background specifies a background image.

1. To define a background color for the entire table, add the bgcolor attribute to the opening <table> tag, setting it equal to a hexadecimal value or a predefined color name. For example:

   ```
   <table bgcolor="#003399">
   ```

2. To define the background color for an individual row, apply the bgcolor attribute to the <tr> tag and, for a single cell, apply it to the <td> or <th> tag. For example:

   ```
   <tr bgcolor="#003399">
   <td bgcolor="#003399">
   <th bgcolor="#003399">
   ```

   Figure 48-1 shows the effect of applying the bgcolor attribute to the <table>, <tr>, and <td> tags simultaneously.

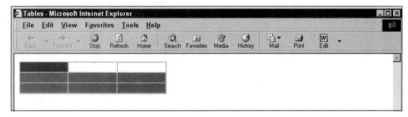

Figure 48-1: Red table, white row, blue cell

3. To define a background image for a table, add the `background` attribute to the `<table>` tag and set it equal to the pathname of the image you want to use. For example:

```
<table background="images/bg.gif">
```

Figure 48-2 shows a background image applied to a table.

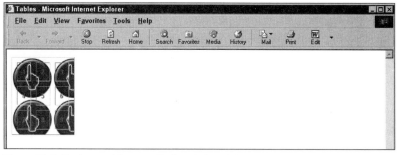

Figure 48-2: Background images tile from left to right and top to bottom across the element they're applied to.

4. To define a background image for an individual row, apply the `background` attribute to the `<tr>` tag and, for a single cell, apply it to the `<td>` or `<th>` tag. For example:

```
<tr background="images/bg.gif">
<td background="images/bg.gif">
<th background="images/bg.gif">
```

cross-reference

- The `<body>` tag also accepts the `bgcolor` and `background` attributes (see Task 9).

Nesting Tables

Nesting tables inside other tables allows you to divide a document into discrete regions. In this way, you gain greater control over page layout.

1. To nest a new table within an existing table cell, place your cursor inside the cell and press Enter once or twice to create space for the code you're about to enter, as shown in Figure 49-1.

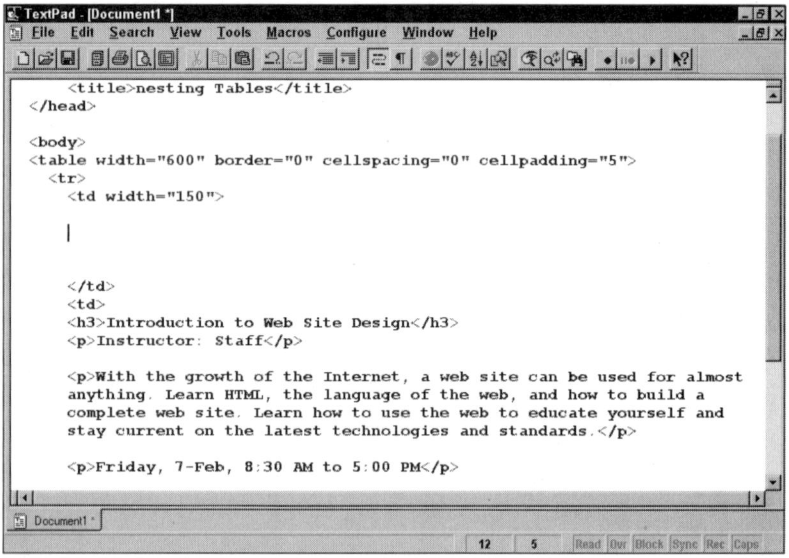

Figure 49-1: An existing table cell ready for nesting

2. Within the cell, enter a comment that describes the content being placed in the nested table. Figure 49-2 shows an example.

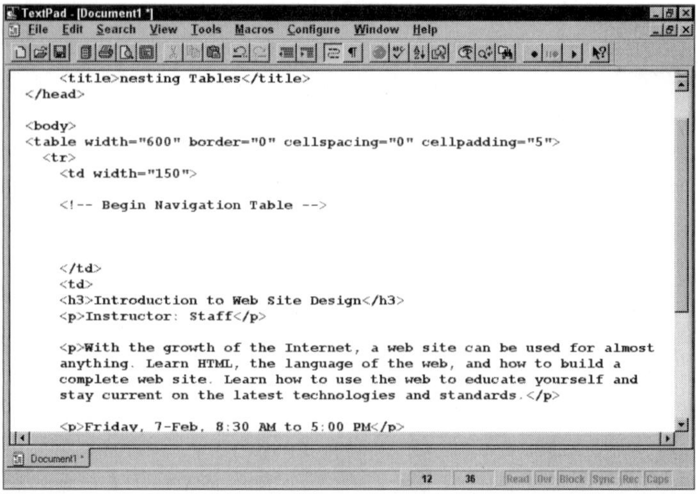

Figure 49-2: A descriptive comment tag ("Begin Navigation Table")

3. Move to the next line and enter the code defining your nested table, as shown in Figure 49-3.

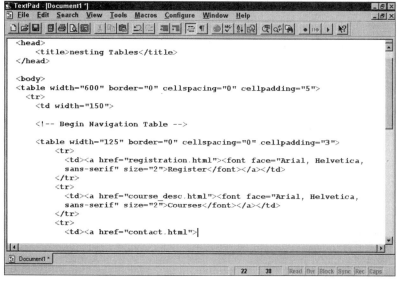

```
<head>
    <title>nesting Tables</title>
</head>

<body>
<table width="600" border="0" cellspacing="0" cellpadding="5">
  <tr>
    <td width="150">

    <!-- Begin Navigation Table -->

    <table width="125" border="0" cellspacing="0" cellpadding="3">
      <tr>
        <td><a href="registration.html"><font face="Arial, Helvetica,
        sans-serif" size="2">Register</font></a></td>
      </tr>
      <tr>
        <td><a href="course_desc.html"><font face="Arial, Helvetica,
        sans-serif" size="2">Courses</font></a></td>
      </tr>
      <tr>
        <td><a href="contact.html">|
```

Figure 49-3: Code for a nested table

4. After the closing tag of the nested table, move to the next line and insert another comment tag demarking the end of the nested table, as shown in Figure 49-4.

```
        <td><a href="contact.html"><font face="Arial, Helvetica, sans-
        serif" size="2">Contact
            Us</font></a></td>
      </tr>
      <tr>
        <td><font face="Arial, Helvetica, sans-serif" size="2"><a
        href="index.html">Home</font></a></td>
      </tr>
    </table>

    <!-- End Navigation Table -->|

</td>
<td>
<h3>Introduction to Web Site Design</h3>
<p>Instructor: Staff</p>

<p>With the growth of the Internet, a web site can be used for almost
anything. Learn HTML, the language of the web, and how to build a
complete web site. Learn how to use the web to educate yourself and
stay current on the latest technologies and standards.</p>

<p>Friday, 7-Feb, 8:30 AM to 5:00 PM</p>
```

Figure 49-4: A comment indicating the end of a nested table ("End Navigation Table")

tips

- When you place multiple tables within a single document, and tables within tables as well, reading through the code and keeping track of which tag is governing what becomes a real challenge. The solution is to place comments within your code, calling out where nested tables begin and end. Comments are written inside opening and closing comment tags (`<!--` and `-->`), which hide any content in between from the browser.

- The general practice of indenting table code makes your document easier to read.

- Comment tags can be used anywhere within a document. They're typically used to explain to others what the author is doing. You can also use them to hide chunks of code temporarily while you're testing a document in the browser.

cross-reference

- As this task demonstrates, comments help organize your code. There are other tags specific to organizing table content (see Task 50).

Organizing Table Data

In Task 49, you learned how to use comment tags to make nested table code easier to read. HTML also has some tags for organizing individual parts of a table: `<thead>`, `<tbody>`, `<tfoot>`, `<caption>`, and `<summary>`. These tags are generally used when the table you're creating is meant to display tabular data.

notes

- The `<tfoot>` content must precede the `<tbody>` content. Even though the footer information is written first, the footer row is still rendered at the bottom of the table. You supply the header and footer first so the browser can render them prior to rendering the body, in case the table is extremely big.

- By default, caption text is centered above the table. To align the caption below the table, add an `align` attribute to the `<caption>` tag and set it equal to `bottom`. Internet Explorer allows you to use both `align` and `valign` attributes, using `valign` to set the top or bottom value and `align` to place the caption to the `left`, `right`, or `center`.

1. To indicate a region of a table containing heading data, place opening and closing `<thead>` tags around the code, as shown in Listing 50-1.

```
<thead>
  <tr>
    <th align="center">MON</th>
    <th align="center">MEAN TEMP</th>
    <th align="center">HIGH</th>
    <th align="center">DATE</th>
    <th align="center">LOW</th>
    <th align="center">DATA</th>
    <th align="center">RAIN</th>
    <th align="center">AVE.WIND SPEED</th>
  </tr>
</thead>
```

Listing 50-1: A table row marked as a header

2. To indicate the table code that makes up the footer, wrap it in opening and closing `<tfoot>` tags, as shown in Listing 50-2.

```
<tfoot>
  <tr>
    <td colspan="8">
    *calculations based on 5 of 7 report zones
    </td>
  </tr>
</tfoot>
```

Listing 50-2: A table footer

3. To indicate the body of the table content, place opening and closing `<tbody>` tags around the remaining table rows, as shown in Listing 50-3.

```
<tbody>
  <tr>
    <td align="center">1</td>
    <td align="center">23.8</td>
    <td align="center">43.2</td>
    <td align="center">30/1/03</td>
```

(continued)

```
        <td align="center">13.7</td>
        <td align="center">1/25/03</td>
        <td align="center">17.00</td>
        <td align="center">7</td>
    </tr>
  </tbody>
```

Listing 50-3: The body section of a table

4. To describe the data within a table, include `<caption>` tags directly following the opening `<table>` tag, as shown here:

```
<table width="100%" border="0" cellspacing="0"
cellpadding="3">
<caption><b>First Quarter Measurements</b></caption>
```

Figure 50-1 shows how captions appear in the browser.

Figure 50-1: A table caption appearing below a table

5. To include a summary of the table data for text-to-speech browsers and Braille-based devices, define a summary attribute for the `<table>` tag, as shown here:

```
<table width="100%" border="0" cellspacing="0"
cellpadding="3" summary="First quarter weather
measurements, 5 of 7 zones reporting.">
```

cross-reference

- The W3C prefers you to use Cascading Style Sheets to format captions (see Part 9).

Part 7: Working with Forms

Defining Form Elements

It seems that forms exist everywhere on the Web. They allow people to sign up for newsletters, purchase goods, and send e-mail. Any HTML document that contains a form has a section inside it containing opening and closing <form> tags. Within this section lies the regular content and its markup, as well as specific form-related elements called *form controls* (check boxes, radio buttons, menus, and so on).

Users fill in "the form" by entering information into text fields, making selections from menus, and clicking check boxes and radio buttons. Clicking the "submit" button sends the data they dutifully entered to a Web server, which sends the collected form data to a processing script. The most important thing to understand about Web forms is that they consist of two parts: the HTML-based interface that visitors use to enter information (that is, the Web page) and a program on the Web server that processes that collected information behind the scenes.

Web forms typically make use of something called the Common Gateway Interface (CGI), a standard system for using external programs to communicate with Web servers. Programs (called *scripts*) can be written in any number of programming languages. The most common is Perl. The form page on the Web site packages the information that users enter and sends it to the Web server where the script resides. The script then processes the information and either has the Web server send a response back to the visitor or holds and maintains the data for some future purpose.

There is no single script that everyone uses to create forms. The Web page form and the script on the server are unique little programs on each Web site. This means that if you want to create your own forms, you need to learn how to program — but that's a topic for another book. In this task, you simply learn how to define the opening and closing <form> tags, which instruct browsers where to submit the data and how the data should be sent.

1. Within the body section of the document, enter an opening <form> tag.

2. Add an action attribute and set it equal to the URL of the processing script, as shown in Listing 51-1.

```
<html>
<head>
   <title>Forms</title>
</head>

<body>

<form action="/cgi-bin/guest.pl">

</body>
</html>
```

Listing 51-1: The opening <form> tag and action attribute

notes

- The get method appends the form data to the URL defined in the action attribute, while the post method sends the data as a transaction body message. Use the get attribute when you're sending a small amount of data and no type of response is scripted to come from the Web server. Use the post attribute when you're sending large amounts of data and the script is sending a response. The World Wide Web Consortium has deprecated the get method.

- The rest of the code that makes up the form (normal content, form controls, and so on) is placed between the opening and closing <form> tags.

3. Follow the `action` attribute with the `method` attribute, setting it equal to `post` or `get`, as shown in Listing 51-2.

```
<html>
<head>
   <title>Forms</title>
</head>

<body>

<form action="/cgi-bin/guest.pl" method="post">

</body>
</html>
```

Listing 51-2: A <form> tag with action and method attributes defined

4. To mark the end of the form, insert a closing `</form>` tag. Listing 51-3 shows a completed form container.

```
<html>
<head>
   <title>Forms</title>
</head>

<body>

<form action="/cgi-bin/guest.pl" method="post">

<!-- The elements that create the physical form the user
sees are placed between these opening and closing form tags.
-->

</form>

</body>
</html>
```

Listing 51-3: A completed form container

cross-reference

- The application on the Web server that processes user-inputted information is typically referred to as a *CGI script*, a program written in one of a number of programming languages. (Perl is the most common.) To learn more about CGI scripting and the Perl programming language, see *Perl For Dummies, 4th Edition* by Paul Hoffman (Wiley Publishing, Inc., 2003).

Formatting Text Fields

If you've ever filled out a Web-based form, you've noticed that more often than not the information you're providing is textual — names, addresses, passwords, and comments — as well as numeric values like ZIP codes and phone and credit card numbers. Form controls that accept this data are generically referred to as *text boxes*. This task shows you how to examine the first of these three types: the basic text field. These form controls are most commonly used for single-line responses, like a name and address, and for short numeric values.

1. Enter an `<input>` tag.

2. Define a `type` attribute and set it equal to `text`, as shown here:

   ```
   <input type="text">
   ```

3. Define a `name` attribute and set it equal to the appropriate value specified by the processing script. For example:

   ```
   <input type="text" name="first_name">
   ```

4. To specify how wide the text field should be, define a `size` attribute, setting it equal to a numeric value representing the width of the text field in characters. For example:

   ```
   <input type="text" name="first_name" size="20"
   ```

5. To specify a maximum number of characters the user can enter into the text field, define a `maxlength` attribute and set it equal to a numeric value, as shown here:

   ```
   <input type="text" name="first_name" size="20"
   maxlength="20">
   ```

6. If you want an initial value displayed in the text field when the document loads, define a `value` attribute and set it equal to the text you want the field to contain. For example:

```
<input type="text" name="first_name" size="20"
maxlength="20" value="First Name Here">
```

7. To make the `<input>` tag compatible with XHTML and keep it recognizable to non-XHTML browsers, conclude the tag by inserting a space after the last attribute value and adding a forward slash and closing bracket, as shown here:

```
<input type="text" name="first_name" size="20"
maxlength="20" value="First Name Here" />
```

Figure 52-1 shows some typical text fields in a browser.

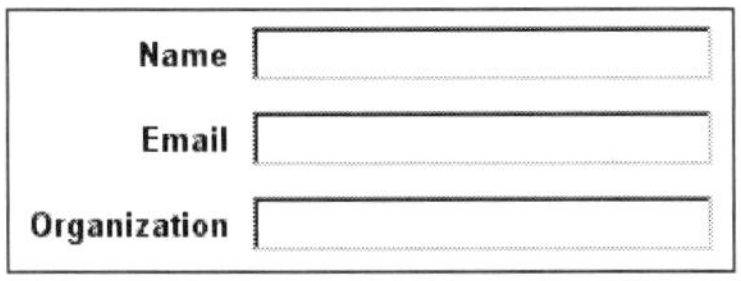

Name	
Email	
Organization	

Figure 52-1: Typical text fields rendered in the browser

cross-reference

- Somewhere in your Internet travels you have likely entered a password and seen it appear onscreen as a row of asterisks or bullets. This is accomplished by another form of text field — the password field, covered in Task 53.

Formatting Password Fields

Password fields, logically enough, accept passwords. They respond to the same size, maxlength, and value attributes as the text field but require the type attribute to equal password so that any text entered into the password field appears onscreen as asterisks (Windows) or bullet points (Macintosh). Other than obscuring password text visually, a password field offers no sophisticated security. It doesn't encrypt or scramble the information in any way.

1. Enter an `<input>` tag.

2. Define a `type` attribute and set it equal to `password`. For example:

    ```
    <input type="password">
    ```

3. Define a `name` attribute and set it equal to the appropriate value specified by the processing script, as shown here:

    ```
    <input type="password" name="password">
    ```

4. To specify the width of the password field, define a `size` attribute, setting it equal to a numeric value representing the width of the password field in characters:

    ```
    <input type="password" name="password" size="12">
    ```

5. To specify a maximum number of characters the user can enter into the password field, define a `maxlength` attribute and set it equal to a numeric value:

    ```
    <input type="password" name="password" size="12"
    maxlength="12">
    ```

6. To make the `<input>` tag compatible with XHTML and keep it recognizable to non-XHTML browsers, conclude the tag by inserting a space after the last attribute value and adding a forward slash and closing bracket. Listing 53-1 shows an example of a simple login screen. Figure 53-1 displays the resulting document in a browser.

Task 53

```html
<html>
<head>
   <title>Password Fields</title>
</head>
<body>

<form action="/cgi-bin/login.pl" method="post">

User Name:<br>
<input type="text" name="user_name" size="20" maxlength="20"
/>

<br>

Password:<br>
<input type="password" name="password" size="20"
maxlength="20" />

<br>
<br>

<!-- Submit and Reset Buttons -->

<input type="submit" value="Login" name="submit">

<input type="reset" value="Clear" name="reset">

</form>
</body>
</html>
```

Listing 53-1: Code behind a simple login screen

Figure 53-1: Simple login screen rendered in the browser

cross-references

- This example includes Submit and Reset buttons. To learn more about them, see Task 60.

- Text boxes that allow more than a single line of text are called text areas (see Task 54).

Formatting Text Areas

A *text area* is a large, scrollable, multiline text window. It is most commonly used for collecting extended written comments. Unlike text and password fields, the text area is not created with the `<input>` tag. Instead, it has its own set of opening and closing `<textarea>` tags.

1. Somewhere within the confines of your `<form>` tags, enter an opening `<textarea>` tag.

2. Define a `name` attribute and set it equal to the appropriate value specified by the processing script. For example:

```
<textarea name="comments">
```

3. To specify the width of the text area, add a `cols` attribute and set it equal to a numeric value representing the width of the text area in characters:

```
<textarea name="comments" cols="50">
```

4. To specify the height of the text area, add a `rows` attribute and set it equal to a numeric value representing the height of the text area in characters:

```
<textarea name="comments" cols="50" rows="10">
```

5. To control how text wraps within the text area, add a `wrap` attribute and set it equal to `off`, `virtual`, or `physical`:

```
<textarea name="comments" cols="50" rows="10"
wrap="virtual">
```

6. To complete the text area, add a closing `</textarea>` tag:

```
<textarea name="comments" cols="50" rows="10"
wrap="virtual">
</textarea>
```

7. If you want an initial value displayed in the text area when the document loads, place the text between the opening and closing `<textarea>` tags, for example:

```
<textarea name="comments" cols="50" rows="10"
wrap="virtual">
Place Your Comments Here...
</textarea>
```

Listing 54-1 shows a completed text area within the context of a small form. Figure 54-1 renders the code in a browser.

```
<html>
<head>
   <title>Text Areas</title>
</head>

<body>
<form action="/cgi-bin/comments.pl" method="post">

User Name:<br>
<input type="text" name="user_name" width"30"
maxlength="20">
<br>
<br>
Enter Your Comments Here:<br>
<textarea name="comments" cols=40 rows=7 wrap></textarea>

<br>
<br>
<!-- Submit & Reset Buttons -->
<input type="submit" value="Send Me" />

<input type="reset" value="Clear Me" />

</form>
</body>
</html>
```

Listing 54-1: A text field followed by a text area

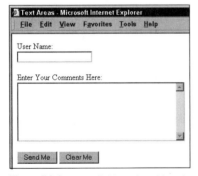

Figure 54-1: A text field rendered in a browser

cross-references

- Browsers respect any white space between characters entered within the `<textarea>` tags. This is similar to the `<pre>` tag (see Part 2).

- The form ends with a Submit and a Reset button. To learn how to use these, see Task 60.

Formatting Check Boxes

The check box form control acts as a switch that the user can toggle on or off (check or uncheck). You create a check box by setting the <input> tag's type attribute equal to checkbox. Check boxes require a value attribute, which supplies the value that gets passed to the script if the check box is clicked. By defining the name and value attributes, you're supplying both halves of the name/value pair; the user decides whether it's sent to the server by how they respond to it — by checking it or not.

note

• HTML allows you simply to define the word checked, while XHTML requires the checked="checked" syntax.

1. Enter an <input> tag.

2. Define a type attribute and set it equal to checkbox:

   ```
   <input type="checkbox">
   ```

3. Define a name attribute and set it equal to the appropriate value specified by the processing script:

   ```
   <input type="checkbox" name="fav_flavor">
   ```

4. Define a value attribute and set it equal to the value that will be passed to the processing script if the user clicks the check box:

   ```
   <input type="checkbox" name="fav_flavor"
   value="chocolate">
   ```

5. If you want a check box to be preselected when the browser loads the page, include the checked attribute:

   ```
   <input type="checkbox" name="fav_flavor" value="chocolate"
   checked>
   ```

6. To make the checked attribute compatible with XHTML, render it like a traditional attribute and set it equal to checked:

   ```
   <input type="checkbox" name="fav_flavor" value="chocolate"
   checked="checked">
   ```

7. To make the <input> tag compatible with XHTML and still keep it recognizable to non-XHTML browsers, conclude the tag by inserting a space after the last attribute value and adding a forward slash and closing bracket:

   ```
   <input type="checkbox" name="fav_flavor" value="chocolate"
   checked="checked" />
   ```

Listing 55-1 provides a simple check box example. Figure 55-1 renders the document in a browser.

```html
<html>
<head>
<title>Checkboxes</title>
</head>

<body>

<form action="/cgi-bin/ice_cream.pl" method="post">

<p>What are your preferred ice cream flavors? </p>

<input name="flavors" type="checkbox" value="chocolate"
checked> Chocolate<br>

<input name="flavors" type="checkbox" value="strawberry">
Strawberry<br>

<input name="flavors" type="checkbox" value="vanilla">
Vanilla

</form>
</body>
</html>
```

Listing 55-1: Code that generates three check boxes

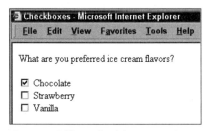

Figure 55-1: Three check boxes to select our preferred ice cream flavor: chocolate, strawberry, or vanilla

tip

- Multiple check boxes typically share a common name attribute, allowing the visitor to supply multiple answers to a single question.

cross-reference

- Check boxes supply users with multiple-choice options. Radio buttons supply either/or choices. To learn more about radio (or option) buttons, see Task 56.

Task **56**

Formatting Radio Buttons

note

- HTML allows you to simply define the word checked, while XHTML requires the checked="checked" syntax.

Whereas check boxes supply users with multiple-choice options in a form, radio buttons supply either/or choices. You create radio buttons by setting the <input> tag's type attribute equal to radio. Radio buttons require the same attributes as check boxes (type, name, and value) but when multiple radio buttons share identical name attribute values, users can select only one at a time. If the user has already selected one, clicking another deselects it.

1. Enter an <input> tag.

2. Define a type attribute and set it equal to radio:

   ```
   <input type="radio">
   ```

3. Define a name attribute and set it equal to the appropriate value specified by the processing script:

   ```
   <input type="radio" name="hand">
   ```

4. Define a value attribute and set it equal to the value that will be passed to the processing script if the user selects the radio button:

   ```
   <input type="radio" name="hand" value="right">
   ```

5. If you want a radio button to be preselected when the browser loads the page, include the checked attribute:

   ```
   <input type="radio" name="hand" value="right" checked>
   ```

6. To make the checked attribute compatible with XHTML, render it like a traditional attribute and set it equal to checked:

   ```
   <input type="radio" name="hand" value="right"
   checked="checked">
   ```

7. To make the <input> tag compatible with XHTML and keep it recognizable to non-XHTML browsers, conclude the tag by inserting a space after the last attribute value and adding a forward slash and closing bracket:

   ```
   <input type="radio" name="hand" value="right"
   checked="checked" />
   ```

Listing 56-1 provides a simple three-button example. Figure 56-1 shows the resulting page in a browser.

```
<html>
<head>
<title>Radio Buttons</title>
</head>

<body>

<form action="/cgi-bin/dexterity.pl" method="post">

<p>Which is your dominant hand?</p>

<input type="radio" name="hand" value="right" checked>
Right <br>

<input type="radio" name="hand" value="left">
Left <br>

<input type="radio" name="hand" value="both">
Ambidextrous

</form>
</body>
</html>
```

Listing 56-1: A series of radio buttons

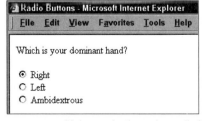

Figure 56-1: Make a selection using radio buttons to specify your dominant hand

tip
- Use radio buttons when you want a visitor to make only one selection from a number of choices. Include at least two radio buttons with identical `name` attribute values.

cross-reference
- Not only can you offer users choices with check boxes and radio buttons, you can provide users with pop-up menus. These are called selection menus in HTML (see Task 57).

Task **57**

Formatting Selection Menus

Selection menus allow users to select one of several items in a pop-up list. You define a selection menu with the `<select>` tag. Each menu option is laid out in much the same way as you would create a list, using opening and closing `<option>` tags to define each menu choice.

note

- HTML allows you to simply define the word `selected`, while XHTML requires you to define it as `selected="selected"`.

1. Insert an opening `<select>` tag.

2. Define a `name` attribute and set it equal to the appropriate value specified by the processing script:

```
<select name="weaponry">
```

3. To define a menu option, move to the next line, indent, and enter the item between opening and closing `<option>` tags:

```
<select name="weaponry">
  <option>Vorpal Sword</option>
  <option>Pointed Stick</option>
  <option>Bare hands</option>
```

4. To specify an initial value for an option, define a `value` attribute for the `<option>` tag and set it equal to the value to be sent to the processing script. If this attribute is not defined, the initial value is set to the content you placed between the `<option>` tags:

```
<select name="weaponry">
  <option value="good">Vorpal Sword</option>
  <option value="bad">Pointed Stick</option>
  <option value="pointless">Bare hands</option>
```

5. To specify one option as preselected, define a `selected` attribute for the `<option>` tag and set it equal to `selected`:

```
<select name="weaponry">
  <option value="good" selected="selected">Vorpal
Sword</option>
  <option value="bad">Pointed Stick</option>
  <option value="pointless">Bare hands</option>
```

6. Once you've defined all your menu options, complete the selection menu with a closing `</select>` tag. Listing 57-1 provides an example of a simple selection menu. Figure 57-1 shows the resulting page in a browser.

```
<html>
<head>
<title>Select Menus</title>
</head>

<body>

<form action="/cgi-bin/good_sense.pl" method="post">
What would you use to stop a Jabberwocky?
<br>
<select name="weaponry">
    <option>Pick a weapon</option>
    <option>-----------------------</option>
    <option value="good">Vorpal Sword</option>
    <option value="bad">Pointed Stick</option>
    <option value="pointless">Bare hands</option>
  </select>

</form>
</body>
</html>
```

Listing 57-1: A simple selection menu

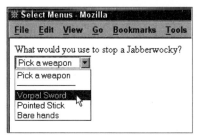

Figure 57-1: The selection menu listing your choice of weapon to stop a Jabberwocky headed your way

tip
- Selection menus save on screen real estate, offering many choices while occupying only one line. If you want to conserve even more screen space, instead of devoting a portion of your document to traditional HTML text that informs the user what the menu is for, make the first option an instruction, as our example shows. To make a visual break between this instructional text and the rest of the menu options, make the second option a line by typing dashes between the `<option>` tags, as our example also shows.

cross-reference
- Forms need to be well laid out, clear, and concise. Tables are the most commonly used elements for structuring not only forms but any type of HTML document. To learn more about tables, see Part 6.

Formatting Selection Lists

When you format a selection menu as a list, the form control becomes a box from which a visitor can make one or more selections. Depending on how you format the list, the box can sprout a scroll bar that allows users to move through the list options. To turn a selection menu into a menu list, simply add the size attribute to the <select> tag. This attribute accepts a numeric value that signifies the number of list options to display. If there are more options in the list than the number of lines defined, the list sprouts a scroll bar so the user can read them all.

notes

- If there are more options in the list than the number of lines defined by the size attribute, the list sprouts a scroll bar on the right side.

- HTML allows you to simply define the word multiple, while XHTML requires the multiple="multiple" syntax.

1. Insert an opening <select> tag.

2. Define a name attribute and set it equal to the appropriate value specified by the processing script:

```
<select name="pets">
```

3. To format the menu as a multiline list, add a size attribute to the opening <select> tag and set it equal to a numeric value signifying the number of list options you want to make visible:

```
<select name="pets" size="4">
```

4. To permit users to make multiple selections from the list, add a multiple attribute and set it equal to multiple:

```
<select name="pets" size="4" multiple="multiple">
```

5. To define your list options, move to the next line, indent, and enter the items between the opening and closing <option> tags:

```
<select name="pets" size="4" multiple="multiple">
  <option>Dogs</option>
```

6. To specify an initial value for an option, define a value attribute for the <option> tag and set it equal to the value to be sent to the processing script. If this attribute is not defined, the initial value is set to the content you placed between the <option> tags:

```
<select name="pets" size="4" multiple="multiple">
  <option value="k9">Dogs</option>
```

7. To specify one option as preselected, define a selected attribute for the <option> tag and set it equal to selected:

```
<select name="pets" size="4" multiple="multiple">
  <option value="k9" selected="selected">Dogs</option>
```

8. Once you've defined all your list options, complete the selection list with a closing `</select>` tag. Listing 58-1 provides an example of a simple selection list. Figure 58-1 displays the resulting page in a browser.

```html
<html>
<head>
    <title>Selection Lists</title>
</head>
<body>

<form action="/cgi-bin/pet_count.pl" method="post">

<p>What kinds of pets do you have?</p>

<select name="pets" size="4" multiple="multiple">
  <option value="canine">Dogs</option>
  <option value="feline">Cats</option>
  <option value="avian">Birds</option>
  <option value="equine">Horses</option>
</select>

<p>To make multiple selections, hold down your Ctrl key
(Win) or your Command key (Mac)</p>

</form>
</body>
</html>
```

Listing 58-1: A simple multiple-choice selection list

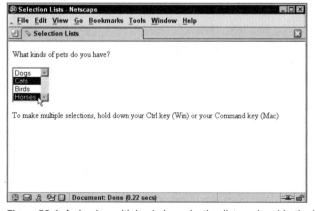

Figure 58-1: A simple multiple-choice selection list rendered in the browser

tip

▪ Let users know that multiple selections are possible, and tell them how to make them. Windows users hold down the Control key and Mac users hold down the Command key.

cross-reference

▪ Web forms can contain file fields, which allow users to upload files to a Web server (see Task 59).

Formatting File Fields

File fields allow your site's visitors to upload files from their hard drive to the Web server. The file field appears as a text field with a Browse button to the right. The file field form control uses the `<input>` tag. Here the `type` attribute is set equal to `file`.

1. Insert an `<input>` tag.

2. Add a `type` attribute and set it equal to `file`:

   ```
   <input type="file">
   ```

3. Define a `name` attribute, setting it equal to the appropriate value specified by the processing script.

   ```
   <input type="file" name="upload">
   ```

4. To specify how many characters wide the file field should be, define a `size` attribute and set it equal to a numeric value representing the width of the text field in characters:

   ```
   <input type="file" name="upload" size="20">
   ```

5. To specify a maximum number of characters the user can enter into the field, define a `maxlength` attribute and set it equal to a numeric value:

   ```
   <input type="file" name="upload" size="20" maxlength="50">
   ```

6. To limit the type of files a visitor can upload, define an `accept` attribute and set it equal to the MIME type of the files you want to allow:

   ```
   <input type="file" name="upload" size="20" maxlength="50"
   accept="image/gif">
   ```

7. To make the `<input>` tag compatible with XHTML and keep it recognizable to non-XHTML browsers, conclude the tag by inserting a space after the last attribute value and adding a forward slash and closing bracket:

   ```
   <input type="file" name="upload" size="20" maxlength="50"
   accept="image/gif" />
   ```

Listing 59-1 provides a simple file field example. Figure 59-1 displays the result in a browser.

```
<html>
<head>
   <title>File Fields</title>
</head>
<body>

<form action="/cgi-bin/image_files.pl" method="post">

<p>Upload Your GIF Images Here:</p>

<input type="file" name="upload" size="20"
accept="image/gif" />

</form>
</body>
</html>
```

Listing 59-1: A simple file field

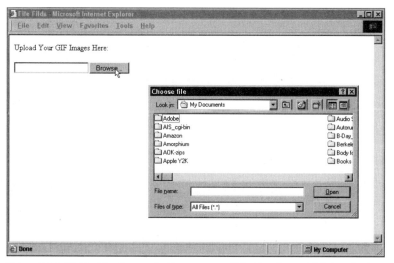

Figure 59-1: Clicking the Browse button opens a dialog box from which to select a file for uploading

cross-reference

- MIME stands for Multi-purpose Internet Mail Extensions. To see a complete list of MIME types, visit our Web site: www .wiley.com/compbooks/ 10simplestepsorless.

Formatting Submit and Reset Buttons

Site visitors click buttons either to send the completed form to the server (the Submit button) or to clear the form if they've made a mistake (the Reset button). You don't get many choices to style basic form buttons, other than what text you put on them. They're typically rendered with beveled edges, in neutral gray with black text on the face.

1. To create a Submit button, insert an `<input>` tag.

2. Add a `type` attribute and set it equal to `submit`:

   ```
   <input type="submit">
   ```

3. To specify the text on the button face, add a `value` attribute and set it equal to the text you want:

   ```
   <input type="submit" value="Submit">
   ```

4. To create a Reset button, insert an `<input>` tag and add a `type` attribute set equal to `reset`. Use the `value` attribute to specify the text on the button face:

   ```
   <input type="reset" value="Reset">
   ```

5. If the processing script demands it, define a `name` attribute, setting it equal to the appropriate value:

   ```
   <input type="submit" value="Submit" name="submit">
   <input type="reset" value="Reset" name="reset">
   ```

6. To make the `<input>` tag compatible with XHTML and keep it recognizable to non-XHTML browsers, conclude the tag by inserting a space after the last attribute value and adding a forward slash and closing bracket:

   ```
   <input type="submit" value="Submit" name="submit" />
   <input type="reset" value="Reset" name="reset" />
   ```

   Listing 60-1 shows a simple form with Submit and Reset buttons in place. Figure 60-1 renders the resulting page in a browser.

Task 60

```
<html>
<head>
   <title>Submit & Reset Buttons</title>
</head>
<body>

<form action="/cgi-bin/message.pl" method="post">
E-mail Address:<br>
<input type="text" name="email" size="20" />

<br>
<br>

Message:<br>
<textarea cols="50" rows="10" wrap="virtual" name="message">
</textarea>

<br>
<br>

<input type="submit" value="Send Me" />

<input type="reset" value="Clear Me" />

</form>
</body>
</html>
```

Listing 60-1: A simple form with Submit and Reset buttons

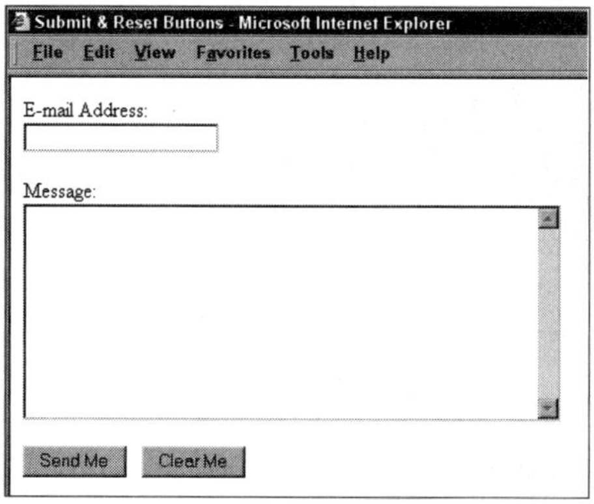

Figure 60-1: A simple form with Submit and Reset buttons rendered by the browser

cross-reference

- You can use an image in place of the Submit button (see Task 61).

Using Graphic Images for Submit Buttons

If the browser's neutral-gray, rectangular Submit button isn't to your liking, you can substitute it for a graphic using a form control called an *image field*.

1. Insert an `<input>` tag.

2. Add a `type` attribute and set it equal to `image`:

   ```
   <input type="image">
   ```

3. To specify the image to be used, add a `src` attribute and set it equal to the image's pathname. For example:

   ```
   <input type="image" src="images/button.gif">
   ```

4. Specify the image's dimensions with `width` and `height` attributes, setting them equal to numeric pixel values:

   ```
   <input type="image" src="images/button.gif" width="25"
   height="25">
   ```

5. To specify an image border, define a `border` attribute:

   ```
   <input type="image" src="images/button.gif" width="25"
   height="25" border="1">
   ```

6. If the processing script requires it, define a `name` attribute:

   ```
   <input type="image" src="images/button.gif" width="25"
   height="25" border="1" name="submit_image">
   ```

7. Define the `alt` attribute and set it equal to your chosen alternate text for the image:

   ```
   <input type="image" src="images/button.gif" width="25"
   height="25" name="submit_image" alt="Submit">
   ```

8. To make the `<input>` tag compatible with XHTML and keep it recognizable to non-XHTML browsers, conclude the tag by inserting a space after the last attribute value and adding a forward slash and closing bracket:

   ```
   <input type="image" src="images/button.gif" width="25"
   height="25" name="submit_image" alt="Submit" />
   ```

note

- Just as with ordinary images, always define the `alt` attribute for visitors with nonvisual browsers.

Listing 61-1 shows an example of an image field in use. Figure 61-1 displays the finished work in a browser.

```html
<html>
<head>
    <title>Graphic Submit Buttons</title>
</head>
<body>

<form action="/cgi-bin/message.pl" method="post">

E-mail Address:<br>
<input type="text" name="email" size="20" />

<br>
<br>

Message:<br>
<textarea cols="50" rows="10" wrap="virtual" name="message">
</textarea>

<br>

<input type="image" src="images/button.gif" width="25"
height="25" name="submit_image" alt="Submit" />

</form>
</body>
</html>
```

Listing 61-1: An image field substituting for the generic Submit button code

tip
- The regular Submit button isn't overly large to begin with, so it's advisable to keep your button graphic relatively small.

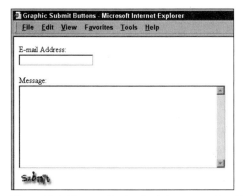

Figure 61-1: The graphical submit button rendered in the browser

cross-reference
- Many attributes defined here are identical to those used in the `<img>` tag. To learn more about images, see Part 3.

Using Hidden Fields

Each of the form controls you've seen so far sends data to a script in response to an action taken by the visitor, who types something into a field, clicks a check box or radio button, selects something from a menu or list, and so forth. HTML provides a mechanism by which you can include values in your form to be sent to the script that visitors never see. These values are defined using *hidden fields*.

note

- In this example, the URL of the processing script (see the `<form>` tag's `action` attribute) is on another Web site. The hidden field tells the script which Web site this data came from.

1. Insert an `<input>` tag.

2. Define a `type` attribute and set it equal to `hidden`:

   ```
   <input type="hidden">
   ```

3. Define a `name` attribute and set it equal to the appropriate value specified by the processing script:

   ```
   <input type="hidden" name="customer_site">
   ```

4. Define a `value` attribute and set it equal to whatever information you want the field to pass to the script when the form is submitted:

   ```
   <input type="hidden" name="customer_site" value="Alpha-Gizmo">
   ```

5. To make the `<input>` tag compatible with XHTML and keep it recognizable to non-XHTML browsers, conclude the tag by inserting a space after the last attribute value and adding a forward slash and closing bracket:

   ```
   <input type="hidden" name="customer_site" value="Alpha-Gizmo" />
   ```

   Listing 62-1 shows an example of a hidden field that sends data to a script. Figure 62-1 shows how that data could be used by a script to generate a special message to the visitor.

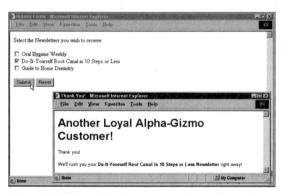

Figure 62-1: The script returns a second page that makes use of the information supplied by the hidden field

```
<html>
<head>
   <title>Hidden Fields</title>
</head>
<body>

<form action="http:// www.some-domain.com/cgi-bin/dental.pl"
method="post">

<input type="hidden" name="web_site" value="Alpha-Gizmo" />

Select the Newsletters you wish to receive:<br>
<br>
<input type="checkbox" name="newsletter"
value="oral_hygiene" /> Oral Hygiene Weekly<br>

<input type="checkbox" name="newsletter" value="root_canal"
/> Do-It-Yourself Root Canal in 10 Simple Steps or Less<br>

<input type="checkbox" name="newsletter"
value="home_dentistry" /> Guide to Home Dentistry

<br>
<br>

<input type="submit" name="Submit" value="Submit" />
<input type="reset" name="reset" value="Reset" />

</form>
</body>
</html>
```

Listing 62-1: A hidden field that tells the script which Web site this form is from

Task **62**

tips

- If you use a single script located on one server to process forms from a number of different Web sites, you could include a hidden field in each instance of the form to indicate which Web site the data came from.

- Sometimes Web pages that visitors see are generated dynamically by scripts. For example, visitors enter information on one page and click a Submit button marked "Continue," which takes them to the next part of the form that's tailored to the information they submitted on the previous page. If the next form page requires any previously submitted information, you don't want to make visitors enter it a second time. This is where hidden fields come in handy: When the script generates the second page, it can include the required information inside hidden fields.

cross-reference

- To learn more about CGI scripting, see *Perl For Dummies* (Wiley Publishing, Inc., 2003).

Specifying the Focus Order of Form Controls

On a page with several form controls, pressing Tab moves the cursor from the first form control to the last. By default, the page's *focus* is the first form control on the page. You can control not only the Tab order but also the specific keys that bring the focus to a particular form control. Both of these methods allow users to bypass the mouse when they enter information on the form, and they are typically included for visitors with speaking browsers.

notes

- By default, most browsers allow users to tab through the form in the order the form controls appear in code.

- The key you specify with the accesskey attribute must be pressed in conjunction with either the Alt key (Windows) or the Control key (Mac). Older browsers do not support the accesskey attribute.

1. Define a tabindex attribute for each form control you want to affect.

2. Set each tabindex attribute equal to a numeric value, in the order you want them to be focused on when people press the Tab key. For example, tabindex="1" is first, tabindex="2" is second, and so on, as shown in Listing 63-1.

3. To make a specific key bring a form control into focus, define an accesskey attribute for the form control and set it equal to the key letter or number. For example:

```
<input type="text" name="organization" size="20"
accesskey="o" />
```

4. Include explicit notes about your access key assignments within your site (see Figure 63-1).

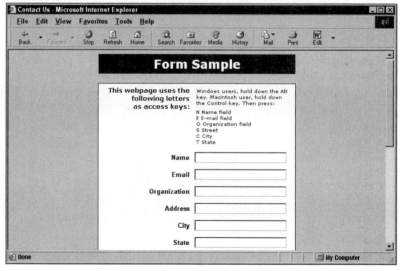

Figure 63-1: Instructional text that helps people navigate the form without the mouse

```
<html>
<head>
<title>Focus Order</title>
</head>

<body bgcolor="#FFFFFF" text="#000000">
<form action="/cgi-bin/newsletters.pl" method="post">

User Name: <br>
<input type="text" name="user" size="20" tabindex="7" />
<br>

E-mail Address:<br>
<input type="text" name="email" size="20" tabindex="6" />

<br>

Join the Mailing list?<br>
<input type="radio" name="mailing" value="yes" checked
tabindex="5" />
Yes<br>
<input type="radio" name="mailing" value="no" tabindex="4"
/>
No<br>

Select a Newsletter:<br>
<select name="select" tabindex="3">
  <option>Chiropractic Accidents</option>
  <option>Medical Love Stories</option>
  <option>Dental Torture made Easy</option>
</select>
<br>
<br>
<input type="submit" name="Submit" value="Submit"
tabindex="2" />
<input type="reset" name="Submit2" value="Reset"
tabindex="1" />

</form>
</body>
</html>
```

Listing 63-1: Defining tabindex attributes in reverse order

tip

▪ To remove a form control from the tab order, set the `tabindex` attribute equal to -1.

cross-reference

▪ Access keys can also be assigned to hyperlinks (see see Part 5).

Using Field Sets

Field sets allow you to group a series of related form controls visually and structurally. Doing so gives users (of visual browsers) a greater understanding of the form by wrapping related controls inside a gray or black border with an accompanying caption (rendered with the <legend> tag). Text-to-speech and Braille browsers use the captions to inform users about the section of the form they're in.

notes

▪ Netscape 7.x and all versions of Internet Explorer render the fieldset borders in gray. Netscape 6.x renders them in black, and Netscape 4.x doesn't render them at all.

▪ Netscape renders field set outlines with more white space around form controls than Internet Explorer does.

1. Insert the opening <fieldset> tag above the first form control in the group.

2. Insert opening and closing <legend> tags immediately following the the opening fieldset tag. For example:

```
<fieldset>
    <legend></legend>
```

3. Place the text you want displayed as the fieldset's caption between the <legend> tags:

```
<fieldset>
    <legend>Personal Information</legend>
```

4. At the end of the group of form controls, insert a closing </fieldset> tag.

   Listing 64-1 shows a completed form using a field set. Figure 64-1 shows how Netscape renders the field set.

```
<html>
<head>
<title>Field Sets</title>
</head>

<body>
<form action="/cgi-bin/data.pl" method="post">
<fieldset>
<table>
  <tr>
   <td>Last Name:</td>
   <td><input name="personal_lastname" type="text"
tabindex="1" /></td>
  </tr>
  <tr>
   <td>First Name:</td>
   <td><input name="personal_firstname" type="text"
tabindex="2" /></td>
  </tr>
  <tr>
   <td>Address:</td>
   <td><input name="personal_address" type="text"
tabindex="3" /></td>
  </tr>
</table>
</fieldset>
</form>
</body>
</html>
```

Listing 64-1: A sample form using a field set

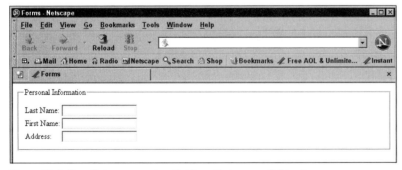

Figure 64-1: How Netscape renders the form that uses a field set

cross-reference

- You can use tables to influence fieldset borders. To learn more about tables, see Part 6.

Part 8:   Working with Frames

Defining Frameset Documents

A frameset document is a set of instructions for dividing the browser window into separate panes. Each pane is called a *frame*. The frameset document defines the orientation of each frame, their physical properties, and the filenames of the other HTML documents displayed within them. In this task, we lay out a base frameset document. Subsequent tasks demonstrate how to flesh the document out.

notes

▪ A frames-based layout requires multiple documents to make it work. For example, a three-framed layout requires a minimum of four HTML documents: the frameset document and one document for each frame that the frameset creates.

▪ A frameset is simply a set of instructions for how the browser window should be divided, rather than a Web page with its own visible content. This is because a frameset has no `<body>` tags.

1. In your text editor, open a new document and define the opening and closing `<html>` tags, including a simple head section, as shown in Listing 65-1.

```
<html>
<head>
    <title>Frames</title>
</head>


</html>
```

Listing 65-1: Basic tags of any Web page, without <body> tags

2. Below the closing `</head>` tag, insert an opening `<frameset>` tag, as shown in Listing 65-2.

```
<html>
<head>
    <title>Frames</title>
</head>

<frameset>

</html>
```

Listing 65-2: An opening <frameset> tag

3. Move to the next line, indent, and add a `<frame>` tag for each frame you want to define, as shown in Listing 65-3.

```
<html>
<head>
    <title>Frames</title>
</head>

<frameset>
    <frame>
    <frame>

</html>
```

Listing 65-3: Adding empty frame tags

4. To specify which document should be displayed in a frame, define a `src` attribute for the `<frame>` tags and set them equal to the chosen document's pathname, as shown in Listing 65-4.

```
<html>
<head>
    <title>Frames</title>
</head>

<frameset>
    <frame src="nav.html">
    <frame src="opening_main.htm">

</html>
```

Listing 65-4: Defining src attributes for each <frameset> tag

5. To make the `<frame>` tag compatible with XHTML and keep it recognizable to non-XHTML browsers, conclude the tag by inserting a space after the last attribute value and adding a forward slash and closing bracket, as shown here:

```
<frame src="nav.html" />
```

6. To close the frameset, move to the next line, return to the left margin, and insert a closing `</frameset>` tag. This initial document appears in Listing 65-5.

```
<html>
<head>
    <title>Frames</title>
</head>

<frameset>
    <frame src="nav.html" />
    <frame src="opening_main.htm" />
</frameset>

</html>
```

Listing 65-5: Building a basic frameset document

cross-references

- Frames can be defined as rows or columns. Mixing the two requires nesting the framesets. To learn how to define rows and columns, see Task 66. To learn about nesting framesets, see Task 69.

- Defining a `src` attribute, be it for a frame or an image, is no different than defining the `href` attribute for a hyperlink (see Part 5).

- This frameset document is merely skeletal. There's much more that needs to be done to it to make it truly functional. For example, we haven't even defined whether the frames will be displayed as rows or columns (see Task 66).

Task 66

Specifying Frame Dimensions

A frame's dimensions and their orientation are defined by two attributes: `rows` and `cols`. Their values don't correspond to the number of rows or columns you want to create. Instead, these attributes accept multiple column width and row height values, separated by commas. The syntax works like this:

```
cols="width of the first column, width of the second
column, etc."

rows="height of the first row, height of the second row,
etc."
```

1. To create a frameset of columns, add the `cols` attribute to the `<frameset>` tag:

```
<frameset cols>
```

2. Set the `cols` attribute equal to the widths of each column you want to create. Separate each value with commas. For example:

```
<frameset cols="150, *">
```

3. To create a frameset of rows, add the `rows` attribute to the `<frameset>` tag:

```
<frameset rows>
```

4. Set the `rows` attribute equal to the height of each row you want to create. Separate each value with commas, as shown here:

```
<frameset rows="75, *, 30">
```

5. For each row or column defined by the `rows` or `cols` attribute, include a `<frame />` tag within the frameset.

notes

- The values you define for the `cols` and `rows` attributes can take any of three possible forms: numeric pixel values, percentages, or relative values.

- Using an absolute pixel value ensures that a row or column is always an exact size. Percentage values create frames that take up the specified percentage of the browser window.

- Relative values allow you to set a frame's dimensions relative to the other frames in the frameset. Written using an asterisk, a value written as `<frameset rows="3*, 2*, 1*">` creates three rows that are relative sixths of the browser window height: 3/6, 2/6, 1/6. (Why sixths? Because 3+2+1=6.)

caution

- You need to be careful how you use pixel values. If you create a frameset defining your `cols` or `rows` attribute all with pixel values (for example, `<frameset cols="100, 100, 100">`), the browser will create a three-column frameset with each column 100 pixels wide. Because you have no control over the size of a visitor's browser window, the browser compensates and makes each frame one third of the screen, effectively giving you percentage widths.

Listing 66-1 shows the completed code for a two-column frameset.
Figure 66-1 shows that frameset displayed in a browser.

Task 66

```html
<html>
<head>
   <title>Frames</title>
</head>

<frameset cols="150, *">
   <frame src="left.html" />
   <frame src="right.html" />
</frameset>
```

Listing 66-1: Code for a two-column frameset

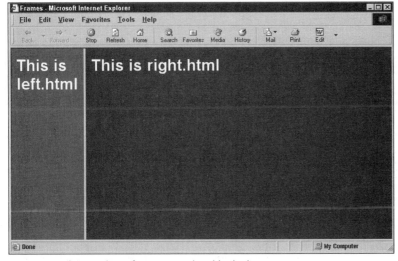

Figure 66-1: A two-column frameset rendered in the browser

tips

- To ensure that a frame stays at a specific pixel dimension, you need to mix absolute pixel values with relative values. For example, the code shown in Step 2 creates a first fixed column that is 150 pixels wide and leaves the rest of the browser window over to the second frame, which expands and contracts as the browser window resizes.

- Although not typically done, you can define both the cols and rows attributes simultaneously. For example, `<frameset rows="1*,1*,1*" cols="1*,1*,1*">` would create a three-row, three-column frameset of equally sized frames.

cross-reference

- As you define a row or column, instead of using a `<frame />` tag, nest a whole other frameset (see Task 69).

Specifying Border Properties

However you define a frame's border properties has a large impact on the look and feel of your layout. You can leave borders to their default settings — free to be repositioned by the visitor — or you can lock them in place to enforce a specific boundary. You can also modify their color, set their thickness, make them flat, or hide them completely.

1. To disable borders, define a `frameborder` attribute for the `<frameset>` tag and set it equal to `no`:

   ```
   <frameset cols="150, *" frameborder="no">
   ```

   Figure 67-1 shows the result.

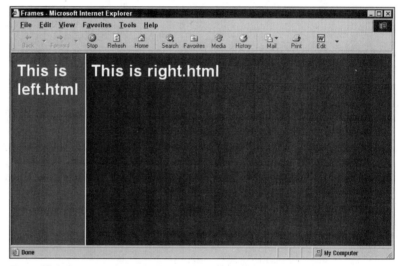

Figure 67-1: Disabling the frame border in Internet Explorer

2. To modify the thickness of frame borders, add a `border` attribute to the `<frameset>` tag and set it equal to a numeric value representing the border's width in pixels:

   ```
   <frameset cols="150, *" frameborder="no" border="0">
   ```

   Figure 67-2 shows the result.

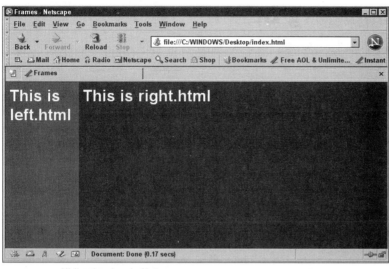

Figure 67-2: Hiding borders in Netscape

3. To prevent users from resizing the border of a specific frame by drag-
    ging on it, add a `noresize` attribute to the `<frame>` tag represent-
    ing the frame you want to lock. For example:

    ```
    <frame src="left.html" noresize />
    ```

4. To make the `noresize` attribute compatible with XHTML, set it
    equal to `noresize`, as shown here:

    ```
    <frame src="left.html" noresize="noresize" />
    ```

5. To specify border colors, add a `bordercolor` to either the `<frame>`
    tag (to modify a specific frame) or the `<frameset>` tag (to govern all
    borders in the layout). Set the attribute equal to either a hexadecimal
    value or predefined color name. For example:

    ```
    <frame bordercolor="#000000">
    ```

    ```
    <frameset bordercolor="black">
    ```

cross-reference

- Some of the early browsers
  didn't support frames, which
  required Web designers to
  include `noframes` content
  (see Task 71).

Controlling Frame Margins and Scroll Bars

The content inside a frame impacts scroll bar behavior. Scroll bars appear whenever there's more content than can fit within the defined dimensions of the frame. This means that scroll bars often pop up when a browser window is resized or if the visitor's monitor resolution is set sufficiently low. The margin settings you specify can add to or subtract from the volume of content in a frame.

1. Open the frameset document you want to edit.

2. To specify the width of a frame's left and right margins, add a marginwidth attribute to its `<frame>` tag and set it equal to a numeric value that represents the margin's pixel width.

3. To specify the height of a frame's top and bottom margins, add a `marginheight` attribute to its `<frame>` tag and set it equal to a numeric value that represents the margin's pixel width. Listing 68-1 shows margin width and height defined for one frame. Figure 68-1 shows the result in Internet Explorer.

```
<html>
<head>
<title>Frame Margins</title>
</head>

<frameset cols="150, *" framborder="no" border="0">
    <frame src="left.html" />
    <frame src="right.html" marginwidth="50"
marginheight="25" />
</frameset>

</html>
```

Listing 68-1: Margin attributes set for one frame

caution

- If you set the `scrolling` attribute to `no`, be sure to test your site across as many browsers and platforms as you can. Text, borders, and the browser window all appear differently in different browsers, operating systems, and monitor resolutions. Therefore, your layout can vary from visitor to visitor. Avoid having a visitor get to your site and not be able to see all the content in one of your frames because you've disabled scrolling.

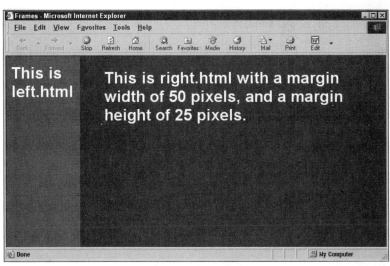

Figure 68-1: Margin effects displayed in Internet Explorer

4. To control the scroll behavior of a frame, add a `scrolling` attribute to the `<frame>` tag:

```
<frame src="left.html" scrolling>
```

5. Set the attribute equal to one of the following three values:

- `yes` displays scroll bars regardless of the amount of content in the frame

- `no` disables scroll bars entirely

- `auto` displays scroll bars if the frame content is sufficient to require them (this is the default browser behavior)

cross-reference

- Coding frames can take some time to get used to. Many WYSIWYG editors make the process a bit easier. If you're curious about those editors, see Part 15 (Working with Dreamweaver) and Part 16 (Working with FrontPage).

Nesting Framesets

Tables allow you to span columns and rows, but the `colspan` and `rowspan` attributes aren't available for the `<frameset>` tag. To achieve similar results, you'd instead nest a frameset in place of a `<frame>` tag.

1. Create that initial frameset, defining either columns or rows with the `cols` or `rows` attribute, as shown in Listing 69-1.

```
<frameset rows="75, *">
    <frame src="top.html" />

</frameset>
```

Listing 69-1: Beginning a basic frameset

2. In place of one of the frame tags, insert an opening `<frameset>` tag, as shown in Listing 69-2.

```
<frameset rows="75, *">
    <frame src="top.html" /> <!-- First row: 75 pixels -->

    <!-- Second row: to be filled by nested frameset -->
    <frameset cols="150, *">

</frameset>
```

Listing 69-2: The parent frameset's second row occupied by the nested frameset

3. Enter the `<frame>` tags for the nested frameset, as shown in Listing 69-3.

```
<frameset rows="75, *">
    <frame src="top.html" /> <!-- First row: 75 pixels -->

    <!-- Second row: to be filled by a nested frameset -->
    <frameset cols="150, *">
        <frame src="left.html" />
        <frame src="right.html" />

</frameset>
```

Listing 69-3: Nesting frames inside the frameset

note

- Typically, if your main frameset (called the parent frameset) is rows, then the frameset you nest is columns, and vice-versa.

caution

- Although having two closing `</frameset>` tags back to back looks a little odd, it is necessary. Forgetting the second tag is the first mistake most beginning coders make.

4. Close the nested frameset with a closing `</frameset>` tag. Listing 69-4 shows the completed code, and Figure 69-1 shows the results in a browser.

```html
<html>
<head>
    <title>Nesting Frames</title>
</head>
<frameset rows="75, *">
    <frame src="top.html" /> <!-- First row: 75 pixels -->

    <!-- Second row: filled by the nested frameset -->

    <frameset cols="150, *">
       <frame src="left.html" />
       <frame src="right.html" />
    </frameset>

</frameset>
</html>
```

Listing 69-4: Completed code for nested frames

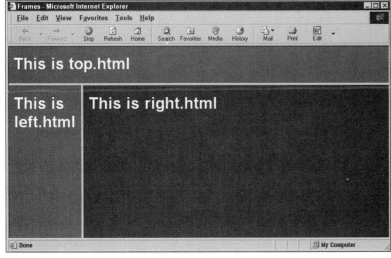

Figure 69-1: Nested frames in Internet Explorer

cross-reference

• Most frame-based layouts place the main navigation links in one frame and the documents they point to in another (see Task 70).

Task 70

Targeting Frames

Hyperlinks displayed in one frame can be written in such a way that the documents they point to are opened within other frames in the frameset. By giving your frames names (via the name attribute), you can reference those frames using the `<a>` tag's `target` attribute, setting it equal to the name of a particular frame.

1. In the frameset document, add `name` attributes to each `<frame>` tag and set them equal to a descriptive term. For example, `left_frame` or `right_frame`, as shown in Listing 70-1.

```
<html>
<head>
    <title>Targeting Frames</title>
</head>
<frameset rows="75, *">
    <frame src="top.html" name="top_frame" />

    <frameset cols="150, *">
        <frame src="left.html" name="left_frame" />
        <frame src="right.html" name="right_frame" />
    </frameset>

</frameset>
</html>
```

Listing 70-1: Describing each <frame> tag with name attributes

2. In the document containing the hyperlinks you want to target, add the `target` attribute to each `<a>` tag and set it equal to the frame name you want the linked documents to be displayed in. For example, `target="right_frame"`, as shown in Listing 70-2.

```
<html>
<head>
<title>Left Frame</title>
</head>

<body bgcolor="red" text="white">

<!-- This is left.html -->

<a href="home.html" target="right_frame">Home</a> <br>
<a href="about.html" target="right_frame">About Us</a><br>
<a href="contact.html" target="right_frame">Contact Us</a>

</body>
</html>
```

Listing 70-2: Targeting each <a> tag with a target attribute

3. To make all links in a document open in a specific frame without using the `target` attribute, add a `<base>` tag to the document's head section, as shown here:

```
<head>
    <title>Targeting Frames</title>
    <base />
</head>
```

4. Define a `target` attribute for the `<base />` tag and set it equal to the frame name you want the linked documents to be displayed in. For example:

```
<head>
    <title>Targeting Frames</title>
    <base target="right_frame" />
</head>
```

5. To make a link's document open in a new browser window, set the `target` attribute equal to "_blank":

```
<a href="contact.html" target="_blank">Contact Us</a>
```

tip

- Besides the `_blank` value, HTML offers other predefined target names that produce various effects. If the link is in a nested frameset:

  `target="_parent"` opens the document in the next outside frameset.

  `target="_self"` opens the document in the current frame (this is the default value).

  `target="_top"` displays the new document in the entire browser window, replacing the frameset altogether.

cross-reference

- You can use the `target="_blank"` method to open links in a new window whether the link is part of a frameset or not. To learn more about the `<a>` tag, see Part 5.

Providing noframes Content

rames weren't initially part of the HTML specification. They were introduced in Netscape 2.0 and adopted shortly thereafter in Internet Explorer 3.0. Earlier browsers don't support frames. To provide content for these older browsers, *noframes* content has been the traditional method of making frames-based sites backwards-compatible.

note

- The common practice is to simply inform the visitors that they have reached a frames-based site and redirect them to another version of your site that isn't frames-based.

1. Open the frameset document in your text editor.

2. Below the closing `</frameset>` tag, enter an opening `<noframes>` tag, as shown in Listing 71-1.

```
<html>
<head>
    <title>No Frames</title>
</head>
<frameset rows="75, *">
    <frame src="top.html" />

    <frameset cols="150, *">
        <frame src="left.html" />
        <frame src="right.html" />
    </frameset>

</frameset>

<noframes>

</html>
```

Listing 71-1: Start after the closing </frameset> tag

3. Enter any type of text you'd place in the body section of a normal HTML document, as shown in Listing 71-2.

```
<html>
<head>
    <title>No Frames</title>
</head>
<frameset rows="75, *">
    <frame src="top.html" />

    <frameset cols="150, *">
        <frame src="left.html" />
        <frame src="right.html" />
    </frameset>

</frameset>

<noframes>
<p>Your browser doesn't support frames.<br>
Don't panic. Simply go <a href="index-2.html">here...</a>
</p>

</html>
```

Listing 71-2: Adding text to explain to people what to do if their browsers don't support frames

4. Close the noframes section with a closing </noframes> tag:

```
<noframes>
<p>Your browser doesn't support frames.<br>
Don't panic. Simply go <a href="index-2.html">here...</a>
</p>
</noframes>
```

tip

▪ If you don't have a copy of an older browser to test your noframes content with, copy and paste the content into an ordinary document, save it, and test it that way.

cross-reference

▪ The likelihood that anyone has a browser so old that it doesn't support frames is pretty slim. But there is a good chance that most folks have Internet Explorer. Task 72 covers a frame option that only it can handle: inline frames.

Working with Inline Frames

Inline frames are an invention of Microsoft. When rendered, they create a floating, scrollable pane within the body of a regular HTML file. Microsoft must have figured that since Netscape invented frames, they could do them one better. The only problem is that, unlike frames which are supported by virtually all browsers, no one but Internet Explorer supports inline frames. Still, developers do occasionally make use of them. For example, when designing for an intranet (a closed group of users, typically within an office, who have access to a private Web server), where the browser being used is identical to all members, taking advantage of a proprietary feature isn't such a risk.

1. To insert an inline frame, insert an opening `<iframe>` tag within the body section of a document.

2. Add a `src` attribute and set it equal to the pathname of the document you want displayed within the frame:

   ```
   <iframe src="content.html">
   ```

3. Add a name attribute to allow the inline frame to be targeted and set it equal to an appropriate value:

   ```
   <iframe src="content.html" name="iframe_1">
   ```

4. To specify the inline frame's dimensions, include `width` and `height` attributes and set them equal to pixel or percentage values:

   ```
   <iframe src="content.html" name="iframe_1" width="400"
   height="200">
   ```

5. To control the margins inside the inline frame, add `marginwidth` and `marginheight` attributes as you would to a standard `<frame>` tag:

   ```
   <iframe src="content.html" name="iframe_1" width="400"
   height="200" marginwidth="25" marginheight="25">
   ```

6. To float the inline frame to the left or right, similar to an image or table, add an `align` attribute and set it equal to `left` or `right`:

   ```
   <iframe src="content.html" name="iframe_1" width="400"
   height="200" marginwidth="25" marginheight="25"
   align="left">
   ```

7. Follow the opening `<iframe>` tag with some form of instructional content you want rendered by browsers that don't support this tag.

notes

- An inline frame aligned to the left makes any body text on the same line wrap down the right side. If it's aligned to the right, text wraps down the left side.

- Any content placed between the opening and closing `<iframe>` tags is rendered by non-Microsoft browsers.

8. Insert a closing `</iframe>` tag to complete the inline frame. Listing 72-1 shows a simple inline frame document. Figure 72-1 shows the effect in Internet Explorer.

```
<html>
<head>
<title>Inline Frames</title>
</head>

<body bgcolor="#333333" text="#FFFFFF">

<iframe src="http://www.highstrungproductions.com"
width="50%" height="50%" align="left">

<a href="http://www.highstrungproductions.com"> Go here!
</a>

</iframe>
<p>
<font face="Arial, Helvetica, sans-serif" size="2">
<b>This is one of my favorite web sites. It hasn't been
updated in years...</b></font></p>

</body>
</html>
```

Listing 72-1: A simple inline frame document.

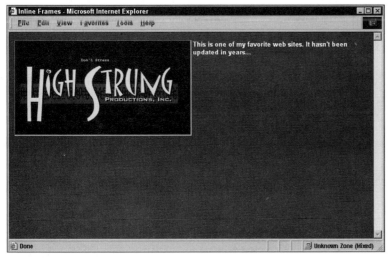

Figure 72-1: Showing a simple inline frame in Internet Explorer

cross-reference

▪ See Part 3 to learn about aligning images. Part 6 covers aligning tables.

Part 9: Cascading Style Sheets

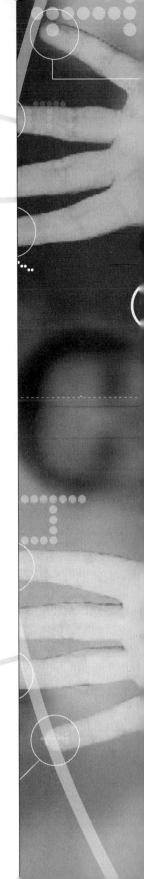

Task **73**

Writing Style Rules

note

- Value types vary with the property. See our Web site at www.wiley .com/compbooks/ 10simplestepsorless for more information.

To quote its creators, "Cascading Style Sheets (CSS) is a simple mechanism for adding style (e.g., fonts, colors, spacing) to Web documents." The purpose is to separate structure from style, leaving HTML to deal with the former while CSS takes over the latter. With the birth of CSS, any HTML markup that deals purely with how things should look is *deprecated* (no longer approved of). Instead, CSS should be used. CSS's syntax is slightly different from HTML. Angle brackets, equal signs, and quotation marks disappear in favor of curly braces, colons, and semicolons. Where HTML uses tags and attributes, CSS rules use *selectors* (the element that the style defines), selectors have *declarations* (which contain properties), and properties are assigned values (see Figure 73-1).

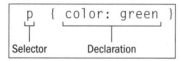

Figure 73-1: Anatomy of a CSS style rule

1. Define a selector for the style rule.

2. Follow the selector with an opening curly brace.

3. Enter a property name, followed by a colon.

4. Follow the colon with a space, supply a value for the property, and conclude the property/value pair with a semicolon.

5. Move to a new line, and enter the second property/value pair. Conclude each pair with a semicolon.

6. When the declaration contains all the properties you want to add, end the declaration with a closing curly brace.

Listing 73-1 shows a style rule for the <p> tag.

```
p { font-family: Arial, Helvetica, sans-serif;
    font-size: 12px;
    color: #000000 }
```

Listing 73-1: A style rule with three defined properties

7. To assign a single declaration to a series of selectors, simply enter the selectors as a comma-separated list, as shown here:

```
h1, h2, h3 { font-family: Arial, Helvetica, sans-serif }
```

8. To set selectors so that they only affect a tag when it appears under specific circumstances, separate a number of selectors with a space. For example:

```
h1 b { color: red }
```

This type of style definition (called a *descendant style*) tells the browser only to apply this style to bold text used with level-1 headings.

9. To use CSS syntax within the flow of an HTML document, add a style attribute to the tag you want to affect and set it equal to an appropriate series of property/value pairs, each separated by semi-colons, as shown in Listing 73-2.

```
<p style="font-family: Arial, Helvetica, sans-serif; font-
size: 12px; color: #000000">
```

Listing 73-2: CSS syntax applied inline to a paragraph tag

cross-references

- You can see a list of CSS property names and value types on our Web site, www .wiley.com/compbooks/ 10simplestepsorless.

- You can embed style definitions in the head section of an HTML document (see Task 74), place them in their own CSS document and link to them (see Task 75), or define them inline, using the style attribute, as shown in Step 7.

Task 74

Creating an Embedded Style Sheet

By embedding a style sheet we mean placing CSS code within the HTML document itself. The code is written within a style element (defined by opening and closing `<style>` tags) located in the head section of the document (defined by opening and closing `<head>` tags). Embedded style sheets affect only the specific HTML document in which the CSS code resides.

1. In the head section of an HTML document, enter an opening `<style>` tag.

2. Define a `type` attribute for the `<style>` tag and set it equal to `text/css`.

3. Insert one or two new lines and enter an opening comment tag, so that your head section resembles Listing 74-1.

```
<head>
    <title>Embedded Styles</title>

<style type="text/css">
<!--

</head>
```

Listing 74-1: The opening <style> tag

4. Insert another line or two and begin entering selectors and declarations, as described in Task 73.

5. To close the embedded style sheet, enter a closing comment tag, followed by a closing `</style>` tag.

caution
- Each declaration must be encapsulated within opening and closing curly braces. Each property/value pair must be separated by semicolons.

Listing 74-2 shows a completed embedded style sheet.

```
<head>
    <title>Embedded Style Sheets</title>

<style type="text/css">
<!--

p { font-family: Verdana, Arial, Helvetica, sans-serif;
    font-size: 11px;
    color: #000000; }

h1 { font-family: Verdana, Arial, Helvetica, sans-serif;
    font-size: 22px;
    color: #000000; }

h2 { font-family: Verdana, Arial, Helvetica, sans-serif;
    font-size: 18px;
    color: #000000; }

h3 { font-family: Verdana, Arial, Helvetica, sans-serif;
    font-size: 14px;
    color: #000000; }

-->
</style>
</head>
```

Listing 74-2: An embedded style sheet

tip

▪ To define an identical style for a series of selectors, separate each selector by a comma. For example:

```
p, td { font-
family: Verdana }
```

To create something called a contextual selector, enter a series of selectors in a row, separated only by spaces, then follow it with a declaration, like so:

```
td p { font-family:
Verdana }
```

This creates a style for paragraphs only when they occur inside a table cell.

cross-reference

▪ An embedded style sheet only defines styles for the specific document. You can use an external style sheet to attach styles to multiple documents. The advantage of this approach is that you only need to edit a single style sheet document to affect style changes across all linked documents (see Task 75).

Creating an External Style Sheet

External style sheets are separate documents containing nothing but style rules. You attach these style sheets to HTML documents using a link reference, effectively allowing you to attach a single style sheet document to as many Web pages as you like. This way you only need to change one style sheet document to update the formatting of elements across every page to which the style sheet document is attached.

1. Open a new blank document in your editor and enter the styles you wish to define. Listing 75-1 provides an example.

```
body { color: #000000;
       background: #FFFFFF;
       margin-left: 100px;
       margin-right: 100px;
       margin-top: 100px }

h1 { font-family: Arial, Helvetica, sans-serif;
     font-size: 20px;
     font-weight: bold }

p { font-family: Arial, Helvetica, sans-serif;
    font-size: 12px;
    text-align: Justify }
```

Listing 75-1: A sample style sheet

2. Save the file with a .css extension within the directory you're using for your local site files (see Figure 75-1).

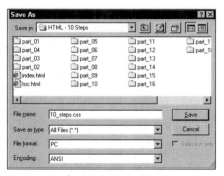

Figure 75-1: Saving the style sheet

3. Open the HTML documents to which you want to attach the style sheet. Within the head section of each document, insert a `<link>` tag with a `rel` attribute set equal to `stylesheet`, and a `type` attribute set equal to `text/css`.

4. Add a final attribute to the `<link>` tag, `href`, and set it equal to the appropriate pathname of the .css file you saved in Step 2. Listing 75-2 shows the complete code and Figure 75-2 shows the document rendered in a browser.

```
<html>
<head>
    <title>External Style Sheets</title>
    <link rel="stylesheet" type="text/css"
href="10_steps.css" />
</head>

<body>
<h1>Creating an External Style Sheet</h1>
<p>External style sheets are separate documents containing
nothing but style rules. These types of style sheets are
attached to HTML documents using a link reference,
effectively allowing you to attach a single style sheet
document to as many web pages as you like. Using this
approach you only need to make change to the individual
style sheet document to update the formatting of elements
across every page to which the style sheet document is
attached.</p>
</body>
</html>
```

Listing 75-1: A sample HTML document containing a link reference to an external style sheet

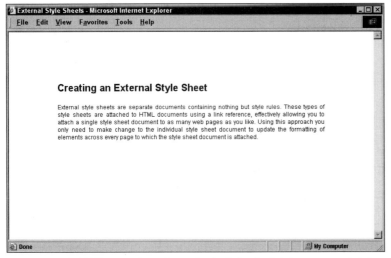

Figure 75-2: An HTML page whose formatting is defined solely in an external style sheet

tips

- When you develop a Web site, structure your local files as they would appear on the Web server. This allows you to assign relative pathnames when creating hyperlinks and other file references within your HTML code.

- The `rel` attribute stands for "relationship." The `text/css` value of the type attribute indicates that the code is text-based and written in CSS.

cross-reference

- As these code samples indicate, CSS provides many different properties that HTML doesn't duplicate. To learn more about margin properties, see Task 94. To learn more about font properties, see Tasks 77–81. To learn more about background properties, see Tasks 82 and 88.

Task **76**

Defining Style Classes

When you create a style class, you specify your own unique selector name and attach a style declaration to it. You can apply your classes to any tag by using the class attribute.

1. Type a period followed by a unique class name in the selector position of your style rule. For example:

   ```
   .citation
   ```

2. Follow the class selector with a declaration by entering an opening curly brace, defining your desired properties, and completing the declaration with a closing curly brace:

   ```
   .citation { font-family: "Times New Roman", Times, serif;
               font-size: 12px;
               font-style: italic }
   ```

3. Apply the class to your chosen HTML tag by adding a class attribute and setting it equal to the class name (without the period):

   ```
   <div class="citation">
   ```

4. Limit classes to a particular tag by preceding the class selector with the tag character. The following example makes sure the class can only be implemented with the <p> tag:

   ```
   p.citation { font-family: Times New Roman, Times, serif;
                font-size: 12px;
                font-style: italic }
   ```

5. Specify unique ID classes by preceding a class name selector with a pound sign and applying them to a tag using the ID attribute:

   ```
   #preamble { font-family: Arial, Helvetica, sans-serif;
               font-size: 20px; }

   <h1 ID="preamble">Preamble</h1>
   ```

Listing 76-1 shows an embedded style sheet that makes use of both a standard and ID class. Figure 76-1 displays the results in a browser.

caution

- An ID class can only be used by a single element per document, so its use is more limited than standard classes.

```
<html>
<head>
   <title>Style Classes</title>

<style type="text/css">
<!--

.citation { font-family: "Times New Roman", Times, serif;
            font-size: 12pt;
            font-style: italic }

#preamble { font-family: Arial, Helvetica, sans-serif;
            font-size: 20pt; }
-->
</style>

</head>

<body>

<h1 ID="preamble">Preamble</h1>

<p class="citation">"We the People of the United States, in
Order to form a more perfect Union, establish Justice,
insure domestic Tranquility, provide for the common defense,
promote the general Welfare, and secure the Blessings of
Liberty to ourselves and our Posterity, do ordain and
establish this Constitution for the United States of
America." </p>

</body>
</html>
```

Listing 76-1: Example of standard and ID classes

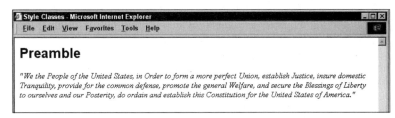

Figure 76-1: A standard class (the citation) and an ID class (the heading) rendered in the browser

tip
- Define your classes in embedded or external style sheets. Because style classes require a selector, it isn't possible to create an inline style class.

cross-reference
- For more coverage of CSS, see our Web site at www .wiley.com/compbooks/ 10simplestepsorless.

Defining the font-family Property

The font-family property in CSS functions identically as the face attribute of the <font> tag in HMTL. Use this property to specify a prioritized list of fonts with which the browser should attempt to render an element. Just as it does with the face attribute, the browser renders text with the first font that matches the one installed on the visitor's computer.

1. Within the declaration of your style rule, include a font-family property as shown here:

   ```
   p { font-family: }
   ```

2. Follow the semicolon with the name of your first choice font. For example:

   ```
   p { font-family: "Times New Roman" }
   ```

3. Enter a comma and follow your first font choice with a second or third, as shown here:

   ```
   p { font-family: "Times New Roman", Times }
   ```

4. Conclude the list with the generic font family name to which the other fonts belong. For example:

   ```
   p { font-family: "Times New Roman", Times, serif }
   ```

   Listing 77-1 shows an embedded style sheet sample. Figure 77-1 shows the resulting document in a browser.

```
<html>
<head>
<title>The font-family Property</title>

<style type="text/css">
<!--

.code { font-family: Courier, monospace }

h1 { font-family: Arial, Helvetica, sans-serif }

p (font-family: "Times New Roman", Times, serif }

-->
</style>
</head>

<body>
<h1>Defining the <span class="code">font-family</span>
Property</h1>
<p>The <span class="code">font-family</span> property in CSS
is similar in function to the <span class="code">face</span>
attribute of the <span class="code">&lt;font&gt;</span> tag
in HMTL. Use this property to specify a prioritized list of
fonts with which the browser should attempt to render the
element. Identically to the <span class="code">face</span>
attribute, a browser renders text with the first font that
matches one installed on the visitor's computer.</p>

</body>
</html>
```

Listing 77-1: The font-family property in practice

Figure 77-1: Rendering the font-family property in the browser

tips

- Capitalize all font names. Any font name that contains more than one word should be placed in quotes. Otherwise, browsers may ignore the spaces between words and not recognize the font name you request.

- By concluding the list of fonts with the generic font family name, you ensure that even if the visitor's computer lacks any of your initial choices, it will still use whatever default font it has that falls within that family. Common generic families include serif (e.g., Times), sans-serif (e.g., Arial), and monospace (e.g., Courier).

cross-reference

- The example in this task uses an embedded style sheet, but an external style sheet could be used just as easily (see Task 75).

Defining the font-size Property with Keywords

As you might have guessed, the CSS `font-size` property fulfills the same function as the `size` attribute of the `<font>` tag in HTML.

1. Within the declaration of your style rule, include a `font-size` property.

2. Use the absolute-size keyword values `xx-small`, `x-small`, `small`, `medium`, `large`, `x-large`, and `xx-large` to define values corresponding to the HTML font size scale of 1 to 7, respectively. Listing 78-1 shows seven paragraph style classes using each value. Figure 78-1 shows how the browser renders the code.

```
<html>
<head>
<title>The font-size Property</title>
<style type="text/css">
<!--
p.one { font-size: xx-small }
p.two { font-size: x-small }
p.three { font-size: small }
p.four { font-size: medium }
p.five { font-size: large }
p.six { font-size: x-large }
p.seven { font-size: xx-large }
-->
</style>
</head>
<body>
<p class="one"> font-size: xx-small = size="1" </p>
<p class="two"> font-size: x-small = size="2" </p>
<p class="three"> font-size: small = size="3" </p>
<p class="four"> font-size: medium = size="4" </p>
<p class="five"> font-size: large = size="5" </p>
<p class="six"> font-size: xx-large = size="6" </p>
<p class="seven"> font-size: xx-large = size="7" </p>
</body>
</html>
```

Listing 78-1: Absolute-size keyword values

3. Use the relative-size keyword values `larger` or `smaller` to increase or decrease the size of text relative to the font size of the parent element.

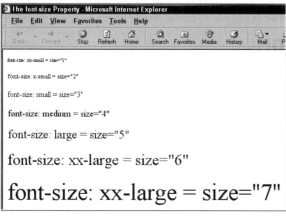

Figure 78-1: Text rendered with absolute-size keyword values

Listing 78-2 shows the <div> tag (the parent element in this case) set to large and two <p> tag style classes which increase and decrease the font size relative to that value.

```
<html>
<head>
<title>The font-size Property</title>
<style type="text/css">
<!--
div { font-size: large }
p.increase { font-size: larger }
p.decrease { font-size: smaller }
-->
</style>
</head>
<body>
<div>
<p class="increase"> This line is larger </p>
<p> This line is large </p>
<p class="decrease"> This line is smaller </p>
</div>
</body>
</html>
```

Listing 78-2: Relative-size keyword values

cross-references

- See Task 14 to learn how to use the size attribute of the <font> tag.

- See Task 76 to create style classes.

- These code listings all demonstrate the use of embedded style sheets. See Task 75 to learn how to define external style sheets.

Task **79**

Defining the font-size Property with Lengths

The CSS specification provides an extensive range of absolute and relative length values not found in HTML. The inclusion of specific units of measure provides greater control over how content is displayed across different output devices (monitors, printers, and so on).

1. Add a `font-size` property to the declaration of your style rule.

2. Set the property equal to an absolute-size length value. Listing 79-1 shows a few possible values. Figure 79-1 displays the results in a browser.

```
<html>
<head>
<title>The font-size Property</title>
<style type="text/css">
<!--
p.point { font-size: 12pt }
p.pica { font-size: 1pc }
p.cent { font-size: .4cm }
p.mill { font-size: 4mm }
p.inch { font-size: .15in }
-->
</style>
</head>
<body>
<p class="point">12 points</p>
<p class="pica">1 picas</p>
<p class="cent">.4 centimeters</p>
<p class="mill">4 millimeters</p>
<p class="inch">.15 inches</p>
</body>
</html>
```

Listing 79-1: Absolute-length values assigned to the font-size property

3. Use relative-size length values to indicate a length relative to some other property. For example:

- **em:** The relative height of the font's uppercase letters

- **ex:** The relative height of the font's lowercase letters

- **px:** The relative pixel resolution of the user's monitor

- **%:** A percentage of the font's default size value

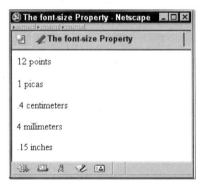

Figure 79-1: Text rendered with absolute-length values assigned to the font-size property

Listing 79-2 shows possible relative values. Figure 79-2 displays the results.

```
<html>
<head>
<title>Font Size</title>
<style type="text/css">
<!--
p.em {font-size: 1em}
p.ex {font-size: 2ex}
p.px {font-size: 16px}
p.percent {font-size: 100%}
-->
</style>
</head>
<body>
<p class="em">1 default uppercase letter high</p>
<p class="ex">2 default lowercase letters high</p>
<p class="px">16 pixels high</p>
<p class="percent">100 percent of the default font size </p>
</body>
</html>
```

Listing 79-2: Relative-length values assigned to the font-size property

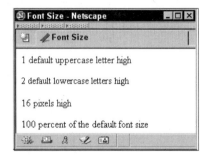

Figure 79-2: Text rendered with relative-length values assigned to the font-size property

tips

- Make sure you don't inadvertently put a space between your numeric value and the abbreviation of the unit of measure.

- Write all units of measure in lowercase.

cross-reference

- To find out more about CSS, check out *CSS For Dummies,* by Damon Dean (Wiley Publishing, Inc., 2001).

Working with Font Styling

Font styling refers to the font-style, font-variant, and font-weight properties. The font-style and font-weight properties correspond loosely to HTML's physical styles <i> and <b>, only in CSS you can control the degree of boldness you prefer. The font-variant property introduces a style possibility lacking from HTML — small caps.

1. To specify whether a selector uses a normal, italic, or oblique font, define a font-style property, as shown here:

   ```
   .citation { font-style: italic }
   ```

2. To specify whether a font uses small-caps, define a font-variant property set equal to small-caps. In a small-caps font, lowercase letters are replaced with uppercase letters of slightly smaller size and proportions.

3. To define a font-variant style that overrides a previous small-caps setting, use a value of normal.

4. To regulate the boldness of text, include a font-weight property in the declaration. For example:

   ```
   { font-weight: bold }
   ```

   The font-weight property accepts relative keyword values of lighter, normal, bold, or bolder.

5. To define the font-weight property using an absolute value, use the following scale, in increments of 100: 100 (the lightest) to 900 (the boldest). Normal font weight is 400; normal bold is 700.

   Listing 80-1 shows each property in use within a style sheet. Figure 80-1 displays the results in a browser.

notes

- Oblique and italic are essentially the same thing, depending on the font. Traditionally, oblique fonts are slanted versions of normal fonts, while italic fonts have been specifically designed to appear slanted. If the font you choose has a specific oblique version, you may see a difference between it and the italic setting.

- If the font you specify with a font-family property doesn't have a specific oblique state, italic will be used instead.

- In many browsers, distinguishing between a font-weight value of 100 and 400 is nearly impossible, as is distinguishing between 400, 500, and 600. Consequently, we recommend using relative keyword values.

```
<html>
<head>
   <title>Font Styling</title>

<style type="text/css">
<!--
h1 { font-family: Arial;
     font-style: italic;
     font-variant: small-caps;
     font-weight: bold }

em { font-family: Courier;
     font-size: smaller;
     font-style: normal;
     font-variant: normal;
     font-weight: normal }

 p { font-family: Arial;
     font-style: normal;
     font-variant: small-caps;
     font-weight: 500 }
-->
</style>
</head>
<body>
<h1>Working with the <em>font-style</em>, <em>font-
variant</em>, and <em>font-weight</em> Properties</h1>

<p>These properties allow the designer to control font
styling.</p>
</body>
</html>
```

Listing 80-1: Examples of the font-style, font-variant, and font-weight properties

Figure 80-1: Text rendered with the font-style, font-variant, and font-weight properties

cross-reference

▪ When you know how to
define CSS styles manually,
implementing them in
WYSIWYG editors like
Macromedia Dreamweaver
is easy (see Part 15).

Using the Font Property Shorthand

In CSS, you can define each of the various font properties' values discussed in Tasks 77–80 all under one inclusive property name, called font. CSS requires that the properties be entered in the order provided here, each separated by a space.

1. Within the declaration of your style rule, enter the font property, as shown here:

   ```
   h1 { font:
   ```

2. Define your desired font-style value (normal, oblique, or italic):

   ```
   h1 { font: normal
   ```

3. Add a font-weight value using either keywords (lighter, normal, bold, and bolder) or values from the 100–900 scale (400 = normal, 700 = bold):

   ```
   h1 { font: normal bold
   ```

4. Provide any desired font-variant value (normal or small-caps):

   ```
   h1 { font: normal bold small-caps
   ```

5. Include the font-size property value you want:

   ```
   h1 { font: normal bold small-caps 24pt
   ```

6. To combine a line-height value with your font-size value, insert a forward slash (/) immediately after the font-size value and then add a line-height value:

   ```
   h1 { font: normal bold small-caps 24pt/48pt
   ```

7. Conclude the list with your desired font-family property, using commas and quotation marks as required:

   ```
   h1 { font: normal bold small-caps 24pt/48pt Arial,
   Helvetica, sans-serif }
   ```

   Listing 81-1 provides examples of the font property shorthand technique. Figure 81-1 displays the results in a browser.

```
<html>
<head>
    <title>Font Property Shorthand</title>
<style type="text/css">
<!--
h1 { font: normal bold small-caps 24pt/48pt Arial,
Helvetica, sans-serif }

p { font: 16pt/24pt Arial, Helvetica, sans-serif }

em { font: bold italic }
-->
</style>
</head>
<body>
<h1>Font Property Shorthand</h1>

<p>The CSS specification <em>requires</em> that the
properties be defined in the order laid out in this task.
Even though some browsers don't care which order you define
them in, others do, so it's best to stick by the rules.</p>
</body>
</html>
```

Listing 81-1: Different implementations of the font property shorthand

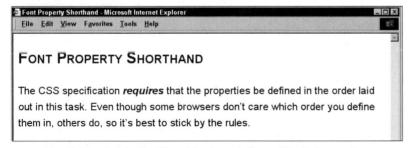

FONT PROPERTY SHORTHAND

The CSS specification *requires* that the properties be defined in the order laid out in this task. Even though some browsers don't care which order you define them in, others do, so it's best to stick by the rules.

Figure 81-1: Text rendered with different implementations of the font property shorthand

tips

- If you do not include a value for a specific property, it will be reset to its default value.

- The only properties required when using the shorthand method are font-size and font-family.

cross-reference

- To learn more about the line-height property, see Task 84.

Task **82**

Working with Foreground and Background Colors

Screens aren't black-and-white; your text needn't be either. The CSS `color` and `background-color` properties allow you to specify the foreground color of an element's text content and the color of an element's background.

1. To specify a color for an element's text, include a `color` property in the style declaration. For example:

```
p { color:
```

2. To specify the color of an element's background, include a `background-color` property in the style declaration. For example:

```
body { background-color:
```

3. To define the value of these properties, use either:

   - **Hexadecimal notation:** `{ color: #FF0000 }`

   - **Predefined color name:** `{ color: red }`

4. CSS also allows the use of *RGB triples*, using either range or percentage values:

   - **RGB range:** `{ color: rgb(255, 0, 0) }`

   - **RGB percentage:** `{ color: rgb(100%, 0%, 0%) }`

   Listing 82-1 provides an example of these two properties in use. Figure 82-1 gives you an idea of how each element implements them.

```
<html>
<head>
    <title>Color and Background Color</title>
<style type="text/css">
<!--
p.inverted { color: #FFFFFF;
             background-color: #000000 }

td.shaded { color: #000000;
             background-color: #666666 }
-->
</style>
</head>
<body>
<table cellpadding="5" cellspacing="0" border="1">
    <tr>
        <td class="shaded">
        The cell's background is completely filled...
        </td>

    </tr>
    <tr>
        <td>
        <p class="inverted">
        while the background color of  the paragraph text
        only covers the text itself</p>
        </td>
    </tr>
</table>

</body>
</html>
```

Listing 82-1: Style classes using color and background-color properties

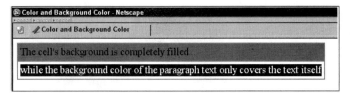

Figure 82-1: Different uses of style classes using color and background-color properties

cross-references

- For a further discussion of color, see our Web site's coverage of both color and CSS: www.wiley .com/compbooks/ 10simplestepsorless.

- The amount of padding an element has (see Task 89) impacts how far the background color extends outward from the text.

- CSS allows elements to use image backgrounds also (see Task 88).

Controlling Character and Word Spacing

The space between letters, words, and lines can be increased or decreased using the letter-spacing, word-spacing, and white-space properties.

1. To specify the distance between characters in text, include a letter-spacing property in the style declaration. For example:

```
p { letter-spacing:
```

2. Specify a length value for the property using any of the allowed units of measure. For example:

```
{ letter-spacing: 2ex }
{ letter-spacing: 1em }
{ letter-spacing: 16px }
{ letter-spacing: 1pc }
{ letter-spacing: 12pt }
{ letter-spacing: 4.2mm }
{ letter-spacing: .42cm }
{ letter-spacing: .165in }
```

3. To specify the distance between words in text, include a word-spacing property in the style declaration. For example:

```
p { word-spacing:
```

4. Supply a length value using any of the units of measure that CSS supports. For example:

```
{ word-spacing: 1ex }
{ word-spacing: .5em }
{ word-spacing: 8px }
{ word-spacing: .5pc }
{ word-spacing: 6pt }
{ word-spacing: 2.1mm }
{ word-spacing: .21cm }
{ word-spacing: .083in }
```

Listing 83-1 shows examples of different spacings. Figure 83-1 displays the document in a browser.

caution
- Although negative values are permissible in CSS, some older browsers may not support them.

```
<html>
<head>
<title>Spacing</title>
<style type="text/css">
<!--
h1 { letter-spacing: -.25ex;
     word-spacing: -1ex }

p { letter-spacing: .5ex;
    word-spacing: 1ex;
    font-size: 16pt }
-->
</style>
</head>
<body>
<h1> Letter & Word Spacing </h1>
<p>The heading looks to be just overlapping, while this
paragraph is quite liberally spaced</p>
</body>
</html>
```

Listing 83-1: Spacing letters, words, and lines

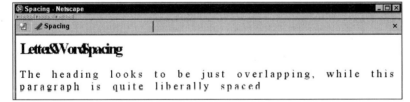

Figure 83-1: Rendering different letter, word, and line spacing in a browser

tip

- Each property can accept the keyword `normal` to return the property to its default value.

cross-reference

- Letter and word spacing can be influenced by the alignment of text. To learn how to align text using CSS, see Task 87.

Controlling Line Spacing and Vertical Alignment

You can manipulate the distance between lines (referred to as *leading*) using the line-height property. The other CSS property that impacts line height calculations is vertical-align, which combines the effects of HTML's align attribute as applied to the <img> tag with the physical style tags that affect line height: <sup> and <sub>.

1. To control the amount of space between lines of text within a given element, include the line-height property in your declaration, as shown here:

   ```
   p { line-height:
   ```

2. Supply a value using any of the following methods:

   • **Keyword value:** line-height accepts the keyword value normal, which tells the browser to use a "reasonable" value based on the font size of the element.

   • **Length value:** a numeric value in any of the units of measure that CSS supports (ex, em, px, pc, pt, mm, cm, in).

   • **Number value:** a multiple of the element's font size. For example:

   ```
   p { line-height: 1.5;
       font-size: 12pt }
   ```

   specifies a computed value of 1.5×12, equaling a line height of 18pt.

   • **Percentage:** a percentage of the element's font size. For example:

   ```
   p { line-height: 125%;
       font-size: 12pt }
   ```

   specifies a computed value 25 percent larger than the current font size, or 15pt ($12 \div 4 = 3$, $3 + 12 = 15$pt, for folks like us who are mathematically challenged).

3. To control the vertical alignment of an element, include the vertical-align property in your declaration. For example:

   ```
   p { vertical-align:
   ```

4. Supply a value using any of the following methods:

   • **Keyword value:** the vertical-align property accepts the keyword values baseline, middle, text-top, and text-bottom (like the align attribute of the <img> tag). It also accepts the values sub and super, creating the same effect as the subscript (<sub>) and superscript (<sup>) tags.

- **Percentage:** raise or lower the element by a percentage of the line-height value.

- **Length value:** raise or lower the element by a specified value in any of the units of measure that CSS supports (ex, em, px, pc, pt, mm, cm, in).

Listing 84-1 provides some examples of line height and vertical alignment. Figure 84-1 displays the results in the browser.

```
<html>
<head>
<title>Line Height & Vertical Alignment</title>
<style type="text/css">
<!--
.math { vertical-align: sub }
p { font: 14pt Verdana;
    line-height: 1.5 }
-->
</style>
</head>
<body>
<p>This paragraph's line height is 1.5 times bigger than its
font size.<br />
With the math class's vertical alignment set to subscript,
it allows me to accurately render H<span
class="math">2</span>O</p>
</body>
</html>
```

Listing 84-1: Examples of the line-height and vertical-align properties

This paragraph's line height is 1.5 times bigger than its font size.
With the math class's vertical alignment set to subscript, it allows me to accurately render H_2O

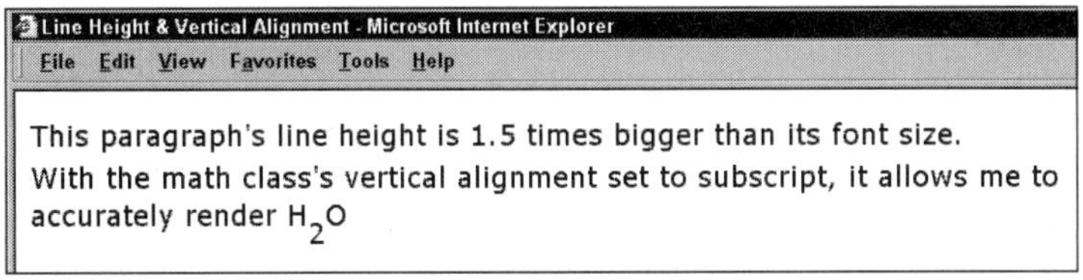

Figure 84-1: Text rendered using the line-height and vertical-align properties

cross-reference

- See Task 16 to learn more about physical styles in HTML. See Task 30 to learn how the align attribute works in the <img> tag.

Defining the text-decoration Property

The `text-decoration` property allows you to add some additional flourishes to text content. You can place a line over, under, or through text; make text blink, or remove any predefined flourishes as well.

note
- The `underline` and `line-through` values are equivalent to HTML's `<u> <s>` tags, respectively.

1. To apply a decorative style to text, include a `text-decoration` property in your declaration, as shown here:

   ```
   em { text-decoration:
   ```

2. Use any of the following keyword values to control the position of a decorative line:

   - Underline text with `underline`
   - Place a line above text with `overline`
   - Strike a line through text with `line-through`

3. To make the text blink, add a value of `blink`.

4. To remove any existing text decoration from an element, add the value `none`.

   Listing 85-1 provides examples of the `text-decoration` property. Figure 85-1 displays the document in a browser.

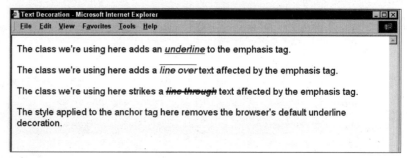

Figure 85-1: Text rendered with the text-decoration property

caution
- The `blink` value is only supported by Netscape. Blinking text also tends to annoy people, giving you two good reasons to avoid using it.

```
<html>
<head>
<title>Text Decoration</title>
<style type="text/css">
<!--
body { font: 14pt Arial }
em.u { text-decoration: underline }
em.o { text-decoration: overline }
em.lt { text-decoration: line-through }
a { text-decoration: none }
-->
</style>
</head>
<body>
<p>The class we're using here adds an <em
class="u">underline</em> to the emphasis tag.</p>

<p>The class we're using here adds a <em class="o">line
over</em> text affected by the emphasis tag.</p>

<p>The class we're using here strikes a <em class="lt">line
through</em> text affected by the emphasis tag.</p>

<p>The style applied to the <a href="css.html">anchor
tag</a> here removes the browser's default underline
decoration.</p>

</body>
</html>
```

Listing 85-1: Examples of the text-decoration property

tip

- Setting the text-decoration property to none is often done to the CSS *pseudo classes* a:link, a:visited, a:active and a:hover to control the underlining of hyperlinks.

86 Defining the text-transform Property

CSS allows you to define styles that affect the capitalization of text. Not only can you force all text to appear in UPPERCASE or lowercase, but you can make the First Letter Of Each Word Capitalized As Well.

1. To control text case, include a `text-transform` property in the declaration. For example:

```
p { text-transform:
```

2. Use any of the following keyword values to control the case of text affected by the style:

   - Render all text in uppercase letters with `uppercase`

   - Render all text in lowercase letters with `lowercase`

   - Render the first letter of each word in uppercase with `capitalize`

3. To remove any previous transformations for an element, use the value `none`.

   Listing 86-1 provides examples of the `text-transform` property. Figure 86-1 displays the document in a browser.

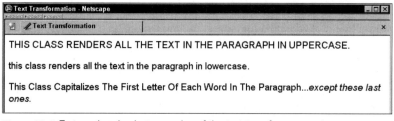

Figure 86-1: Text rendered using examples of the text-transform property

```
<html>
<head>
<title>Text Transformation</title>
<style type="text/css">
<!--
body { font: 14pt Arial }
p.up { text-transform: uppercase }
p.low { text-transform: lowercase }
p.cap { text-transform: capitalize }
em { text-transform: none }
-->
</style>
</head>

<body>
<p class="up">This class renders all the text in the
paragraph in uppercase.</p>

<p class="low">This class renders all the text in the
paragraph in lowercase.</p>

<p class="cap">This class capitalizes the first letter of
each word in the paragraph...<em>except these last
ones.</em></p>

</body>
</html>
```

Listing 86-1: Examples of the text-transform property

cross-references

- The small-caps value of the font-variant property replaces lowercase letters with uppercase letters of slightly smaller size and proportions (see Task 80).

- In case you have trouble remembering all these property names, if you use Helios Software TextPad you can install *clip libraries* that put these names all at your fingertips (see Part 12).

- Bare Bones Software BBEdit allows you to define CSS properties using dialog boxes accessed from the CSS submenu (see Part 13).

Task **87**

Controlling Text Alignment and Indentation

In HTML you control the alignment of text elements with the `align` attribute. In CSS you use the `text-align` property instead. One thing that HTML can't do for you is indent the first line of a paragraph. CSS has no such restriction and allows you to do that with the `text-indent` property.

1. To control the alignment of a text element, include a `text-align` property within your declaration, as shown here:

   ```
   p { text-align:
   ```

2. Use the following keyword values `left`, `right`, `center`, or `justify` to instruct the browser how to align the text.

3. To specify the indentation of the first line of text in a block, include a `text-indent` property in your declaration.

4. Supply a length value (ex, em, px, pc, pt, mm, cm, in) to create an indentation of fixed length or a percentage value, which creates an indent relative to the element's overall width.

   Listing 87-1 shows examples of the `text-align` and `text-indent` properties. Figure 87-1 displays the document in a browser.

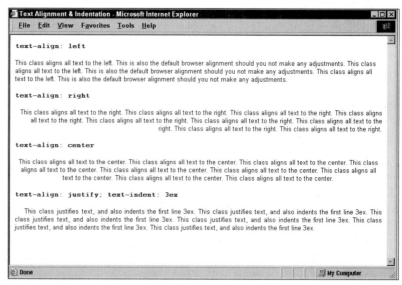

Figure 87-1: Text examples rendered with the text-align and text-indent properties

```
<html>
<head>
<title>Text Alignment & Indentation</title>
<style type="text/css">
<!--
body { font: 88t Arial }
h1 { font: bold 88t Courier, monospace; text-align: left }
p.left    { text-align: left }
p.right   { text-align: right }
p.center  { text-align: center }
p.just    { text-align: justify; text-indent: 3ex }
-->
</style>
</head>
<body>
<h1>text-align: left</h1>
<p class="left">This class aligns all text to the left. This
is also the default browser alignment should you not make
any adjustments. This class aligns all text to the left.
This is also the default browser alignment should you not
make any adjustments. This class aligns all text to the
left. This is also the default browser alignment should you
not make any adjustments. </p>

<h1>text-align: right</h1>
<p class="right">This class aligns all text to the right.
This class aligns all text to the right. This class aligns
all text to the right. This class aligns all text to the
right. This class aligns all text to the right. This class
aligns all text to the right. This class aligns all text to
the right. This class aligns all text to the right. This
class aligns all text to the right. </p>

<h1>text-align: center</h1>
<p class="center">This class aligns all text to the center.
This class aligns all text to the center. This class aligns
all text to the center. This class aligns all text to the
center. This class aligns all text to the center. This class
aligns all text to the center. This class aligns all text to
the center. This class aligns all text to the center. This
class aligns all text to the center. </p>

<h1>text-align: justify; text-indent: 3ex</h1>
<p class="just">This class justifies text, and also indents
the first line 3ex. This class justifies text, and also
indents the first line 3ex. This class justifies text, and
also indents the first line 3ex. This class justifies text,
and also indents the first line 3ex. This class justifies
text, and also indents the first line 3ex. This class
justifies text, and also indents the first line 3ex. </p>
</body>
</html>
```

Listing 87-1: Examples using the text-align and text-indent properties

cross-reference

- See Task 83 for more on
  the letter-spacing
  and word-spacing
  properties.

Working with Background Images

In HTML background images are limited to the document body and the various parts of the table element. In CSS you can make use of background images in virtually all elements.

1. To specify a background image for an element, include a background-image property in your declaration, as shown here:

   ```
   body { background-image:
   ```

2. To specify the path to the image you want to use, define a URL value with the appropriate pathname (in parentheses) identifying the location of the image file on the server. For example:

   ```
   body { background-image: url(images/bg.gif) }
   ```

3. To control how the background image tiles, add a background-repeat property. For example:

   ```
   body { background-image: url(images/bg.gif);
       background-repeat:
   ```

4. Supply the background-repeat property with one of the following four keyword values:

   • repeat tiles the image horizontally and vertically (the default browser behavior)

   • no-repeat prevents the image from tiling at all, displaying only a single instance of the image

   • repeat-x tiles the image horizontally only

   • repeat-y tiles the image vertically only

5. To fix the background image in place, so it appears stationary while the browser window is scrolled, add a background-attachment property and apply the value fixed, as shown here:

   ```
   body { background-image: url(images/bg.gif);
       background-repeat: repeat-x;
       background-attachment: fixed;
   ```

6. Include a background-position property to determine the position of a background image. Use this in conjunction with the background-image property and the background-repeat property, indicating no-repeat. For example:

   ```
   body { background-image: url(images/bg.gif);
       background-repeat: no-repeat;
       background-position:
   ```

7. Define a value for the `background-position` property using the following value types:

- Length values: ex, em, px, pc, pt, mm, cm, in

- Percentage values

- Keyword values: top | center | bottom and left | center | right

Listing 88-1 shows a sample style rule for the `<body>` tag, and Figure 88-1 shows the effect in the browser.

```
body { background-image: url(flower.gif);
       background-repeat: no-repeat;
       background-position: center center }
```

Listing 88-1: Three related properties governing a background image and its placement

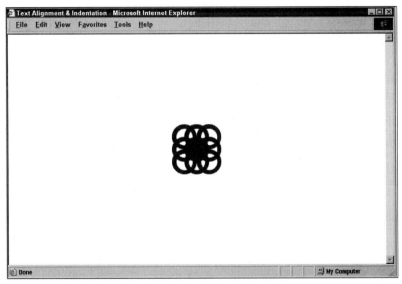

Figure 88-1: Displaying a non-repeating background flower image in the center of the browser window

tip

- To enforce the default browser behavior so that the background image scrolls with the content of the document, set the `background-attachment` property to `scroll`.

cross-reference

- Microsoft FrontPage makes building style sheets simple (see Part 16).

Defining CSS Padding Properties

notes

- The examples in this task use a background-color property to emphasize the area affected by the padding.

- In this style class, we aligned the paragraph to the right to see the effect of the padding-right property.

In the HTML table model, you have the ability to increase the spacing between a cell's content and the cell walls using the cellpadding attribute. The CSS box model (explained on the book's Web site) is very similar to a table cell. It provides a mechanism for increasing or decreasing the spacing around content through the use of padding properties. Unlike HTML, where padding is simultaneously increased on all sides around the cell content, CSS allows you to specify the padding values for all fours sides independently using length (ex, em, px, pc, pt, mm, cm, in) or percentage values. A value of zero collapses the padding area completely. Negative values are not permitted.

1. To specify the amount of padding above the element, include a padding-top property in your declaration.

2. To specify the amount of padding on the right side of the element, include a padding-right property.

3. To specify the amount of padding below the element, include a padding-bottom property.

4. To specify the amount of padding on the left side of the element, include a padding-left property.

5. To render padding properties in shorthand, simply include a padding property in your declaration, followed by one to four values:

   - **One value:** Applies the stated padding equally to all sides of the element

   - **Two values:** Sets the top and bottom padding to the first value and the right and left padding to the second

   - **Three values:** Sets the top padding to the first value, the left and right padding to the second value, and the bottom padding to the third

   - **Four values:** Applies the stated padding to the top, right, bottom, and left sides, respectively

Listing 89-1 shows an example of the padding properties while Figure 89-1 displays each property in action.

```
<html>
<head>
<title>Padding</title>
<style type="text/css">
<!--
p.top { padding-top: 100px;
        font: bold 12pt Courier;
        background-color: #CCCCCC }
```

(continued)

```
p.right { padding-right: 100px;
        font: bold 12pt Courier;
        text-align: right;
        background-color: #CCCCCC }

p.left { padding-left: 100px;
        font: bold 12pt Courier;
        background-color: #CCCCCC }

p.bottom { padding-bottom: 100px;
        font: bold 12pt Courier;
        background-color: #CCCCCC }
-->
</style>
</head>
<body>
<p class="top">padding-top: 100px</p>

<p class="right">padding-right: 100px</p>

<p class="left">padding-left: 100px</p>

<p class="bottom">padding-bottom: 100px</p>

</body>
</html>
```

Listing 89-1: Examples of the four padding properties

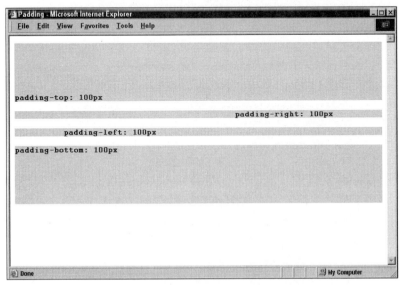

Figure 89-1: Rendering the four padding properties in the browser

cross-reference

- The cellpadding attribute discussed in the introduction to this task is discussed in Task 44.

note

* Netscape 6 supports all border styles.

Task 90

Defining Border Style Properties

In HTML only images and tables have definable borders. The CSS box model extends borders to the entire spectrum of page content. The first step to define a border is to specify a border style. There are eight styles to choose from and, as with all properties relating to the CSS box model, you can specify them for each side individually, or all four sides at once.

1. To specify the style of the border above an element, include a `border-top-style` property in your declaration.

2. To specify the style of the border on the right side of the element, include a `border-right-style` property.

3. To specify the style of the border below the element, include a `border-bottom-style` property.

4. To specify the style of the border on the left side of the element, include a `border-left-style` property.

5. To render border style properties in shorthand, simply include a `border-style` property in your declaration.

6. Define a value for your border style properties using any of the following keyword values:

   * `none` removes all borders; this value forces the border width to 0 (see Task 91)

   * `dotted` renders the border in dots

   * `dashed` renders the border as a dashed line

   * `solid` renders the border as a solid line

   * `double` renders the border as two solid lines

   * `groove` renders the border as an engraved line

   * `ridge` renders the border as an embossed border

   * `inset` renders the entire box to look as though it were embedded in the page

   * `outset` renders the entire box to look as though it were embossed (the opposite of `inset`)

Listing 90-1 demonstrating the use of border style properties. Figure 90-1 shows the effects of each value.

cautions

* Internet Explorer 5.5 and later support all border styles. IE4 and IE5 do not support the `dotted` and `dashed` values.

* The `border-style` property is not recognized in Netscape 4.

```
<html>
<head>
<title>Border Styles</title>
<style type="text/css">
<!--
```

(continued)

```
body { font: bold 16pt Courier }
p.none { border-style: none }
p.dotted { border-style: dotted }
p.dashed { border-style: dashed }
p.solid { border-style: solid }
p.double { border-style: double }
p.groove { border-style: groove }
p.ridge { border-style: ridge }
p.inset { border-style: inset }
p.outset { border-style: outset }
-->
</style>
</head>
<body>
<p class="none">none </p>
<p class="dotted">dotted</p>
<p class="dashed">dashed</p>
<p class="solid">solid</p>
<p class="double">double</p>
<p class="groove">groove</p>
<p class="ridge">ridge</p>
<p class="inset">inset</p>
<p class="outset">outset</p>
</body>
</html>
```

Listing 90-1: Examples of the shorthand border-style property

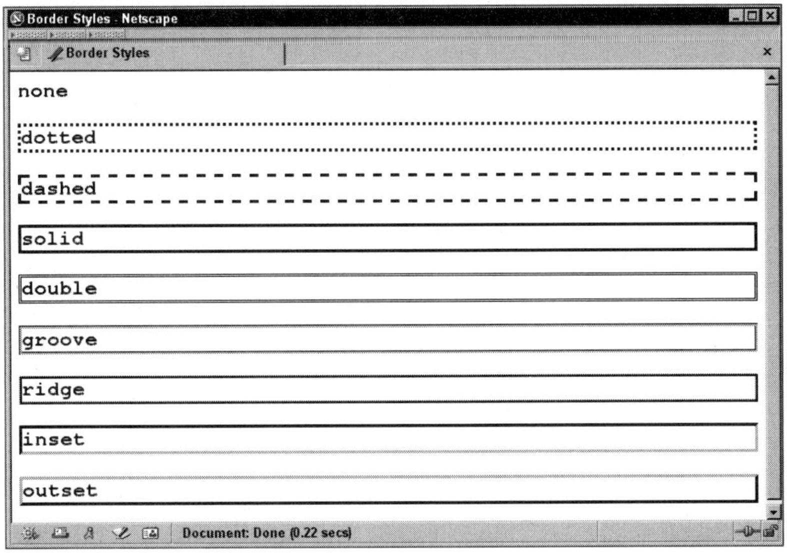

Figure 90-1: Border styles rendered in the browser

cross-references

- To learn how to control border thickness, see Task 91.

- To learn how to color borders, see Task 92.

- To learn how to control the width of elements, see Task 95.

Defining Border Width Properties

In Task 90 you saw how to specify a border using the border style properties. In this task you learn how to control the width (or more accurately, thickness) of an element's borders. These properties accept keyword values (`thin`, `medium`, `thick`) as well as any positive length value (ex, em, px, pc, pt, mm, cm, in). A value of zero collapses the border area completely. Negative values are not permitted.

1. To specify the width of an element's top border, include a `border-top-width` property in your declaration.

2. To specify the width of the right border, include a `border-right-width` property.

3. To specify the width of the bottom border, include a `border-bottom-width` property.

4. To specify the width of the top border, include a `border-left-width` property.

5. To render border width properties in shorthand, simply include a `border-width` property in your declaration, followed by one to four values:

   - **One value:** Applies to all sides of the element

   - **Two values:** Sets the top and bottom paddings to the first value and the right and left paddings to the second

   - **Three values:** Sets the top padding to the first value, the left and right paddings to the second value, and the bottom padding to the third

   - **Four values:** Applies to the top, right, bottom, and left paddings, respectively

Listing 91-1 shows the code demonstrating the values. Figure 91-1 displays the effects of each potential value in a browser.

```
<html>
<head>
<title>Border Width</title>
<style type="text/css">
<!--
body { font: bold 16pt Courier }

p.thin { border-style: dotted;
        border-width: thin }

p.medium { border-style: dashed;
        border-width: medium }
```

(continued)

```
p.thick { border-style: solid;
          border-width: thick }

p.length { border-style: double;
           border-width: 25px }
-->
</style>
</head>
<body>
<p class="thin">border-style: dotted; border-width: thin</p>

<p class="medium">border-style: dashed; border-width:
medium</p>

<p class="thick">border-style: solid; border-width:
thick</p>

<p class="length">border-style: double; border-width:
25px</p>
</body>
</html>
```

Listing 91-1: Code demonstrating border-width properties

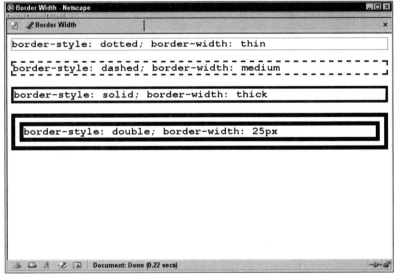

Figure 91-1: Border widths rendered in the browser

cross-reference

- HTML only provides borders for images (see Part 3) and tables (see Part 6).

Defining Border Color Properties

Besides specifying the style of a border, and its width, you can govern its color. As with all border properties discussed in previous tasks, CSS allows you to define the border color of each side of an element independently. Values are expressed in hexadecimal, color name, or RGB triple (see Task 82). Use the keyword `transparent` to render a border invisible.

1. To specify the color of an element's top border, include a `border-top-color` property in your declaration.

2. To specify the color of the right border, include a `border-right-color` property.

3. To specify the color of the bottom border, include a `border-bottom-color` property.

4. To specify the color of the left border, include a `border-left-color` property.

5. To render border color properties in shorthand, simply include a `border-color` property in your declaration, followed by one to four values:

   • **One value:** Applies to all sides of the element

   • **Two values:** Sets the top and bottom paddings to the first value and the right and left paddings to the second

   • **Three values:** Sets the top padding to the first value, the left and right paddings to the second value, and the bottom padding to the third

   • **Four values:** Applies to the top, right, bottom, and left paddings, respectively

   Listing 92-1 shows sample code that uses these properties, while Figure 92-1 displays the effects of border color properties in a browser.

```
<html>
<head>
<title>Border Color</title>
<style type="text/css">
<!--
body { font: bold 16pt Courier;
       color: #FFFFFF;
       background-color: #000000 }
p.hex { border-color: #CCCCCC;
        border-style: dotted;
        border-width: 5px }
```

(continued)

```
p.color_name { border-color: SlateGray;
               border-style: dashed;
               border-width: 5px }

p.triple { border-color: rgb(50, 50, 50);
           border-style: solid;
           border-width: 5px }
p.mixed { border-top-color: #FFFFFF;
          border-right-color: #333333;
          border-bottom-color: SlateGray;
          border-left-color: rgb(50, 50, 50);
          border-style: double;
          border-width: 10px }
-->
</style>
</head>
<body>
<p class="hex">border-color: #CCCCCC</p>
<p class="color_name">border-color: SlateGray</p>
<p class="triple">border-color: rgb(50, 50, 50)</p>
<p class="mixed">border-top-color: #FFFFFF; border-right-
color: #333333; border-bottom-color: SlateGray;
border-left-color: rgb(50, 50, 50);</p>
</body>
</html>
```

Listing 92-1: Code demonstrating border-color properties

Figure 92-1: Border colors rendered in the browser

cross-reference

▪ To learn how to combine all border properties in a shorthand declaration, see Task 93.

Using the Border Property Shorthand

You can render CSS border properties in shorthand two different ways. You can define the style, width, and color of a single side in one declaration, or the style, width, and color for all sides with one declaration.

1. To specify the style, width, and color for the single side of an element, include a `border-top`, `border-right`, `border-bottom`, or `border-left` property in your declaration.

2. Define the width, style, and then color (separated by spaces) as a single value. For example:

   ```
   div { border-top: thin dashed #FF0000 }
   ```

3. To specify the style, width, and color for all sides of an element's border, include a `border` property in your declaration.

4. Define the width, style, and then color (separated by spaces) as a single value, as in Step 2.

   Listing 93-1 shows the code required to render this shorthand method displayed in Figure 93-1.

note

* The `border` property cannot set different values of the four borders, as the `padding` and `margin` properties can.

```
<html>
<head>
<title>Border Shorthand</title>
<style type="text/css">
<!--
body { font: bold 16pt Courier }

p.four-sides { border-top: thick dashed #FF0000;
               border-right: medium dotted green;
               border-bottom: thin solid rgb(0, 0, 255);
               border-left: 5px double #000000 }


p.all-sides { border: thin dashed SlateGray }
-->
</style>
</head>
<body>
<p class="four-sides">
border-top: thick dashed #FF0000;<br />
border-right: medium dotted green;<br />
border-bottom: thin solid rgb(0, 0, 255);<br />
border-left: 5px double #000000 </p>

<p class="all-sides">
border: thin dashed SlateGray
</p>
</body>
</html>
```

Listing 93-1: Shorthand border definitions in code

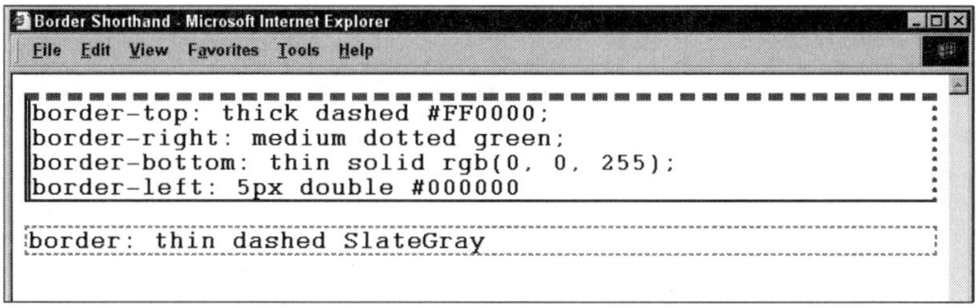

Figure 93-1: Shorthand border properties rendered in the browser

cross-references

- See Task 89 on the padding property shorthand.

- See Task 94 on the margin property shorthand.

Working with Margin Properties

Margin properties allow you to expand and contract the outermost area in the CSS box model, the margin area — just as you would the padding area. You can define the top, right, bottom, and left margin independently using individual properties. A shorthand margin property allows you to define all margins simultaneously. Each property accepts length (ex, em, px, pc, pt, mm, cm, in) and percentage values. A value of zero collapses the padding area completely. Negative values are permitted.

notes

- We've used colors to distinguish between the padding and margin settings. The gray regions around each paragraph mark the area affected by the padding property. The black regions indicate the area affected by the margin property.

- Margin properties are supported equally by Internet Explorer and Netscape.

1. To specify the width of the top margin, include a `margin-top` property in your declaration.

2. To specify the width of the right margin, include a `margin-right` property.

3. To specify the width of the bottom margin, include a `margin-bottom` property.

4. To specify the width of the left margin, include a `margin-left` property.

5. To render margin properties in shorthand, simply include a `margin` property in your declaration, followed by one to four values:

   - **One value:** Applies to all sides of the element

   - **Two values:** Sets the top and bottom paddings to the first value and the right and left paddings to the second

   - **Three values:** Sets the top padding to the first value, the left and right paddings to the second value, and the bottom padding to the third

   - **Four values:** Applies to the top, right, bottom, and left paddings, respectively.

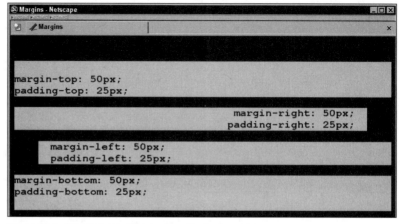

Figure 94-1: Margin properties rendered in the browser

Listing 94-1 shows the code illustrating these properties. Figure 94-1 displays the effects of margin properties in a browser.

```html
<html>
<head>
<title>Margins</title>
<style type="text/css">
<!--
body { background-color: black;
       font: bold 16pt Courier }

p.top { margin-top: 50px;
        padding-top: 25px;
        background-color: #CCCCCC }

p.right { margin-right: 50px;
          padding-right: 25px;
          text-align: right;
          background-color: #CCCCCC }

p.left { margin-left: 50px;
         padding-left: 25px;
         background-color: #CCCCCC }

p.bottom { margin-bottom: 50px;
           padding-bottom: 25px;
           background-color: #CCCCCC }
-->
</style>
</head>
<body>
<p class="top"> margin-top: 50px;<br />
padding-top: 25px;</p>

<p class="right">margin-right: 50px;<br />
padding-right: 25px;</p>

<p class="left">margin-left: 50px;<br />
padding-left: 25px;</p>

<p class="bottom">margin-bottom: 50px;<br />
padding-bottom: 25px;</p>
</body>
</html>
```

Listing 94-1: Different margin properties

cross-reference

- For a full discussion of the CSS box model, see our Web site at www.wiley .com/compbooks/ 10simplestepsorless.

Defining Element Dimensions

While HTML has width and height attributes, CSS has width and height properties. You can define values in length measurements (ex, em, px, pc, pt, mm, cm, in) or percentages of the parent element. Negative values are not permitted.

note

• Both width and height properies allow the keyword value auto, which assumes the instrinsic dimensions, for example, of an image.

1. To specify the width of an element, include a width property in your declaration.

2. To specify the height of an element, include a height property.

3. To specify the maximum width of an element, include a max-width property.

4. To specify the minimum width of an element, include a min-width property.

5. To specify the maximum height of an element, include a max-height property.

6. To specify the minimum height of an element, include a min-height property.

   Listing 95-1 shows sample code with defined width and height properties, while Figure 95-1 displays these elements in a browser.

caution

• To date, no browser supports the max- or min-versions of the width and height properties. However, this could change as new browser versions are released.

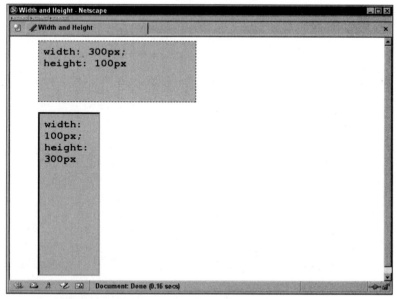

Figure 95-1: Widths and heights rendered in the browser

```
<html>
<head>
<title>Width and Height</title>
<style type="text/css">
<!--
p.one { width: 300px;
        height: 100px;
        border: thin dashed black;
        padding: 88x;
        background-color: rgb(200, 200, 200);
        margin-left: 50px;
        font: bold 16pt Courier }

p.two { width: 100px;
        height: 300px;
        border-style: inset;
        padding: 88x;
        background-color: rgb(200, 200, 200);
        margin-left: 50px;
        font: bold 16pt Courier }
-->
</style>
</head>
<body>
<p class="one">width: 300px;<br />
height: 100px
</p>

<p class="two">width: 100px;<br />
height: 300px</p>
</body>
</html>
```

Listing 95-1: Examples of using the width and height properties

cross-reference

▪ Width and height are
  properties integral to
  creating layered content.
  See Task 99.

Task 96

Working with the float Property

The float property functions much like the align attribute of a `<table>` or `<img>` tag. Using the float property, you shift an element either to the left or right side and flow content down the opposite side.

note

- The clear property can only be specified for block-level elements, like paragraphs, tables, and divisions (`<div>`).

1. To float an element, include a float property in your declaration.

2. Define one of the three following keyword values:

   - left places the element on the left margin and wraps content to the right

   - right places the element on the right margin and wraps content to the left

   - none disables the float property

3. Specify which side of an element may not be adjacent to a floating element using the clear property.

4. Define one of the four following keyword values:

   - left prevents content from wrapping down the right side of left-floated elements

   - right prevents content from wrapping down the left side of right-floated elements

   - both prevents content from wrapping around any floated elements

   - none disables the clear property

Listing 96-1 shows sample code that uses these properties while Figure 96-1 displays floated and cleared content.

caution

- A floated element must have an assigned value using the width property.

```
<html>
<head>
<title>Float and Clear</title>
<style type="text/css">
<!--
img.one { float: left;
          width: auto;
          height: auto }

p.one { width: 300px;
        height: 100px;
        border: thin dashed black;
        padding: 88x;
        background-color: rgb(200, 200, 200);
        margin-left: 50px;
        font: bold 16pt Courier }
```

(continued)

```
p.two { clear: left;
        width: 300px;
        height: 100px;
        border: thin dashed black;
        padding: 88x;
        background-color: rgb(200, 200, 200);
        margin-left: 50px;
        font: bold 16pt Courier }
-->
</style>
</head>
<body>
<img class="one" src="flower.gif" />

<p class="one">This paragraph wraps down the right-hand side
of the floated image.
</p>

<img class="one" src=" flower.gif" />

<p class="two">Because this paragraph has a clear: left, it
doesn't...</p>
</body>
</html>
```

Listing 96-1: Examples of the float and clear properties

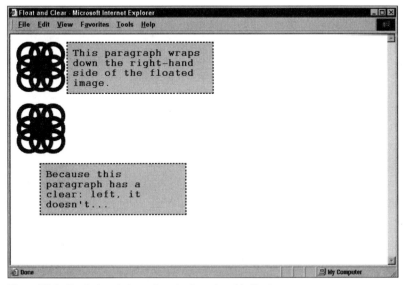

Figure 96-1: Floated and cleared content rendered in the browser

cross-reference

▪ To learn about the width
  and height properties,
  see Task 95.

Controlling List-Item Bullet Styles

In HTML you control the bullet styles of unordered lists using the `type` attribute of the `<ul>` tag. In CSS you use the `list-style-type` property instead. With CSS, you can even use images as bullets.

1. To specify the list item style for an unordered list, create a style rule for the `<ul>` tag and include a `list-style-type` property. For example:

   ```
   ul { list-style-type:
   ```

2. Define any of the following keyword values:
   - `disc` is a solid round disc (the default)
   - `circle` is a hollow circle
   - `square` is a solid square

3. To control the position of a bullet, include a `list-style-position` property.

4. Define either of the following keyword values:
   - `inside` places the bullet inside the list item block (see Figure 97-1)
   - `outside` places the bullet outside the list item block

5. To specify an image as a bullet style for an unordered list, include a `list-style-image` property in your declaration.

6. To specify the path to the image you want to use, define a URL value with the appropriate pathname (in parentheses) identifying the location of the image file on the server. For example:

   ```
   ul { list-style-image: url(images/triangle.gif) }
   ```

Listing 97-1 shows the code using these properties. Figure 97-1 displays various list item bullet styles.

```
<html>
<head>
<title>List Item Bullet Styles</title>
<style type="text/css">
<!--

body { font:  16pt Arial }

ul.square { list-style-type: square }

ul.compact { list-style-position: inside }
```
(continued)

```
ul.triangle { list-style-image: url(triangle.gif) }
-->
</style>
</head>
<body>

<ul class="square">
  <li>The bullet style <br>is square</li>
  <li>The bullet style <br>is square</li>
</ul>

<ul class="compact">
  <li>The bullet position <br> is "inside"</li>
  <li>While the other lists <br>are defaulting to
outside</li>
</ul>

<ul class="triangle">
  <li>The bullet style <br>uses a triangular image</li>
  <li>The bullet style <br>uses a triangular image</li>
</ul>

</body>
</html>
```

Listing 97-1: Examples of the list-style-type, list-style-position, and list-style-image properties

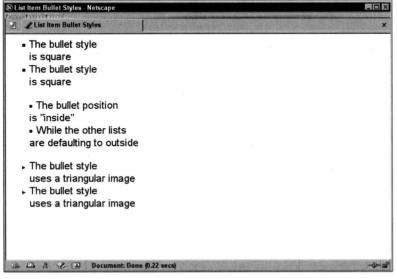

Figure 97-1: Various bullet styles rendered in the browser

cross-reference

▪ To learn how to control the list item styles for ordered lists, see Task 98.

Controlling List-Item Number Styles

Just as you saw in Task 97, in HTML the style of numbering in an ordered list is governed by the type attribute of the <ol> tag. In CSS you use the list-style-type property.

notes

▪ The CSS specification calls for Georgian, Armenian, Hebrew, Chinese, Korean, and Japanese numbering styles, but no browser yet supports these options.

▪ The W3C advises that numbered lists improve document accessibility by making lists easier to navigate.

1. To specify the list item style for an ordered list, create a style rule for the <ol> tag and include a list-style-type property. For example:

   ```
   ol { list-style-type:
   ```

2. Define any of the following keyword values:

   - decimal uses Arabic numerals (1, 2, 3)
   - lower-roman uses lowercase Roman numerals (i, ii, iii)
   - upper-roman uses uppercase Roman numerals (I, II, III)
   - lower-alpha uses lowercase letters (a, b, c)
   - upper-alpha uses uppercase letters (A, B, C)
   - none disables list styles

3. To control the position of a bullet, use the list-style-position property.

4. Define either of the following keyword values:

   - inside places the bullet inside the list item block
   - outside places the bullet outside the list item block

   Listing 98-1 shows sample code for different effects you can create with ordered lists. Figure 98-1 displays the ordered lists in a browser.

```
<html>
<head>
<title>List Item Numbering Styles</title>
<style type="text/css">
<!--
body { font: bold 12pt Arial }
ol.decimal { list-style-type: decimal }
ol.lower-roman { list-style-type: lower-roman;
                 list-style-position: inside }
ol.upper-roman { list-style-type: upper-roman }
ol.lower-alpha { list-style-type: lower-alpha }
ol.upper-alpha { list-style-type: upper-alpha }
ol.none  { list-style-type: none }
-->
</style>
</head>
```

(continued)

```
<body>
<ol class="decimal">
   <li>decimal</li>
   <li>decimal</li>
   <li>decimal</li>
</ol>
<ol class="lower-roman">
   <li>lower-roman;<br> inside</li>
   <li>lower-roman;<br> inside</li>
   <li>lower-roman;<br> inside</li>
</ol>
<ol class="upper-roman">
   <li>upper-roman</li>
   <li>upper-roman</li>
   <li>upper-roman</li>
</ol>
<ol class="lower-alpha">
   <li>lower-alpha</li>
   <li>lower-alpha</li>
   <li>lower-alpha</li>
</ol>
<ol class="upper-alpha">
   <li>upper-alpha</li>
   <li>upper-alpha</li>
   <li>upper-alpha</li>
</ol>
</body>
</html>
```

Listing 98-1: Different styles of ordered lists

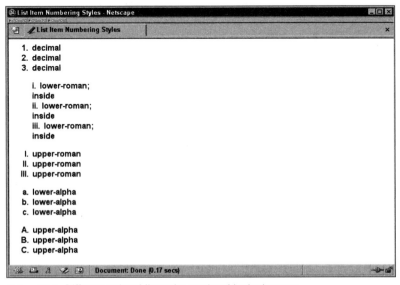

Figure 98-1: Different ordered-list styles rendered in the browser

cross-reference

- To learn about creating lists in HTML, see Part 2.

Creating Layers with Absolute Positions

The `<div>` tag is a generic tag that contains no inherent formatting abilities. Simply short for *division*, the `<div>` tag is meant to be used wherever you intend to begin a block-level section of page content. Although not exclusively meant for layering, by using inline CSS syntax, the `<div>` tag is ideal for creating layers with an absolute position.

notes

- Absolute positioning places the layer in a specific location with respect to its parent element, using the coordinates supplied with the `top` and `left` properties. If the parent element is the body of the document, the element is positioned in relation to the browser window. For example, the `left` and `top` values shown in Figure 99-1 place the upper-left corner of the layer 150 pixels over from the left and 50 pixels down from the top of the browser window.

- Layers mimic three-dimensional space. The `left` and `top` properties position the layer along the *x* and *y* axes. The *z* axis is controlled by the `z-index` property, which defines a layer's place in the stacking order and accepts a numeric value. The lower a layer's `z-index` number, the "deeper" its position in the stack. For example, if you have three layers in a document — with `z-index` of 1, 2, and 3, respectively — layer 3 will be on the top of the stack, layer 2 will be in the middle, and layer 1 will be at the bottom.

1. Within the body section of your document, insert an opening `<div>` tag.

2. To apply a name to the layer, add an `id` attribute and set it equal to the name you want to give the layer.

3. To begin including inline style syntax, add a `style` attribute. The value of this attribute will contain the various style declarations.

4. To specify an absolute position for the layer, define a `position` property and supply a value of `absolute`. Follow this declaration with a semicolon to continue adding to the `style` attribute value.

5. To specify the actual coordinates for the layer's position, define `left` and `top` properties and supply pixel values for them, as shown in Listing 99-1.

```
<html>
<head>
<title>Layered Content</title>
</head>

<body>

<div id="rain_text" style="position: absolute; left: 150px;
top: 50px">

</body>
</html>
```

Listing 99-1: Defining the left and top properties

6. To define the layer's dimensions, define `width` and `height` properties, as shown here:

```
<div id="rain_text" style="position: absolute; left:
150px; top: 50px; width: 265px; height: 25px">
```

7. To control a layer's stacking order, define the `z-index` property and supply it a numeric value.

8. Insert the content you want displayed within the layer and close the layer with a closing `</div>` tag, as shown in Listing 99-2. Figure 99-1 displays these two layers in a browser.

```
<div id="rain_text" style="position: absolute; left: 150px;
top: 50px; width: 400px; height: 200px; z-index: 2">
<h1><font color="red">The Rain in Spain Stays Mainly in the
Plain.</font></h1>
</div>

<div id="shadow_text" style="position: absolute; left:
145px; top: 55px; width: 400px; height: 200px; z-index: 1">
<h1>The Rain in Spain Stays Mainly in the Plain.</h1>
</div>
```

Listing 99-2: Code for two completed layers of text

Figure 99-1: Displaying the two layers of text in the browser

cross-reference

- The properties shown in this task can be expanded upon. To learn more about CSS properties, see our Web site, at www.wiley.com/compbooks/10simplestepsorless.

Creating Layers with Relative Positions

Generally you use the `<span>` tag to apply an inline style to a small section of page content, instead of defining a larger, block-level element — as you do with the `<div>` tag. By setting the position property to `relative`, you place the content that falls between the opening and closing `<span>` tags in a location relative to its normal position within the flow of the document.

1. Within the body section of your document, insert an opening `<span>` tag.

2. To apply a name to the layer, add an `id` attribute and set it equal to the name you want to give the layer.

3. To begin including inline style syntax, add a `style` attribute. The value for this attribute will contain the various style declarations.

4. To specify an absolute position for the layer, define a `position` property and supply a value of `relative`. Follow this declaration with a semicolon to continue adding to the `style` attribute value.

5. To specify the coordinates for the layer's position, define `left` and `top` properties and supply pixel values for them.

6. To control a layer's stacking order, define the `z-index` property and supply it a numeric value.

7. Insert the content you want displayed within the layer and close the layer with a `</span>` tag.

Listing 100-1 shows a code example and Figure 100-1 shows the results in the browser.

note

- When specifying coordinates for layers, you can assign both positive and negative values. In Listing 100-1, observe how the negative value locates the span to the left of the text's normal inline position.

caution

- The id attribute gives an element its unique name. For that reason, no two elements can have the same value assigned to this attribute.

```
<html>
<head>
<title>Layered Content</title>
</head>

<body>

<h1> The Rain in Spain Stays
<span id="plain" style="position: relative; left: -167px;
top: 40px">Mainly in the Plain.</span>
<h1>

</body>
</html>
```

Listing 100-1: Example of a relative span

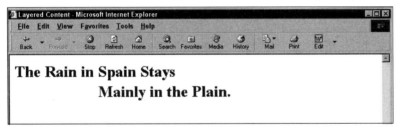

Figure 100-1: A relative span displayed in the browser

cross-reference

■ Code editors like
Macromedia Dreamweaver
and Microsoft FrontPage
make working with layers
simple because the layer
becomes something you
can physically see and
manipulate on the screen.
To learn more about these
tools, see Parts 15 and 16.

Defining a Layer's Clipping Area

Defining a clipping area masks off content within a layer, leaving a rectangular area within the layer visible in the browser window. By defining a clipping area, you don't actually delete content, you simply hide it from view.

- The rect value indicates a rectangular clipping area. This is currently the only available shape value supported by browsers.

- The syntax for the rect property is rect(top right bottom left). Figure 101-1 shows how the pixel values you supply are rendered.

- The second measurement is off the left side of the layer. So if your layer is 110 pixels wide and you want to mask off 10 pixels on the right side of the layer, enter a value of 100.

- The third measurement is down from the top of the layer. So if you have a layer 110 pixels high and want to mask off the bottom 10 pixels, assign a value of 100.

1. To begin a clipping area, , add a clip property and supply a rect value.

   ```
   clip: rect
   ```

2. Follow the rect value with parentheses, where you add the four coordinate values (see Figure 101-1).

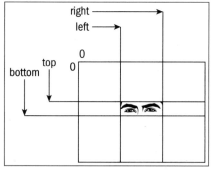

Figure 101-1: Diagram of clipping area values

3. Within the parentheses, enter the first value indicating how many pixels down from the top should be masked off. Enter a space before assigning the second value.

   ```
   clip: rect (35 )
   ```

4. Enter a second value indicating where the right side of the layer's clipping area should begin. Enter a space before assigning the third value.

   ```
   clip: rect (35 48 )
   ```

5. Enter a third value indicating where the bottom side of the layer's clipping area should begin.

   ```
   clip: rect (35 48 45 )
   ```

6. Enter a fourth value indicating how many pixels in from the left side of the layer should be masked off.

   ```
   clip: rect (35 48 45 18)
   ```

Listing 101-1 shows a completely defined clipping area.

```
<html>
<head>
<title>Clipping Areas</title>
</head>

<body>

<div id="kitty" style="position:absolute; width:100px;
height:100px; z-index:1; left: 48px; top: 46px; clip:
rect(35 48 45 18)"><img src="catcube3.jpg" width="100"
height="100"></div>

</body>
</html>
```

Listing 101-1: A layer with a clipping area defined

tip

- Clipping areas are typically defined to create visual effects where simply cropping the image in an image editor won't do. For example, JavaScript can be used to change a defined clipping area dynamically, thereby creating an animated effect where different parts of the image are alternately revealed and hidden.

Part 10: Simple JavaScript

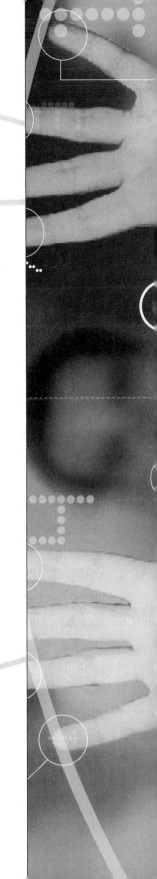

Task **102**

Preparing Documents for Scripting

This may seem obvious, but HTML and JavaScript are two different animals. One is a markup language, and the other is a form of programming language. Consequently, when you add JavaScript to an HTML document, you need to embed the code within `<script>` tags. This way, when the browser reads the JavaScript code, it knows what it's looking at. Otherwise, the browser will assume that what you've written is regular document text that should be displayed in the browser window. In this task, you set up a container to house JavaScript code.

1. Enter an opening `<script>` tag, as shown here:

   ```
   <script
   ```

2. Define a language attribute for the `<script>` tag and set it equal to JavaScript, as shown here:

   ```
   <script language="JavaScript">
   ```

3. Old browsers don't recognize JavaScript code. To hide your code from these browsers, place it between HTML comment tags by moving to the next line and entering an opening HTML comment tag, as shown here:

   ```
   <script language="JavaScript">
   <!--
   ```

4. Enter a few blank lines and enter two forward slashes, followed by a closing HTML comment tag (see Listing 102-1).

   ```
   <script language="JavaScript">
   <!--


   //-->
   ```

Listing 102-1: Opening and closing comment tags within a JavaScript code section

notes

- Netscape introduced JavaScript in Navigator 2.0. Microsoft came out with their own flavor, called JScript, in Internet Explorer 3.0. The likelihood that you know anyone who uses either JavaScript-unaware browser, which dates back to 1996, is rare but it's still considered good form to place your JavaScript code inside comment tags so that those browsers don't inadvertently display it onscreen.

- The double forward-slash in step 4 is actually a JavaScript single-line comment. Why place it in front of the closing HTML comment tag? Because JavaScript recognizes it as just two minus signs followed by a greater-than symbol. The comment tags just hide the last HTML comment from JavaScript, and they hide the JavaScript code from old browsers. And you wonder why programmers have the reputation they do!

5. Move to the next line and enter a closing `</script>` tag.

Listing 102-2 shows a finished container in the head section of an HTML document, awaiting JavaScript code.

```
<html>
<head>
<title>Java Script</title>

<script language="JavaScript">
<!--


//-->
</script>

</head>

<body>


</body>
</html>
```

Listing 102-2: A JavaScript container in the head section of an HTML document

tip

- The `<script>` tags can be placed in either the body or head section of a document. If it consists of code that needs to be executed before the page loads, place the `<script>` tags in the head section; if it should be executed after the page loads, place the `<script>` tags in the body section.

cross-reference

- Most text editors allow you to set up frequently used code snippets as macros, which means that by either clicking a menu command or by pressing a combination of keystrokes you can input the proper code instantly into a document. To learn how to set a container like this up as a macro, see Parts 12 through 16.

Inserting Simple Time Stamps

JavaScript is an *object-based* language, meaning there are a number of predefined components (objects) the programmer can access and manipulate. One of these is the Date object. Essentially, when you reference the Date object, the browser looks at the date and time setting of the computer. In this task, you'll learn how to invoke the Date object and make it appear on the screen.

note

- Variables are temporary locations in memory for storing data. For example, here we're storing the date and time from the computer's system clock. You can then manipulate this data throughout your code — like writing it to the screen.

1. In the head section of the HTML document, insert a script container like that in Task 102, as shown here:

```
<script language="JavaScript">
<!--

//-->
</script>
```

2. Place your cursor within the container and define a variable by entering var, as shown here:

```
<script language="JavaScript">
<!--
    var
//-->
</script>
```

3. Give the variable an appropriate name so it's easier to understand. For example, because this variable stores the visitor's current date and time settings, name the variable right_now, as shown here:

```
<script language="JavaScript">
<!--
    var right_now
//-->
</script>
```

4. Set the variable equal to a new Date object, as shown here:

```
<script language="JavaScript">
<!--
    var right_now = new Date()
//-->
</script>
```

5. In the body section of your document, place a script container where you want the time stamp to appear, and inside it enter a `document.write` statement and reference the variable name inside parentheses.

Listing 103-1 shows the sample code and Figure 103-1 shows the resulting document displayed in a browser.

```html
<html>
<head>
<title>A Simple Time Stamp</title>
<script language="JavaScript">
<!--
    var right_now = new Date()
//-->
</script>
</head>
<body>
<script language="JavaScript">
<!--
    document.write(right_now)
//-->
</script>
</body>
</html>
```

Listing 103-1: Place the <script> tags and document.write() statement anywhere in the body section where you want them to appear

Sun Mar 16 13:53:27 EST 2003

Figure 103-1: A simple time stamp. The value of the Date() object typically appears as *Day, Month, Date, Hour (24-hour clock) : Minute : Seconds, Time Zone, Year*

tip

- There are rules when naming variables in JavaScript. You can't use words that are part of the language, like `var`, `function`, and `if`. Variables also can't have spaces or special punctuation characters, like +, =, %, or –. To use two or more words in a variable name, insert an underscore character, as we did in the example. Another common practice is to use capitalization to separate words, as in *rightNow*.

cross-reference

- Want to find more information on JavaScript? Add a Google Search to your Web page and use it to research the subject. See Task 110.

Changing Content Based on Time

In Task 103 you learned how to make the date and time appear onscreen. With the right JavaScript code, you can also show visitors a different page based on the time of day they come to your site.

1. In the head section of a new document, enter opening and closing `<script>` and comment tags:

   ```
   <script language="JavaScript">
   <!--

   // -->
   </script>
   ```

2. Within the scripting area, declare a variable to hold the `Date()` object. For example:

   ```
   <script language="JavaScript">
   <!--
   var time = new Date()

   // -->
   </script>
   ```

3. Move to a new line and begin your `if` statement, as shown here:

   ```
   <script language="JavaScript">
   <!--
   var time = new Date()

   if ()

   // -->
   </script>
   ```

4. Within the parentheses you entered, insert the variable's name and the `getHours` method, as shown here:

   ```
   <script language="JavaScript">
   <!--
   var time = new Date()

   if (time.getHours() )

   // -->
   </script>
   ```

5. Set the method less than or equal to 12:

```
<script language="JavaScript">
<!--

var time = new Date()

if (time.getHours() <= 12 )

// -->
</script>
```

6. Follow the argument with curly braces. Inside it instruct the browser to send the visitor to a specific document (see Listing 104-1).

```
<script language="JavaScript">
<!--
var time = new Date()

if (time.getHours() <= 12 ) {
    location = index-am.html
    }
// -->
</script>
```

Listing 104-1: A completed if statement

7. After the closing curly brace, enter an `else` statement (see Listing 104-2), which tells the browser which document to display if the initial conditions aren't met.

```
<script language="JavaScript">
<!--
var time = new Date()

if (time.getHours() <= 12 ) {
    location = index-am.html
    }

else {
    location = index-pm.html
    }
// -->
</script>
```

Listing 104-2: The completed if and else statements

tips

- The if/else combination effectively says, "If the time is between 1 AM and 12 noon, send visitors to this page, otherwise send them to another page." Place the code from Step 7 in the head section of your home page, leaving the body section empty because JavaScript will load one of two pages. Alternatively, place it in the head section of one of the two pages you want displayed. If the time is right, the current document will stay in the browser, otherwise the script will load the other document.

- Because we're asking the browser to perform a certain task when the right conditions are met — if it's one time of day, display this page, or else display a different page — we use a standard programming element frequent in languages, called an *if statement* in Step 3.

- In JavaScript, the parentheses mark what's called an *argument* — meaning the conditions we're trying to meet.

Writing to the Browser's Status Bar

Every browser has something called a status bar that typically runs along the bottom of the window and displays what the browser is currently doing. For example, when you run your mouse over a link, the link's URL appears. When you click a link, the status of the download's progress appears. Using JavaScript, you can control the contents of the status bar. In this task, you'll learn how to customize text in the status bar using event handlers.

note

- JavaScript responds mainly to users' actions, called *events*. JavaScript uses elements called *event handlers* to reference these actions. For example, a loading page is an event, which you reference in code using the onLoad event handler. Moving a mouse over an image is also an event, which you reference in code using the onMouseOver event handler. A mouse moving off an image is also an event, which you reference using the onMouseOut event handler.

1. To customize text in the status bar when a page loads, add the onLoad event handler to the opening <body> tag, as shown here:

   ```
   <body onLoad
   ```

2. Set the onLoad handler equal to window.status, as shown here:

   ```
   <body onLoad="window.status
   ```

3. In turn, set window.status equal to the string of text you want to display in the status bar when the page loads. Use single quotes around this value and double quotes around the entire onLoad value, as shown below. Figure 105-1 shows how the browser's status bar appears after the document loads.

   ```
   <body onLoad="window.status='The Rain in Spain Falls
   Mainly on the Plain'">
   ```

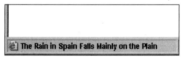

Figure 105-1: The status bar displays this text until the next event triggers a new handler.

4. To customize text in the status bar when an image is moused over, add the onMouseOver event handler to the `<img>` tag and set it equal to a `window.status` statement, as shown here:

```
<img src="daisy.gif" width="100" height="100" alt="Daisy"
onMouseOver="window.status='This is Daisy!'">
```

5. To change the status bar text when the mouse moves off the image, add an onMouseOut event handler and define it as you require. For example:

```
<img src="daisy.gif" width="100" height="100" alt="Daisy"
onMouseOver="window.status='This is Daisy!'"
onMouseOut="window.status='Meow!'">
```

Figure 105-2 shows the mouseover effect.

Figure 105-2. Changing the status bar with an onMouseOver event so that it reads "This is Daisy!" when the picture is moused over

tips

- The order of a tag's attributes and event handlers doesn't matter. If you have a series of exiting attributes already defined for your `<body>` tag, simply add the event handler to the end of the tag.

- If you simply want to clear the status bar using the onMouseOut handler, set its `window.status` statement equal to a space: `window.status=' '`

Hiding E-mail Addresses from Spammers

note

- The values for each of these variables are called *strings* — in other words, simply a series of characters. Adding the two variable values together, along with the @ symbol, is an example of *string concatenation*.

One of the ways spammers harvest e-mail addresses is by setting up programs (called *bots*, short for robots) that crawl across Web sites searching for mailto: links, which indicate the presence of e-mail addresses. You can circumvent this trick by breaking an e-mail address down into its component parts, setting each part equal to a variable name, and then putting it all back together again using a document.write statement.

1. In the body section of your document, place a script container where you want the e-mail address to be written.

2. Between the comment tags of your container, enter a variable to hold whatever name or word appears before the @ symbol in the e-mail address. For example:

```
<script language="JavaScript">
<!--

var myName  = "robert"

//-->
</script>
```

3. Define another variable to hold the domain name which appears after the @ symbol in the e-mail address, as shown here:

```
<script language="JavaScript">
<!--

var myName  = "robert"
var myDomain = "highstrungproductions.com"

//-->
</script>
```

4. Define a third variable which adds the two variables together with an @ symbol. For example:

```
<script language="JavaScript">
<!--

var myName  = "robert"
var myDomain = "highstrungproductions.com"
var myAddress  = myName + "@" + myDomain


//-->
</script>
```

5. Enter a `document.write` statement which concatenates the anchor tag and last variable. Listing 106-1 shows the complete code and Figure 106-1 shows the corresponding code displayed in a browser.

```
<script language="JavaScript">
<!--

var myName   = "robert"
var myDomain = "highstrungproductions.com"
var myAddress  = myName + "@" + myDomain
document.write("<a href='mailto:" + myAddress + "'>Write
Me</a>")

//-->
</script>
```

Listing 106-1: Breaking an e-mail address into variable values, which keeps spammers from collecting a usable address

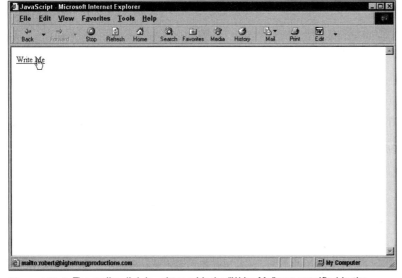

Figure 106-1: The mailto: link is written with the "Write Me" text specified in the document.write statement, and when it's moused over, the completed link is referenced in the status bar.

tip

- In a `document.write` statement, what appears between double quotes is written exactly as you type it, so don't enter a space where you don't want one.

cross-references

- There's much more to JavaScript than the few tricks we cover in this book. To learn more about JavaScript, read *Beginning JavaScript* by Paul Wilton (Wrox Press).

- To learn more about the script container, see Task 102.

Preloading Images

When a browser reads an HTML document and comes across an `<img>` tag, it begins downloading the image file from the Web server in order to display it in the flow of the document. The time it takes to do this varies on the size of the image and the speed of the visitor's Internet connection. In Task 29 you learned that defining width and height attributes speeds the loading of the overall document by letting the browser know just how much space each image requires — so the rest of the document can load in the meantime. Using JavaScript, you can inform the browser of all the images in your document and have them loaded into memory before the browser begins loading the page. The result is that the browser loads the entire page at once after it's downloaded all the image files.

notes

- As mentioned in Task 102, the head section is where you place scripts that need to be processed prior to the visible page loading.

- The pathname you define here is no different than the pathname you use when defining the `src` attribute for an `<img>` tag as if you are going to insert this.

1. In the head section of your document, enter a script container, as discussed in Task 102.

2. Define a variable within the comment tags of the script container and give it a name that describes the image it's going to store. For instance:

   ```
   <script language="JavaScript">
   <!--

   var orangeCat

   //-->
   </script>
   ```

3. Set the variable name equal to a new image object, as shown here:

   ```
   <script language="JavaScript">
   <!--

   var orangeCat = new Image()

   //-->
   </script>
   ```

4. Inside the parentheses, enter the dimensions for the image — width followed by height, separated by a comma:

   ```
   <script language="JavaScript">
   <!--

   var orangeCat = new Image(150, 50)

   //-->
   </script>
   ```

5. On the next line, define the pathname of the source file for the image object:

```
<script language="JavaScript">
<!--

var orangeCat = new Image(150, 50)
orangeCat.src = "images/japser.jpg"

//-->
</script>
```

6. Repeat Steps 2 through 5 for each image in your document, as shown in Listing 107-1.

```
<script language="JavaScript">
<!--

var orangeCat = new Image(150, 50)
orangeCat.src = "images/japser.jpg"

var crazyCat = new image(150, 50)
crazyCat.src = "images/daisy.jpg"

var bwCat = new image(150, 50)
bwCat.src = "images/calvin.jpg"

var babyCat = new image(150, 50)
babyCat.src = "images/willow.jpg"

//-->
</script>
```

Listing 107-1: Multiple Image() objects defining image download details

7. In the body of your document, define your `<img>` tags as you normally would. When the browser calls up the images it will do so from the copies in local memory it downloaded prior to loading the page.

cross-reference

- To learn how to insert images, see Task 29.

Creating Simple Image Rollovers

An image rollover is the result of swapping one image for another in response to a mouseover. Images should be preloaded so that when the mouse event triggers the swap there isn't a blank spot onscreen while the browser downloads the image file.

1. In the head section of your document, enter a script container.

2. Define a variable within the comment tags of the script container and give it a name that describes the first image displayed in the rollover. For example:

```
<!--
var homeButtonUp
//-->
```

3. Set the variable name equal to a new image object and, inside the parentheses, enter the dimensions for the image, as shown here:

```
var homeButtonUp = new Image(100, 50)
```

4. On the next line, define the pathname of the source file for the image object, as shown here:

```
var homeButtonUp = new Image(100, 50)
homeButtonUp.src = "images/home_up.gif"
```

5. Repeat Steps 2 through 4 to define the image to be displayed when the mouse rolls over the image. For example:

```
var homeButtonUp = new Image(100, 50)
homeButtonUp.src = "images/home_up.gif"

var homeButtonOvr = new Image(100, 50)
homeButtonOvr.src = "images/home_ovr.gif"
```

6. In the body of the document, create an image link using the first image displayed in the rollover, and add a `name` attribute set equal to a word describing the image:

```
<a href="index.html"><img src="images/home_up.gif"
width="100" height="50" alt="Home Page" border="0"
name="home"></a>
```

7. Add `onMouseOver` and `onMouseOut` event handlers to the `<a>` tag:

```
<a href="index.html"
onMouseOver="document.home.src=homeButtonOvr.src"
onMouseOut="document.home.src=homeButtonUp.src"><img
src="images/home_up.gif" width="100" height="50" alt="Home
Page" border="0" name="home"></a>
```

caution

- The two images you use for each rollover effect must have the same dimensions. If they don't, the second image will be forced into the dimensions taken up by the first image and so appear either stretched or scrunched. The end result is a distorted second image.

8. Repeat Steps 6 through 7 for each rollover image for which you've defined image objects. Listing 108-1 shows the complete code for the document. Figure 108-1 shows the effect in action.

```html
<html>
<head>
    <title>JavaScript</title>
<script language="JavaScript">
<!--
var homeButtonUp = new Image(100, 50)
homeButtonUp.src = "images/home_up.gif"

var homeButtonOvr = new Image(100, 50)
homeButtonOvr.src = "images/home_ovr.gif"
//-->
</script>
</head>

<body>
<a href="index.html"
onMouseOver="document.home.src=homeButtonOvr.src"
onMouseOut="document.home.src=homeButtonUp.src"><img
src="images/home_up.gif" width="100" height="50" alt="Home
Page" border="0" name="home"></a>
</body>
</html>
```

Listing 108-1: Image rollover code

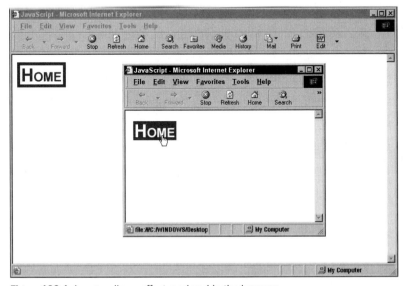

Figure 108-1: Image rollover effect rendered in the browser

cross-references

- Read about script containers in Task 102.

- Now that you have some control over images, do you want to learn how to mess around with windows? See Task 109.

- JavaScript can access the time and use that information to effect a Web page. To learn more, see Tasks 103 and 104.

Creating Simple Pop-up Windows

Before you read onward, you should understand why pop-up blocking software is so popular. When used intrusively, pop-up windows aggravate your visitors' experience of your Web site. Use them, if at all, to enhance the viewing experience, not to pummel viewers into submission. In this task you learn how to open a small window with a mouse click.

note
- You need the hyperlink to create an element that the mouse interacts with. Instead of opening a document, you can enter a little JavaScript that creates a new window object.

1. Within the body of your document, insert an anchor tag:

   ```
   <a>
   ```

2. Define an `href` attribute for the tag and set it equal to #:

   ```
   <a href="#">
   ```

3. Follow the attribute with an `onClick` event handler, as shown here:

   ```
   <a href="#" onClick>
   ```

4. Set the event handler equal to `window.open()`, as shown here:

   ```
   <a href="#" onClick="window.open()">
   ```

5. Inside the parentheses, enter the name of the document inside single quotes that you want displayed in the pop-up window. For example:

   ```
   <a href="#" onClick="window.open('dingo.html')">
   ```

6. Enter a comma and follow the name of the document with the name you want to assign the window object. For example:

   ```
   <a href="#" onClick="window.open('dingo.html',
   'myWindow')">
   ```

7. Enter a comma and define the window properties you want to include within single quotes, separated by commas. For example:

   ```
   <a href="#" onClick="window.open('dingo.html', 'myWindow',
   'width=300, height=200')">
   ```

Your choices are as follows:

- `width` specifies the width of the window in pixels

- `height` specifies the height of the window in pixels

- `location=yes` includes the window's address bar

- `toolbar=yes` includes the window's standard toolbar buttons

- `scrollbars=yes` includes the window's scrollbars

8. Follow the opening anchor tag with the image or text you want affected and complete the link with a closing anchor tag.

Listing 109-1 shows such a link in a document. Figure 109-1 shows the results in a browser.

```html
<html>
<head>
   <title>Pop-up Windows</title>
</head>
<body>

<a href="#" onClick="window.open('dingo.html', 'myWindow',
'width=300, height=200')">Dingo? What Dingo?</a>

</body>
</html>
```

Listing 109-1: Link code that opens a 300 × 200 window

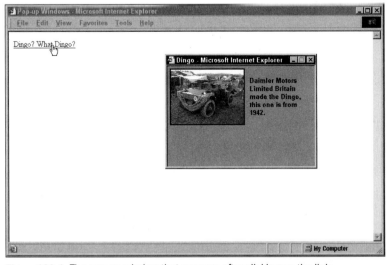

Figure 109-1: The pop-up window that appears after clicking on the link

tip

- If you don't want to define one or more of these properties, simply don't include them in your code.

cross-reference

- If you want your code editor to write JavaScript for you, see Task 215, which describes how to create a pop-up window in Macromedia Dreamweaver.

Part 11: Adding Third-Party Elements

Adding a Free Google Search Bar

Google is the most widely used search engine on the Web. With just a little bit of code pasted into your site's documents, you can add a Google search bar to your site free of charge.

note

- Google's SiteSearch option allows visitors to search your Web site specifically. To activate this functionality, your site must first be registered with Google. To add your URL to Google's database, go to www .google.com/addurl.html.

1. Go to www.google.com. Beneath the main Google search field, click the Business Solutions link.

2. On the following page, scroll to the bottom and locate the Free Solutions category. Click the Free Search link.

3. At the "Google's Free Web WebSearch and SiteSearch" heading, click the Sign Me Up for Free Search link directly beneath the heading. The next page to appear begins, "Step 1 of 4: Select a Search Option."

4. On the Step 1 of 4 page, check the Free WebSearch radio button and then click the Continue button at the bottom of the page.

5. On the Step 2 of 4 page (see Figure 110-1), use the form to customize how the results page will appear. Enter color options, supply Google with the URL of your site's logo, and preview the results. When you're satisfied with your modification, or choose to leave the default settings as they are, click the Continue button to proceed.

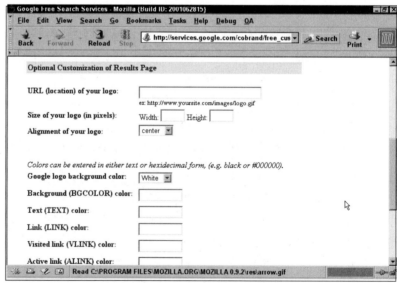

Figure 110-1: The form fields that customize how your Google search results page will appear

6. On the Site 3 of 4 page, enter your first and last name, your e-mail address, a chosen password, a company name if you have one, and the URL of your Web site. Click the Continue button to move ahead.

7. The Step 4 of 4 page (see Figure 110-2) displays the source code required to place a Google Search bar onto your site. Select the code with your cursor and copy and paste it into your chosen HTML document.

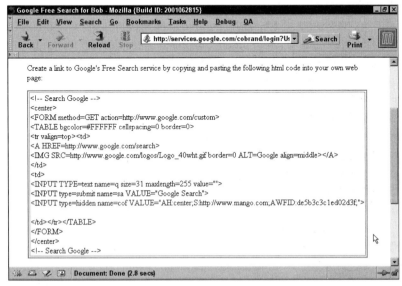

Figure 110-2: The source code Google provides for you to copy and paste into a document on your Web site

tip

▪ Be careful about the color schemes you choose. You want your results page to be easily read by your site's visitors.

cross-reference

▪ You'll notice that the source code Google gives you is a small form. Forms are covered in Part 7.

Adding a Free News Ticker

7am.com offers a free news ticker you can easily place on your Web pages. The ticker is a small Java applet that you add to pages by copying and pasting a few lines of code.

1. Go to www.7am.com/ticker/ to read about the features of the 7 a.m. ticker, shown in Figure 111-1.

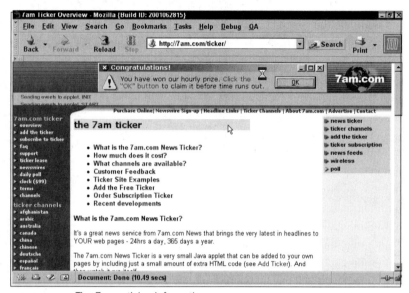

Figure 111-1: The 7 a.m. ticker information page

2. When you're ready to add the free ticker to your page, click the Add the Free Ticker link (sixth link down the bulleted list when we wrote this book) to take you to the installation instructions.

3. Read the instructions thoroughly. Copy and paste the applet code from the first field into your Web page's source code, shown in Figure 111-2.

4. Add any of the available parameters you want to include, as described in the All Users section.

5. Follow the instructions to add your own headlines and corresponding URLs to the ticker.

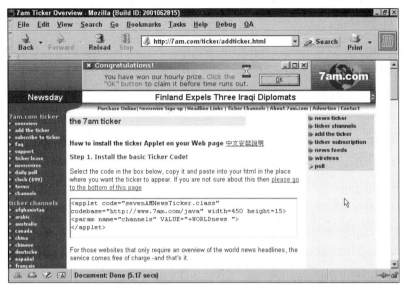

Figure 111-2: Getting the code for the 7 a.m. news ticker: the first field contains the applet code; the rest of the page describes the available parameters for the applet

6. Test your document in a browser and make any modifications to the width and height attributes of the applet tag you see fit. Figure 111-3 shows the applet at work.

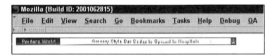

Figure 111-3: The 7 a.m. news ticker in action

tip

- To copy, select the code and press Ctrl+C (Windows) or Command+C (Mac). To paste, click in your document and press Ctrl+V (Windows) or Command+V (Mac).

cross-references

- To learn more about Java applets, see Task 38.

- To add a poll to your site, see Task 112.

Task 112

Adding a Web Poll

Freepolls.com provides free, customizable, form-based polling for your site. With an account you set up on the Freepolls.com Web site, you can administer your poll from their site — changing poll questions and layout — and see your changes executed on your site.

1. Go to www.freepolls.com and click the Sign Up button to start the registration process. On the Step 1 page, choose a username and enter it into the field provided. Click the Next button to advance and choose your account type.

2. When your username is accepted, the next page displays all the different account types that Freepolls offers. Choose the 100% Free account option at the bottom of the page by clicking its Sign Up button. Doing so takes you to the Account Info page.

3. In the fields provided on the Account Info page (see Figure 112-1), enter your vital statistics (name, e-mail address, preferred password, etc.). Choose any Special Deal information you want to receive, complete the Terms of Service section, and click Next.

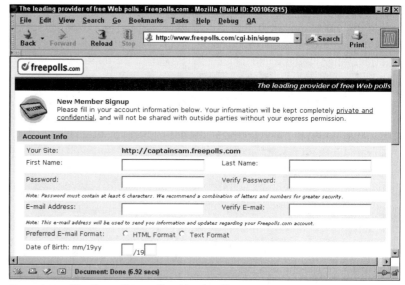

Figure 112-1: The Freepolls.com New Member Signup page

cautions

- If your username is already taken, try again. Click the Back button on the right side of the screen and enter a new username.

- Make sure your chosen password is six or more characters long.

4. The next page of the Poll Wizard is another Deals page, which has one option prechecked. If you don't want this stuff, deselect it and click Next to proceed.

5. Go to the middle of the next page where it says Create a New Poll and click the Create New Poll button.

6. On this page (see Figure 112-2), enter your poll question and possible answers into the fields provided. Once you're finished, click Next.

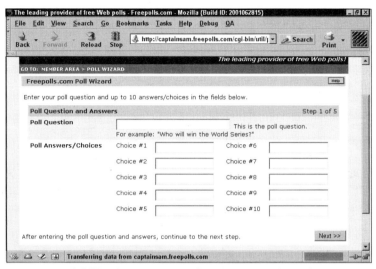

Figure 112-2: Poll Wizard page where you formulate your poll question and answers

7. On the following page, enter your poll title, the URL of your page where the poll will appear, and the name of your site. Select the category that best fits your site. Click Next to proceed.

8. In the next two pages, choose a color scheme and then a layout. Click the Get HTML button to move to the last page in the Poll Wizard.

9. The last page provides different options for displaying your poll (see Figure 112-3). Choose the option that best suits your needs and then copy and paste the source code from the provided field into your document.

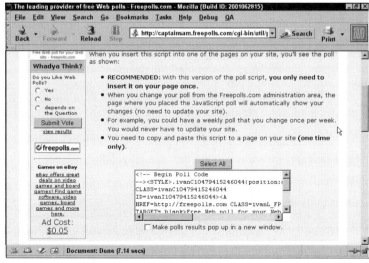

Figure 112-3: The JavaScript option shown first seems to be the most eye-catching; it also has the most upfront advertising

10. Test your document in a browser.

cross-reference

▪ Want to become an Amazon.com Associate? See Task 113.

Becoming an Amazon.com Associate

To become an Amazon.com associate, place a properly configured link to Amazon.com on your Web site. When your site's visitors click through to Amazon.com from your site, you earn up to 15 percent in referral fees.

notes

▪ The first page you see provides an overview of the Associates program. Read it in detail to make sure this is something you're interested in pursuing.

▪ The operating agreement gives explicit details about how the program works, what type of content options are available to you, and their payment details.

1. Go to www.amazon.com and scroll all the way down to the text links that begin with Directory of All Stores, shown in Figure 113-1. Here you see the Join Associates link. Click this one to begin.

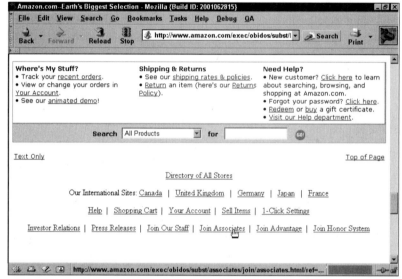

Figure 113-1: The Amazon.com Join Associates link (Image © 2002 Amazon.com, Inc. All Rights Reserved.)

2. Having read through the overview information, click the Read Our Operating Agreement link at the bottom of the page and read that information as well. Once you've read through the pertinent documentation, scroll to the top of the page and click the Join Now link. A dialog box appears, informing you that you're about to access a secure server. Click Yes to continue and advance to the first part of the registration process.

3. In the fields displayed on the next page (see Figure 113-2), enter your e-mail address, check Create a New Password for Associates Central, enter and confirm your password, and then click Submit.

4. On the following page, read the instructions thoroughly and complete the form. Click the Submit button at the bottom of the page when you're done. Depending on the payment option you chose on the previous page, the next page you see may request banking information. The other options sends you gift certificates or checks.

5. You'll be shown your account summary. Choose the Edit button if there are any errors, or Submit if the information is correct.

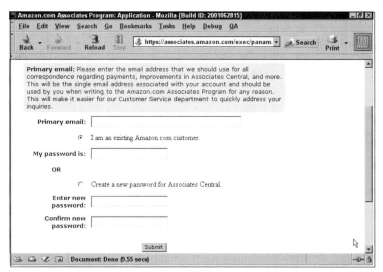

Figure 113-2: Entering your e-mail address and creating a password (Image © 2002 Amazon.com, Inc. All Rights Reserved.)

6. The next page provides you with instructions for putting the Amazon. com link and graphics in your page. Click the Build-It button below the Amazon.com graphic of your choice. You'll be asked to log in to Associates Central, at which point you are presented with the necessary HTML code, already embedded with your Associates ID.

7. On the next page (see Figure 113-3), copy the source code from the top field in the document. Copy the graphic to your computer for uploading to your Web site. Depending on where you place the graphics within your site, you may need to edit the `<img>` tag code that Amazon.com supplies.

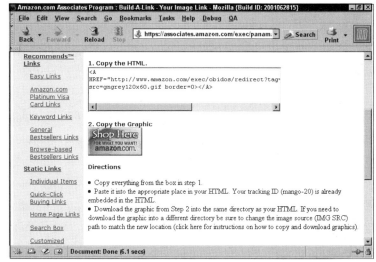

Figure 113-3: Copying and pasting the code, and saving the graphic (Image © 2002 Amazon.com, Inc. All Rights Reserved.)

tips

- If you ever bought something at Amazon.com before, you already gave them your e-mail address and created a password. You don't have to create a separate Associates account.

- The easiest way to copy a graphic from a Web page is to right-click (Windows) or Command-click (Mac) and then choose Save Picture As (Internet Explorer) or Save Image As (Netscape) from the context menu.

cross-reference

- To learn about the `<img>` tag, see Task 29.

Task

Adding a Free Hit Counter

Free-Hit-Counters.com gives you a free hit counter, and they get an opportunity to advertise their product on your site. Their hope is that you'll drive traffic to their site and those folks (or you) will sign up for the upgrades, which does cost something.

1. Go to www.free-hit-counters.com and click their Sign Up link. In the first page (see Figure 114-1), enter your name, e-mail address, site URL, etc. in the fields provided. Click the Join button.

Figure 114-1: The Free-Hit-Counters.com initial sign-up page

2. Select an image from the list of choices (see Figure 114-2) and click the Choose button.

3. Select the code on the following page (see Figure 114-3) and copy and paste it into the body of your document where you want it to appear.

caution

- The Free-Hit-Counters.com code is written in JavaScript and needs to be placed in the body section of your document.

Task 114

Figure 114-2: Image options available for your counter

4. Click the Finish button.

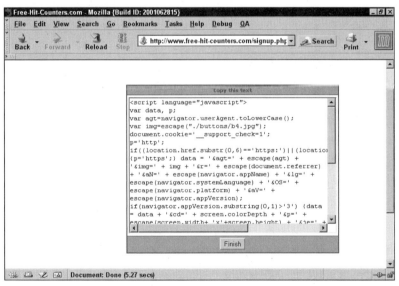

Figure 114-3: Copying the hit counter's JavaScript code from the field provided

cross-references

- To learn more about simple JavaScript usage, see Part 8.

- Want to add weather information to your site? See Task 115.

Task 115

Adding Weather Data to Your Site

If you want to provide your site's visitors with a local four-day forecast, or the ability to search for that information, TimeTemperature.com has the solution for you.

1. Go to www.timetemperature.com and click the link at the top of the page that adds a free weather chart on your site. The first page shows you the three options available to you: a free weather image, a free custom weather page, and a weather search box.

2. To insert an image containing a four-day forecast for your location, enter your City, State, or ZIP code in the fields provided at the bottom of Method 1. Click the Go button.

3. On the following page, you see the current weather and four-day forecast for that locale. To add this information to your Web page, click the link in the middle of the page that reads, "Click here to add this forecast to your web site!"

4. The next page (see Figure 115-1) offers you the source code required to place both images (current weather and four-day forecast) in your Web site. Simply copy the HTML to your page where you want the images to appear.

Figure 115-1: The Method 1 source code page for adding weather information to your Web site

5. To order a free custom weather page, click the order link beside the sample under Method 2. Enter your e-mail address, Web site URL, city and state, and your name in the fields provided. You'll be sent the

URL of your custom weather page within two or three business days. Then just link from your site to that page.

6. To insert a weather search box, go to Method 3 (see Figure 115-2) and copy and paste the provided code into your document.

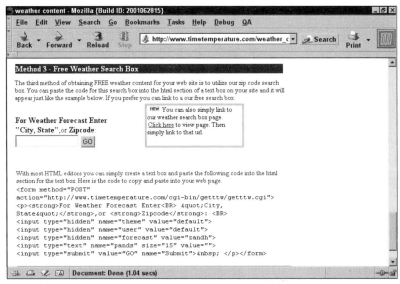

Figure 115-2: The Method 3 source code page for adding weather information to your Web site

tips

- You can customize the background and text color using the radio buttons at the bottom of the page. Make your selections and click the Submit button to get the revised code.

- To find more weather resources, go to your favorite search engine and enter "web pages" + "add weather".

cross-reference

- What text editor have you been using so far? Are you a Windows user? See Part 12. On a Mac? See Part 13.

Part 12: TextPad

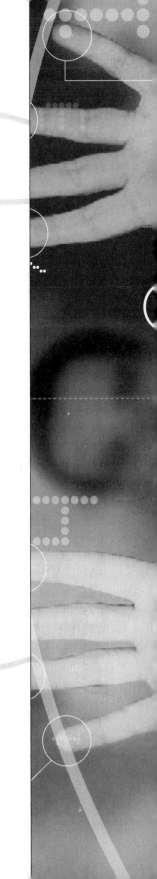

Downloading and Installing TextPad

notes

- TextPad has similar functionality to other applications, including spell checking (in 10 languages), the ability to work with multiple files simultaneously, drag-and-drop text, redo and undo back to the first change made, and the ability to create keyboard macros.

- When starting the program after installation, you'll see a short Help message and Tip of the Day. The tip can be disabled by deselecting the Show tips at Startup check box on the tip dialog box. The Help message will not disappear until you purchase and register the program.

caution

- Make sure you acknowledge the license agreement, or the installation will cease.

TextPad from Helios Software Solutions is, in our opinion, the best Windows-based text editor on the market. It functions seamlessly in any modern Windows OS (95, 98, ME, NT, 2000, and XP), it loads quickly, and it's designed in accordance with the Microsoft Windows Guidelines for Accessible Software Design. What that means is that it looks and behaves similarly to any Microsoft product you've installed, so learning how to use it doesn't require mastering a new user interface from square one. If you've used any Microsoft Office application, you can figure out TextPad's basics in one sitting.

You download the full application on a trial basis. After evaluating the program, if you want to keep using it, you can purchase and register it online. Before you can start using TextPad, you need to download and install it. The download takes only a few minutes, even when using a dial-up connection, and the installation is completed in seconds.

1. Go to www.textpad.com.

2. Click the Download link at the top of the page (see Figure 116-1).

Figure 116-1: The navigation link to the download page on the TextPad site

3. Click the link titled TextPad Downloads from the bulleted list at the top of the page or scroll down to the heading of that same name.

4. From the table (see Figure 116-2), select the language you want and click the link for the download method you prefer. For readers in North America we suggest either HTTP (USA) option to download the installation file.

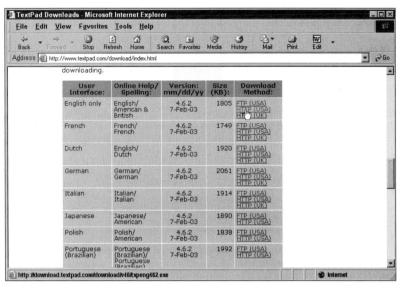

Figure 116-2: The table of download options

5. A dialog box will ask you if you want to save the file or open it. Choose Save to begin the download and specify where on your hard drive you want the file saved. Make sure you choose a location you can find later on.

6. Once the file has downloaded itself, double-click the file's icon to begin the installation process.

7. Follow the prompts provided in the installation wizard until the installation is complete (see Figure 116-3). Depending on when you download your copy, your version number may differ from the one shown here.

tip

- As a coding tool, TextPad provides plenty of useful ways to work in HTML and other programming languages, including syntax checking and coloring, as well as clip libraries that store reusable pieces of code to save on typing.

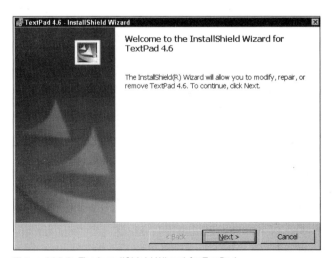

Figure 116-3: The InstallShield Wizard for TextPad

cross-reference

- TextPad is all well and good for the Windows crowd but what about Mac users? Bare Bones Software makes a fantastic text editor for Macintosh called BBEdit. To learn more about it, see Part 13.

Creating and Opening Files

When you first open TextPad, you see a new blank file. You also see various interface elements at your disposal to generate HTML files.

1. To create a new *unnamed* document, choose File ➪ New or click the New Document button (see Figure 117-1) on the tool bar. You will see a blank screen awaiting your code.

Figure 117-1: TextPad's New Document button

2. To create a new *named* document, choose File ➪ Open or click the Open button (see Figure 117-2). This displays the Open File(s) dialog box.

Figure 117-2: TextPad's Open button

3. In the field that lists all your folders (see Figure 117-3), double-click a folder where you want to create the file.

Figure 117-3: The Open File(s) dialog box

4. Type the filename in the File Name field.

5. Use the Files of Type list to select the file type (HTML) and then click OK (see Figure 117-4).

Figure 117-4: The Files of Type list

6. Click Yes in the message box that appears, which tells you that the file does not exist and asks whether you want to create it.

7. To open an existing file, choose File ⇨ Open from the menu or click the Open button to display the File Open dialog box.

8. Locate the file you want to open from within your file system and click OK.

tip

- To select multiple files, hold down the Ctrl button to select each in turn, or the Shift button to select a range of files.

cross-reference

- You can instantly fill a new file with structural tags of a blank HTML document using TextPad's clip libraries. To learn more, see Task 128.

Task **118**

Moving Around in Text

Programmers don't touch the mouse much. Why should they? When you code, you type a lot so why should your hands ever leave the keyboard? TextPad, like any good text editor, provides keystrokes that can move the cursor quickly through your code so your fingers don't have to waste precious seconds moving to the mouse to perform basic functions. (Well, almost never.)

1. To move the cursor to the beginning of a file, press Ctrl+Home (see Figure 118-1).

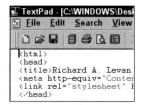

Figure 118-1: Pressing Ctrl+Home jumps the cursor to the start of the document.

2. To move the cursor to the end of the file, press Ctrl+End (see Figure 118-2).

Figure 118-2: Pressing Ctrl+End jumps the cursor to the end of the document.

3. To move the cursor forward one word (or tag, attribute, or value), press Ctrl+W.

4. To move the cursor back one word, press Ctrl+B.

5. To move the cursor back to the end of the previous word, press Ctrl+D.

6. To move the cursor to the start of the next paragraph, press Alt+↓.

7. To move the cursor to the start of the previous paragraph, press Alt+↑.

8. To scroll down one line, press Ctrl+↓.

9. To scroll up one line, press Ctrl+↑.

10. To move the cursor to a specific line number, press Ctrl+G to open the Go To dialog box and enter the line number.

tips

- To get a feel for the features discussed in this task, open a hefty HTML file to play with. Any HTML file saved directly from the browser while surfing to any site will do the trick.

- Press the Home key to move to the beginning of a line and End to move to the end of a line.

- To move forward or backward a single character, or up and down a single line, press the Right, Left, Up, and Down arrow keys, respectively.

- To view line numbers, select View ⇨ Line Numbers from the menu or press Ctrl+Q, followed by the L key.

cross-reference

- Now that you know how to move the cursor around quickly, you could learn how to actually select the text. See Task 119.

Selecting Code

Creating code is a matter of typing it out. But after that you need to be able to manipulate it. In order to edit the contents of your HTML file, you need to learn how to select it. TextPad provides the following methods for selecting code.

1. As you're likely used to doing in your favorite word processor, selecting code with your mouse is as easy as holding the left button down at the start of the code you want to select and dragging the pointer to the end of the selection (see Figure 119-1).

```
C:\WINDOWS\Desktop\RLA\site-as_of_12-09-02\vn_default.html
<form method="GET" action="http://www.google.com/custom">
    <table border="0" cellspacing="0" cellpadding="3" align="right">
        <tr>
            <td class="deunderline"> </td>
            <td><font face="Arial, Helvetica, sans-serif" size="2">
                <input type="radio" name="sitesearch" value="">
                <font color="#FFFFFF"> Web</font>
                <input type="radio" name="sitesearch" value="www.rlevan.com"
                checked>
                <font color="#FFFFFF"> rlevan.com </font></font></td>
        </tr>
```

Figure 119-1: Dragging across a selection to highlight it

2. To select a single word, double-click it with the left mouse button (see Figure 119-2).

```
C:\WINDOWS\Desktop\RLA\site-as_of_12-09-02\vn_default.html
<form method="GET" action="http://www.google.com/custom">
    <table border="0" cellspacing="0" cellpadding="3" align="right">
        <tr>
            <td class="deunderline"> </td>
            <td><font face="Arial, Helvetica, sans-serif" size="2">
                <input type="radio" name="sitesearch" value="">
                <font color="#FFFFFF"> Web</font>
                <input type="radio" name="sitesearch" value="www.rlevan.com"
                checked>
                <font color="#FFFFFF"> rlevan.com </font></font></td>
        </tr>
```

Figure 119-2: Double-clicking a word to select it

3. To select a whole line, move the cursor to the left margin until it changes to a right-pointing arrow, then double-click at the start of the line.

4. To select a whole paragraph, triple-click in the left margin at the start of any line in the paragraph.

5. To select the entire document, hold the Ctrl key and click anywhere in the left margin of the document. Alternatively, press Ctrl+A or select Edit ⇨ Select All from the menu (see Figure 119-3).

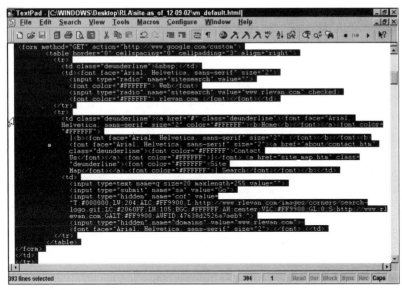

Figure 119-3: Selecting the entire document

6. To select code with the keyboard, hold the Shift key down while using the arrow keys to move the cursor to the end of your selection.

7. To cancel your selections, press the Esc key.

tips

- You can also click the mouse at the start of the selection, hold down the Shift key, and then click the mouse at the end of the selection.

- You can use the Shift key in conjunction with any of the keystrokes discussed in Task 118 to select a word, paragraph, or line at a time.

cross-reference

- Because HTML coding can become repetitious, you'll probably be doing a lot of copying and pasting. That's a function of the Clipboard, covered in Task 120.

Using the Clipboard

TextPad offers the same Clipboard functionality you're accustomed to in other applications (Ctrl+C = Copy, Ctrl+V = Paste, and Ctrl+X = Cut). TextPad also provides a few unique Clipboard functions you'll wish your word processor possessed.

notes

▪ TextPad not only generates the primary structural tags for an HTML document but includes embedded CSS code.

▪ If the text you copy is formatted using external CSS code, TextPad can't include the formatting.

1. With no code selected, copying the line the cursor is currently on is a simple matter of choosing Edit ⇨ Copy Other ⇨ Line. Cut the line to the Clipboard using Edit ⇨ Cut Other ⇨ Line.

2. To copy the word the cursor is currently in, choose Edit ⇨ Copy Other ⇨ Word. Cut the word to the Clipboard using Edit ⇨ Cut Other ⇨ Word (see Figure 120-1).

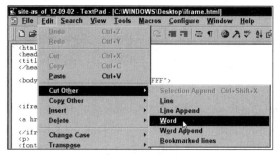

Figure 120-1: The Copy Other menu

3. To add more code to whatever you currently have in the Clipboard buffer, select a range of code and choose Edit ⇨ Cut Other ⇨ Cut Word Append, or Cut Line Append, or Edit ⇨ Copy Other ⇨ Copy Line Append or Copy Word Append.

4. To copy a line of code from one document and paste it into a new document, including the necessary tags to render an HTML document, choose Edit ⇨ Copy Other ⇨ As a HTML Page (see Figure 120-2).

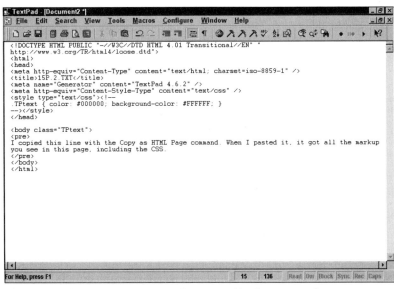

Figure 120-2: Code copied into a new document with all necessary document tags

5. To paste text from a browser and have it maintain its HTML formatting, select the text in the browser window, move to TextPad and choose Edit ➪ Insert ➪ Paste HTML (see Figure 120-3).

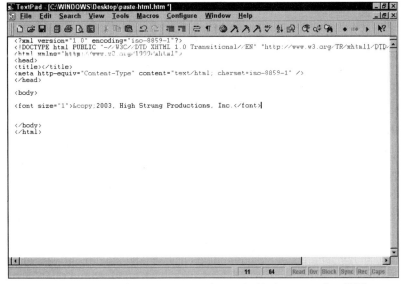

Figure 120-3: Text copied from a browser and pasted with the appropriate HTML formatting

tip

▪ If you want to copy or cut only part of a line, use Word. If you want the entire line, use Line.

cross-reference

▪ To learn more about Cascading Style Sheets, see Part 9.

Managing Files

TextPad allows you to manage multiple files using the Manage Files dialog box. From this little interface, you can duplicate, delete, and rename files, as well as update their timestamps. All of these functions come in extremely handy when you work within a large Web site.

note

• If you have a document open, its path will appear in the Files field.

1. To access the Manage Files dialog box (see Figure 121-1), click the Manage Files button on the toolbar (it looks like a filing cabinet, fourth button from the left) or choose File ➪ Manage Files.

Figure 121-1: The Manage Files dialog box

2. Click the Browse button to locate the file you want to work with. Then click OK to accept the file you select.

   The following steps assume you've selected some file in the Manage Files dialog box.

3. To copy the selected file somewhere else in your folder structure, click the Copy button to display the Copy dialog box (see Figure 121-2).

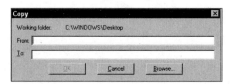

Figure 121-2: The Copy dialog box

4. From here, click the Browse button to choose where you want to copy the file. Click OK to complete the copy.

caution

• You can't rename multiple files simultaneously.

5. To delete a file, click the Delete button to display the Delete dialog box (Figure 121-3). Click the OK button to confirm the deletion.

Figure 121-3: The Delete dialog box

6. To rename a file, click the Rename button to display the Rename/Move dialog box (see Figure 121-4).

Figure 121-4: The Rename/Move dialog box

7. Enter a new filename in the To field to rename it in the same folder as the original file, or click the Browse button to move the file to a different folder.

8. To update the file's timestamp, click the Touch button and then click OK in the Touch dialog box to change the document's last modified date and time to the current system settings.

tip

- To copy multiple files, click the Browse button in Manage Files dialog box. In the Open dialog box that appears, locate the folder containing the files you want to copy and then either hold down the Shift key to select a range of files or press the Ctrl key to select noncontiguous files. This method can also be used to delete and update the time-stamps of multiple files.

cross-reference

- TextPad has a number of interface elements for working with multiple files. See Task 126.

Task **122**

Using the Find and Replace Tools

Find-and-replace functionality is vital for Web site maintenance. You might have multiple documents with multiple instances of identical link code and now you have to change all the links to a specific page throughout the site. Don't panic — TextPad's find and replace functionality is second to none.

1. To find code, choose Search ⇨ Find from the menu to open the Find dialog box (see Figure 122-1).

Figure 122-1: The Find dialog box

2. In the Find What field, type in the search string, or choose a previous string from the drop-down list.

3. Set the options you want to control the search.

4. Click the Find Next button to scroll to a found instance of your search criteria. If the string is not within the document, TextPad prompts you that the string was not found.

5. To replace code, choose Search ⇨ Replace from the menu to open the Replace dialog box (see Figure 122-2).

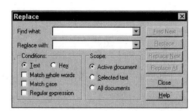

Figure 122-2: The Replace dialog box

6. Enter the string you want to locate in the Find What field and the code you want to replace it with in the Replace With field.

7. Click the Scope options to choose whether the search is done within the currently active document, a selected range of text, or across all currently open files.

8. Click Find Next to select the next instance of the string in the document, and click Replace to change that instance. Clicking Replace Next replaces the current selection and jumps to the next occurrence. Clicking Replace All replaces all instances of the string within the current scope.

cross-reference

- TextPad has a way to locate matching tag brackets. To learn more, see Task 124.

Task **123**

Searching for Strings in Multiple Files

I f you need to know all the occurrences of a particular string within a given set of files, use the Find in Files command. This command generates a report that details each occurrence of the string by filename and line number.

1. Choose Search ⇨ Find in Files from the menu bar to open the Find in Files dialog box (see Figure 123-1).

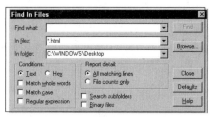

Figure 123-1: The Find in Files dialog box

2. Enter the search string in the Find What field.

3. Enter the file extension for the files you want to search in the In Files field, preceded by an asterisk. For example, ***.html** or ***.htm**.

4. Click the Browse button to open the Browse for Folder dialog box (see Figure 123-2). From here, locate the folder you want to search. The folder's pathname is entered in the In folder field.

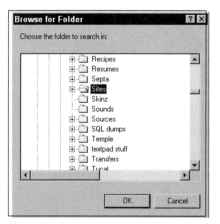

Figure 123-2: The Browse for Folder dialog box

5. Click the Find button to begin the search and generate the report, shown in Figure 123-3.

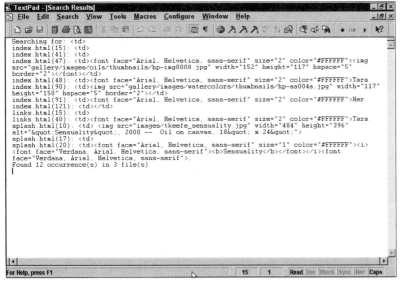

```
TextPad - [Search Results]
File   Edit   Search   View   Tools   Macros   Configure   Window   Help

Searching for: <td>
index.html(15): <td>
index.html(41): <td>
index.html(47): <td><font face="Arial, Helvetica, sans-serif" size="2" color="#FFFFFF"><img
src="gallery/images/oils/thumbnails/hp-img0008.jpg" width="152" height="117" hspace="5"
border="2"></font></td>
index.html(48): <td><font face="Arial, Helvetica, sans-serif" size="2" color="#FFFFFF">Tara
index.html(90): <td><img src="gallery/images/watercolors/thumbnails/hp-aa004a.jpg" width="117"
height="150" hspace="5" border="2"></td>
index.html(91): <td><font face="Arial, Helvetica, sans-serif" size="2" color="#FFFFFF">Her
index.html(121): <td></td>
links.html(15): <td>
links.html(40): <td><font face="Arial, Helvetica, sans-serif" size="2" color="#FFFFFF">Tara
splash.html(10): <td> <img src="images/tkeefe_sensuality.jpg" width="484" height="396"
alt="&quot;Sensuality&quot;, 2000 -- Oil on canvas, 18&quot; x 24&quot;">
splash.html(17): <td>
splash.html(20): <td><font face="Arial, Helvetica, sans-serif" size="1" color="#FFFFFF"><i>
<font face="Verdana, Arial, Helvetica, sans-serif"><b>Sensuality</b></font></i><font
face="Verdana, Arial, Helvetica, sans-serif">,
Found 12 occurrence(s) in 3 file(s)

For Help, press F1                              15    1    Read  Ovr  Block  Sync  Rec  Caps
```

Figure 123-3: An example of a report using the All Matching Lines option in the Report Details section

6. To open all the files returned in the report, right-click the report window and choose Open All from the context menu.

tips

* Each of the fields in the Find in Files dialog box are drop-down lists you can click to reselect previously used values.

* To open only some of the files, select their lines in the report first.

cross-reference

* You can find and replace strings across multiple files too (see Task 122).

Finding Matching Brackets

Coding languages, especially HTML, are loaded with brackets. There are times when finding an opening bracket's closing match can give you a headache. TextPad, like any good coding tool, has the solution.

1. To find a matching bracket, place the cursor on the left side of the bracket you want to match, as shown in Figure 124-1.

Figure 124-1: Placing the cursor to the left of the bracket

2. From the menu bar, choose Search ⇨ Match Bracket, or press Ctrl+M. If there is a matching bracket, the cursor will jump to it and select it (see Figure 124-2).

Figure 124-2: A selected bracket.

notes

- In TextPad, (, [, {, and < represent potential opening brackets. The characters),], }, and > are the corresponding closing brackets.

- If the matching bracket is found forward of the cursor position, TextPad also selects the brackets. If the matching bracket is found behind the cursor position only the intervening text is selected.

3. To toggle back and forth between the two brackets, press Ctrl+M.

4. In a long stretch of code, place the cursor within the line and choose Search ⇨ Match Bracket to send the cursor to the next closing bracket in the document.

5. To select all text between brackets, place the cursor on the left side of the bracket you want to match, and press Ctrl+Shift+M. If TextPad locates a matching bracket, all text in between will be selected (see Figure 124-3).

```
<td>
<input type="text" name="textfield2">
<input type="button" name="Button2" value="Go">
</td>
```

Figure 124-3: Text selected between brackets

cross-reference

• If you're like us, you appreciate a good spell-checking feature. See Task 125 to find out more.

Using the Spelling Checker

TextPad can check the spelling of your document against 11 language dictionaries, including Legal English and Medical English dictionaries.

note

- If you want to download other dictionaries, go to www.textpad.com/ add-ons/dictionaries.html.

1. To check the spelling of a document, open the file and choose Tools ➪ Spelling from the menu bar. If TextPad finds a misspelled word, it launches the Spelling dialog box (see Figure 125-1). The Spelling dialog box displays the misspelled word in the Not in Dictionary field and its closest guess in the Change To field.

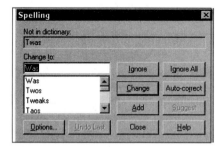

Figure 125-1: The Spelling dialog box

2. If the correct spelling is available in the scrolling list of options beneath the Change to: field, select it and click the Change button.

3. If the correct spelling is not available, enter it manually into the Change To field and click the Change button.

4. To change all occurrences of the misspelled word, click the Auto-Correct button.

5. To add the word to the dictionary, click the Add button.

6. To undo the last changed word, click the Undo Last button.

7. To change the current working dictionary, click the Options button to open the Spelling Preferences dialog box (see Figure 125-2). Here you can change the current working dictionary and modify the spell-checking preferences.

8. To edit a dictionary, click the Edit button in the Spelling Preferences dialog box to display the Edit Dictionary dialog box (see Figure 125-3).

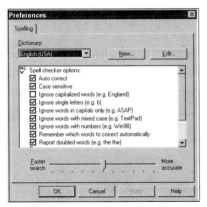

Figure 125-2: The Spelling Preferences dialog box

tip

■ To check the spelling of a single word or range of text, simply select it prior to running the Spelling command.

9. To add a word to the dictionary, select the dictionary file from the Files field at the bottom, type the word you want to add in the Words field, and click the Add Word button.

10. To delete a word, select it from the scrolling list of words and click Delete Word.

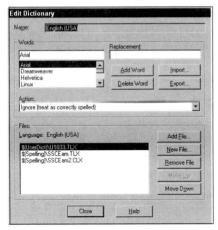

Figure 125-3: The Edit Dictionary dialog box

cross-reference

■ To learn about formatting text with HTML, see Part 2.

Working with the Document Selector

The Document Selector is a handy tool for selecting open documents quickly and activating their windows in the applications. When you turn the Document Selector on, you see a list box on the left side of the TextPad window, showing you each currently open document in alphabetical order.

note

* When you see an asterisk beside a filename in the Document Selector, that indicates the file has unsaved changes.

1. To display the Document Selector, choose View ➪ Document Selector from the menu bar, or press F11. All currently open documents are displayed (see Figure 126-1). To activate a document, simply click its filename.

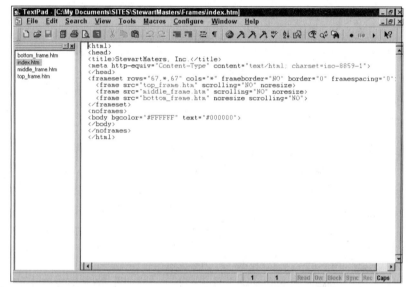

Figure 126-1: Files displayed in the Document Selector (left side of the screen)

2. To increase the width of the Document Selector, move the cursor over the right border until the cursor changes to a double-headed arrow. Click and drag the border.

3. To select multiple files in the Document Selector (see Figure 126-2), Ctrl-click individual filenames. Click on a filename and Shift-click on another to select all filenames in between. You can also highlight multiple filenames by clicking the mouse and dragging it over the names you want to select.

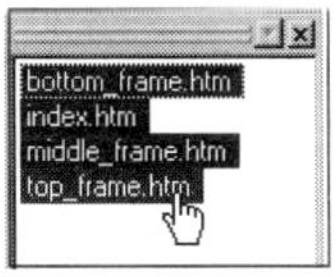

Figure 126-2: Multiple files selected in the Document Selector

4. To move the selector among the filenames, click within the Document Selector and then use the arrow keys to move up and down the list of files. Press Home to jump to the first file in the list and End to jump to the last.

5. To see the full pathnames of files (see Figure 126-3), right-click in Document Selector and choose Show Full Paths from the context menu.

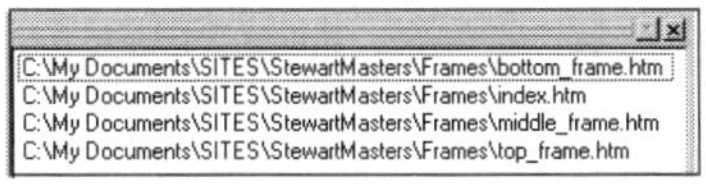

```
C:\My Documents\SITES\StewartMasters\Frames\bottom_frame.htm
C:\My Documents\SITES\StewartMasters\Frames\index.htm
C:\My Documents\SITES\StewartMasters\Frames\middle_frame.htm
C:\My Documents\SITES\StewartMasters\Frames\top_frame.htm
```

Figure 126-3: Full pathnames displayed in the Document Selector

6. To close a selected file, click in the Document Selector and press the Delete key, or right-click in the Document Selector and choose Close Document(s) from the context menu.

tips

- If the Document Selector is the only tool open it will occupy the full height of the application window. If you also have the clip library open (see Task 128), the two interfaces will split the height of the window between them. You can drag the border between the Document Selector and the clip library to adjust their relative heights.

- Select multiple files in the Document Selector when you want to perform an action on all the files simultaneously, such as saving, closing, or printing.

- Selecting View ⇨ Document Tabs from the menu bar, TextPad also places named tabs along the bottom of the application window. Clicking on a tab activates the file.

cross-reference

- The Document Selector works nicely with TextPad workspaces. To learn more about workspaces, see Task 127.

Task 127

Creating Workspaces

When you're developing a Web site, you typically create a directory (folder) somewhere on your hard drive that contains all your Web site's files. This folder mimics the root folder of your Web server. In TextPad, you can save any series of files you're currently working on as a "workspace." You could have 5, 10, or 20 documents open that represent an entire Web site, save them all in a TextPad workspace, and then later open all these related files simultaneously using a single menu command. This saves you the hassle of continually using the File menu to open files. You'll see all open documents either in the Document Selector or in the Document Tabs.

notes

■ Only one file defines a TextPad workspace. It remembers the state of all files you open, no matter where they reside on your hard drive. These workspace files have the extension ".tws."

■ If you have a different workspace currently open, it is saved automatically and is closed before the new workspace opens.

1. To create a workspace, open all the files you want the workspace to contain.

2. Choose File ⇨ Workspace ⇨ Save As from the menu. This opens the Save As dialog box (see Figure 127-1), with the workspace name initialized to the current folder.

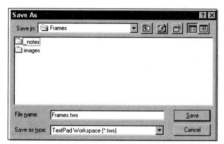

Figure 127-1: The Save As dialog box with the workspace filename set to that of the current working folder

3. If necessary, browse to where you want to save the workspace file or change the filename, then click Save to save the file and close the dialog box.

4. To add or remove files from the workspace, simply open or close files while in the workspace and choose File ⇨ Workspace ⇨ Save (or Save As).

5. To open a saved workspace, choose File ⇨ Workspace ⇨ Open. This displays a File Open dialog box, from which you can locate the .tws file and click the Open button. The Workspace submenu also displays recently opened workspace files which you can open immediately (see Figure 127-2).

| Open... |
| Save |
| Save As... |
| Close |
| 1 Frames.tws |
| 2 ...\site-as_of_12-09-02.tws |

Figure 127-2: A recently opened workspace listed on the Workspace submenu

6. To close a workspace, choose File ⇨ Workspace ⇨ Close. TextPad asks if you want to save your changes and closes the workspace and all its related documents.

tip
- You can choose Save As from the Workspace submenu to save the workspace with a different filename.

cross-reference
- Being able to hop around all the files in a workspace is facilitated by the Document Tabs and Document Selector (see Task 126).

Working with the Clip Library

TextPad's clip library is an interface that gives you access to predefined snippets of code. These snippets are organized into files, which TextPad calls "books." These books typically refer to a particular programming language, or pertain to a specific aspect of a programming language. TextPad comes with a number of clip library books installed, most notably one for inserting HTML tags and another for HTML character entities.

notes

* When you first install and run TextPad, the clip library is visible by default. You'll know it's open if you see a checkmark next to Clip Library in the View menu.

* As of this writing, the code in the HTML clip library is compliant with HTML 4.01/XHTML 1.0. Newer clip libraries are available for download from the Web site at www.wiley .com/compbooks/ 10simplestepsorless (see Task 130).

1. To open the clip library, choose View ⇨ Clip Library from the menu or press Ctrl+F3. The clip library appears on the left side of the TextPad application window (see Figure 128-1).

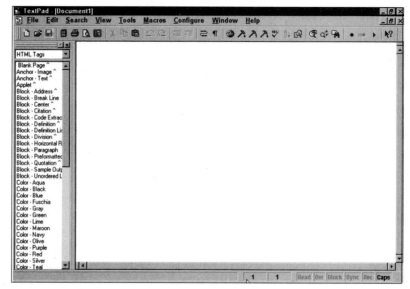

Figure 128-1: The clip library

2. To select a different book, click the drop-down list at the top of the clip library interface (see Figure 128-2).

Figure 128-2: The clip library's drop-down list

3. Use the scrolling list of clips below the drop-down list to locate the one you want to insert (see Figure 128-3).

Figure 128-3: The scrolling list of clippings

Mousing over a clip in the scrolling list displays a tool tip containing the code that will be inserted (see Figure 128-4).

Figure 128-4: A clipping's tool tip

4. To insert a clip, double-click its name in the scrolling list, select the clip, and press Enter. Alternatively, right-click the clip and choose Insert from the context menu.

Task 128

tips

- Want to quickly start a new HTML document? Open a new blank file, open the clip library, choose the HTML Tags book, and click the Blank Page clip.

- For a clip that represents a container tag, select text in the document window and then insert the clip. Doing so wraps the tags around the selected text.

cross-reference

- To edit a clip, see Task 129.

Editing Clip Libraries

You can edit existing clips, as well as create whole new clip libraries, all with a minimum of effort, using the clip library's context menu.

1. To edit an individual clipping, right-click its name in the scrolling list and choose Edit from the context menu. This opens the Clip Library Entry dialog box (see Figure 129-1).

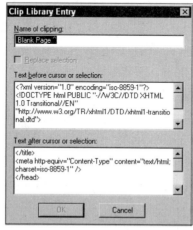

Figure 129-1: The Clip Library Entry dialog box

2. In the fields provided, edit the part of the clip that appears before the cursor location, as well as the code to be placed after the cursor location. Clips that don't insert wrapping content will only show code in the upper field.

3. To rename a clip, choose Rename from the context menu to open the Clip Library dialog box (see Figure 129-2). From here, simply enter a new name for the clip.

Figure 129-2: The Clip Library dialog box

4. To delete a clip, choose Delete from the context menu. TextPad displays a prompt asking you to confirm the deletion.

5. To add a new clip to a book, right-click the scrolling list of clips and choose Paste New Entry from the context menu. This displays the Clip Library Entry dialog box again with the current contents of your system's Clipboard entered in the Text Before Cursor or Selection field. If the Clipboard is empty, the field is blank awaiting your input. From here, simply enter a name for your clip and content in the appropriate fields.

6. To edit an entire book, right-click the book's name in the drop-down list and choose Edit Book. This opens the text file for the entire book in the application window. You can manually edit the document now. Simply edit the entries and choose Save from the File menu when you're done.

7. To create a new empty book, choose New Book from the context menu. TextPad displays a Save As dialog box, prompting you for its filename, followed by a prompt for the name to be displayed in the drop-down list (see Figure 129-3). From, here you can right-click the scrolling list and choose Paste New Entry to create new clips as described in Step 5.

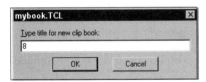

Figure 129-3: Prompts when creating a new book

tip

- The Replace Selection check box is selected by default, and the Text After Cursor or Selection field grayed out, allowing you to create only a clip that inserts a single item or replaces a selected item. To create a clip that wraps content around a selection, deselect the Replace Selection check box to activate the Text After Cursor or Selection field.

cross-reference

- Download new clip libraries from the TextPad Web site (see Task 130).

Downloading Clip Libraries

New clip libraries aren't necessarily something you have to create yourself. There are many available libraries for download at the TextPad Web site — specifically, about HTML/XHTML tags, predefined color name values, CSS properties, and JavaScript libraries.

1. Go to www.textpad.com.

2. Click the Add-ons link at the top of the page (see Figure 130-1).

Figure 130-1: The Add-ons link

3. Click the Clip Libraries link on the subsequent page (see Figure 130-2).

4. Read the descriptions of the clip libraries offered from the table and then click the link on the left side to begin the download process.

5. Once the zipped file is downloaded, choose Configure ➪ Preferences from TextPad's menu to open the Preferences dialog box. Choose Folders to see what folder on your hard drive TextPad uses to access the clip libraries (see Figure 130-3).

Figure 130-2: The Clip Libraries link

tip

- When using WinZip, all you have to do is double-click the zip file's icon to open a WinZip application window. From here, you can drag and drop the clip library file (*.tcl) into the folder using Windows Explorer.

6. Extract the new clip library file into the folder indicated in the Preferences dialog box.

7. To activate the new clip libraries you've installed, restart TextPad and go to the Clip Library drop-down list. The new book names appear in the list in alphabetical order.

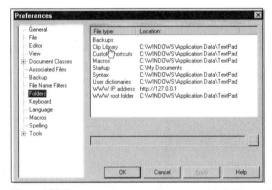

Figure 130-3: The Preferences dialog box with Folders selected

cross-reference

- A text editor is only one part of your development environment. Obviously, you need to test your code in browsers. TextPad allows you to conjure browser support straight from TextPad to launch your documents in any browser you have installed (see Task 131).

Configuring TextPad with Web Browsers

TextPad has a reconfigured button on its standard toolbar that looks like a little globe. When you click it, it launches the current document in your system's default Web browser. Of course, when you create Web content, you want to test your document in more than a single browser. Fortunately, you can configure TextPad to launch the current document in as many different browsers as you have installed on your computer. The following series of steps add a command to the Tools menu and configure a button on the Tools toolbar (which you can always move later to the toolbar of your choice).

1. Choose Configure ➪ Preferences to open the Preferences dialog box. Click Tools on the left to view the Tools options (see Figure 131-1).

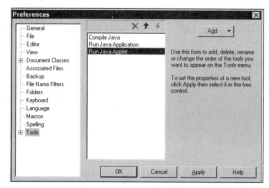

Figure 131-1: The Preferences dialog box with the Tools option selected

2. In the upper-right corner, click the Add button and choose Program from the menu that appears. This opens the Select a File dialog box (see Figure 131-2).

Figure 131-2: The Select a File dialog box

3. From here, locate the executable program file for the browser you want to add to the Tools menu and click the Open button to close the dialog box. The program name now appears in the Preferences dialog box.

4. Click Apply to confirm the operation. To change the order of commands, click the up and down arrow buttons at the top of the list. Click OK to close the Preferences dialog box.

5. To view the Tools toolbar, choose View ⇨ Toolbars ⇨ Tools from the menu. Sixteen user-defined tool buttons appear as little hammer icons on the toolbar. Each tool corresponds to the commands in the order they are defined.

6. To copy buttons to other toolbars, choose View ⇨ Toolbars ⇨ Customize. This displays the Customize dialog box (see Figure 131-3).

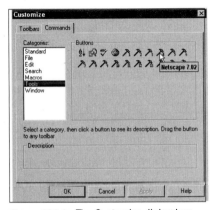

Figure 131-3: The Customize dialog box

7. Click the Commands tab and select the Tools category to see all the buttons on that toolbar. Drag the button icons to any toolbar visible in TextPad.

Task **131**

tip

- If you want to modify the name, click once and then click a second time to highlight the program name. From here you can edit the name to your satisfaction.

cross-reference

- Test in multiple browsers to make sure your designs are clean and accessible to the widest possible audience. If you're just starting out in Web design, check out www.webpagesthatsuck .com so your sites won't get listed there.

Configuring an HTML Validator

TextPad has been designed to integrate with the AI Internet Solutions CSE HTML Validator. Validation software allows you to find and correct invalid markup, such as improperly nested tags, missing quotation marks, and misspelled tag and attribute names. This task covers how to download and install the Validator and configure it for use with TextPad.

1. Go to www.htmlvalidator.com.

2. Click the Download link in the top navigation bar (see Figure 132-1).

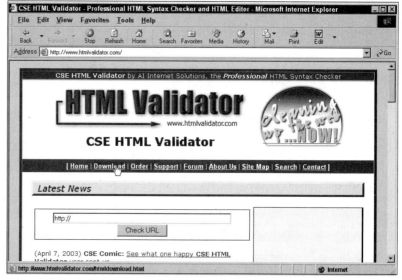

Figure 132-1: The Download link on the CSE HTML Validator site

3. Click the appropriate link to download the version of your choice: the Trial version, the Lite version, or the Registered version (requires prior online purchase). The next screen you see depends on the version you choose.

4. In the subsequent page, click the appropriate link to begin the download. The Save As dialog box (see Figure 132-2) appears, allowing you to choose where to save the installation file.

Figure 132-2: The Save As dialog box

5. Once the installer executable is downloaded, double-click its icon to begin the installation process, and follow the prompts in the installation wizard. Once installation is complete, TextPad adds a command to run the Validator to the Tools menu.

6. To add commands to the Tools menu that allow access to the Validator's configuration dialog boxes, select Configure ➪ Preferences. Click the Tools category.

7. Click the Add button and select HTML Validator Commands from the drop-down list (see Figure 132-3). Click OK.

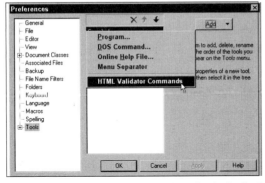

Figure 132-3: The Add button drop-down list in the Preferences dialog box

tip

▪ You can use the trial version of CSE HTML Validator for 30 days or to validate 100 documents, whichever comes first. After that time, you must purchase a license to keep it functioning.

cross-reference

▪ TextPad's color syntax checking also helps you notice when code has errors. To modify the colors TextPad uses, see Task 135.

133

Creating Keystroke Macros

The purpose of a macro is to let you record any frequently repeated editing command (including the typing of text) and play it back whenever you need it. This saves you time doing repetitive tasks. In TextPad, you can create up to 64 named macros.

notes

* If you have an unsaved macro in memory, you'll be asked if you want to erase it.

* While recording the macro you can use any command in the File and Window menus, all commands in the Edit menu (except Undo and Redo), and all commands in the Search menu except Find in Files.

1. To begin recording a macro, either choose Macro ⇨ Record, click the Record On/Off button on the toolbar (see Figure 133-1), or press Ctrl+Shift+R.

Figure 133-1: The Record On/Off button

2. With the recorder running, type out your code as you would normally, or make your menu command selections. When finished, choose Macro ⇨ Stop Recording, click the Record On/Off button on the toolbar, or press Ctrl+Shift+R again.

3. To save the macro, choose Macro ⇨ Save from the menu to open the Save Macro dialog box (see Figure 133-2).

Figure 133-2: The Save Macro dialog box

Task 133

4. Provide a filename for the macro, being sure not to obliterate the .tpm file extension. By default TextPad uses MACRO*xx*.tpm, where *xx* is a number.

5. Provide a name for the macro in the Display Name field. This name appears in the Macro menu. You can also include the macro author's name and a description of what the macro does.

6. Select an option from the Default Play Mode list and click OK to close the dialog box.

7. To play the macro, go to the Macros menu and select its name from the list of choices.

tips

- If where the cursor is located in the document is important to the playback of the macro, position the cursor where you want it before you begin the recording process.

- For macros that simply type text, selecting Play Once is typically the best Default Play Mode option. For macros that perform a task throughout a document, for example finding and replacing text, choose Repeat Through Selection or Repeat to End of File.

cross-reference

- Creating macros that wrap selected text within tag containers can be a real timesaver. See Task 134 to create such a macro and assign it a keyboard shortcut.

Task 134

Creating a Tag-Wrapping Macro

In this task, you'll learn how to define a macro that wraps selected text in the tags of your choice. You can then create a series of these macros for nearly every container tag combination HTML requires. What's more, you can assign keyboard shortcuts to the macros, turning TextPad into a dedicated HTML authoring tool.

1. Open TextPad and begin a new blank document. Enter a single line text into the document and select it.

2. Open the Replace dialog box (see Figure 134-1) by choosing Search ⇨ Replace or pressing F8.

Figure 134-1: The Replace dialog box

3. In the Find What field, type a backward slash (\) and ampersand (&), as shown in Figure 134-2.

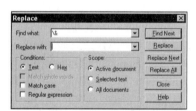

Figure 134-2: Entering \& in the Find What field

4. In the Replace With field, enter a container tag set with an ampersand in the middle. For example, <p>&</p>.

5. Click the Regular Expression check box and then start the recorder by clicking the Record On/Off button on the toolbar, or pressing Ctrl+Shift+R.

6. With the macro now recording, go back to the Replace dialog box and click the Find Next button, followed by the Replace button.

7. Stop the recording by clicking the Record On/Off button or pressing Ctrl+Shift+R, and follow the prompts to save the macro, giving it an appropriate name.

8. To assign a keyboard shortcut to the macro, select Configure ⇨ Preferences. This opens the Preferences dialog box. In the Preferences list on the left, choose Keyboard (see Figure 134-3).

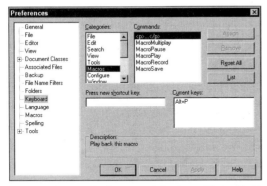

Figure 134-3: The Preferences dialog box with the Keyboard option selected

9. Select Macros from the Categories field. This displays all the commands currently in the Macros menu in the Commands field. From here, select the name of the macro you just created.

10. Enter a key combination in the Press New Shortcut Key field — for example, Alt+P — and click the Assign button to match the macro to your shortcut key choice.

Task **135**

Working with Color Syntax Checking

TextPad recognizes the type of code you're writing through the use of document classes. TextPad comes with a number of predefined classes — most notably for you, the HTML document class. These classes color-code different parts of HTML. For example, tags, attributes, and values each have their own color in TextPad. When you make a typographic or HTML syntax error, the color of all code following the error changes to a single color so that the error stands out. You can easily modify these colors to suit your own taste.

1. To modify the HTML document class colors, choose Configure ⇨ Preferences to open the Preferences dialog box.

2. Click the plus sign beside Document Classes in the options list to expand the list of currently installed classes.

3. Click HTML to examine the HTML class (see Figure 135-1).

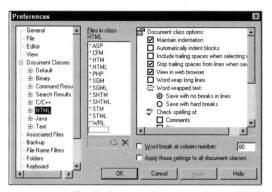

Figure 135-1: The Preferences dialog box with the HTML class selected

4. Click the plus sign beside HTML to expand the class options.

5. Select the Colors option from beneath the HTML class (see Figure 135-2).

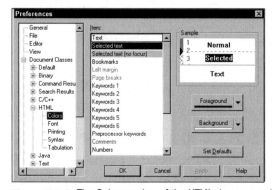

Figure 135-2: The Colors option of the HTML document class

6. Choose the item whose color you want to modify.

7. Change the text color and the color behind it by clicking the Foreground and Background buttons to the right and selecting a color option from the color picker that appears (see Figure 135-3).

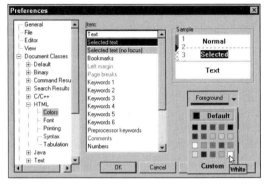

Figure 135-3: The Foreground color picker

8. Click Apply to change the color and keep the dialog box open, or click OK to change the color and close the dialog box.

9. To return the colors for a selected item to their original values, click the Set Defaults button.

tips

- To modify the font of a class, select its Font page. You can change both the font used onscreen as well as the printed font.

- Use the Sample field to preview the effect of your color selections.

Part 13: Working with BBEdit

Downloading and Installing BBEdit

Any company that sells its software under the tag line "It doesn't suck" is a winner with us. BBEdit is the premiere HTML and text-editing application for Macintosh OS. Downloading the fully functioning, 30-day trial version of BBEdit 7.0 is fairly simple.

notes

- BBEdit 7.0.2 runs on Mac OS 9.1 or later but Mac OS 9.2.2 or later is recommended. If you are using Mac OS X, version 10.1.5 or later is required although version 10.2.3 or later is recommended.

- BBEdit requires CarbonLib 1.5 or higher on your system. If you need to download it, get the most-recent versions of CarbonLib at http://docs.info.apple.com/article.html?artnum=120047.

1. Go to www.barebones.com (see Figure 136-1) and click on the Products link and select BBEdit.

Figure 136-1: The Bare Bones Software home page

2. On the main BBEdit page, look for the vertical list of links on the right side of the screen and click on Demo.

3. In the "Please Sign Up!" form, enter the information they request and click the Register button (see Figure 136-2).

4. Click the Demo Package download link to begin downloading the installation file and choose a location on your system to save it (see Figure 136-3).

5. With the executable installation file downloaded, double-click the file to unpack the installer. Double-click the installer to install BBEdit on your system.

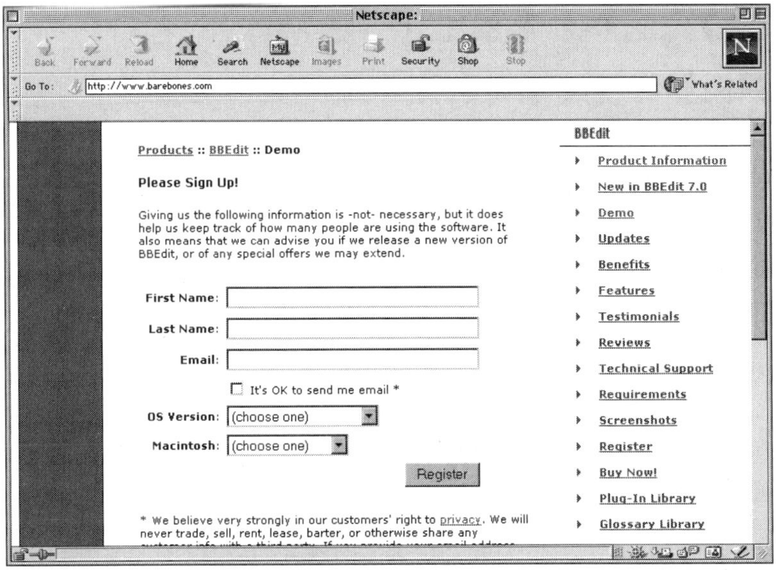

Task **136**

Figure 136-2: Registering for BBEdit

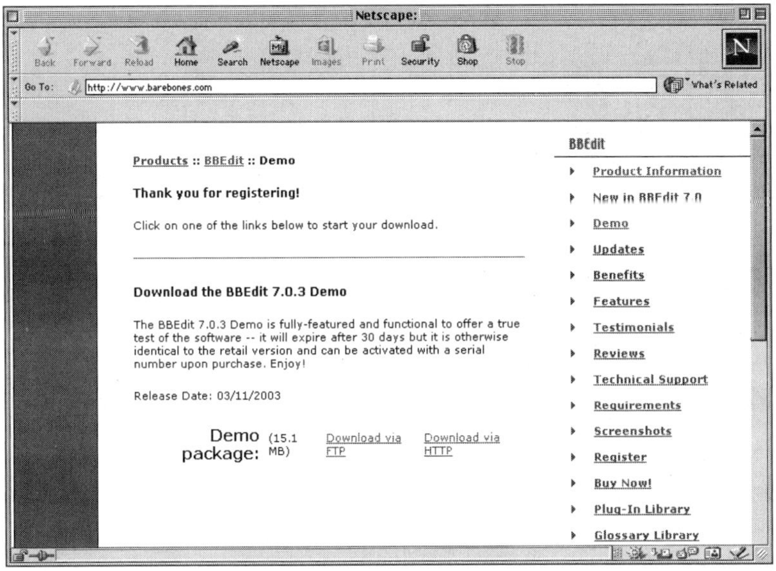

Figure 136-3: Selecting the download option you prefer

tips

- To download the user manual, click the Technical Support link in the vertical list and then scroll down to the Resources section on the next page. Here you find a link to the user manual in PDF format. You need Adobe Reader to view it, which you can download for free at www.adobe .com/products/acrobat/ readstep2.html.

- If you're interested in purchasing BBEdit, go to www.barebones.com/ store/index.shtml.

cross-reference

- If you're a PC user running Windows, then you cannot use BBEdit, which is for Mac OS only. Read about TextPad, an equivalent product, in Part 12.

Task 137

Configuring BBEdit for Web Site Development

notes

- BBEdit uses the URL to determine which links point to the files on your Web server.

- If you haven't got a Web server yet, don't worry. You can always go back and update any of these fields later.

- The root filename is the name of the file sent to a browser that visits (requests) a domain name. For example, when a browser visits www.domain_name.com, the Web server returns the root document because no specific filename was requested. Your Web hosting company or server administrator knows what the proper root filename is. Common ones include "index," "default," "main," and "home" — followed by the extension .htm or .html.

Although you ultimately copy your files to a remote Web server when you publish your Web site, you develop your site (and edit it after publication) on your local computer. This task shows you how to develop your local file structure and set up your site in BBEdit.

1. On your hard drive, create a folder that will contain all the files and directories of your Web site.

2. Choose Edit ⇨ Preferences to open the BBEdit Preferences panel (see Figure 137-1). Scroll down to HTML Web Sites in the left-hand list.

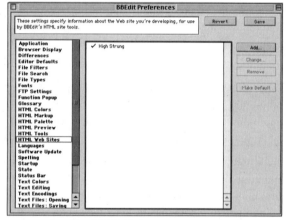

Figure 137-1: The BBEdit Preferences panel with HTML Web Sites selected

3. Click the Add button on the right to display the Web Site Settings dialog box (see Figure 137-2).

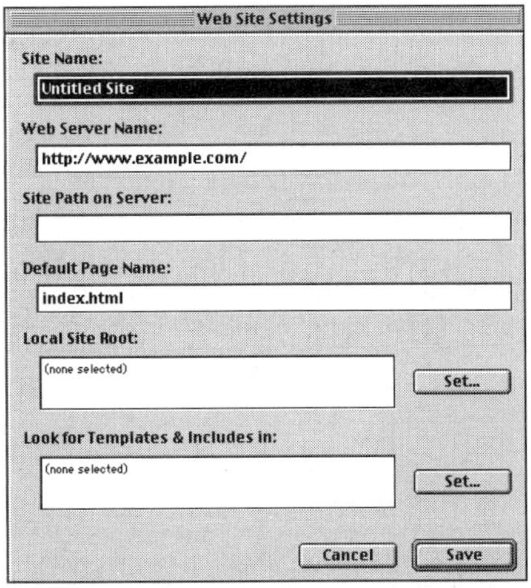

Figure 137-2: The Web Site Settings dialog box

4. In the Site Name field, enter a descriptive name for your site. This is the name that the site will appear later as in the HTML Web Sites category of the BBEdit Preferences panel.

5. In the Web Server Name field, enter the URL of your Web server, if you have one (*http://www.domain_name.com/*).

6. In the Site Path on Server field, enter any subfolders that lead to the index.html home page. For example, if the path to the home page is www.domain_name.com/alpha/beta/index.html, enter **alpha/beta**.

7. In the Default Page Name field, enter your Web server's default root filename.

8. Beside the Local Site Root field, click the Set button to select the folder you created in Step 1.

cross-reference

- Regardless of which editing tool you use, developing a sound folder structure on your local machine is the first step to building a Web site. This book contains overviews of other development tools as well: Helios Software's TextPad (Part 12), Macromedia HomeSite (Part 14), Macromedia Dreamweaver MX (Part 15), and Microsoft FrontPage (Part 16).

Creating New HTML Documents

Y ou can create an HTML document in any text editor just by entering markup code and saving the file with an .htm, or .html extension. However, using BBEdit allows you to insert the main structural tags of an HTML document quickly and easily.

1. Click New Document on the HTML Tools Palette or choose File ⇨ New ⇨ HTML Document from the main menu to open the New HTML Document dialog box (see Figure 138-1). If you choose, you can simply click OK here and insert the document tags. Otherwise, continue to define other properties of the document.

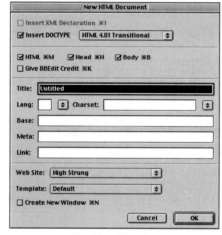

Figure 138-1: The New HTML Document dialog box

2. To specify a DOCTYPE declaration, select an option from the pop-up menu beside the Insert DOCTYPE check box.

3. Using the check boxes provided, deselect any standard container tags you want to leave out.

4. Enter the title of the HTML document in the Title field.

5. To indicate what language the document is written in, make a selection from the Lang menu.

6. To define a `<meta>` tag, enter the necessary code into the Meta field.

7. To include a `<link>` tag, for example to reference an external style sheet, enter the necessary code in the Link field.

8. To specify the Web site this file is part of, use the Web Site pop-up menu to select one of the sites you've defined.

9. To specify a template you want this file based on, select it from the Templates pop-up menu.

10. Click OK to close the dialog box and open the new document. A new document opens on the desktop (see Figure 138-2). The code contains information you entered in the New HTML Document dialog box.

Figure 138-2: A new HTML document

cross-reference
- To learn how to define a Web site in BBEdit using file groups, see Task 155.

Using the Tag Maker Edit Tag Tools

BBEdit provides two context-sensitive tools for inserting and modifying tags: Tag Maker and Edit Tag. "Context-sensitive" means that BBEdit looks at where the cursor is currently positioned in the code and only provides tags, attributes, or CSS options that make sense for that location.

1. Place your cursor within the flow of your document code.

2. To open the Tag Maker (see Figure 139-1), click the Tag Maker button on the HTML Tools palette, choose Markup ⇨ Tag Maker from the main menu, or press Command+M.

notes

- If there is only one possible tag that can be inserted at the current cursor location, BBEdit simply inserts the tag without displaying the Tag Maker. If there are no appropriate tags, a system alert sounds.

- If the cursor is located between `<style>` tags, Tag Maker displays a list of possible selectors. Option-clicking the Insert button brings up a dialog box of possible style properties. If the cursor is within the brackets of a style declaration, the Tag Maker displays style properties right away.

Figure 139-1: The Insert Tag dialog box

3. Select the appropriate tag you want to insert from the list of tags.

4. To bring up an attribute dialog box appropriate to the selected tag (see Figure 139-2), hold down the Option key and click the Insert button.

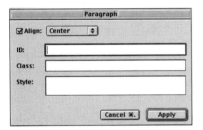

Figure 139-2: An attribute dialog box appropriate to the selected tag — in this case the <p> (paragraph) tag

5. Enter any attribute values you require and click the Apply button to close the dialog box.

6. To display attributes for preexisting tags (see Figure 139-3), place the cursor within the tag and invoke the Tag Maker using any of the methods described in Step 1.

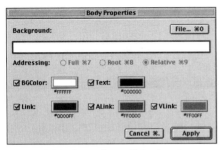

Figure 139-3: An attribute dialog box for a preexisting <body> tag

7. To modify the most common attributes of a tag, click Edit Tag on the HTML Tools palette. Enter the appropriate values and click Apply.

tip
- Clicking in the Insert Tag dialog box's scrolling list and typing a letter scrolls you quickly to the tags beginning with that letter.

cross-reference
- To learn more about Cascading Style Sheets, see Part 9.

Formatting Text

If there's a tag, the HTML Tools Palette has a button to insert and format it. To mark up text, simply click a button and, where applicable, modify the tag's attributes in the resulting dialog box. Occasionally you have to wander up to the BBEdit menu bar to find a command, but not often.

note
- All dialog boxes that deal with color have a color button that you click to open the color picker. Simply choose a color from the picker to close it to return to the dialog box.

1. To insert a paragraph, click the Paragraph button on the HTML Tools Palette or choose Paragraph from the Block Elements submenu. This opens the Paragraph dialog box (see Figure 140-1). Here you can modify the tag's `align`, `ID`, `class`, and `style` attributes.

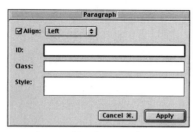

Figure 140-1: Modifying the <p> tag with the Paragraph dialog box

2. To insert headings, click the Heading button and select one of the six heading tags from the submenu that appears.

3. To insert `<font>` tags, click the Font button to open the Font dialog box (see Figure 140-2). Specify values for the `face`, `size`, and `color` attributes by clicking the appropriate check boxes and entering values in the fields provided.

Figure 140-2: Modifying the <font> tag with the Font dialog box

4. To insert physical style tags, click the Font Style Elements button and select the style of your choice from the submenu.

5. To insert logical styles, click the Phrase Elements button and select the appropriate style from the submenu.

6. To insert preformatted text (with the `<pre> </pre>` tags), click the Block Elements button and choose Preformatted from the submenu.

7. To modify the default body text and text link colors, click the Body Properties button to open the Body Properties dialog box (see Figure 140-3). Place check marks next to the attributes you want to specify and use the color tools to select a color.

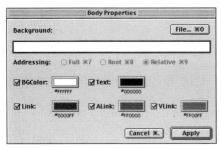

Figure 140-3: Modifying default body text and text link colors in the Body Properties dialog box

8. To format selected text as a hyperlink, click the Anchor button to open the Anchor dialog box (see Figure 140-4). Enter values for the appropriate attributes in the fields provided.

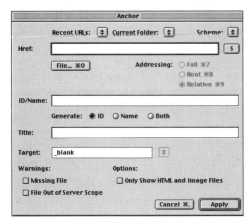

Figure 140-4: Hyperlinking text with the Anchor dialog box

tip

- The Recent URLs menu allows you to select from a list of files you've recently linked to. Click the File button to browse your site folder for a file, or enter the complete URL of another site.

cross-reference

- To learn more about the tags that BBEdit inserts for each of these options, see Part 2.

Creating Lists

HTML requires a series of structured tag pairings to render lists in the browser. BBEdit makes manipulating list code a pretty simple proposition.

1. To convert existing text to a list, select the text comprising the list items and click the List button on the HTML Tools Palette to open the Lists submenu (see Figure 141-1).

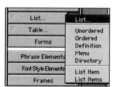

Figure 141-1: The HTML Tools Palette List submenu

Select List from the submenu to open the Lists dialog box (see Figure 141-2).

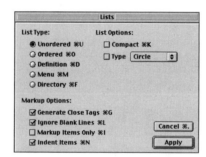

Figure 141-2: Selecting list options in the Lists dialog box

2. Select the list type, attribute settings, and markup options using the radio buttons, check boxes, and pop-up menus in the dialog box.

3. Click Apply to close the dialog box and wrap the selected text in the appropriate markup.

4. To build a list from scratch, choose the list type from the List button submenu to insert the appropriate opening and closing tags (`<ul> </ul>`, `<ol> </ol>`, or `<dl> </dl>`), along with an empty pair of list items tags (`<li> </li>`, or `<dt> </dt>` and `<dd> </dd>`). (See Figure 141-3.)

Figure 141-3: List tags inserted using the HTML Tools Palette

5. Enter the text required for your list items.

6. To modify the attributes of any tag in the list, place the cursor within the tag and click the Tag Maker button to view a list of possible attributes in the Insert Attribute dialog box (see Figure 141-4).

Figure 141-4: Modifying attributes in the Insert Attribute dialog box

cross-reference

- To learn more about creating lists, see Tasks 22–28.

Inserting Images

BBEdit makes it easy to insert images and enter values for the `<img>` tag's associated attributes.

1. Click the Image button on the HTML Tools Palette to open the Image dialog box (see Figure 142-1).

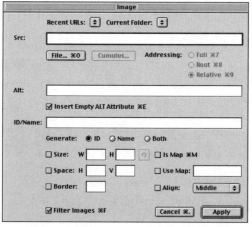

Figure 142-1: Inserting images using the Image dialog box

2. In the Src field, enter the pathname of the image file or click the File button to browse for one on your hard drive. Alternatively, use the Recent URLs pop-up menu to select among image files you've recently inserted.

3. In the Alt field, enter the alternate text you want to specify for the image.

4. To specify the dimensions of the image, click the Size check box and enter width and height values in the W and H fields, respectively.

5. To specify hspace and vspace attributes, click the Space check box and enter values in the H and V fields, respectively.

6. To align the image, click the Align check box and choose an option from the pop-up menu to the right.

7. Click Apply to close the Image dialog box and insert the appropriate code into your document (see Figure 142-2) that makes the image appear on your Web page.

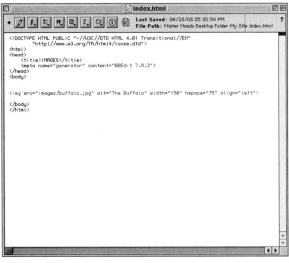

Figure 142-2: Code inserted using the Images dialog box

8. To center-align an image, insert a `<div>` tag with an `align` attribute set to "`center`" by selecting the `<img>` tag, clicking the Div button, and modifying the `align` attribute in the Division dialog box (see Figure 142-3).

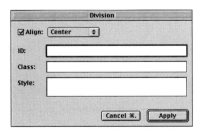

Figure 142-3: Setting values for the `<div>` tag using the Division dialog box

9. To see how the image appears in a browser, click the Preview button at the bottom of the HTML Tools Palette and choose one of the installed browsers on your system to open the HTML document (see Figure 142-4).

Figure 142-4: Options for previewing your page in a browser

cross-reference

- To learn more about inserting images on Web pages in HTML, see Part 3.

Creating Tables

BBEdit provides you with a number of features to generate HTML tables. You can modify every attribute of the table-related tag (`<table>`, `<tr>`, `<td>`, and `<th>`). Of course, you can also access these attributes using the Tag Maker and Edit Tag tools.

note

- BBEdit provides fields for the `char` value of both the `align` and `charoff` attributes. Although technically part of the HTML 4 specification, browsers have never supported them. Be aware also that browsers prior to the 4.*x* versions of Internet Explorer and Netscape Navigator don't support attributes of the `<tr>` tag; they only recognize attributes of the `<td>` tag.

1. To insert a table, click the Table button on the HTML Tools Palette, and select table from the submenu. This opens the Table dialog box (see Figure 143-1).

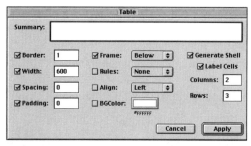

Figure 143-1: Setting table values in the Table dialog box

2. To specify a value for the table border, click the Border check box and enter a pixel value in the field provided.

3. To define the table's width, click the Width check box and enter either a pixel or percentage value in the provided field.

4. To specify values for cell padding and cell spacing, select the appropriate check boxes and supply pixel values in the associated fields.

5. To specify the table's alignment, click the Align check box and use the pop-up menu to the right to set the alignment to left, right, or center.

6. To define a background color for the table, click the BGColor check box, click the color picker, and choose a color value from the palette.

7. Click Apply to close the dialog box and insert the opening and closing `<table>` tags with your attributes already defined.

8. To insert a new row — which HTML defines with the `<tr>` tag — click Tables and choose Row from the submenu to open the TR dialog box (see Figure 143-2). Specify the `<tr>` tag's `align` and `valign` attribute values, as well as a background color.

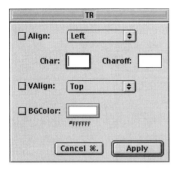

Figure 143-2: Setting attribute values for the <tr> tag in the TR dialog box

9. To insert a new cell — which HTML defines with the `<td>` or `<th>` tag — click Tables and choose TD or TH to open the corresponding dialog box (see Figure 143-3). Specify the dimensions of the cell, the number of rows or columns the cell spans, its horizontal and vertical alignment, and its background color.

Figure 143-3: Setting table cells in the TD dialog box

tip

- If you want to insert a complete table with rows and columns, click the Generate Shell check box and enter values in the Columns and Rows fields. Selecting the Label Cells check box fills the cells with label text: for example, _Row_1_Cell_1_, _Row_1_Cell_2_, _Row_1_Cell_3_, etc.

cross-reference

- To learn more about building tables, see Part 6.

Building Forms

BBEdit makes inserting and formatting form controls easy using the Forms submenu of the HTML Tools palette.

1. To generate the opening `<form>` tag, click the Forms button and choose Form from the submenu to open the Form dialog box (see Figure 144-1).

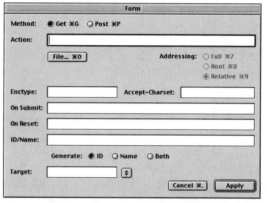

Figure 144-1: Defining a form control in the Form dialog box

2. Click the relevant radio button for the Method attribute (Post or Get).

3. In the Action field, enter the URL of the processing CGI script that runs the form control.

4. Click the Apply button to close the Form dialog box and insert the generated code into the current document.

5. To insert any of the form controls created with the `<input>` tag, click the Forms button and choose Input from the submenu to display the Input dialog box (see Figure 144-2).

6. Select the type of form control in the Type pop-up menu. Supply the value for the `name` and the `value` attributes, if applicable, in the fields provided.

7. To create a selection menu, choose Select from the Forms button submenu to display the Select dialog box (see Figure 144-3). Supply the `name` attribute value, activate multiple selections, and modify the `size` attribute in the fields provided. Click Apply to insert the code.

8. To insert selection menu `<option>` tags, place the cursor between the opening and closing `<select>` tags and choose Option from the Forms submenu. This opens the Option dialog box, where you define the `label` and/or `value` attributes in the fields provided.

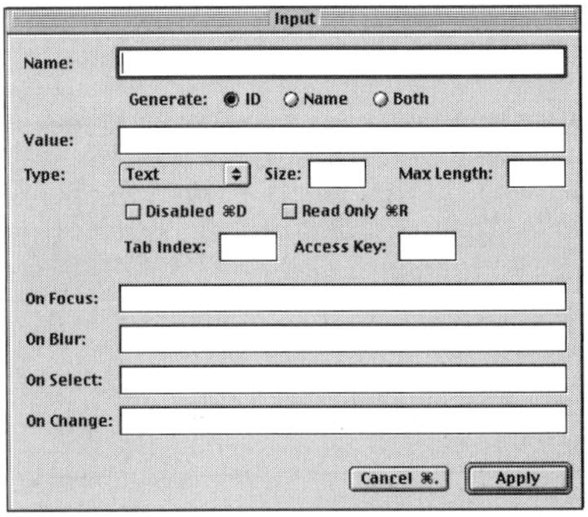

Figure 144-2: Setting <input> tag attributes in the Input dialog box

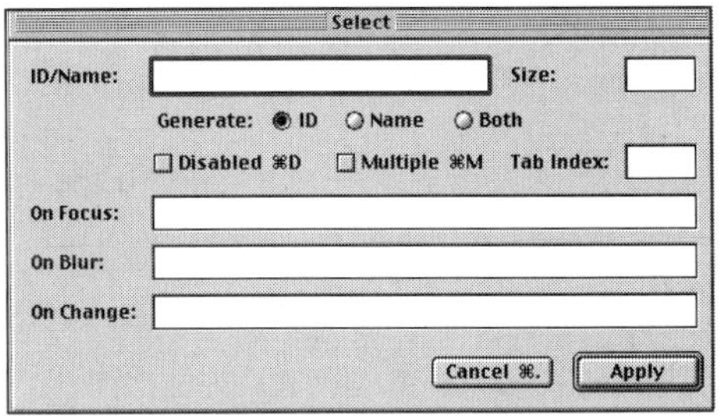

Figure 144-3: Defining a selection list in the Select dialog box

9. To insert a text area, click Text Area on the Forms submenu to open the Text Area dialog box (see Figure 144-4). Specify the values of the `rows` and `cols` attributes in the fields provided and click Apply.

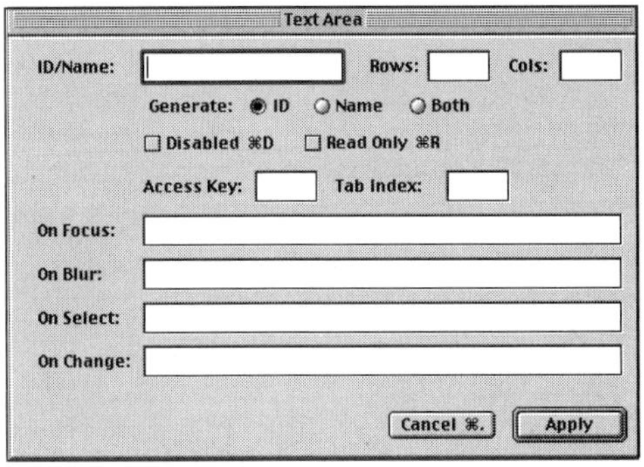

Figure 144-4: Defining a text area using the Text Area dialog box

cross-reference

- Learn more about forms using HTML in Part 7.

Working with Frames

In a frames-based layout, one document (the frameset document) defines the properties of the various frames on the page, each of which are separate documents. From the Frames submenu on the HTML Tools Palette you can invoke a number of dialog boxes that allow you to insert and modify the various tags that make up the frameset document.

1. To insert the `<frameset>` tags, click the Frames button on the HTML Tools Palette and choose Frame Set from the submenu to open the Frameset dialog box (see Figure 145-1).

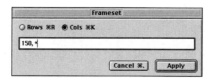

Figure 145-1: The Frameset dialog box

2. Select either Rows or Cols, and enter your dimension values in the field provided. Click Apply to close the dialog box and insert the code.

3. To insert `<frame>` tags, click the Frames button and choose Frame from the submenu to open the Frame dialog box (see Figure 145-2).

4. Click the File button to locate the document you want to display in this frame, or enter the pathname manually.

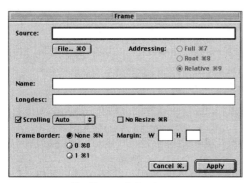

Figure 145-2: The Frame dialog box

5. To define the `name` attribute of the frame, enter a value in the Name field.

6. To modify the `scrolling` attribute of the frame, select the Scrolling check box and set the associated pop-up menu to Yes, No, or Auto.

7. To prevent the user from resizing a frame, click the No Resize check box.

8. To modify the `frameborder` attribute, select a value of None, 0, or 1. None removes the `frameborder` attribute from the tag, while 0 and 1 set the attribute equal to those respective pixel values.

9. To specify frame margins, enter values in the fields provided.

10. To insert `<noframes>` tags, place your cursor outside the `<frameset>` tags and choose No Frames from the submenu.

cross-reference
- To learn more about HTML frames, see Part 8.

Task 146

Defining CSS Font Properties

The HTML Tools Palette provides a means of editing Cascading Style Sheet code, whether the code is inline, embedded, or in an external style sheet document. To modify CSS `<font>` tag properties, follow these steps.

note

- If you initially place the cursor within an existing style declaration, the corresponding selector appears in the Selector field and the properties you define are added to the existing declaration.

1. Place the cursor in the current document at the point you want to insert the style definition. Click the CSS button and choose Font from the submenu to open the Font dialog box (see Figure 146-1).

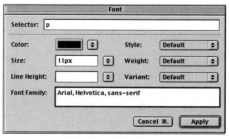

Figure 146-1: The Font dialog box

2. Enter a selector of your choice in the Selector field.

3. To specify a `color` property, click the color picker and select a color from the color palette.

4. To define a `font-size` property, click the pop-up menu beside the Size field to select a unit of measure and then enter a value in the field.

5. To define a `line-height` property, click the pop-up menu beside the Line Height field to select a unit of measure and enter a value in the field.

6. To define a `font-family` property, enter a value in the Font Family field.

7. To define a `font-style` property, choose Italic, Oblique, or Normal from the Style pop-up menu. The Default value leaves the property undefined.

8. To define a `font-weight` property, choose a value from the Weight pop-up menu. The Default value leaves the property undefined.

9. To define a `font-variant` property, choose Small-Caps or Normal from the Variant pop-up menu. The Default value leaves the property undefined.

10. When you've completed you choices, click the Apply button to insert the style declaration (see Figure 146-2).

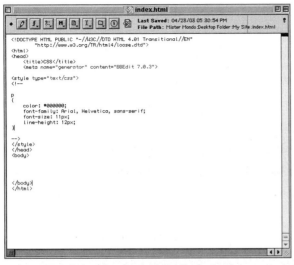

Figure 146-2: A completed style definition in the document window

tips

- The best unit of measure for cross-platform usage is pixels.

- Define font family property just as you would the `face` attribute of the `<font>` tag — for example, in a comma-delimited list of three or more font names, like "`Arial, Helvetica, sans-serif`".

cross-reference

- To learn more about Cascading Style Sheets, go to the book's Web site at www.wiley .com/compbooks/ 10simplestepsorless.

Defining CSS Text Properties

BBEdit's CSS editing tools allow you to adjust text properties in CSS, which affect the physical characteristics of the text itself — spacing of characters, words, and lines as well as alignment and indentation. Defining these properties in BBEdit is simply a matter of accessing the appropriate dialog box and entering your chosen values.

notes

- If you initially place the cursor within an existing style declaration, the corresponding selector appears in the Selector field and the properties you define are added to the existing declaration.

- For some reason, BBEdit duplicates the line-height property in both the Font and Text dialog boxes. To define it here, select a unit of measurement and enter a value in the Line Height field.

1. Place the cursor in the current document at the point you want to insert the style definition. Click the CSS button and choose Text from the submenu to open the Text dialog box (see Figure 147-1).

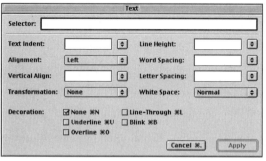

Figure 147-1: The Text dialog box

2. Enter a selector of your choice in the Selector field.

3. To define a `text-indent` property, click the pop-up menu beside the Text Indent field to select a unit of measure, and then enter a value in the field.

4. To define a `text-align` property, choose a value from the Alignment pop-up menu.

5. To define a `vertical-align` property, choose a value from the corresponding pop-up menu, or select a percentage from the menu and enter a numeric value in the field.

6. To define a `text-transform` property, choose a value from the transformation pop-up menu.

7. To define `word-spacing` and `letter-spacing` properties, select a unit of measure from their respective pop-up menus and enter a value in their fields.

8. To define a `white-space` property, choose a value from the White Space pop-up menu.

9. To define a `text-decoration` property, select each of the check boxes you want to include from those listed at the bottom of the dialog box.

10. Click Apply to close the dialog box and insert the definition in the current document (see Figure 147-2).

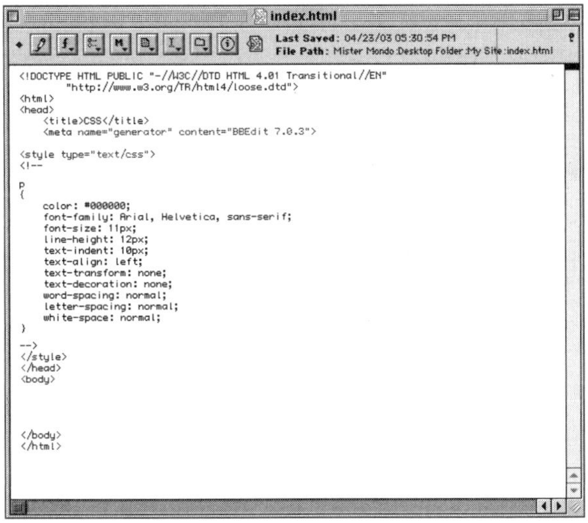

Figure 147-2: Text properties added to a style definition

tip

- The best unit of measure for cross-platform usage is pixels.

cross-reference

- To learn more about Cascading Style Sheets, see Part 9.

Task **148**

Defining CSS Background Properties

In HTML you can assign a background color or image to several areas of the document, including various parts of a table (cells, rows, or the entire table) and layered content. In CSS, by comparison, you can determine the background of any element in the document including individual words, paragraphs, headings — anything. If there's a tag for it, you can modify its background.

1. Place the cursor in the current document at the point you want to insert the style definition. Click the CSS button and choose Background from the submenu to open the Background dialog box (see Figure 148-1).

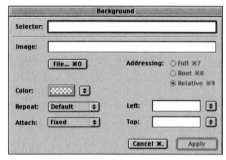

Figure 148-1: The Background dialog box

2. Enter a selector of your choice in the Selector field.

3. To define a `background-image` property, click the File button to browse your hard drive for an image file you want to use.

4. To define a `background-color` property, click the dialog box's color picker and choose a color from the palette.

5. To control how a background image tiles, define a `background-repeat` property by selecting a value from the Repeat pop-up menu.

6. To specify the location of a background image, define a `background-position` property by entering Left and Top coordinates in the fields provided and specifying the unit of measure with the corresponding pop-up menus.

7. To specify whether the background image is fixed or scrolls with the browser window, define a `background-attachment` property using the Attach pop-up menu.

8. To insert the new definitions, click the Apply button. The code is written to the document (see Figure 148-2).

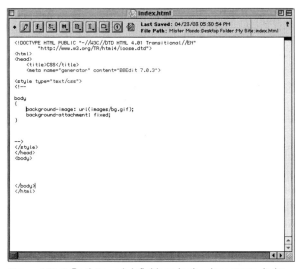

Figure 148-2: Background definitions in the document window

tip

- Any image you intend to use in a Web site should be copied into the local site's root directory.

cross-reference

- To learn more about Cascading Style Sheets and the background properties, see Part 9.

Defining CSS Padding and Margin Properties

BBEdit makes it easy to define padding and margin properties in CSS. You do it all in the same dialog box.

notes

- If you initially place the cursor within an existing style declaration, the corresponding selector appears in the Selector field and the properties you define are added to the existing declaration.

- BBEdit does not support the properties padding-top, padding-right, padding-bottom, or padding-left. Instead, it uses the single padding property, which accepts four values to represent these separate properties, respectively (padding: top right bottom left). If you don't want to assign a padding value to a particular side, you must enter 0 in the corresponding field.

1. To define padding properties, place the cursor in the current document at the point you want to insert the style definition. Click the CSS button on the HTML Tools Palette and choose Padding from the submenu to open the Padding dialog box (see Figure 149-1).

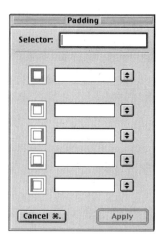

Figure 149-1: The Padding dialog box

2. Enter the selector you're defining the property for in the Selector field.

3. To supply an identical value for each of the four possible sides, type a value in the first field and choose a unit of measure from the accompanying pop-up menu.

4. To define a value for any combination of sides, enter individual values in each of the subsequent fields — top, right, bottom, or left — as indicated by the field's icon on the left.

5. To define margin properties, place the cursor in the current document at the point you want to insert the style definition. Click the CSS button on the HTML Tools Palette and choose Padding from the submenu to open the Padding dialog box (see Figure 149-2).

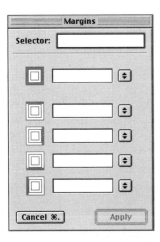

Figure 149-2: The Margins dialog box

6. As described just previously for the Padding dialog box, enter the selector in the Selector field and type margin values in the fields provided.

cross-reference

- To learn more about Cascading Style Sheet properties, see Part 9. For a discussion of CSS syntax, see the book's Web site at www.wiley .com/compbooks/ 10simplestepsorless.

Defining CSS Border Properties

Before CSS came into style, so to speak, the only HTML elements that could possess borders were tables and images. Now any element can possess a border. You can determine the width of an element's border, the border color, and the border style using BBEdit's CSS border tools. The properties defined for the selector are border-width, border-color, and border-style, respectively.

1. Place the cursor in the current document at the point you want to insert the style definition.

2. Click the CSS button on the HTML Tools Palette and choose Border from the submenu to open the Border dialog box (see Figure 150-1).

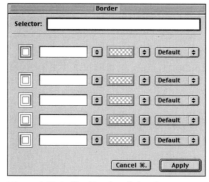

Figure 150-1: The Border dialog box

3. Enter the selector you're defining the property for in the Selector field.

4. Use the fields on the left side of the dialog box to enter border-width values, specifying units of measure with the pop-up menus directly to their right.

5. To specify border-color values, click the color pickers and make selections from the color palette. To select one of the 16 predefined color names, use the pop-up menus to the right of the color pickers.

6. To specify border-style values, make selections from the pop-up menus on the extreme right side of the dialog box.

7. To insert the values and close the dialog box, click the Apply button. The generated code is entered into the document (see Figure 150-2).

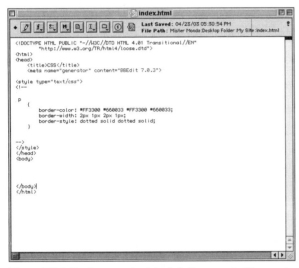

Figure 150-2: Border property style definitions applied to a page

tip

- To define values for all sides concurrently, use the first row of interface elements. To define values for any combination of sides, enter individual values in each of the subsequent fields — top, right, bottom, or left, as indicated by the field's icon on the left.

cross-reference

- BBEdit's color picker defaults to the Web-safe palette when first installed. To learn how to change the color picker preferences, see Task 158.

Defining CSS Box Properties

The box model of Cascading Style Sheets surrounds every element by a kind of rectangular "bull's-eye," with four zones radiating out from a central area that holds the element itself — text, image, table, or whatever. This central area is known as the *content area*. The next zone out from this is the *padding area* (governed by padding properties covered in Task 149), followed by the *border area* (Task 150), and then the *margin area* (Task 149 again). Instead of bundling the box properties into a single dialog box, BBEdit breaks them up for easier access but leaves the last five box properties (width, height, float, clear, and display) to themselves.

notes

▪ If you initially place the cursor within an existing style declaration, the corresponding selector appears in the Selector field and the properties you define are added to the existing declaration.

▪ If the element you assign a width or height to requires more space than the values allow, the element will override your settings.

1. Place the cursor in the current document at the point you want to insert the style definition. Click the CSS button on the HTML Tools Palette and choose Box from the submenu to open the Box dialog box (see Figure 151-1).

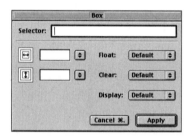

Figure 151-1: The Box dialog box

2. Enter the selector you're defining the property for in the Selector field.

3. To specify a width property, enter a value in the Width field and choose a unit of measure from the pop-up menu.

4. To specify a `height` property, enter a value in the Height field and choose a unit of measure from its pop-up menu.

5. To specify a `float` value, make a selection from the corresponding pop-up menu.

6. To specify a `clear` value, make a selection from the relevant pop-up menu.

7. To specify a `display` value, make a selection from the pop-up menu.

8. To close the dialog box, click the Apply button. The generated code is inserted into the document (see Figure 151-2).

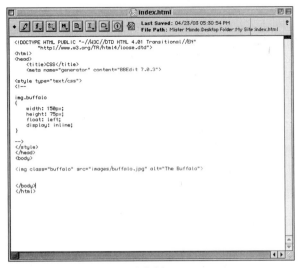

Figure 151-2: Box property definitions.

cross-reference

- Dreamweaver generates style sheet code using the Style Definition dialog box, which provides a single interface for defining all style properties. To learn more, see Part 15.

Validating HTML

BBEdit has a feature that debugs your HTML syntax and link references. This prevents you from creating code with errors or broken links that will affect the look of your page when you publish it to the Web. You can validate HTML on an individual document or on an entire folder or site.

1. To validate the current document's code, click the Check Syntax button on the HTML Tools Palette. If BBEdit finds any errors, the HTML Syntax Errors panel (see Figure 152-1) appears.

Figure 152-1: When BBEdit encounters errors, it displays the HTML Syntax Errors panel in the code window.

2. Click the warning or error in the upper portion of the dialog box to see the corresponding line of code displayed in the lower portion.

3. To make corrections to the code, double-click the error or warning to jump to the document containing the document. The line is highlighted in the document window.

4. To check the syntax of all documents in a given folder, click the Check button on the HTML Tools Palette and choose Folder Syntax from the submenu to display the Check Folder Syntax dialog box (see Figure 152-2).

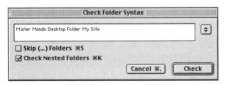

Figure 152-2: The Check Folder Syntax dialog box

5. By default the dialog box defaults to the folder containing the currently active document. To select a different folder, click the pop-up menu arrow to the right of the dialog box and choose Other. This opens the Choose a Folder dialog box in which you locate your folder.

6. Click the Check button in the Check Folder Syntax dialog box. Errors appear in the HTML Syntax Errors dialog box. Click to see the referenced code in the lower portion, and double-click to open the specified document at the indicated line to edit it.

7. To check an entire site's syntax, choose Site Syntax from the Check button's submenu to display the Check Site Syntax dialog box. It too defaults to the site of the currently active document. To switch sites, use the same pop-up menu mentioned in Step 5. Click the Check button in the Check Site Syntax dialog box to display errors in the HTML Syntax Errors dialog box as we previously discussed.

tip

- Along with various syntax checks, BBEdit checks links in the document, folder, and site. Run these checks from the Check button submenu. They operate identically to the syntax-checking discussed in these steps. If a hyperlink, image reference, or other attribute that accepts a pathname value comes up unresolved (because there's no corresponding file or the pathname is incorrect), BBEdit opens the HTML Link Errors dialog box (identical to the Syntax Error dialog box). Simply double-click the error to open the document and make the necessary edits.

cross-reference

- Macromedia Dreamweaver checks links automatically every time you rename a document or move a file. To learn more about Dreamweaver, see Part 15.

Task 153

Using BBEdit Utilities

BBEdit contains a number of practical utilities that help you add or remove markup tags quickly. Use Translate to mark up a plain-text document quickly with basic paragraph tags. Conversely, use Remove Markup to strip markup tags from an HTML document. You can also wrap content within comments and change the case of text.

1. To convert plain text to HTML, select the text in the document window, click the Utilities button on the HTML Tools Palette, and choose Translate from the submenu to open the Translate dialog box (see Figure 153-1).

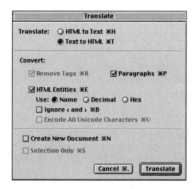

Figure 153-1: Converting plain text to HTML using the Translate dialog box

2. Click the Text to HTML option, choose your conversion parameters, and click the Translate button.

3. To strip all tags from a document, choose Remove Markup from the Utilities submenu.

4. To wrap content in comment tags (see Figure 153-2), select a range of content and choose Comment from the submenu.

Figure 153-2: Comment tags inserted using the Utilities submenu

5. To remove all comment tags from a document, choose Remove Comments from the submenu.

6. To convert all tags in a document to uppercase or lowercase, select the corresponding command from the Utilities submenu.

7. To specify what case BBEdit defaults to, open the HTML Preferences category of the BBEdit Preferences panel (see Figure 153-3) and click either the Upper Case or Lower Case radio button. You can then use the Normalize Tag Case command on the Utilities submenu to convert all tags to that choice.

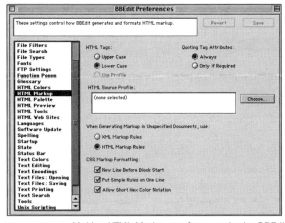

Figure 153-3: Making HTML Markup preferences in the BBEdit Preferences panel

tips

- Remove all markup from an HTML document to convert it to plain text.

- Selecting Uncomment removes comment tags from the current selection.

cross-reference

- Macromedia HomeSite 5 is another excellent text-based HTML editor. For more information, see Part 14.

Task **154**

Using Find and Replace

Your marketing department is sure to change their minds seven times today about some magic phrase they had you place in 200 locations on the company Web site before you finally crawled home to bed. Now you have to change it one more time — quickly. That's exactly where the Find and Replace tool is a real lifesaver.

1. Choose Search ➪ Find from the BBEdit menu bar to open the Find & Replace dialog box (see Figure 154-1).

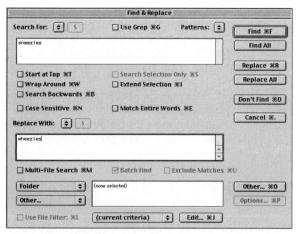

Figure 154-1: The Find & Replace dialog box

2. In the Search For field, enter the string you want to search for.

3. In the Replace With field, enter the string you want the found text to be replaced with.

4. Use the central check boxes to modify your search parameters as necessary.

5. To display the search results in a search results window (see Figure 154-2), select the Batch Find check box.

6. To return only the files that don't have the search string present, click the Exclude Matches check box.

7. Use the controls at the bottom part of the Find & Replace dialog box to specify the set of files to search.

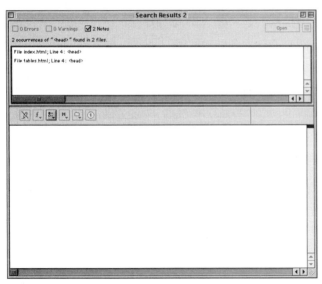

Figure 154-2: The Search Results window

8. To do a multifile search, click the Multi-File Search check box and make a selection from the pop-up menu beneath it to specify a category: Folder, Open Documents, or Web Site. Choose the specific folder or Web site from the second pop-up menu.

9. Click the Options button to display the Multi-File Search Options dialog box (see Figure 154-3). Choose the folder parameters and file types through which you want to search.

Figure 154-3: The Multi-File Search Options dialog box

10. Click the appropriate button on the right side of the dialog box (Find, Find All, Replace, or Replace All).

tips

- BBEdit remembers the last 12 find-and-replace terms you use each session. To repeat a recent choice, choose it from the pop-up menus above the Search For and Replace With fields. To paste the document's current selection into these fields, click the corresponding § button.

- If the folder you want to search is not in the pop-up menu, choose Other and select the folder from the Choose a Folder dialog box. You can also drag a folder from the Finder directly into the path box at the bottom of the Find & Replace dialog box.

cross-reference

- For UNIX fans, BBEdit supports grep searches. To learn more, see the BBEdit user manual at www.barebones.com/support/bbedit/.

Working with File Groups

For those situations where you find yourself working with a large number of related Web pages, consider using a file group. Creating a file group generates a small BBEdit file that references the files and directories comprising the group. When you access the file group, BBEdit opens the corresponding files and folders for easy editing.

1. To create a file group, choose File ➪ New ➪ File Group from the BBEdit menu bar to display a new file group window (see Figure 155-1).

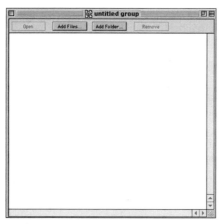

Figure 155-1: A new file group window

2. To add files to the file group, click the Add Files button to display an Open dialog box or drag a file into the file group window from the Finder.

3. To add folders to a file group, click the Add Folder button. This opens the Add Folder to Group dialog box:

4. Click Choose to locate a folder in the Open dialog box or drag it from the Finder into the field on the left. Click Add to complete the selection and close the dialog box.

5. To save the file group, choose File ➪ Save from the menu bar and save the file group to a chosen location.

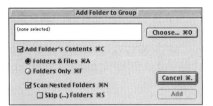

Figure 155-2: The Add Folder to Group dialog box

6. To open a file group, choose File ⇨ Open from the menu bar.

7. To access files and folders in the File Group window, simply double-click them or select them and click the Open button. Files are opened in a document window, while folders are opened in disk browser windows (see Figure 155-3).

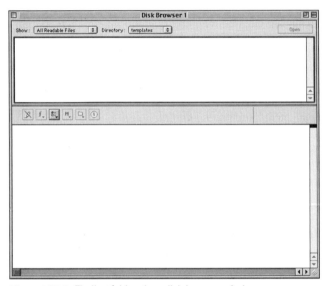

Figure 155-3: Finding folders in a disk browser window

8. To remove a file or folder from a file group, drag it into the Trash or select it and click the Remove button.

tip
- Use the check boxes and radio button to choose folder, files, or both.

cross-reference
- Helios Software's TextPad (see Part 12) and Macromedia HomeSite (see Part 14) both offer similar functionality for Windows users.

Setting Menu Keys

Each function in the HTML Tools Palette we've covered here in Part 13 is mirrored as a command on the Markup menu. BBEdit makes it easy to define keyboard shortcuts ("equivalents") for them.

1. Choose Edit ➪ Set Menu Keys from the BBEdit menu bar to open the Set Menu Keys dialog box (see Figure 156-1).

Figure 156-1: The Set Menu Keys dialog box

2. To access the commands for the Markup menu, scroll down and click the disclosure triangle next to Markup (see Figure 156-2).

3. To add a menu key, select a command and click the Set button. This displays the Set Key dialog box (see Figure 156-3).

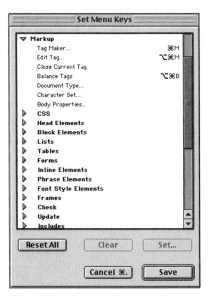

Figure 156-2: Exposing the various Markup commands

tip
- You know you've made a typo when the code coloring turns solid. You can customize those colors (see Task 157).

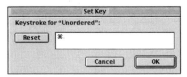

Figure 156-3: Creating a keyboard shortcut in the Set Key dialog box

4. Type a key combination and click OK. If the key combination is in use already, a prompt tells you which keystroke it's currently assigned to and asks if you want to replace it (see Figure 156-4).

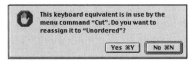

Figure 156-4: A keyboard shortcut already in use

5. To reset an accepted keystroke, click the Reset button and try another keystroke combination.

cross-references
- Helios Software's TextPad (see Part 12) offers similar menu key-setting functionality.

- If you want to use a WYSIWYG HTML editor for the Mac, try Macromedia Dreamweaver MX (see Part 15) at www .macromedia.com/ software/dreamweaver.

Modifying Color Syntax Checking

BBEdit allows you to modify the colors it uses to color the HTML code. Although there is no objective, functional benefit to changing these colors, doing so gives you the freedom to impose your personal style (favorite colors, etc.) on your editing environment.

note

- This topic isn't about coding per se but you should make a habit of commenting code. Code needs to be legible to humans and machines alike.

1. To enable color syntax checking, open the BBEdit Preferences panel by choosing Edit ⇨ Preferences from the menu bar or pressing Command+; on the keyboard. Choose Editor Defaults to view these options (see Figure 157-1). Make sure you click the Syntax Coloring check box.

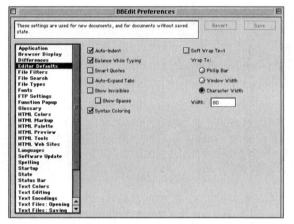

Figure 157-1: Setting the code editor's default preferences

2. To modify the colors used in syntax-checking, choose Text Colors in the BBEdit Preferences panel (see Figure 157-2) to view these options.

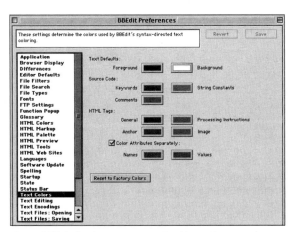

Figure 157-2: Setting the syntax-checking colors

Task **157**

3. To modify the background color, select a new color from the Background color picker.

4. To modify HTML tags, select a new color from the General color picker.

5. To change the color of comment tags, select a new color from the Comments color picker.

6. To change the color of `<a>` tags, select a new color from the Anchor color picker.

7. To change the color of `<img>` tags, select a new color from the Image color picker.

8. To assign unique colors to attributes, click the Color Attributes Separately check box, Assign attribute colors with the Names color picker and values with the Values color picker.

9. To save your changes, click the Save button in the upper right and then close the BBEdit Preferences panel.

tip

- A text editor is something you could find yourself staring at for a long time when the HTML bug really grabs you. Use colors that don't make you bug-eyed.

cross-reference

- Color syntax-checking is standard in most editors. TextPad (see Part 12), Macromedia HomeSite (see Part 14), Macromedia Dreamweaver (see Part 15), and Microsoft FrontPage (see Part 16) all use it.

Task 158

Modifying HTML Color Preferences

By default, BBEdit's color picker uses a 216-color, Web-safe palette. These 216 colors are guaranteed not to shift or dither on any platform, running any browser, when running in 8-bit color mode. There's just one small problem with that: Personal computers advanced beyond 8-bit color nearly a decade ago. Consequently, using colors outside the Web-safe palette isn't as risky as it was in 1995. For this reason, you may want to change BBEdit's color picker to gain a little leeway.

1. Choose Edit ⇨ Preferences from the menu bar or press Command+; to open the BBEdit Preferences panel. Select HTML Colors (see Figure 158-1) to view those options.

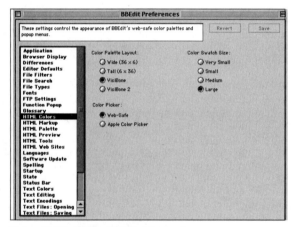

Figure 158-1: Making HTML color preferences

2. Under Color Picker, click Apple Color Picker. The next time you invoke a color picker, the Apple color opens (see Figure 158-2).

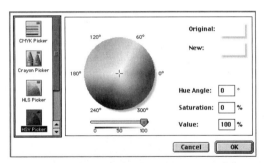

Figure 158-2: The Apple Color Picker

3. In the Apple Color Picker, scroll down the list of options on the left side and select the HTML Picker (see Figure 158-3).

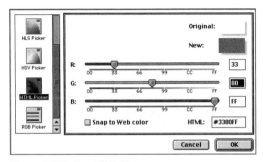

Figure 158-3: The HTML Picker

4. Use the RGB sliders to specify levels of red, green, and blue. Corresponding hexadecimal color values appear in the HTML field.

5. To restrain the sliders to a Web-safe palette, click the Snap to Web Color check box.

6. Once you choose a color, click OK to close the dialog box and insert the color value.

tip

▪ If you prefer to use the Web-safe color picker, you can display it horizontally or vertically, and in various swatch sizes. Choosing the VisiBone or VisiBone 2 option in the BBEdit Preferences panel displays the color picker as a square swatch radiating out from the center in order of hue.

cross-reference

▪ To learn more about color and the Web, see the book's Web site at www.wiley.com/compbooks/10simplestepsorless.

Part 14: Working with HomeSite

Exploring the HomeSite Environment

At first glance, Macromedia HomeSite 5 looks like a simple text editor — a place to type your HTML code, save your files, and create other types of code that are added to your HTML document. Looks can be deceiving, however. HomeSite is a very powerful program that offers a variety of automated features, views, tools, and commands found throughout a fairly complex (yet easy to use) interface. In this task, you take a tour of that interface, checking out each of the main areas of the workspace and learning to navigate HomeSite efficiently. If you'd like to give HomeSite a test-drive, go to the Macromedia Web site (www.macromedia.com) and download an evaluation version. It will only work for 30 days, after which you must purchase the application in order to keep using it.

note

- HomeSite is not a WYSI-WYG ("what you see is what you get") design tool like Dreamweaver is. If you want to access Dreamweaver's graphical interface to do your design work or to enhance a page you've started in HomeSite, click the Open Macromedia Dreamweaver button at the foot of the Editor's toolbar.

1. Display HomeSite's screen tips. Hover your mouse over the buttons on the main toolbars, on all the tabs on the right side (top) of the window, and across the bottom of the left-most panel. Figure 159-1 shows the entire workspace.

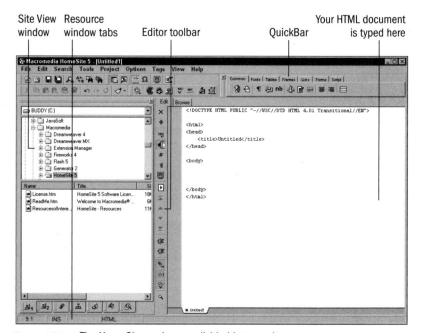

Figure 159-1: The HomeSite workspace divided into sections

2. Click the Help button (the purple book with a "?" on it) among the tabs at the bottom of the Resource panel. The Help tools appear (see Figure 159-2).

3. Click the Projects tab on the Resource panel to see your project files and folders.

4. To see a tree-like display of your project files, click the Site View tab, also found in the Resource panel. Figure 159-3 shows an index page (Home Page) and two subpages (About Us and Contact Us).

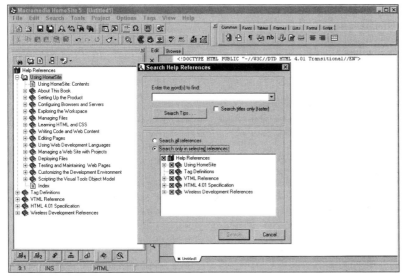

Figure 159-2: Click the plus signs next to the various topic groups to find the help you need.

tips

- Click the Search button (the one with the tiny binoculars in the top tool bar) to search the help files using keywords or phrases.

- You can insert a set of paragraph tags by pressing Shift+Ctrl+P. Any time there's a shortcut for a command, you'll find it in the menu.

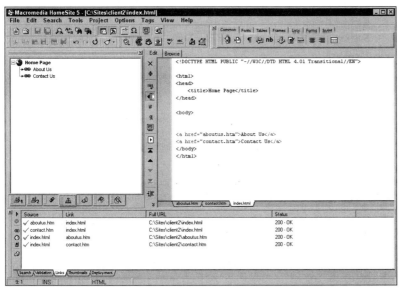

Figure 159-3: Use the view in the upper left to get a sense of the relationship among your pages and to establish links between them.

cross-reference

- BBEdit provides a similar set of tools for Mac users. Learn to insert tags quickly in Part 13.

5. Experiment with the Quickbar. Click the Fonts tab (also called the Fonts toolbar) to see your text formatting tools and then check out the Tables tab (Tables toolbar).

Creating a New Project

In HomeSite, a project is the same as a site. It's called a project because, typically, the development of a Web site — rather than just a few ad hoc pages — is a project unto itself. If you think about a project as being a site, you'll find it very easy to understand HomeSite's tools.

1. Choose Project ➪ New Project. The New Project dialog box opens (see Figure 160-1).

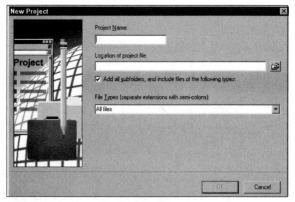

Figure 160-1: Starting a new project

2. Type a name for your project in the Project Name field.

3. Type or browse to the location of the project folders. If you click the yellow folder button at the right end of the Location of Project File field, the Select Directory dialog box opens (see Figure 160-2).

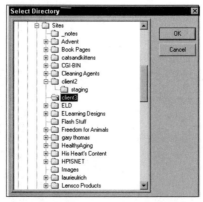

Figure 160-2: Selecting a directory for your project and its files and subfolders

4. Click a directory (or folder) where you want to store your project files and click OK. The project files will appear in the Projects tab of the Resource panel (see Figure 160-3).

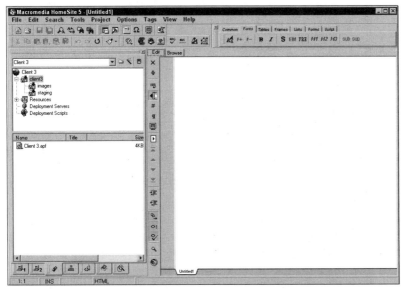

Figure 160-3: The main project folder and two subfolders are ready to store the HTML documents and other files you create and use with the project.

tips

- Creating a real project in HomeSite is important for when you later want to upload your site's files to a Web server. If you just create a group of linked pages, you will make more work for yourself when it comes time later to establish a workable folder structure on the Web server to run your Web site.

- Because the Select Directory dialog box offers no "New Folder" button, you should create the project folder before beginning this process. You can do this in Windows Explorer or any other file-management tool.

- When setting up your project folders, be sure to create an images folder as well as a site_content folder for storing non-HTML documents containing text that you may use on your Web pages. The images folder, obviously, is the repository for all images used in your Web pages.

cross-reference

- Setting up a site in FrontPage is a very similar process. See Part 16.

Organizing a Project with Folders

O nce you've set up a project, you can add folders to the project folder, creating a filing system for your HTML documents, images, and site content files (documents, worksheets, and other files that your client may send you or that you may accumulate yourself). Although the number of folders you can create is unlimited, don't add so many folders and subfolders that you create a filing system that's difficult to manage, navigate, and understand.

1. With the Projects tab displayed in the Resources panel, right-click the main project folder. A submenu appears (see Figure 161-1).

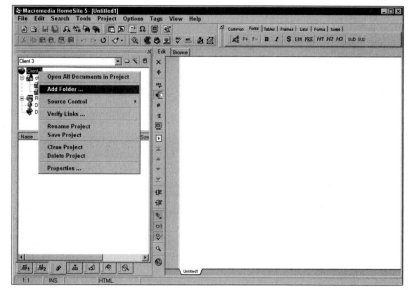

Figure 161-1: Accessing folder-related tools by right-clicking your existing folders

2. To create a new subfolder for your projects folder, choose Add Folder. The Add a Project Folder dialog box opens (see Figure 161-2).

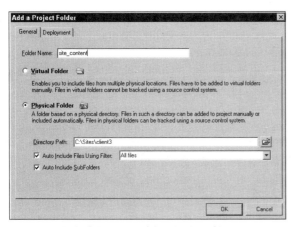

Figure 161-2: Defining a new folder in HomeSite

3. In the Add a Project Folder dialog box, click the Folder Name text box and type a name for the folder. The name should be in lowercase and contain no spaces or punctuation.

4. Click the Physical Folder option.

5. As needed, type or browse to (using the browse button) the Directory Path that contains your folder.

6. Click the Auto Include Files Using Filter option and leave All Files selected.

7. Click the Auto Include Subfolders option if it's not already selected.

8. Click OK to create the folder.

tips

- These folder-naming rules exist so that any server that could host these folders would be able to support them. Some servers don't allow capital letters in names and, for the Web, using underscores instead of spaces (as in "site_content" rather than "site content") helps prevent problems later on.

- The same shortcut menu that allowed you to add folders can be used to delete them, too. Right-click an unwanted folder (from within the Project tab of the Resource panel) and choose Remove Folder. No dialog box results — the folder is simply deleted.

cross-reference

- Creating folders to store site files is easy in Dreamweaver, too. Check Part 15 for all the details.

Starting a New HomeSite Document

After you create your project and build your folders to store HTML documents and related files, you can start your first HomeSite document. This task shows you how to start a new page, work within the automatically-inserted tags, and begin entering page content.

notes

■ The text between the
  `<title>` tags appears
  in the title bar of the
  browser when it displays
  your Web page.

■ Choose `<h1>` (Heading 1),
  `<h2>` (Heading 2), or
  `<h3>` (Heading 3) tags in
  the Tags menu. Once the
  heading tags are inserted,
  add the actual heading text
  between them.

1. With your project displayed in the Project tab of the Resource panel, choose File ➪ New. The New Document dialog box opens (see Figure 162-1).

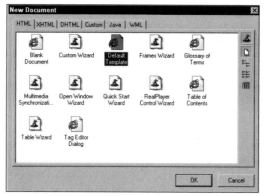

Figure 162-1: Picking the kind of page you want to create

2. Double-click the Default Template icon. This creates a new HTML document with the starting tags already inserted (see Figure 162-2).

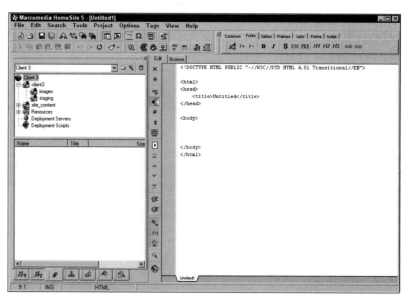

Figure 162-2: The starting page with <html> and <body> tags already in place

3. Once the page is onscreen, enter a title for the page between the `<title> </title>` tags.

4. Click inside the `<head> </head>` tags to insert your `<meta>` tags, where you include the keyword or description text.

5. Click between the `<body> </body>` tags to begin building your page and inserting text and graphics. Use the Tags menu to choose from some commonly used tags (see Figure 162-3).

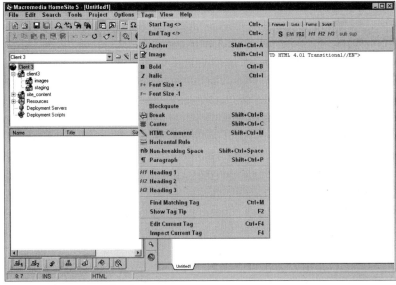

Figure 162-3: Inserting heading tags so you can enter your first heading text and format it

tips

- Choosing File ➪ New Document opens a blank document with no tags built in at all. If you prefer this, use this method instead of choosing the default template.

- To help people find your site in search engines, provide keywords and description text in `<meta>` tags. Search engines use this text, along with body text, to categorize your site.

cross-reference

- TextPad offers automatic tag insertion tools. Find out more about them in Part 12.

Creating and Using Web Page Templates

When you start a new document with the default template, your HTML document already contains some basic tags. This is more helpful than starting out with a blank document; otherwise you must insert all tags manually. The benefit of using templates is that they do some of the work for you. The same goes for templates that do a lot of the work for you. Instead of repeatedly building pages that contain many of the same elements you want to appear throughout your Web site, just save one file as a template and create the others from it. Doing so will save you from having to reinvent the wheel every time you create a page for your Web site.

1. Build a Web page that contains the components you could use to start another page for the same Web site (see Figure 163-1).

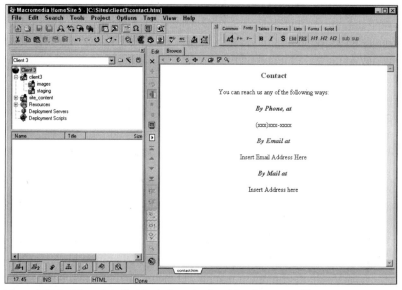

Figure 163-1: A template that includes a basic table with text and images you can replace later

2. To save a page that contains the necessary elements with which to create subsequent Web pages, choose File ➪ Save As Template.

3. In the Save as Template dialog box, type a name for your template (see Figure 163-2).

Figure 163-2: Saving your template with a descriptive name

4. To use a template that you or someone else already created, choose File ➪ New and click the Custom tab in the New Document dialog box (see Figure 163-3).

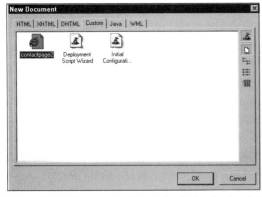

Figure 163-3: User-created templates in the Custom tab

5. Select the template and click OK to see it appear as a new, untitled page.

tips

- When you build a template, don't just think of pages you build all the time; consider any special pages that you build at least once in most of your projects, such as a Contacts page or a frameset with a particular layout. Templates speed you through basic page development.

- Because a new document is based merely on the underlying template, changes you make to the document have no effect on the template. To edit a template, start a new document based on it, make your changes, and then save it as a template, giving it the same name as the existing file. This ensures that your modified version replaces the existing one.

cross-reference

- Learn to create and use FrontPage templates in Part 16.

Inserting and Converting Files

HomeSite makes it easy to incorporate an existing HTML document into an open file. You can also insert a text file or other type of document into a Web page.

1. To insert an existing HTML document into the one you're currently working on, click where you want the inserted document's code to start.

2. Choose File ➪ Insert File. In the Open dialog box, navigate to the file you want to insert (see Figure 164-1).

Figure 164-1: Finding the HTML file you want to insert into your open document

3. Double-click the file you want to insert in your existing document.

4. To add content to your file by converting another file, such as a text (.txt) file, to HTML first and then inserting it, click where the new content should go.

5. Choose File ➪ Convert File.

6. In the Open dialog box navigate to the file you want to convert, such as a comma or tab-delimited text file. Click Open to insert the file (see Figure 164-2).

note

- By default the Files of Type setting is All Web Documents. Click the drop-down list to see everything from HTML to TXT files.

caution

- You may have to do some serious formatting to make the converted text useful after it's inserted. For example, delimited data won't appear in a nice grid, nor will it be placed automatically in a table (as it would if you used Dreamweaver to import tabular data; see Part 15).

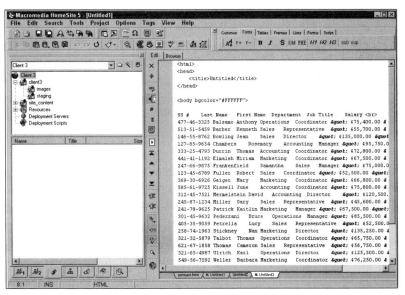

Figure 164-2: Converted text file inserted into an open HTML document

7. Once your text is inserted, edit the text as desired and apply formatting using <font> tags and related attributes (see Figure 164-3).

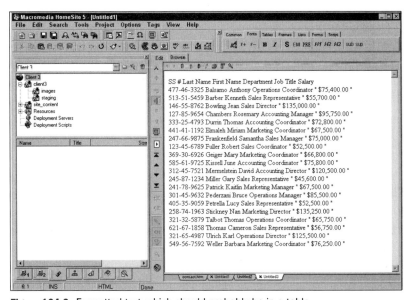

Figure 164-3: Formatted text, which should probably be in a table

tip

- You may have to strip out redundant tags, such as extra <html> or <body> tags; you only need one set per HTML page. HomeSite's CodeSweeper gets rid of extraneous or redundant code (see Task 166).

cross-reference

- Speaking of Dreamweaver's tools for converting delimited text file data and putting it in a table, see Part 15 to find out more.

Finding and Inserting Tags and Attributes

Even if you know HTML like the back of your hand, you needn't always type it out. The Tags menu contains many tags and attributes that you can insert with the click of a button.

1. In an open document, click where you want to insert a tag or attribute. Figure 165-1 shows `<font>` tags in need of the bold attribute and some text to display in bold.

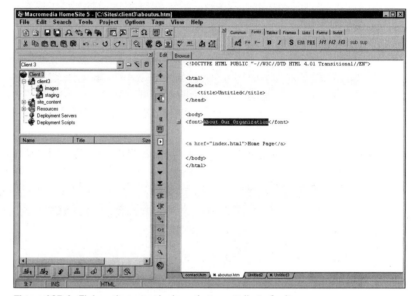

Figure 165-1: Elaborating a tag by inserting an attribute for it

2. Click the Tags menu to display the tags and attributes that you can insert (see Figure 165-2).

3. Click the tag or attribute you want to insert from the menu. It appears where your cursor was positioned (see Figure 165-3).

4. As needed, insert your text between the tags/attributes.

5. Continue inserting tags and attributes from the Tags menu, as needed.

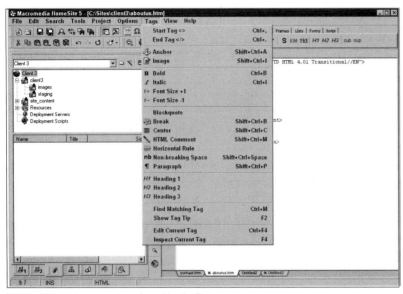

Figure 165-2: Common tags found in the Tags menu

tip

- Unless you're working with one of the few tags that don't require a closing tag, be sure to place your cursor between the opening and closing tags before inserting an attribute. If you're inserting a tag, watch your placement and be sure that if you're within another set of tags, that they won't conflict or cancel each other out.

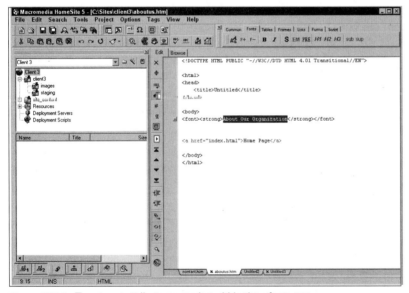

Figure 165-3: The strong attribute appearing within the <font> tag

cross-reference

- TextPad offers some automatic tag insertion commands. Find out more about them in Part 12.

Cleaning Code with CodeSweeper

CodeSweeper does just what its name implies. It sweeps code, cleaning out redundancies and getting rid of extraneous code inserted by various development tools. You can choose which sort of code to sweep (you'll be sweeping HTML here) and then let the CodeSweeper do its thing.

1. Open a document that needs sweeping and make it visible in the Edit tab of the main window. Choose Tools ➪ CodeSweeper.

2. From the submenu (see Figure 166-1), choose the language you want CodeSweeper to sweep. Here choose HTML CodeSweeper (Optimized for HTML Only).

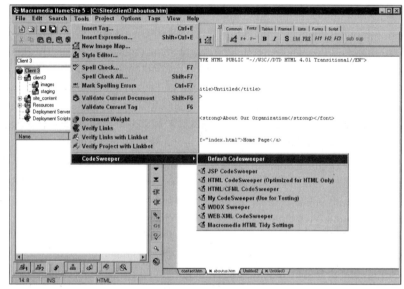

Figure 166-1: You can sweep HTML, JSP, Web-XML, and WDDX.

3. In the CodeSweeper dialog box (see Figure 166-2), click Run CodeSweeper. Figures 166-3 and 166-4 show before and after views of a code page that's been "swept."

Figure 166-2: Click Run CodeSweeper to continue the process.

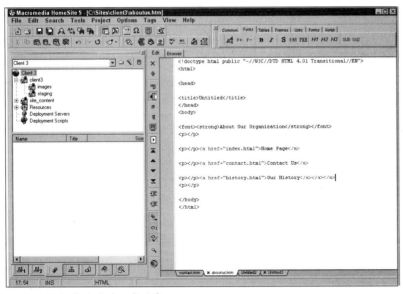

Figure 166-3: Code before CodeSweeper

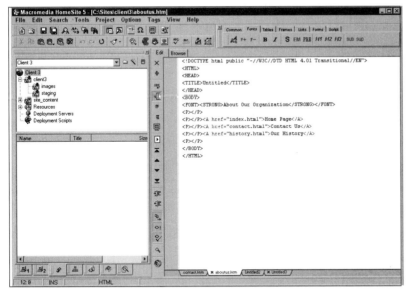

Figure 166-4: Same code after CodeSweeper

4. To clean up a document that you developed in Macromedia Dreamweaver, select Tools ➪ CodeSweeper ➪ Macromedia HTML Tidy Settings. The same CodeSweeper dialog box appears, with Run or Configure buttons. If you choose to run the CodeSweeper, your Dreamweaver-created code will be cleaned up.

cross-reference

• TextPad offers many tools that assist in cleaning up code. Check them out in Part 12.

Task 167

Editing Cascading Style Sheets with the Style Editor

The Style Editor utilizes a third-party program called TopStyle Lite. Through this program, you can view and edit Cascading Style Sheets (CSS) and save them for use in your HTML documents.

note

- Once you've edited and saved a .css document, copy it to your Project folder and make use of it in any of your project files by invoking it through your HTML code.

1. Click the Style Editor button, which you can find on the toolbar shown in Figure 167-1. TopStyle Lite opens (see Figure 167-2). The application window consists of a large panel where the CSS appears, a Preview panel area below that, and a two-tabbed section on the right for viewing the details of your style sheet.

Style Editor button

Figure 167-1: Next-to-last in the toolbar is the Style Editor button

Start a new file

View style sheet here

Add new selectors

Word wrap

Toggle style inspector

Save

Toggle preview on and off

Preview style sheet effects

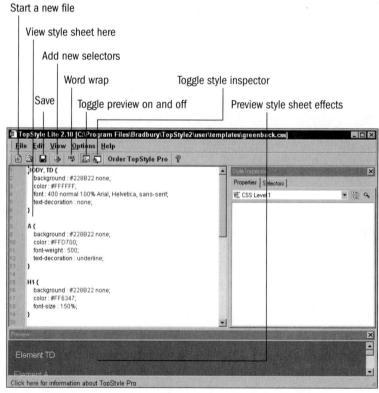

Figure 167-2: Opening a style sheet and viewing it in the TopStyle workspace

2. Choose File ➪ Open to select a style sheet to edit. The Open dialog box (see Figure 167-3) lists only files with a .css extension, by default.

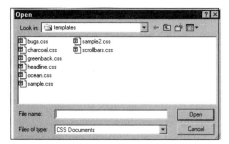

Figure 167-3: Choosing the CSS file you want to view

3. Edit the style sheet, as desired. Use the New Selector button or type directly in the panel displaying the style sheet.

4. To save your changes to the style sheet, select File ➪ Save. This overwrites the existing version. To preserve the original version and create a second version that reflects your latest changes, choose File ➪ Save As. This opens the Save As dialog box. Give the CSS file a new name or choose a new location (like your Project folder) in which to save it.

tip

• Experts recommend purchasing TopStyle Pro, a more elaborate version of TopStyle Lite. If your CSS needs are simple, however, or if you find that you know CSS well enough to create style sheets on your own without any automation or extra tools, you'll be happy with TopStyle Lite.

cross-reference

• A comprehensive set of CSS skills is offered in Part 9 and Appendix D, found on the Web site at www.wiley.com/ compbooks/ 10simplestepsorless.

Previewing in External Browsers

Previewing Web pages in an actual browser window (rather than just through HomeSite's Browse tab) is an essential step in the Web design process. As you work in a text-based development environment like HomeSite, viewing pages, images, formatting, and all visual elements is key to spotting mistakes, seeing the need for layout changes, and recognizing opportunities perhaps to use more color, different fonts, more or fewer graphics, and to test animated GIFs and movie files on your page. By previewing your files in actual browsers, you help ensure that what you designed is what your visitors actually see.

1. Choose Options ➪ Configure External Browsers.

2. In the External Browsers dialog box, view the currently selected browsers (see Figure 168-1).

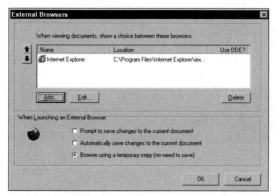

Figure 168-1: Seeing which browsers you have installed, and which ones you need to add

3. Assuming you want to add a browser, click the Add button and use the Browser dialog box (see Figure 168-2) to select a new browser.

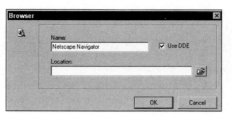

Figure 168-2: Selecting a browser to add to the list

caution

▪ The Automatically Save Changes to the Current Document option is risky. You could end up saving a file, only to find out later that you preferred an earlier version.

4. In the Name box, type the name by which you want to list the browser when you click the View External Browser List button or open the External Browsers dialog box. Click OK.

5. Back in the External Browsers dialog box, choose one of three options affecting how external browsers are launched. Your best choice is to leave the default (third option) selected.

6. If you want to rename or redirect the path to a browser application — perhaps to open a more recent (or older) version than the one you set up — select one of the listed browsers and click the Edit button. The aforementioned Browser dialog box opens, showing the settings for the selected browser, which you can edit right there.

7. Click OK to return to the External Browsers dialog box.

8. Repeat Steps 3 through 5 for any other browsers you wish to add to your External Browsers list. In order to set them up, make sure they are installed on your computer.

9. To preview your page in a selected browser, be sure the page is open and in Edit view. Click the View List of External Browsers button (see Figure 168-3). Choose a browser from the list. Your page will appear in the appropriate browser window.

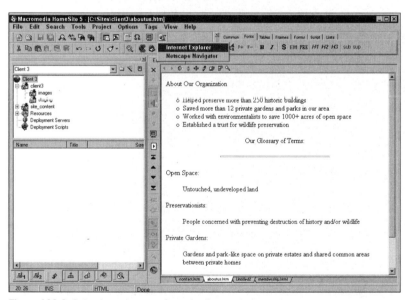

Figure 168-3: Selecting a browser from the list

tips

▪ Make sure you have at least two browsers installed, Internet Explorer and Netscape. Additional browsers are great; so is loading multiple versions of a browser. Testing your pages on computers with alternate versions of browsers is a great way to troubleshoot your pages in old and new versions.

▪ If you want to be prompted to save the HTML file before previewing it, choose the first option. If not, leave the last one (the default, Browse Using a Temporary Copy) selected.

▪ Browsers appear in the order you installed them. Use the blue up and down arrows to move the selected browser (click it to select it) up or down the list. The one listed in this dialog box is the first one listed in the View List of External Browser button's drop-down list.

cross-reference

▪ Read about Dreamweaver's tools for previewing Web pages in a browser, in Part 15.

Formatting Body Text

In Part 2 you learned how to format text in HTML. In this task, you learn how to format text using the Fonts tab in HomeSite. You can enhance your code with a single click of a button.

1. In an open document, select the body text you wish to format. If the text is not there, type it in first or refer to Task 164, "Inserting and Converting Files." You can also copy and paste text from word-processing documents as needed.

2. Click the Fonts toolbar (see Figure 169-1).

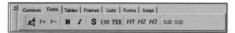

Figure 169-1: Thirteen different formatting options appear on the Fonts tab.

3. To apply a new font, click the Font button (the first button) and view the Tag Editor - FONT dialog box (see Figure 169-2).

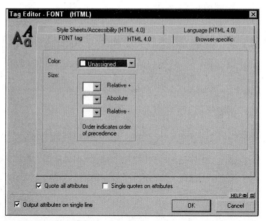

Figure 169-2: Choose your font and its attributes through the Tag Editor dialog box.

4. On the FONT Tag tab, select a color for the font and choose a size by selecting Relative+, Absolute, or Relative– values.

5. Click the Browser-Specific tab to see whether there are any issues for your particular installed browsers. In Figure 169-3, it appears that Netscape needs a point-size equivalent for the font size chosen in the FONT Tag tab. Enter a number to satisfy this requirement.

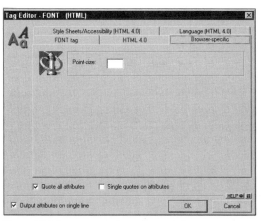

Figure 169-3: Entering information that your installed browsers require

6. Use the HTML 4.0 tab (see Figure 169-4) to select individual fonts, font combinations (using the Combo field), and Generic fonts.

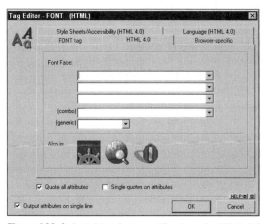

Figure 169-4: Satisfying font specifications for HTML 4.0

7. Work with the remaining tabs like Language and Style Sheets/ Accessibility (for assigning a style sheet to the font) as needed. For most simple text formatting, however, Steps 1 through 8 more than suffice.

8. Click OK to return to the document and Fonts toolbar.

9. Click the buttons for any formatting you wish to apply. As you click any of these buttons, the proper attributes appear in the code.

tip

- If you paste text from a word-processing document, any formatting that may already appear there will not appear in the text in HomeSite. To recreate the formatting you had, you have to use HomeSite's formatting tools.

cross-reference

- Learn about writing your own HTML code (without the help of buttons) in Part 1.

Creating Lists

There are four types of lists you can create in HomeSite and two ways to create them. Creating a Quick List uses a dialog box to establish the type of list you're creating. You can also create lists from existing body text.

1. To create a list from scratch and format it at the same time, start by clicking in the document where the list should begin.

2. Click the Lists toolbar (see Figure 170-1).

Figure 170-1: The Lists toolbar provides a quick set of list-creation tools.

3. Click the Quick List button (the first one on the bar). The List dialog box opens (see Figure 170-2).

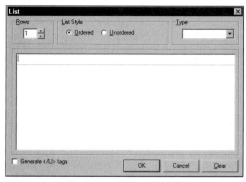

Figure 170-2: Typing and formatting your list in the List dialog box

4. In the Rows field, enter the number of rows in your list, or click the up and down triangles to increment or decrement the default of 1.

5. Choose a List Style: Ordered or Unordered.

6. Choose a Type. The list of items shown depends on whether you choose Ordered or Unordered in Step 5.

7. In the large text box in the middle of the dialog box, click to start typing your list. Type each item in the list and press Enter after each item to start a new line.

8. Click the Generate </LI> Tags check box to set this option.

9. Click OK to create the list. The results appear in Figure 170-3.

note

- If you choose Ordered, a list of numbers (Roman and Arabic) and letters (upper- and lowercase) appears. If you choose Unordered, you get three bullet choices: disc, square, or circle.

caution

- View your page in a browser to make sure your list is properly constructed before you create any similar lists in the document, and certainly before copying the page to a public Web site.

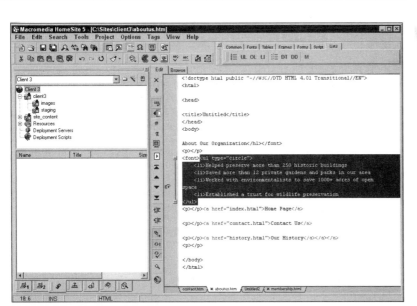

Figure 170-3: The code for a list (and the list itself) is generated and inserted into the document.

10. To convert lines of text you've already typed into a list, select them and click any of the remaining buttons on the Lists tab. A definition list, created from existing text, appears in Figure 170-4.

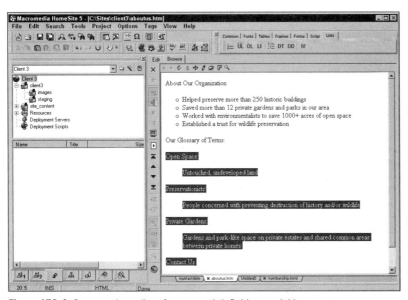

Figure 170-4: Constructing a list of terms and definitions quickly

cross-reference

- Learn about creating lists in a graphical design environment like FrontPage. Check out Part 16.

Checking the Spelling

There aren't too many things more embarrassing than publishing something on the Web that contains a spelling error or typo. Publishing the mistake to a potential audience in the thousands or millions is unthinkable. To avoid this possibility, always use whatever proofing tools you have at your disposal to check your spelling. HomeSite's tool checks for and fixes errors in a selected range of text or across an entire Web page. If you're not sure about certain esoteric or industry-specific terms, flag the (potential) errors with the Mark Spelling Errors command and correct them later after you've consulted a dictionary or online reference.

1. To check the spelling of a selected range of text, start by selecting the text to be checked — drag through it with your mouse and avoid selecting any adjacent tags (see Figure 171-1).

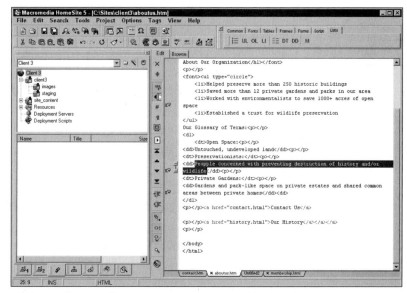

Figure 171-1: Restricting your spell check to a specific portion of text

2. Choose Tools ⇨ Spell Check. The Spell Check dialog box opens (see Figure 171-2) with the first spelling error selected (highlighted in the document and displayed in the dialog box).

note

- You can use the Ignore and Ignore All buttons if you know the word is spelled correctly. This usually applies to names, product names, serial numbers, and foreign words.

caution

- Use the Add button with care. Clicking it adds the allegedly misspelled word to your custom dictionary, which is checked, right along with the main dictionary, each time a spell check is run. If you add a misspelled word to it, you won't be alerted if you use that same misspelling again.

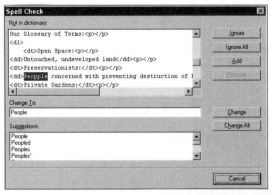

Figure 171-2: Errors shown in context as well as in the Spell Check dialog box

3. Look in the Change To text box. If the word there is the correct spelling, click the Change button next to it. If not, look at the list of words in the Suggestions list, pick one, and then click Change.

4. If none of the suggested words is right, type your own correction in the Change To box and click Change.

5. When all misspelled words have been displayed and either changed, ignored, or added to the dictionary, a prompt appears, telling you the statistics for the spell check session (see Figure 171-3). Click OK.

Figure 171-3: Spell check statistics — how much text was checked and how many mistakes found and corrected — appear at the end of a spell check session.

6. To check your entire page, click anywhere in the text (don't select anything specific) and choose Tools ⇨ Spell Check. Repeat Steps 3 through 5.

7. To check the spelling in your entire project, choose Tools ⇨ Spell Check All. Each document will be opened and checked, one at a time, until all documents have been checked and all errors resolved.

tips

- If there are no spelling errors within the selected text, a prompt informs you so.

- If you think you repeated the same mistake in a document, click Change All. If the other errors are in the selected range of text, they'll be corrected at the same time.

- If your project (site) has many, many pages, you may want to check the spelling in each page individually. Otherwise, you could be in for a very lengthy spell check session as each and every page is checked by Spell Check All.

cross-reference

- Learn about TextPad's spell checking tools in Part 12.

Adding a Horizontal Rule

A horizontal rule is a line that extends across your Web page. Its width and thickness are determined by attributes you apply, and its placement is determined by where you insert the tag, either directly or using a menu command.

1. Click wherever you want the rule to appear, relative to the existing content on the page.

2. Select Tags ⇨ Horizontal Rule. The Tag Editor - HR dialog box opens (see Figure 172-1).

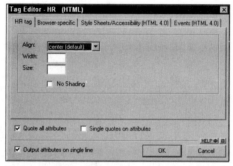

Figure 172-1: The Tag Editor - HR dialog box establishes the appearance and placement of horizontal rules

3. In the HR Tag tab, choose an Align setting. Center is the default, although you can choose Left or Right, depending on your page's layout.

4. Set the Width of the line, meaning how far across the page the rule runs. Enter a percentage, such as **50** for a rule that runs half the width of the page.

5. Enter the size in pixels, indicating the thickness of the rule.

6. Click the No Shading option if you don't want a chiseled, shaded line (which you get by default on lines in excess of 1 pixel).

7. Click OK to create the rule code (see Figure 172-2).

caution

- Only Internet Explorer supports colored horizontal rules. If you want, click the Browser Specific tab before exiting the Tag Editor dialog box and select a color for the border. In Netscape (and presumably other browsers), the line will be gray.

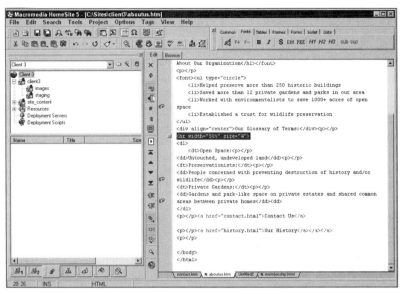

Figure 172-2: The <hr> tag inserted to create the line you want

Figure 172-3 shows the Browse preview of the page.

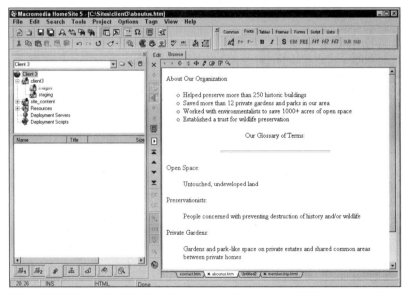

Figure 172-3: The horizontal rule as it appears on the page

tip

- Horizontal rules are a handy element to use when separating paragraphs of text (with more than simply a blank line) or to divide a page into conceptual sections. Thin lines create a subtle effect; thick lines are more dramatic.

cross-reference

- You can create a horizontal rule with FrontPage, quickly and easily. See Part 16 for more information.

Searching an HTML Document

Missing something? Can't find where someone's name appears on a given Web page, or where you used a particular image or applied a specific color? HomeSite has tools for looking for any text — body text, a tag, an attribute, a value — and displaying all occurrences it finds.

1. To look for text within an open document, choose Search ➪ Find or click the Find button on the toolbar (see Figure 173-1).

Find   Extended Find

Figure 173-1: The Magnifying glass works the searching tool.

2. In the Find dialog box (see Figure 173-2), enter the text, number, or tag you're looking for.

Figure 173-2: Search for a name, number, or piece of code.

3. Customize your search by clicking the Match Whole Words or Match Case options.

4. Choose the Direction for your search, Up or Down, based on your current cursor position.

5. Click Find Next to find the first occurrence of the text you're looking for. As each instance is found, click outside the dialog box to edit or delete the text directly and then click back inside the dialog box to activate it, and click Find Next to go to the next occurrence.

6. To do a more elaborate find, click the Extended Find button on the main toolbar, or choose Search ⇨ Extended Find.

7. In the resulting Extended Find dialog box (see Figure 173-3), type the text you're looking for in the Find What box and then use the Find Where options to choose which documents, folders, or projects to use in the search.

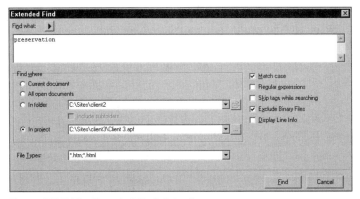

Figure 173-3: The Extended Find dialog box

8. Click the Find button. A list of the occurrences of the text you're searching for appears in the pane below the document window, including a total number of matches found.

tips

- You can also press Ctrl+F to invoke the basic Find tool.

- Match Whole Words helps you find "other" without also finding "mother" or "brother," which also contain that word. Match Case distinguishes between "THE" and "the."

- Making a selection prior to starting Find does not restrict the search to just the selected text.

- Five check boxes on the right help fine-tune your search, including or excluding different types of code from your search.

cross-reference

- FrontPage also offers Find and Replace tools. Read about them in Part 16.

Replacing Web Page Content

Using Find and Extended Find (see Task 173) requires that you act on each found item individually, clicking within the document and making changes to the text that's been found. While this is useful for a few isolated items, you need to use Replace and Extended Replace to make more sweeping changes or to replace every single occurrence of a specific piece of text or code with something else.

1. To replace text in the active document, click the Replace button on the toolbar (see Figure 174-1) or choose Search ➪ Replace.

   Replace   Extended Replace

   Figure 174-1: Using the Replace button to perform a simple search and replace operation

2. In the Replace dialog box (see Figure 174-2), type the text you're looking for in the Find What text box and type the text you want to replace it with in the Replace With text box.

   Figure 174-2: Telling HomeSite what you're looking for and what to replace it with once it's found

3. Choose the direction you want the process to take — Up, Down, or only applying to a selection made beforehand.

4. Click the Replace button to replace each found item individually or Replace All to do a global find and replace in one step.

5. To do a more extensive find and replace, searching within multiple documents and folders, choose Search ➪ Extended Replace. You can also click the Extended Replace button on the toolbar.

6. In the Extended Replace dialog box type the appropriate text in the Find What and Replace With text boxes (see Figure 174-3).

7. Use the Find Where options to control how many files to search: Current Document, All Open Documents, In Folder, or In Project.

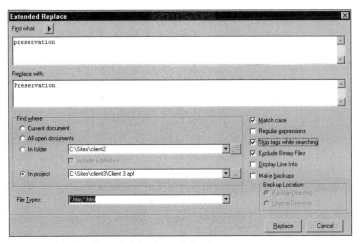

Figure 174-3: The Extended Replace dialog box

8. Make selections from the five check boxes on the right side of the dialog box to restrict what's found.

9. Choose File Types for your extended replace session. For example, you could eliminate .doc files and only search in .htm or .html files.

10. Click Replace. Any items found are listed in the pane beneath the main window (see Figure 174-4). Double-click any items listed to activate them within the text for further manual editing.

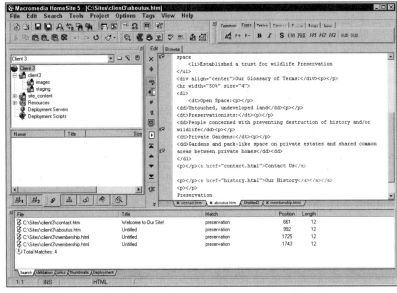

Figure 174-4: See all items found and replaced in a single scrollable list.

tips

- The Replace box offers two options for fine-tuning the Find and Replace process. You can restrict your search by using Match Case and/or Match Whole Words.

- Restrict what to find and replace (even when using Replace All) by selecting just the text you want to search and replace in, prior to activating the feature.

- Ctrl+Shift+R opens the Extended Search dialog box.

- Save searched-for text by clicking the right-arrow button next to Find What. Reuse saved searches in a new search attempt.

- The Make Backups selection remains unavailable until and unless you choose In Project from the Find Where section. The Make Backups option creates a backup of project files. Select the location in which to store the backup.

cross-reference

- FrontPage's Replace tools are not quite as extensive as HomeSite's, but they're worth checking out in Part 16.

Inserting an Image

Inserting an image is as easy as issuing the proper command and selecting an image. All the requisite code is inserted for you.

1. Click within your existing code at the point where the image should appear.

2. Choose Tags ⇨ Image. The Tag Editor - IMG dialog box opens (see Figure 175-1).

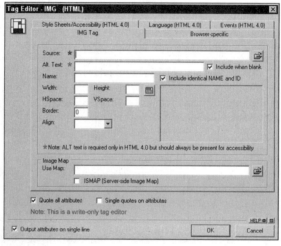

Figure 175-1: Choosing an image and setting its attributes in the Tag Editor - IMG dialog box

3. In the IMG Tag tab, click the Source box and type the pathname of the image you want to insert. To avoid mistakes, click the Folder button at the end of the field and browse for the image. (Doing so opens the Open dialog box.)

4. Enter any text (to appear when you hover the mouse over an image or to accommodate browsers that don't show graphics) in the Alt Text field.

5. Give your image a Name to make it easier to spot code references to it. (This is not the same as the image filename.)

6. Choose a Border thickness (enter a number of pixels) if you want a frame around your image.

7. Choose a Left, Right, Top, Middle, Bottom align setting.

8. If you want to add any white space around the image, enter values in the HSpace (space above and below the image) and VSpace (space to the left and right of the image) fields.

9. Click the Browser-Specific tab to check for any settings that you can establish for particular browsers or versions of browsers (see Figure 175-2).

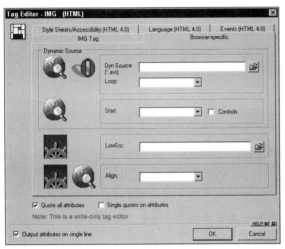

Figure 175-2: Dealing with browser-specific issues for your image

10. Click OK to insert the image and generate the code behind the scenes (see Figure 175-3).

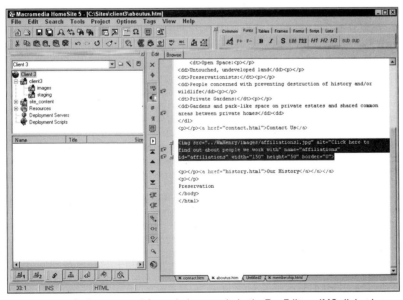

Figure 175-3: Code generated from choices made in the Tag Editor - IMG dialog box

tips

▪ Press Shift+Ctrl+I to open the Tag Editor - IMG dialog box.

▪ Store all images in an "images" folder and place it within your project folder. This makes selecting images easier and gives you a single place to store images you feel may be useful in a particular project. It also makes future Web site posting easier because when you copy your folders to the remote Web server, you will keep all image links intact.

▪ The option to create an identical name and ID is on by default.

▪ You don't have to deal with any of these issues, but you may want to make some choices to eliminate potential problems for some of your visitors. For example, the Align option in Netscape and Internet Explorer provides more alignment options.

cross-reference

▪ The process of inserting images is much quicker in WYSIWYG applications — check out Dreamweaver's approach in Part 15.

Using the Image Map Editor

An image map is a series of "hotspots" drawn on an image to turn areas of it into links that you can use to open other pages or files on the site.

1. Open the document that contains the image you want to turn into an image map.

2. In the document, click the New Image Map button (see Figure 176-1) or choose Tools ➪ New Image Map.

Figure 176-1: The New Image Map button

3. In the Create Image Map dialog box (see Figure 176-2) observe the list of images from the open document — one line per image. Click the one you want to turn into an image map.

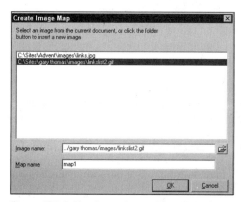

Figure 176-2: The Create Image Map dialog box

4. Click in the Map Name text box to give your map a name. This name will appear with the HTML code for the image map and make it easier to spot the code references to the map. Click OK.

5. In the Image Map Editor window (see Figure 176-3) begin drawing the map areas on your image.

note

- Unlike other page elements that you can name or give an ID, the Create Image Map dialog box requires that you give the map a name.

caution

- Don't cram too many areas into a single image map. If you do, visitors may get confused about exactly where to click to go to a given URL or file. Leave a little space between your maps so that people don't inadvertently click one area when they wanted to click the one next to it.

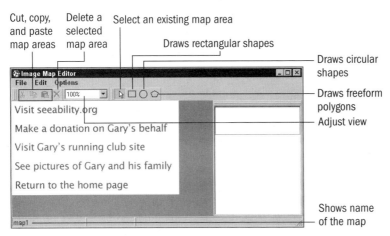

Cut, copy, and paste map areas

Delete a selected map area

Select an existing map area

Draws rectangular shapes

Draws circular shapes

Draws freeform polygons

Adjust view

Shows name of the map

Figure 176-3: All the tools you need to build your image map appear here.

6. Click a shape tool and use it to map out an area by clicking and dragging across the image to create the shape.

7. As soon as the shape in Step 6 is complete the Tag Editor - AREA dialog box appears (see Figure 176-4). With the AREA Tag tab selected, type a URL or pathname in the HREF text box to whatever the map area should link to.

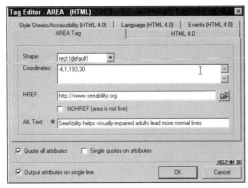

Figure 176-4: The Tag Editor - AREA dialog box sets the <href> tag for the image map.

8. Click OK to finish this particular map area. Back in the Image Map Editor, continue mapping areas of the image.

9. Create as many image maps as you'd like — using one, two, or all three of the shape tools as needed. Repeat Steps 7, 8, and 9 for each newly mapped area you create.

tips

• To draw a polygon, click and drag to draw one side; then keep clicking and dragging each time you want to change direction and draw a new side of the polygon.

• Provide alt text for these links so that all visitors can see what graphics you've put on the site.

• When you're finished drawing maps and exit the Image Map Editor, you'll be prompted to save the map. Click Yes to do so.

cross-reference

• Learn to use Dreamweaver to create hotspots on a selected image. The WYSIWYG technique is very similar to HomeSite's, except that you see the mapped areas on the image itself in Design view. Read Part 15 for more information.

Inserting Tags Automatically

Instead of typing your tags manually, you can choose tags from a list instead, which prevents you from making typos in code. The Tag Chooser helps you select tags to insert in a document, as well as determine a tag's attributes.

1. Click to position your cursor where the tag should appear in code.

2. Choose Tools ⇨ Insert Tag to open the Tag Chooser (see Figure 177-1).

<div class="notes">

notes

- Press Ctrl+E to open the Tag Chooser.

- For tags that require no attributes, clicking Select places the tag in the document right away.

</div>

Figure 177-1: Choose from different categories of tags in the Tag Chooser.

3. In the Tag Chooser, note the plus signs next to the different groups of tags in the left pane: HTML Tags, XHTML Tags, and so on. Click the plus sign next to HTML Tags to see the subcategories (see Figure 177-2).

4. Select a subcategory, such as Page Composition, Formatting and Layout, or Lists.

5. View the tags for each selected subcategory in the right panel and scroll through them until you find the one you want. Click once on the tag and click Select.

<div class="caution">

caution

- After inserting a tag through this method, always view your page in the Browse tab to make sure everything is the way you want it.

</div>

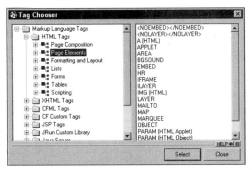

Figure 177-2: Viewing HTML tag categories in the Tag Chooser

6. Assuming the tag you choose has attributes that can be set, click the Select button to open the Tag Editor - [TAG NAME] dialog box (see Figure 177-3, which shows the MARQUEE tag, for example).

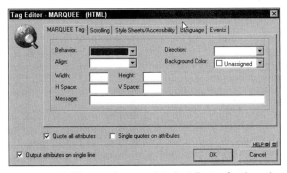

Figure 177-3: Viewing the associated attributes for the selected tag

7. In the Tag Editor dialog box, use the tag name's tab to fill in the relevant fields. These fields and options vary depending on which tag you choose.

8. Click OK to insert the tag and its attributes, based on your settings.

tips

- The plus sign indicates sublevel items that can be displayed. Clicking the plus sign changes it to a minus sign. To hide the displayed subcategories, click the minus sign.

- If you aren't sure which category your tag appears in, just expand the HTML Tags category and scroll through the list alphabetically until you find the tag you want.

- You can preview the attributes that can (and sometimes must) be set for a given tag in a box at the bottom of the Tag Chooser. This gives you some idea of what to expect when you enter values in the Tag Editor. If you see no attributes, you won't see a Tag Editor for that tag.

- The other tabs you see in the Tag Editor depend on which tag you choose. You may not need to change the settings in all the tabs.

cross-reference

- Learn about BBEdit's tag insertion tools in Part 13.

Inserting Tables

Tables are an important structural device in Web sites. HomeSite provides a set of easy-to-use and powerful tools for inserting and formatting tables.

1. In your active document, click to position your cursor where the table should appear.

2. Click the Tables toolbar.

3. To draw a quick table (and insert all the requisite code), click the last button on the Tables tab, called the Table Sizer (Quick Table). A grid appears (see Figure 178-1).

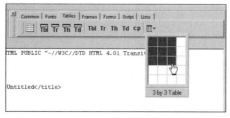

Figure 178-1: Use the Table Sizer to insert a quick table (3 x 3 in this case).

4. Drag through the pop-up grid (it expands for tables larger than 4 x 5) and release the mouse button when the blue cells in the grid and the dimensions listed below the grid match the table you want to create.

5. To have more control over the table you create, as well as its content and attributes, use the Table Wizard (first button on the Tables tab). Click the button to open the Table Wizard dialog box (see Figure 178-2).

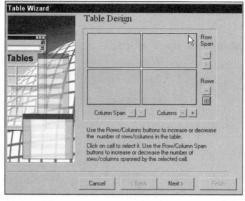

Figure 178-2: Click in the Table Wizard to design your table.

6. Click the Row and Column buttons (the cells in the sample table) and then click the plus and minus buttons to increase or decrease the number of rows or columns in your table.

7. When the grid in the Table Wizard equals the dimensions you require, click Next.

8. In the Table Properties page of the Table Wizard (see Figure 178-3), enter your desired specifications and click Next.

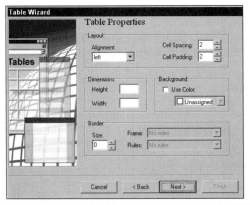

Figure 178-3: Establishing table properties in the Table Wizard

9. In the Cell Properties page (see Figure 178-4), click any individual cells to assign Content, establish the cell's Width, and set up the Content Alignment.

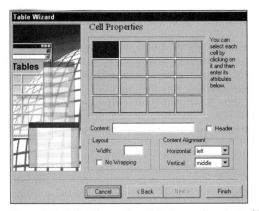

Figure 178-4: Setting up the attributes and content of individual cells

10. Click Finish to create the table.

tips

- The Table Wizard is also accessible from the New Document dialog box (choose File ➪ New).

- Repeat Step 9 for each cell in the table before clicking Finish. Just click in each cell that you want to format and use the settings over and over, once for each selected cell.

cross-reference

- Build a table graphically in FrontPage. See Part 16.

Building Framesets

Frames have their fair share of detractors. Designers don't like how they control page layout. Site visitors don't like how they affect searching and navigating within framesets, not to mention bookmarking them. Still, they are a powerful tool for structuring Web pages. HomeSite makes it relatively easy to set up a frameset in your site.

notes

- Framesets are difficult to find in search engines, such as Google, because they contain little searchable content. They consist only of frame tags — no body text, meta tags, or descriptive text.

- If you want to build content of your own into the frame later, leave the Source URL field blank. To add content to a frame, insert text and images as you would in any regular Web page. Remember, each frame *is* a Web page, at least in terms of how HTML generates content within it.

1. To start a new page with frames (called a *frameset*), choose File ⇨ New. In the New Document dialog box, double-click the Frames Wizard icon.

2. In the Frame Design page of the Frames Wizard (see Figure 179-1), click any one of the four starting frames and use the Col+, Col–, Row+, and Row– buttons to add columns and rows (frames) to your frameset.

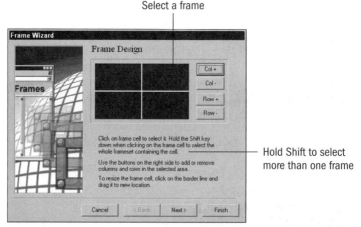

Figure 179-1: Deciding how many frames you want in your frameset

3. Click Next to move to the next step in the Frames Wizard, the Frame Attributes page (see Figure 179-2), which offers tools for setting up content for each frame in the frameset, and for establishing size and scrollability.

4. To set up individual frame attributes, click in each frame and enter a name in the Name text box as well as a Web address in the Source URL text box. Use the Margins and Frame Appearance sections to establish the frame equivalent of cell padding (margins) and determine whether or not the frame will have a scrollbar and if visitors can resize the frame themselves.

5. When each frame is set up, click Finish.

6. Using the Frames toolbar (see Figure 179-3) you can augment and alter the frameset you just created. There are buttons to open tag- and attribute-creating dialog boxes (Set, Fra, If, No); for inserting framesets (Set), frames (Fra), and floating frames (If); and for turning off frames with a set of `<noframes>` tags (No).

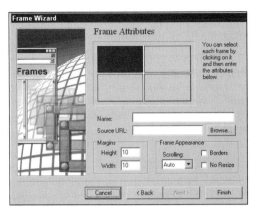

Figure 179-2: Clicking in a frame to set your frame attributes

Figure 179-3: Using the Frames toolbar to add to existing frames, build frames from scratch, or access dialog boxes for customizing existing frames

7. Use the Browse tab to make sure you have the frameset you want, no matter which method you used to build or customize it. Figure 179-4 shows a completed frameset with Web pages displayed in two frames and a blank frame awaiting original content.

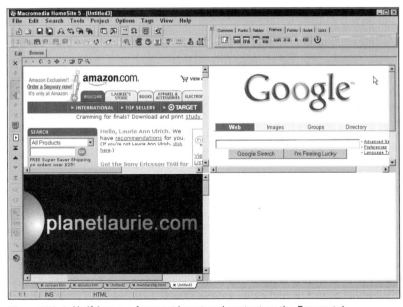

Figure 179-4: Verifying your frameset layout and content on the Browse tab

tips

- Combine two frames by holding down the Shift key to select two frames and then clicking the Col– or Row– button to merge the pair into one.

- If your frame contains a lot of text, set some sort of margin (just a few pixels) so that the text doesn't run right into the frame's walls. The default setting is 10 but you may want more or less, depending on your design goals and frame content.

- The Next button remains dim — there is no subsequent step, which can be confusing — so just click Finish when you've set up your frames.

- Make sure each frame's Source URL setting is correct by viewing the frameset in a browser.

cross-reference

- Frames are easily created in a graphical environment such as the one provided by Dreamweaver — check out Part 15.

Creating Forms

note

- GET is the default, but POST is better if you're sending confidential information, such as credit card numbers or phone numbers and addresses.

Forms allow you to obtain information from your site's visitors. Through text boxes, drop-down lists, check boxes, and radio buttons, you can elicit opinions, vital statistics, thoughts, ideas, and even credit card numbers. HomeSite gives you tools for building forms — from creating the form itself to populating it with interactive tools your visitors need to answer the questions posed by the form.

1. Click within your page code to place the cursor where the form should appear.

2. Click the Forms toolbar (see Figure 180-1).

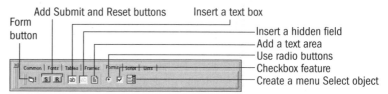

Figure 180-1: Tools needed to build a form and fill it with form objects appear in the Forms toolbar.

3. Click the Form button to open the Tag Editor - FORM dialog box (see Figure 180-2).

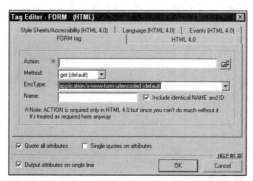

Figure 180-2: The Tag Editor - FORM dialog box

4. Supply an Action for your form — the URL of the processing script. If you don't know this address, check with your Webmaster, or the Web host from whom you purchase space for your Web page.

5. Choose your Method: POST or GET.

6. Give your form a Name and click OK to create the form. The `<form> </form>` tags appear and your cursor is automatically situated between them.

7. Begin adding form objects, using the remaining Forms toolbar buttons. Each addition results in a Tag Editor dialog box with options for the specific object. Figure 180-3 shows the Tag Editor - INPUT dialog box for a text box.

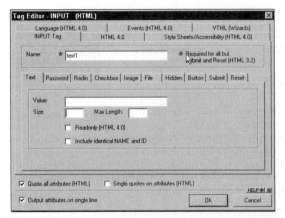

Figure 180-3: Entering settings for a particular form object you're inserting into the form

tip

- Don't forget to end your form with Submit and Reset buttons (inserted by clicking the S and R buttons on the Forms toolbar) so that visitors can send their data to you (Submit) or clear the form and start over (Reset).

8. Click OK to insert the form object with the settings you've established.

9. Repeat Steps 7 and 8 for each form object you want to include in your form.

10. Click the Browse tab to see your finished form (see Figure 180-4).

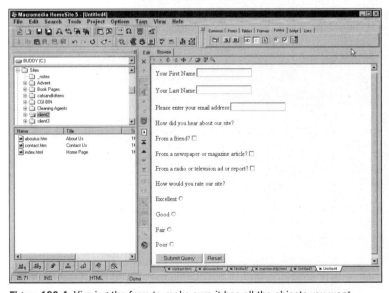

Figure 180-4: Viewing the form to make sure it has all the objects you want

cross-reference

- Learn to create a form with Dreamweaver's WYSIWYG tools. See Part 15.

181

Determining Document Weight

Document weight refers to the size of a Web page, the number of dependent files (images, multimedia files, style sheets), and the estimated time it takes someone to download the document over a dial-up Internet connection. HomeSite's document weight tool shows you how big a Web page is and the estimated time it takes people to download the page to their browser. Depending on what you find out, perhaps you only need to reoptimize your Web graphics (to make them smaller) or eliminate a sound or movie file that's not essential to the page but is slowing its load time. After making your changes, you can review the document weight to see if you're closer to the goal of creating an efficient, fast-loading page.

1. In an open document, select Tools ➪ Document Weight.

2. In the Document Weight dialog box (see Figure 181-1), review the list of dependent files (see the Dependency list), each containing a file size (see the Size column).

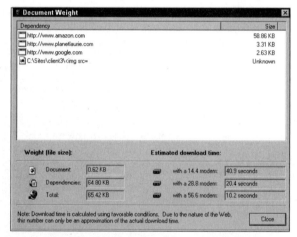

Figure 181-1: Checking your list of dependent files and their sizes

notes

- GIF images can usually be saved at a very low quality and still look OK online. JPG images get choppy and messy looking if they're not saved at high or maximum quality; they're often bad candidates for further file-size reduction through tighter optimization settings.

- At some point, there won't be anything more you can do to make a page load faster, and you'll have to accept the estimates and live with them.

3. Check the Weight and Estimated Download Time statistics and see if they're within acceptable limits.

4. As needed, sort your list of dependent files by clicking the Dependency button or Size button. Whichever button you click, you're sorting the list in that field's order.

5. Double-click any file you want to find more information about. In the Image Properties dialog box (see Figure 181-2), you can see the name of the file, its format and size, and a preview of the image itself.

Figure 181-2: Previewing and finding out more information about a particular dependent file in the Image Properties dialog box

6. Click OK to exit the Image Properties dialog box and go back to the Document Weight dialog box; click OK again.

7. Make any changes to your dependent files — reoptimizing graphics to make them smaller, eliminating nonessential images — and then reopen the Document Weight dialog box to see if your changes appreciably reduced the page's download estimates.

tips

- A page shouldn't take more than 10 seconds to load on an average-speed modem. Although the days of designing for the 14.4 or 28.8 modem crowds are over, aim for the needs of the 56.6 user. If it takes them more than 10 seconds, the page is too big.

- To see the largest dependent files first (and therefore spot the troublemakers immediately), click the Size button so that the largest files appear at the top of the list. Scroll through them to find any that could be made smaller (in file size, not physical dimensions) and make note of them.

cross-reference

- Part 3 discusses the optimization process and how to reduce file sizes so images load quickly.

Validating and Verifying Your Code

There's nothing more frustrating for site visitors (and consequently for Web designers) than links that don't work or some aspect of the page that appears improperly due to a coding error or browser-functionality conflict. Errors reduce a visitor's faith in your site and creates more work for the designer. Instead of putting errors on the Web, use HomeSite's document validation tools to check your code for conflicts and problems, and use the link verification tools to make sure all your links work as intended.

1. To check whether your links work, click anywhere in the document (on the Edit tab) and choose Tools ⇨ Verify Links. The Results pane appears to display a list of links in the page. Figure 182-1 shows the Results pane for a page with many links — some that work and some that don't.

Figure 182-1: A list of page links and the status of each one

2. If you choose, sort the Results pane by clicking the Source, Link, Full URL, and Status buttons at the top of the columns. Sort by

Status to see all nonfunctioning links together or sort by Full URL to see if the problem links are associated with a particular site that may be down since you last checked it.

3. To fix individual links that aren't working, double-click them to go to the code where the link appears.

4. To complete checking the overall page quality, validate the code throughout the page by choosing Tools ➪ Validate Current Document.

5. In the Results pane, observe the list of problems found — if any — and double-click them individually to see the problem in context (see Figure 182-2).

tips

- To avoid typos in URLs, copy the URL directly from a browser's address or locator bar.

- To validate a particular tag, select it (and all of its attributes) and choose Tools ➪ Validate Current Tag.

- You'll see a red circle with an X for invalid tags or attributes and a yellow diamond with an exclamation point for attribute values that are inconsistent or illegal within parameters for that particular tag/attribute.

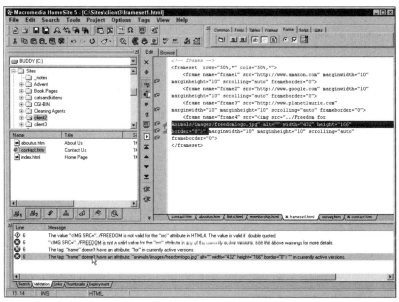

Figure 182-2: Checking the Line column for the status of individual problematic code lines

6. Edit the problematic tags as needed, using Help if you need it, or reinsert the tag using the Tag Chooser (Tools ➪ Insert Tag).

cross-reference

- To find out more about TextPad's HTML validation tools, see Part 12.

Customizing HomeSite

Making an application work the way you do is a big part of using it efficiently. If you constantly have to reset options or work around things that the application does, you're wasting time and effort, and probably getting frustrated with the application as a whole. HomeSite's customization settings allow you to change the appearance of the workspace and tweak the way the program performs various tasks. You may not need or want to make any changes but it's nice to know that you can.

1. To customize the way HomeSite's workspace looks and works, choose Options ➪ Customize.

2. In the Customize dialog box (see Figure 183-1), choose from one of the four tabs: Toolbars, Keyboard Shortcuts, Snippet Shortcuts, and Script Shortcuts.

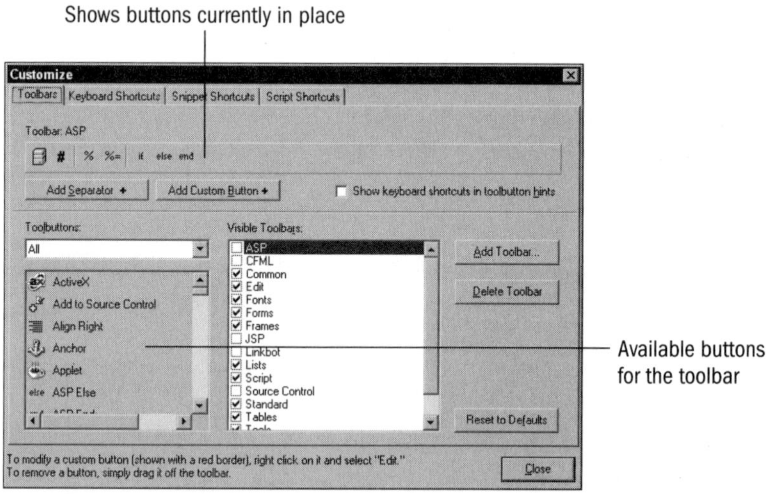

Shows buttons currently in place

Available buttons for the toolbar

Figure 183-1: Customize just about any aspect of HomeSite's workspace and commands

3. On the Toolbars tab, select any toolbar from the Visible Toolbars list and add commands to the bar by dragging buttons from the Toolbuttons list (set to All by default) to the sample bar within the dialog box.

4. Click the Add Separator button to insert vertical breaks between (groups of) buttons as you add them to various toolbars. Figure 183-2 shows the Fonts toolbar with a new separator and a few new buttons added.

5. On the Keyboard Shortcuts tab, view the list of shortcuts. If there are any you want to change, use the text box in the lower left corner to enter a new shortcut. Click Apply to make the change happen.

6. Click Close to apply your changes to the toolbars or shortcuts.

Separates default toolbar buttons from newly added ones   Newly added options

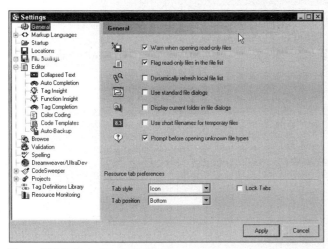

Figure 183-2: Adding more heading styles to the Font toolbar

7. To change the way HomeSite's commands and features work, choose Tools ⇨ Settings.

8. In the Settings dialog box (see Figure 183-3), examine the various categories on the left. For each one you click, the settings on the right change to offer options relevant to the category you've selected.

Figure 183-3: From the general to the very specific, you can change just about anything about the way HomeSite works.

9. Using the options for the selection made on the left panel, make changes to HomeSite's defaults, including its spelling options, which include a checklist of spelling situations that you can make HomeSite ignore (such as words in ALL CAPITAL LETTERS).

10. Click the various categories on the left and make your changes, as needed, on the right. When you've made all the changes you want, click Apply to close the dialog box.

tips

- While the Customize dialog box is open and a toolbar appears, you can drag existing buttons around the toolbar to rearrange them.

- Make changes to the way HomeSite does important things — like editing tags, verifying links, and validating code — only if you're absolutely sure of what you're doing. You may end up wanting to put things back the way they were, and if you went through the Settings dialog box and changed many things, that may not be possible.

cross-reference

- See how TextPad's settings can be customized in Part 12.

Using Auto-Backup

Backing up files is one thing most people forget to do. You think about it and decide you'll get around to it one day, but you never do so. When your computer crashes or you write over a file you didn't mean to, you're out of luck because you have no backup with which to replace the missing or corrupted file. To save you from your own tendency to forget to backup, HomeSite offers an Auto-Backup feature that creates backup versions of your files and saves them to a location you specify.

1. To make sure Auto-Backup is on and working efficiently for your needs, choose Options ⇨ Settings.

2. In the Editor category, click the Auto-Backup subcategory. The Settings dialog box and the default Auto-Backup options appear (see Figure 184-1).

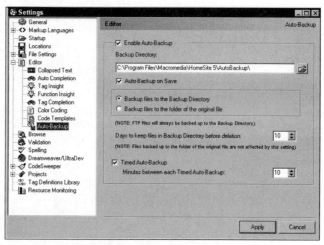

Figure 184-1: Customizing Auto-Backup's settings

caution
- The only potentially danger-ous option in its default set-ting is Days to Keep Files in Backup Directory Before Deletion. A setting of 10 may be too few days if you don't work on a site every day or even every week. Considering that backup files will be rewritten each time the original files are saved (provided you leave the Auto-Backup on Save option checked), there's lit-tle chance you'll store a backup file for too long.

3. Make sure Enable Auto-Backup is checked.

4. Use the Backup Directory box to adjust the location of your backup files. Click the Browse button to open the Browse for Folder dialog box (see Figure 184-2).

Figure 184-2: Choosing a new location for your backup files

5. Select a folder from the dialog box and click OK.

6. Verify the other settings in the dialog box (the rest of these defaults are generally best for most users) and click Apply to confirm your changes, if any.

tips

▪ Create a new folder by clicking the New Folder button in the upper-right corner of the Browse for Folder dialog box. Be sure the parent folder of the new subfolder is selected before you do so.

▪ Access a list of your backed-up files by choosing Options ➪ Auto-Backup File Maintenance. In the resulting dialog box, you can see the files that are backed up (viewed by folder). Delete any files you no longer need.

cross-reference

▪ Using the Save As command in FrontPage to make spare versions of existing files (approximating a backup system) is covered in Part 16.

Establishing Deployment Options

"**D**eployment" is HomeSite's term for uploading a Web site to a Web server. Before deploying your site (or project) to the Web, it's a good idea to make sure your deployment options are set up properly. This prevents last-minute surprises when you deploy the site — such as an inability to log on to the remote server because you have the wrong password or don't have the right folder chosen to store your Web site files. You can avoid these problems and more with a little advance preparation.

1. Open the site (project) you want to deploy and choose Tools ⇨ Settings.

2. In the Settings dialog box, click the Projects category and display the Deployment subcategory (see Figure 185-1).

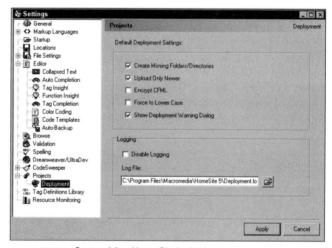

Figure 185-1: Customizing HomeSite's deployment process

3. Although the default settings are generally acceptable for most situations, if you wish to change any of them, check or uncheck settings as needed.

4. If you want to be able to upload all files, regardless of how long ago you or your team worked on them, turn off the Upload Only Newer option.

note

- If your files are in upper- or mixed-case on your local drive and you force them to be lowercased when you deploy them (to accommodate your Web server, which may only recognize lower-case file names), your local and remote file-names won't match. As needed, rename your local files to all lowercase names and make it a practice to use lowercase for all new file names. There are no servers that require upper-case names and many only recognize lowercase — so it's a safe practice to get into.

caution

- If you physically move your project files around using your regular file manager, be sure you move all your dependent files and their folders, too. Validate and verify your code and links to make sure all your paths are updated to reflect the new location of your project files and folders.

5. In the Logging section, leave Disable Logging unchecked because you don't want to not keep logs of your deployments.

6. Use the Browse button at the end of the Log File field to choose a new place to store your log files, as needed.

7. If you want to update the path to your project file so that your deployment goes to the right folder to find your local files, choose Project ➪ Properties.

8. In the Edit Project Properties dialog box (see Figure 185-2), type a path to your project files.

Figure 185-2: View the current path and type a new one if you know it.

9. If you don't know the exact path, click the Browse button at the end of the Deployment Path field to open the Select Directory dialog box (see Figure 185-3).

Figure 185-3: Selecting a folder for your project files

10. Click a folder to select it and click OK to confirm the new location of your project files.

tips

▪ If your Web server only recognizes files in all lowercase letters, be sure that Force to Lower Case is checked.

▪ This option is intended to prevent saving old files stored locally over newer versions on the Web server. It's your choice as to whether or not this is a potential problem-solver or work-creator for you.

▪ Having updated this information, when you choose to deploy your project, the new path will be used to find your project files.

cross-reference

▪ Setting up the process of Putting your files (Dreamweaver's term for uploading to a Web server) is covered in Part 15.

Deploying Files and Folders

Assuming your deployment settings are correct and you're ready to put your locally-stored project up on the Web, you're ready to deploy. It's a rather militaristic-sounding term for the process of uploading files, but the serious tone of the terminology is well-placed. The way you upload your files to the Web can make or break your site's successful appearance online — if dependent files are missing or links to project pages fail because not all the pages are uploaded, you'll have confused visitors and may have created some extra work for yourself in fixing the problems. To make deployment easier, and to help eliminate problems before they occur, HomeSite provides the Deployment Wizard.

note

- "One-time operation" does not mean you can't redeploy your project or some of its content later on. It simply means that no script is used or generated by performing the deployment this time.

1. Choose Project ⇨ Deployment Wizard to open the wizard (see Figure 186-1).

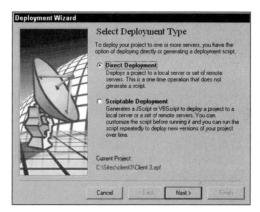

Figure 186-1: Starting the Deployment Wizard

2. In the first page of the wizard, choose whether you'll do a Direct Deployment or a Scriptable Deployment. Direct is the default because it assumes you're uploading local files to a Web server on a one-time basis.

3. Click Next. The Select Deployment Destination and Options page appears (see Figure 186-2).

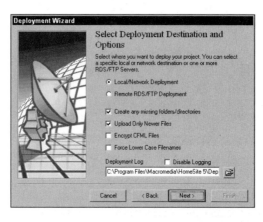

Figure 186-2: Choosing where your project files will end up

4. Choose the type of deployment (Local/Network or Remote/FTP). In this case, choose FTP, because this is how I connect to my Web server. Your choice would be based on your Web server's location and preferred deployment method.

5. Choose which files to upload and whether or not to create folders on the remote location that match the local project files. You would want to create folders and subfolders to match your local folders so that paths to files in those folders would be supported on the Web server, just as they worked locally.

6. Click Next. On the Ready for Deployment page (see Figure 186-3), click Finish to begin deployment.

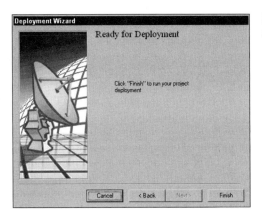

Figure 186-3: Clicking Finish to deploy your site

After deployment finishes successfully, the Results window (see Figure 186-4) opens and shows the success or failure of your attempt. Each step in the process is listed, along with the status of that step.

7. If your deployment failed, repeat the Wizard or check your Project Properties to see if your remote or local settings are incorrect.

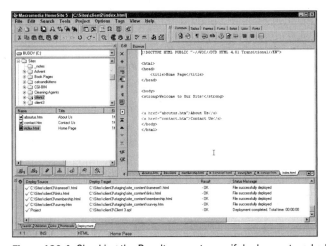

Figure 186-4: Checking the Results pane to see if deployment worked

tips

- You may find HomeSite's deployment feature a bit difficult to work with — and you wouldn't be the first. If you're less than pleased with this feature and its performance, use a third-party FTP program, such as WS_FTP Pro (www.ipswitch .com), CuteFTP (www.cuteftp .com), or any number of shareware applications, like Martin Prikryl's WinSCP (http://winscp.sourceforge .net/eng), to upload your files to the Web server.

- To establish your FTP settings for a particular project (not all projects go to the same Web server), go to the Projects tab in the Resource window and right-click the project folder. Choose Deploy Files in Folder and then click Yes to respond to the prompt. Use the Specify Folder Deployment Location dialog box to establish the FTP location for your project files.

cross-reference

- Check Part 16 for more information on the FrontPage procedure for publishing a site to the Web.

Part 15: Working with Dreamweaver

Assigning Preview Browsers

A good Web designer tests all pages in more than one browser — preferably more than one version of each — before uploading pages to the Web. This allows you to find out if any of your pages don't appear or function properly for visitors who use specific browser software or specific versions of that software. In this task you determine which browsers to use to preview your Web pages.

1. With Dreamweaver MX open and running, choose File ➪ Preview in Browser. From the shortcut menu, choose Edit Browser List.

2. In the Preferences dialog box (see Figure 187-1), select the Preview in Browser category and then choose which browsers you want to use, clicking the plus sign to add them.

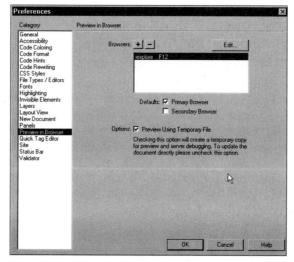

Figure 187-1: Choosing from the list of browsers you have on your computer, adding one, some, or all of them to your preview list

notes

- Macromedia offers free trial versions of software, including Dreamweaver MX, at www.macromedia. com/downloads.

- In order to add browsers to your list, you must install them on your computer. Obtain the latest version of Internet Explorer from Microsoft (www.microsoft .com/downloads) and the latest version of Netscape (http://channels.netscape .com/ns/browsers). An excellent place to find older browsers is http://browsers .evolt.org.

- You really can't have too many browsers to choose from. The more you have, and the more versions of each one you install, the more thoroughly you can test your pages and troubleshoot them before uploading them.

caution

- When choosing which browsers (and versions) to install, consider your audience. If your visitors are largely technical people, you don't need to worry too much about older versions. If your audience is more broad and potentially in possession of old hardware and software, cover your bases by checking your pages in versions of IE and Navigator prior to version 4.0.

3. When you click the plus sign, the Add Browser dialog box appears (see Figure 187-2). Here you enter a browser name, choose which application to run, and designate the browser as your primary or secondary default.

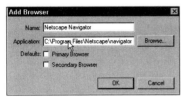

Figure 187-2: Setting options about the browser you add to the preview list

4. Click OK to accept the settings for this browser and return to the Preferences dialog box.

5. Repeat Steps 1 through 4 for each browser/version you want to add to your list.

6. Click OK to close the Preferences dialog box.

cross-reference

- Once your site appears and functions properly in all your browsers, upload it to the Web (see Task 220).

Task **188**

Defining Sites

The first step to build a Web site in Dreamweaver MX is to define it, to tell Dreamweaver what your site is called, the site's domain name, and where its files (images and related content) are stored locally. These same folders are recreated later on the Web server so that the Web site mirrors your local file structure perfectly.

1. Choose Site ➪ New Site to open the Site Definition dialog box (see Figure 188-1). If your screen looks different, click the Basic tab to see the Site Definition wizard.

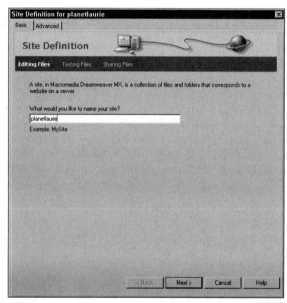

Figure 188-1: Starting the site definition process by naming your new site

2. Enter a name for your site and click Next.

3. Choose what sort of server technology (ColdFusion, ASP, NET, JSP, or PHP) you want to use. Choose Yes to use server technology or No to skip that.

4. Click Next. The third step in the process appears, asking how you edit your pages (locally or on the server).

5. Choose Edit Local Copies on My Machine. You must enter the path to the folder where you will store this site's pages.

6. Click Next and choose how you connect to your Web server. Depending on your response, different options will appear in the dialog box.

7. Click Next and decide if you want to enable Check In and Check Out.

8. Click Next and confirm your settings (see Figure 188-2).

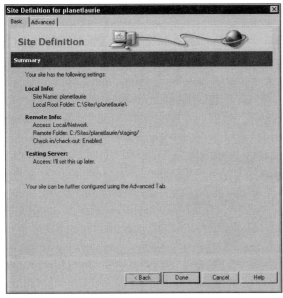

Figure 188-2: Making sure your settings are correct

9. Click Done. Your site is set up and you can begin adding pages to it.

10. To begin building your site, save the blank, new document as index.htm and see how that file appears in the site map (see Figure 188-3).

Figure 188-3: Making your first page, typically saved as index.htm, the official home page

tips

- The name for your site needn't be the same as the domain name; it can be "Bob's site" or "ABC Company Site."

- To turn your first page (or any page you've created and saved within the site) into the home page, right-click the file icon in the site map and choose Set as Home Page from the shortcut menu.

- Dreamweaver alleges that any file named "index.htm" is universally recognized as the site's home page. Experience has shown, however, that this is not reliably the case. It's a good idea to designate a home page manually.

cross-reference

- You can set up a site in FrontPage by choosing a particular site template and building your pages one by one. Read Part 16 for more information.

Task **189**

Using Site Maps

A site map allows you to create and control links between pages and to open particular pages for editing. It also gives you a bird's-eye view of your site so you can discern relationships between your pages and the site's structure. One caveat: You need to establish a site first, with some files saved in it, in order to use a site map. The following steps assume you've created a site and saved at least one file in it — preferably the home page, index.htm.

1. To open an existing site and view its site map, choose Site ⇨ Site Map. If you have more than one site available, click the drop list that lists all of your sites (a list of your available sites appears as shown in Figure 189-1) and choose the one you want to see.

Figure 189-1: Choose which site you want to work with from the Edit Sites dialog box

2. With the site open and the site map displayed, double-click the site folder to display the files within the site. A tree structure appears, similar to the one seen in Windows Explorer, showing the connection between your site files.

3. To open a site file, double-click its icon in the site map. The file opens in its own window, ready for you to edit the page.

4. To create a quick link between two pages in your site, expand the site map window by clicking the Expand/Collapse button (the last button on the toolbar). The site map window expands substantially, based on the overall Dreamweaver window size and any other displayed workspace items (see Figure 189-2).

5. Click the Site Map button (third button from the left) so that a "family tree" version of your site map appears on the left side of the window (see Figure 189-3).

6. Click on the Point-to-File icon (next to the index.htm icon in the site map) and drag it to a file in the site list. If you don't see this icon, click once on the file icon. Once the connection is made, the second file appears in the site window and the link between the files is indicated by a line connecting the two file icons (see Figure 189-4).

7. Continue making connections or close the site map by reclicking the Expand/Collapse button.

Expand/Collapse button

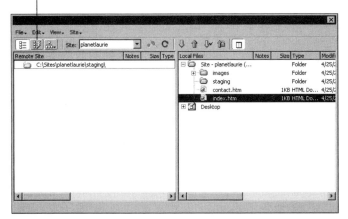

Figure 189-2: Working in the expanded version of the site window

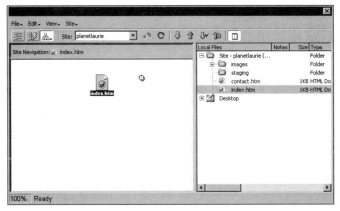

Figure 189-3: Site map of your index.htm file

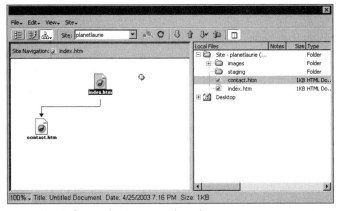

Figure 189-4: Connecting two pages in a site map

tips

- Double-click again to hide the files and see only the site folder.

- When you create a link between pages this way, a text link is added to the target page (in this case, a text link to the aboutus.htm page is created in the index.htm page). You can change that link to a graphic later, or you can leave it as text but reposition and format it as desired.

- In previous versions of Dreamweaver, the site map appeared in a separate window and you had to click its taskbar button to bring it to the top and use the map. The Expand/Collapse button serves much the same purpose, allowing you to see the site map when you need it, and to see a pared-down version (in the far right panel) when you don't need to do anything more than open files within the site.

cross-reference

- FrontPage offers a Navigation view of a Web site, providing many of the same features and functions of Dreamweaver's site map. Read Part 16 to find out how FrontPage provides site support.

Establishing Page Properties

Page properties, which apply to the active page in your site, should be consistent throughout the site. This means you should apply the same properties to each new page you create, or else establish them once and use them when building subsequent pages.

1. Open the page for which you want to establish properties. Choose Modify ⇨ Page Properties.

2. Enter a title for your page in the Page Properties dialog box (see Figure 190-1).

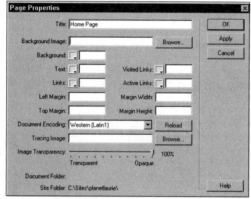

Figure 190-1: Customize virtually anything about the active page in the Page Properties dialog box

3. Choose a background image for your page, if desired. Otherwise choose a background color using the palette (see Figure 190-2).

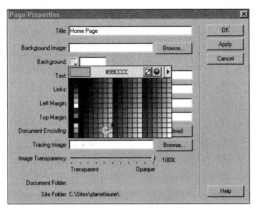

Figure 190-2: Setting the page background as a picture or solid color

4. Using the same palette buttons for each option, set the Text and Links, Visited Links, and Active Links colors.

5. Change page margins as desired.

6. If you're using a tracing image, set its pathname here.

7. Click OK to confirm your settings and see them applied to the page.

Task 190

tips

- You can also right-click the page and choose Page Properties from the short-cut menu.

- The title you enter will appear in the title bar of the browser window whenever a visitor goes to the page. Keep these entries short and relevant. Try not to exceed 50 characters, otherwise the title will not fit on the title bar.

- If you want to see your settings applied and keep the dialog box open for more changes, click the Apply button instead.

cross-reference

- The FrontPage Page Properties dialog box offers many of the same options. Check it out in Part 16.

Setting Code View Options

Trust us when we say there's no substitute for knowing the code. Just because Dreamweaver is a visual editor doesn't mean you never have to look at HTML again. In fact, Dreamweaver *wants* you to. That's why it gives you so much access to it. Half of the document window is devoted to Code view.

1. Open Dreamweaver and go to the document window.

2. On the document window's toolbar, click the Code View button (see Figure 191-1).

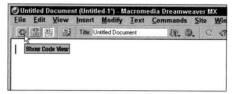

Figure 191-1: The Code View button

3. Choose View ➪ Code View Options. A submenu appears with a check mark beside any currently set option (see Figure 191-2).

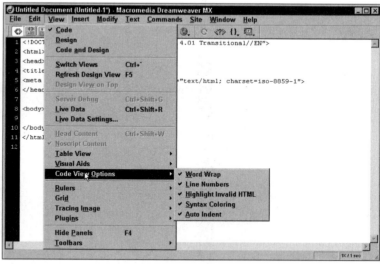

Figure 191-2: The Code View Options submenu

note

▪ You can view both Code and Design views simultaneously with the Design & Code View button, found just to the right of the Code View button. The document window will split horizontally to show both views.

4. Select any of these options from the submenu:

- **Word Wrap:** Wraps code so it can be read without any horizontal scrolling.

- **Line Numbers:** Displays line numbers along the side of the code.

- **Highlight Invalid HTML:** Highlights invalid HTML in bright yellow. When an invalid tag is clicked, information about how to fix it appears in the Property inspector (see Figure 191-3).

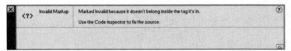

Figure 191-3: Suggested code corrections in the Property inspector

- **Syntax Coloring:** Toggles code coloring on and off.

- **Auto Indent:** Indents code automatically when you press the Enter key while editing or adding code in Code view.

5. To disable a checked option, simply select it to remove the check mark.

tip

- To toggle between Code view and Design view, select View ⇨ Switch View or press Ctrl+tilde (~) (Windows) or Command+tilde (Macintosh).

cross-reference

- Dreamweaver supplies prewritten chunks of HTML for frequently used items. You can also create your own. They're called code snippets (see Task 192).

Working with Code Snippets

In Dreamweaver, a code snippet is just a saved bit of code (HTML, CSS, JavaScript, or any other language). A handy panel allows you easily to create, store, and retrieve these snippets. Dreamweaver also comes with some ready-made snippets you can use as a starting point.

1. To insert a code snippet, place your cursor in the desired location within your document.

2. Select Window ➪ Snippets to open the Snippets panel (see Figure 192-1) and double-click the snippet of your choice.

Figure 192-1: The Snippets panel

3. To create a new snippet, click the New Snippet button (the document with the plus sign) located at the bottom right of the panel to open the Snippet dialog box (see Figure 192-2).

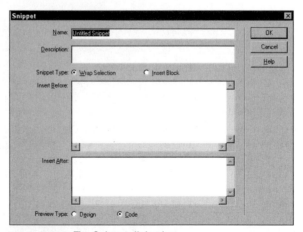

Figure 192-2: The Snippet dialog box

4. Enter a name and description for the snippet in the fields provided.

5. Choose your snippet type:

   • **Wrap Selection:** Enter the code you want to appear in front of the selection in the Insert Before field and the code you want to appear after the selection in the Insert After field

   • **Insert Block:** Simply enter your code into the Insert Code field

6. Choose a preview type:

   • **Design:** When you insert the snippet the Preview pane appears in Design view

   • **Code:** The Preview pane displays the snippet code

7. Click OK to close the Snippet dialog box.

8. To edit or delete a code snippet, select it in the panel and click the Edit Snippet button to reopen the Snippet dialog box, or the Remove button to delete it.

9. To create folders to manage your snippets, click the New Snippet Folder icon at the bottom of the panel and drag your snippets into the new folders or the preexisting folders.

Task 192

tip

• You can also right-click (Windows) or Control-click (Macintosh) the snippet and choose Insert from the context menu.

cross-reference

• Ok, now let's learn how to really put Dreamweaver to work. See Task 193 to learn how to format text.

Inserting and Formatting Text

Text appears on virtually every Web page. It expresses ideas, shares information, sells products, and instructs. Dreamweaver makes it easy to insert text into pages; link text to other pages, files, or sites; and format text so it's legible and color-coordinated with the rest of your page.

1. In the open page, click to position your cursor where the text should begin.

2. Type your text. Word-wrapping forces long lines of text to flow to the next lines (see Figure 193-1).

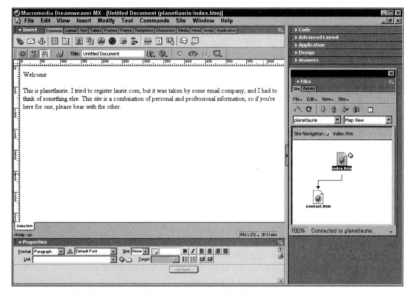

Figure 193-1: Typing a page title or paragraph of information

3. After typing, select any text that you want to format.

4. If it's not already displayed, select Window ➪ Properties to view the Properties inspector. The Font and Size selectors on it adjust the appearance of your text (see Figure 193-2).

5. Click the Text Color button to open the color palette, which you can use to select a color or enter a hexadecimal value for one (see Figure 193-3).

6. Apply bold or italic, as desired, by clicking the B and I buttons, respectively.

Resize text
List and target options
Choose a font/font group
Choose text color
Create links
Enter the color's hexadecimal number here
Format button
Choose bold or italic   Change alignment

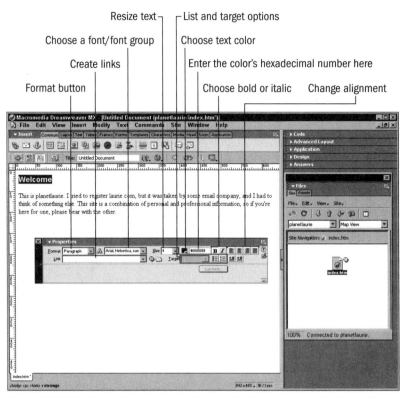

Figure 193-2: The Properties inspector allows you to format any aspect of text

7. Use the alignment buttons (Left, Center, Right, or Justify) to change the horizontal alignment of your text.

8. Repeat Steps 1 through 8 for any other text that needs formatting on the page.

Figure 193-3: Picking a color from the Web-safe palette

tips

▪ The starting point for text can be on any line in the page or table cell, a layer, or a frame. Wherever the cursor appears, the text will appear as soon as you begin to type.

▪ When choosing a font, choose a group, such as Arial, Helvetica/Sans-Serif. This gives you greater assurance that at least one of those fonts will be on your visitor's computer and will appear correctly in the browser.

▪ Click on any color within the Dreamweaver workspace — anything on the active page or a color displayed in the toolbars and palettes. Because the eyedropper pointer indicates you're in sampling mode, anything you click on will be selected as your text color. This works for all color fields: Once the color palette and eyedropper pointer appear, any color onscreen is selectable.

cross-reference

▪ Create heading styles and apply other font attributes to HTML code in Part 2.

Creating Lists

Lists come in three varieties: ordered lists (also called numbered lists), unordered lists (bulleted lists), and definition lists.

1. Select your list — any series of lines of text or paragraphs.

2. To create a bulleted list, click the Unordered List button.

3. To create a numbered list, click the Ordered List button. Figure 194-1 shows an unordered list created from four lines of text.

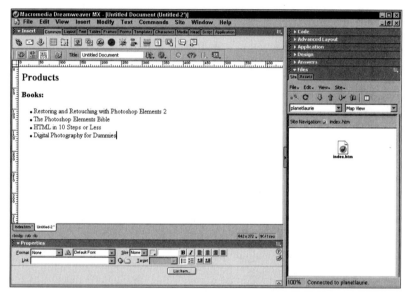

Figure 194-1: An unordered list implies a series of equally-important items with no implied priority between them.

4. Delete items in your list and observe the changes in the list itself. If your list is numbered, the number sequence updates automatically.

5. Add items to your list and observe the changes to the number of bulleted items or the number sequence of list items.

6. To create a definition list, select the text and choose Text ⇨ List ⇨ Definition List.

   As shown in Figure 194-2, the items in the list alternate between being terms and definitions.

notes

- There's a difference between unordered and ordered lists. If you give instructions, such as driving directions, use an ordered list so that readers know how to perform the tasks in sequence. If your list has no order or priority implied, use an unordered list.

- When you build a definition list, every other line is designated as either a term or definition. Definitions are indented automatically to link them clearly to the terms above them.

- If you insert a new line at the end of an unordered or ordered list, you'll get one more bulleted or numbered line. Press Enter twice to exit list mode.

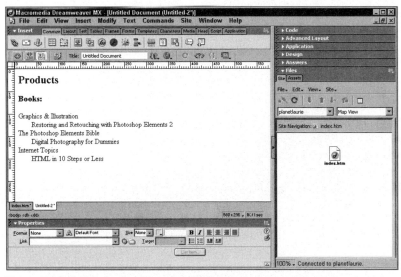

Figure 194-2: Building a list of terms and definitions

tip
- Create a quick Q & A list by placing the questions in the terms and the answers in the definitions.

cross-reference
- Find out how to create bulleted and numbered lists in FrontPage. See Part 16.

Proofing Page Text

Dreamweaver's spell-check feature works very much like that in any word processor. Words not found in the internal dictionary are listed as misspelled, and you have the opportunity to choose an alternate spelling or edit the text directly.

1. To spell-check just one part of your page, select the text and choose Text ⇨ Check Spelling. If you want to check the entire page, just choose the command without first selecting any text.

2. In the Check Spelling dialog box (see Figure 195-1), each misspelled word appears, one by one.

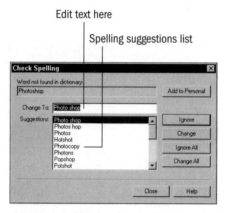

Edit text here

Spelling suggestions list

Figure 195-1: Mistakes found within the selected text or on a page appear in the Word Not Found in Dictionary text box.

3. Select an alternate spelling from the Suggestions list or type a correction in the Change To text box.

4. Click Change or Change All if you want to implement the change.

5. Ignore a word you know is spelled correctly by clicking Ignore or Ignore All.

6. If you spell-check a selection, you'll be prompted that the selection has been checked (see Figure 195-2).

Figure 195-2: Checking just a portion of your text, or checking all of it if you wish

7. When the spell check is complete and the entire page has been checked, the dialog box closes.

Task 195

tips

- Your choices for dealing with spelling errors include Change and Change All to correct one or more errors, and Ignore or Ignore All if you know the word is spelled correctly. To add a word to your personal dictionary (which is checked at the same time the main dictionary is checked), click Add to Personal.

- To stop a spell-check prematurely, click the Close button.

cross-reference

- TextPad offers a spell checker, and you can find out how it works in Part 12.

Using Find and Replace to Edit Page Content

Updating a Web page or Web site for the new year (changing copyright references), changing someone's name, and bringing product or service references up-to-date are all great uses of Find and Replace. It helps you get a tedious, error-prone job done quickly.

note

- To control which replacements are made, use the Find Next button. For each item found, click Replace (to replace it with the Replace With text) or Find Next to skip that occurrence and move on to the next one.

1. To find text and replace it with other text, open any page you want to change.

2. Choose Edit ⇨ Find and Replace. The Find and Replace dialog box opens (see Figure 196-1).

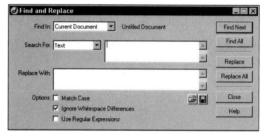

Figure 196-1: The Find and Replace dialog box provides all the controls you need to make global edits to your page or site.

3. In the Find In list box choose the scope of the Find and Replace session: Current Document, Entire Current Local Site, Selected Files in Site, or Folder.

4. In the Search For list box specify if you want to look for anything other than text. Your choices include Source Code and Specific Tag.

5. Type the text you're looking for in the text box to the right of the Search For list box.

6. Type what you want the found content to be replaced with in the Replace With text box.

caution

- Use care when typing your Search For and Replace With text. If spaces, special characters, and capitalization don't match perfectly, no replacements will be made.

Task **196**

7. Click the options below to refine your Find and Replace session.

8. Click Replace All to do a global Find and Replace for the scope of your site selected in the Find In list box.

9. Click OK to respond to the confirming dialog box (see Figure 196-2), which indicates which areas of the site were checked and how many replacements occurred.

Figure 196-2: Results of performing a requested Find and Replace

tips

- Press Ctrl+F to open the Find and Replace dialog box.

- If you first select text before choosing Edit ➪ Find and Replace, that selected text will appear in the Search For field. That's especially handy for specific text phrases that repeat across the site. In Code view, that feature is great for replacing long code strings (or HTML tags) with something else.

- The options Match Case, Ignore Whitespace Differences (selected by default), and Use Regular Expressions control what searched text meets the Find criteria and therefore what's replaced with the Replace With text. Your situation and Web page or site content will dictate which options you need.

cross-reference

- TextPad offers a handy Find and Replace tool, too. Read more about it in Part 12.

Importing Word HTML

Microsoft Word makes it easy to convert Word documents into HTML. Unfortunately, Word adds extraneous code that bloats HTML files. Dreamweaver makes it easy to work with Word-converted HTML files by taking out the code that Word puts in, making a much cleaner HTML file in the process.

1. In the page into which you wish to import a Word HTML document, choose File ⇨ Import ⇨ Word HTML.

    The Clean Up Word HTML dialog box opens (see Figure 197-1).

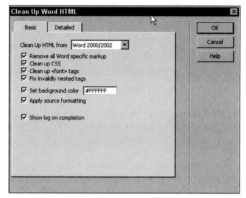

Figure 197-1: The dialog box that says it all: "Clean Up Word HTML"

2. On the Basic tab, view the list of cleanup tasks that will be performed and uncheck any that you don't want done.

3. On the Detailed tab (see Figure 197-2), view the specific Word version information that Dreamweaver will use to clean up the code, and check the CSS cleanup options as well. Uncheck any items you don't want done.

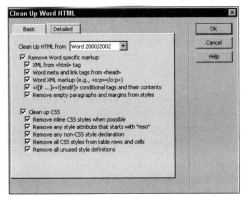

Figure 197-2: Choosing the version of Word used to create the imported HTML document

4. Click OK to perform the cleanup and import the Word HTML file into Dreamweaver. A prompt appears (see Figure 197-3), telling you what was done to the imported document.

Figure 197-3. A rundown of the unnecessary code Dreamweaver stripped out of the Word HTML document

tip
- Leave all the basic cleanup tasks checked. If you turn off any of the cleanup steps, you may cause problems for Dreamweaver, which requires very clean code.

cross-reference
- Find out more about how clean CSS code should look (see Part 9).

Importing Data Tables from Other Applications

S uppose you need to take a Microsoft Excel worksheet or a table from a Microsoft Word document — or even a data table from Microsoft Access or another database management system — and import it into a Web page. This task requires importing the tabular data — located in a table, one piece of data per cell — and inserting it so it's legible and accessible within Dreamweaver. You can easily make that tabular data appear in a Dreamweaver-created table using the Import Tabular Data command.

1. Open the page you want to import tabular data into and choose File ⇨ Import ⇨ Tabular Data.

   This opens the Import Tabular Data dialog box (see Figure 198-1).

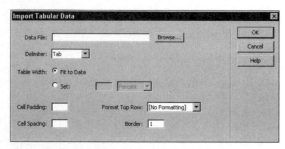

Figure 198-1: Choosing the source of the tabular data and informing Dreamweaver how you want to use and display it

2. Click the Browse button to select your tabular data file. This opens the Open dialog box (see Figure 198-2).

Figure 198-2: Navigating to the data file you want to import into your Web page

3. Select the file you want to import and click OK. This returns you to the Import Tabular Data dialog box.

4. Choose the delimiter that separates the individual pieces of data within your source document. Tab is the default.

5. Leave the Table Width setting in its default condition: Fit to Data.

6. Insert any cell padding or cell spacing you feel enhances the legibility of your data.

7. If your top row is the column headings (field names from the database), you may want to choose Bold from the Format Top Row list box.

8. Click OK to import the tabular data and create a table in the Web page (see Figure 198-3).

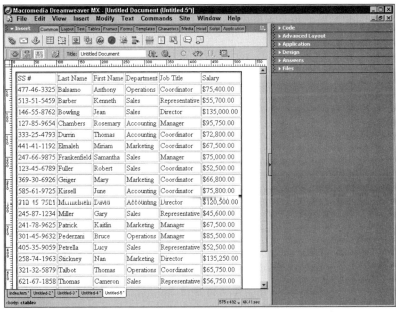

Figure 198-3: A database of employees becomes a table of names and numbers in Dreamweaver

tips

- In case your delimiter isn't listed in the dialog box, go back to your source text file and use Find and Replace to change the delimiter character to something Dreamweaver accepts.

- By telling Dreamweaver to fit the table it creates to the data you're importing, you prevent data in two or more cells from combining into one, or the appearance of extra, empty columns and rows.

cross-reference

- You can paste table content from Word into a FrontPage document. Explore more of the ways that FrontPage is similar to Word in Part 16.

Inserting and Formatting Images

Inserting an image into Dreamweaver is almost too easy. It's also easy to change the image's dimensions and alignment, and apply a border to the image.

1. In Design view, click to position your cursor where the image should be placed.

2. Choose Insert ⇨ Image. The Select Image Source dialog box opens.

3. Navigate to the image you want to use. A preview of it appears to the right (see Figure 199-1).

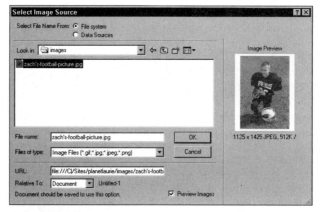

Figure 199-1: Navigating to the folder containing the image you want to use — known as the image source

4. Click OK to insert the selected image on the Web page. If you choose an image that's not already stored in the current site, a prompt appears asking if you want to copy the file to the site folder. Click Yes.

5. Once the image is in place, click to select it (see Figure 199-2). The Properties inspector displays various image-related options (be sure the inspector is in its expanded state).

6. Give your image a name for use within the HTML code by clicking in the text box under the word "Image" and the image size. Type a short name in the box.

Type name for the image here

Change vertical and horizontal alignment

Dimensions

Observe image dimensions   Type alternate text here

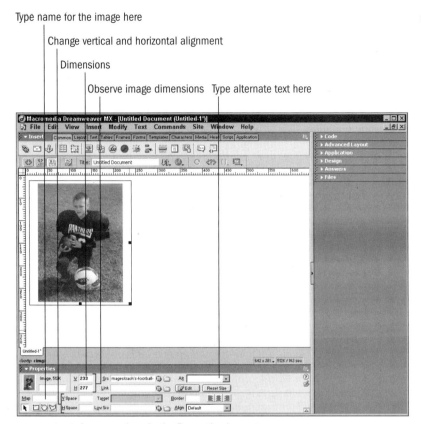

Figure 199-2: Image options in the Properties inspector

7. Use the Alignment tools (three buttons and an Align list box) to reposition the image on the line or within the table cell that contains it.

8. Enter a number in the Border field, indicating the pixel width of any border that surrounds the image.

tips

- Click the Insert Image button on the main toolbar to see the Select Image Source dialog box. (It's the button with a tree against a blue sky.)

- Once you set a default image editing program (see Task 203), clicking the Edit button in the Properties inspector launches that application with the selected image already loaded in it so you can edit it.

- By using a name such as "customerservicerep" (for a picture of a customer service representative), you can spot references to the image quickly and easily within your code.

- After you resize an image in an external image editor, you may see strange artifacts in Dreamweaver — choppy edges or oddly colored pixels along the edge of the image in Design view. Click the Reset Size button in the Properties inspector to snap the image back to its correct size.

cross-reference

- Find out how to insert and position an image through HTML in Part 3.

Task 200

Inserting Flash Text

When you click on Flash text in a browser, it changes color, creating a subtle level of interactivity. Flash text can function as an interactive link too. You can create Flash text quickly and easily in Dreamweaver.

1. In Design view, click to position your cursor where the Flash text should appear.

2. Choose Insert ⇨ Interactive Images ⇨ Flash Text.

   This opens the Insert Flash Text dialog box (see Figure 200-1).

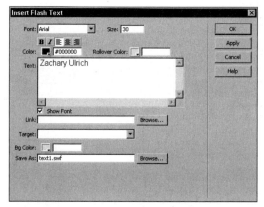

Figure 200-1: All the tools you need to build interactive Flash text in the Insert Flash Text dialog box

3. Choose a font and size for your Flash text. The first font in your operating system's Font folder determines the default font; size 30 is the default size.

4. Apply bold (B), italic (I), or underline (U) styles to your text and set any alignment changes (Left, Center, or Right) to the text. Left is the default.

5. Click the Color button to choose a color for the text in the resulting palette.

6. Click the Rollover Color button to choose the color that the text turns when someone points to it with the mouse.

7. Type the Flash text in the Text field.

8. Type or browse to the URL or file that this Flash text should link to.

9. Establish your target setting for the linked page/file.

10. Click the OK button to create the Flash text and see it on the Web page (see Figure 200-2).

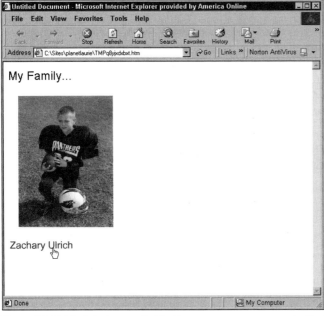

Figure 200-2: Flash text generated by Dreamweaver appears under the image.

Task **200**

tip

- The Show Font option is checked so that you can preview in the dialog box how the Flash text will appear once it's placed onscreen.

cross-reference

- You can insert text buttons in FrontPage, applying interesting color and 3D effects to the buttons. Read about it in Part 16.

Inserting Flash Buttons

Flash buttons are really cool graphic buttons or tabs that contain text (which you provide) in any number of visually compelling styles. You can choose the button style, color, and font, and determine where the button links to.

1. In Design view click to position your cursor where the Flash button should appear.

2. Choose Insert ⇨ Interactive Images ⇨ Flash Button. The Insert Flash Button dialog box appears (see Figure 201-1).

notes

- Size 12 is the default text size, which is based on the average size of the buttons. You may want to stick with this number until and unless you see that the text is too small to be legible at high screen resolutions.

- To preview your button on the page, click the Apply button and move the Insert Flash Button dialog box out of the way so you can see the inserted button on the page. If you want to start over, click Cancel in the dialog box and begin again.

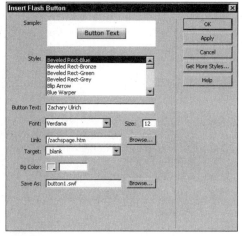

Figure 201-1: Creating a Flash button in the Insert Flash Button dialog box

3. Scroll through the Style list and click on individual style names to see them in the Sample box.

4. When you find one that you like, leave it selected.

5. Click in the Button Text box and type the text that should appear on the button face.

6. Choose a font for the text, and also a size by entering a number in the Size text box.

7. In the Link text box, enter or browse to a URL or file that the Flash Button should link to.

8. Click OK to create the button and see it on the Web page (see Figure 201-2).

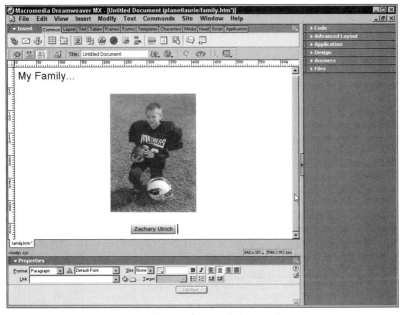

Figure 201-2: Flash button with the text, font, and size you choose

tips

- If you want the linked file or page to appear in a new window, choose "_blank" from the Target list box.

- If there's too much text to fit on the button, consider a text link instead. Flash buttons (and any graphical button, for that matter) are better used for short phrases and single words.

cross-reference

- You can make any graphic (photo, button, anything) into a link (see Part 5).

Testing and Formatting a Flash Button

Once you create a Flash button, you can use the Properties inspector to test and change its appearance and placement on the page. You can also name your button so that the related HTML code is easy to spot within Code view.

1. Click on the Flash button to select it. Handles appear around it.

2. Observe the Properties inspector (see Figure 202-1) and be sure it's expanded to show all of its tools. Once you expand it and leave it that way, it should remain in the expanded view.

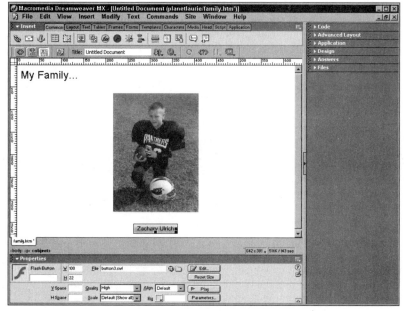

Figure 202-1: Flash button settings in the Properties inspector

3. Click in the text box under the words "Flash Button" on the left side of the Properties inspector. Enter a name for the button. That name will appear in the HTML code that refers to the button (see Figure 202-2).

4. Enter new height and width settings for the button, as needed, using the H and W boxes.

5. Adjust the Quality of the button image. High is the default and your best choice.

6. Click the Play button to see how your button reacts when the mouse pointer goes over it (see Figure 202-3).

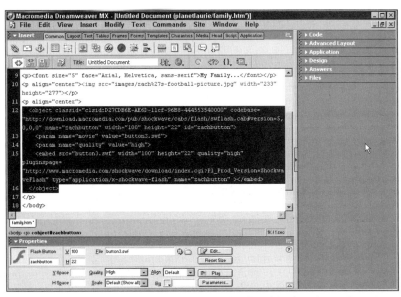

Figure 202-2: References to a Flash button in code after giving it a short, relevant name in the Properties inspector

7. Adjust the alignment of the button. This changes its horizontal alignment on the line or within the table cell that contains it.

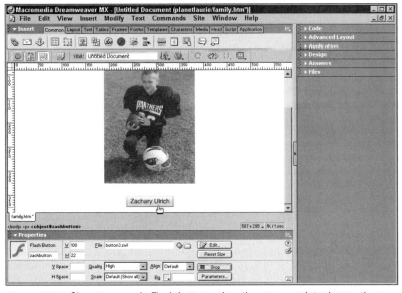

Figure 202-3: Changes occur in Flash buttons when the mouse pointer hovers them

tip

- For a browser's-eye view of the Flash button, use the Preview in Web Browser shortcut (press F12 to open your default browser) and mouse over the button.

cross-reference

- You can preview your pages in a browser window, testing all of their features, through any of the text editors covered in this book. For example, HomeSite has a preview command, discussed in Part 14.

Assigning an External Image Editor

You probably have a favorite application for creating and editing graphics. Dreamweaver displays an Edit button in the Properties inspector (visible whenever a graphic is selected), which you can set to open the graphics-editing application of your choice. Clicking the Edit button launches the designated application and opens the selected graphic to await your changes.

1. Choose Edit ⇨ Preferences to open the Preferences dialog box (see Figure 203-1).

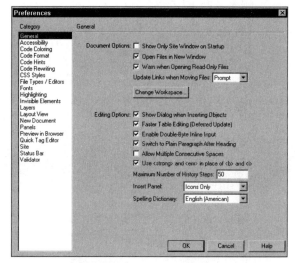

Figure 203-1: Customizing many areas in Dreamweaver

2. In the Category list, select File Types/Editors. The right side of the dialog box changes (see Figure 203-2).

3. In the Extensions list, click once on the first Web-safe graphics file format you see: GIF, JPG, or PNG.

4. Check the Editors list next to the Extensions list; the application (if any) associated with that file type appears.

5. To change programs, select the unwanted application and click the minus-sign button on the Editors side of the dialog box. The current application name disappears from the list.

6. Click the plus-sign button above the Editors list to open the Select External Editor dialog box (see Figure 203-3).

note

- If you want to use Adobe Photoshop to edit your graphics, browse to the Adobe application folder (likely in C:\Program Files) and double-click the Photoshop.exe file.

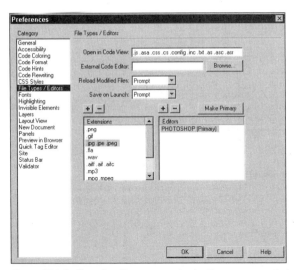

Figure 203-2: Choosing file types and selecting programs that edit them

7. Navigate to the application folder of the program you want to use for editing graphics, and double-click the executable file. You're returned to the Preferences dialog box.

8. Repeat Steps 3 through 7 for each of the file types (GIF, JPG, PNG) you want to assign to a specific editor.

Figure 203-3: Choosing the application you want to associate with a selected file type

tips

- Assuming you have both GIF and JPG images in most of your Web pages, be sure to set up an assigned editor for both types. If you never use PNG images, you can skip that one.

- You can assign more than one program for each file type. Select one in the Editors list and click the Make Primary button above it. The primary editor will launch by default (it becomes the default by being first in the list) when you click the Edit button in the Properties inspector.

cross-reference

- Learn more about image editing in Part 3.

Creating Image Maps

An image map is a group of *hotspots* — geometric shapes drawn on top of an image that you associate with specific URLs or files. This turns the area into a hyperlink.

1. Click once on the image you want to turn into an image map. Handles appear around it and the Properties inspector shows image-related tools (see Figure 204-1).

note

- The "_blank" target makes the linked page open in a new browser window; "_self" opens the link within the existing window, replacing the current content; "_parent" opens the linked window in the parent frameset (only applicable if you use frames); and "_top" replaces the frameset itself. If you're not using frames, "_blank" and "_self" are your only options, but "_blank" is preferable because it doesn't let the visitor entirely leave your site.

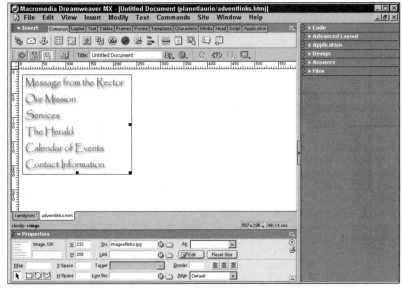

Figure 204-1: Selecting an image in Dreamweaver

2. In the lower half of the Properties inspector, click on the map shape that works for the area you want to turn into an image map (see Figure 204-2).

Figure 204-2: The image map tools

caution

- Although you can link as many areas of an image map as you want, don't cram in too many links. Keep enough space between hotspots so that visitors aren't confused when they click somewhere on the image map.

3. As soon as you draw the map area, the Properties inspector changes its features (see Figure 204-3). Click in the Link box and type the URL or path to the file the image map area should link to.

4. Make a target choice for your link: _blank, _self, _parent, or _top.

5. Repeat Steps 2 through 4 for each area you want to include in the image map.

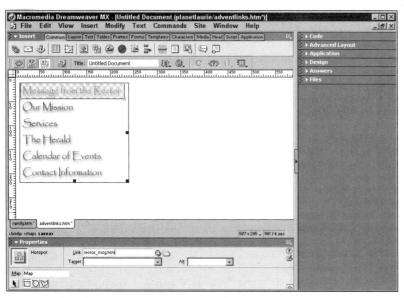

Figure 204-3: Setting the link details for a specific image map area

6. When your image map is complete, press F12 to preview your page
   in a browser. View the links that have been placed in the image map
   (see Figure 204-4).

Figure 204-4: Pointing to areas on an image map

Task 204

tip
- To help visitors decide
  which hotspot to click,
  enter something in the Alt
  text box in the Properties
  inspector so that text
  appears when users mouse
  over the hotspot. Bear in
  mind, however, that Alt text
  on hotspots is not universally supported in all
  browsers or versions
  thereof. As good design
  dictates, always test your
  pages in more than one
  browser.

cross-reference
- Learn to set up hotspots in
  FrontPage — see Part 16.

Creating Image Rollovers

A rollover consists of two images that occupy the same space on your Web page. One image replaces the other when the mouse pointer hovers over it. Rollovers are most useful for images because the image's change in appearance draws attention to the link. A rollover can also provide instructions (such as "Click Here!").

1. In Design view click to position the cursor where the image rollover should appear.

2. Choose Insert ⇨ Interactive Images ⇨ Rollover Image to open the Insert Rollover Image dialog box (see Figure 205-1).

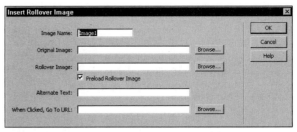

Figure 205-1: The Insert Rollover Image dialog box gives you all the options you need to set up your rollover.

3. Give the rollover a name in the Image Name text box. The name helps you find the code pertaining to the rollover in Code view.

4. Type the name of the file you want to use for the original image, or click the Browse button to find the file manually.

5. Choose the rollover image — the image that appears when someone's mouse rolls over the original image.

6. Type any desired alternate text, such as instructions for following the link, a description of what happens when the link is clicked, or text that serves as a caption for the image that appears.

7. In the When Clicked Go to URL text box, type or browse to the URL that the interactive image should link to.

8. Click OK to create the rollover. The image appears to have shading over it when it first appears in Dreamweaver (see Figure 205-2). This indicates that more than one image is occupying the space.

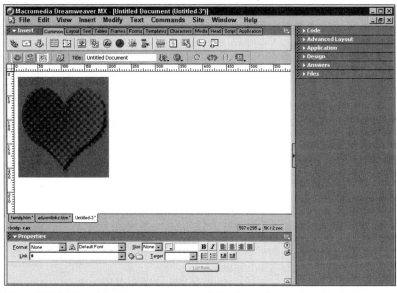

Figure 205-2: The original image appears and shading indicates that another image associated with the same spot appears on the page.

Task 206 Building Navigation Bars

A navigation bar can be very convenient, and depending on your page design, may be essential for providing a consistent list of links to pages within a site. Visitors like "nav bars" because they appear the same on every page (if they're designed correctly) and designers like them because Dreamweaver makes them easy to build.

1. Click to position the cursor where the navigation bar should appear. You should be in Design view (or the Design portion of the Code & Design view).

2. Choose Insert ⇨ Interactive Images ⇨ Navigation Bar to open the Insert Navigation Bar dialog box (see Figure 206-1).

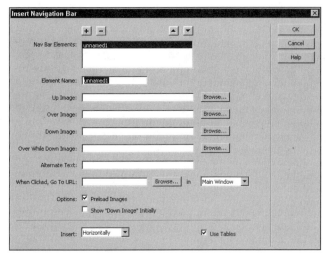

Figure 206-1: Adding several images to a navigation bar, each pointing to a different page in your site

3. Replace the "unnamed1" text in the Element Name text box with the name you want to give the first image in the navigation bar.

4. Click the plus-sign button above the Nav Bar Elements box. This moves the named element into the list of elements.

5. Click the Up Image text box and click the Browse button to select the image you want to appear when there's no mouse pointer hovering over the first element of the navigation bar.

6. Click in the When Clicked Go to URL text box and type the URL of (or browse to) the page that should appear when the first element in the navigation bar is clicked.

7. Choose the direction that the navigation bar should run: Horizontally (the default) or Vertically. You can also leave the Use Tables option clicked at the bottom of the dialog box so that the bar is placed in a table.

8. Repeat Steps 3 through 7 for each element in the navigation bar.

9. Click OK to create the bar (see Figure 206-2).

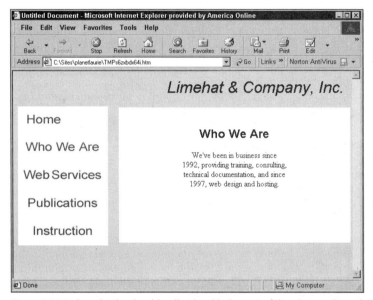

Figure 206-2: A navigation bar blending in with the rest of the page and running vertically, creating a graphical table of contents along the left side of the page

tips

▪ To place the same bar on all the pages in your site, copy and paste it on all pages. Adjust the links on a per-page basis using the Properties inspector, if necessary, to work with individual elements of the bar.

▪ The direction you choose for your bar (horizontal or vertical) should be dictated by the rest of your page and its overall layout.

cross-reference

▪ You can create a navigation bar in FrontPage, too. Find out how in Part 16.

Task 207

Creating Tables

Tables are one of the most powerful tools available to a Web designer. They enable you to structure your pages with considerable precision — placing text and graphics side by side, controlling the space taken up by text or graphics, and creating navigation bars and product listings. Their uses are nearly unlimited. Dreamweaver makes it easy to build them. (As you discover in Task 208, Dreamweaver also makes it easy to change and customize them after they're built.)

notes

- Tables inside other tables are called *nested tables*. Tools for creating and editing tables are identical whether you're dealing with a table on its own, a table inside another table, or a table that houses another table inside it.

- The numbers you enter are interpreted as pixels, so a cell padding of 3 adds three 3 pixels to the inside of each cell, keeping the cell content 3 pixels away from the cell walls.

1. In Design view click to position your cursor, placing it where the table should start. This can be on a page, inside a frame, within a layer, or inside an existing table.

2. Click the Insert Table button on the common toolbar to open the Insert Table dialog box (see Figure 207-1).

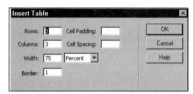

Figure 207-1: Defining the table you want to create in Dreamweaver

3. Enter the number of rows you want in your table.

4. Enter the number of columns you want in your table.

5. Enter any cell padding or cell spacing you think your table needs.

6. Enter the width of the table — a percentage of the page width or an exact pixel width. (The default is 75 percent of the page.)

7. If you want a border on your table, click in the Border cell and enter the pixel width of that border.

8. Click OK to create the table. A new empty table appears (see Figure 207-2).

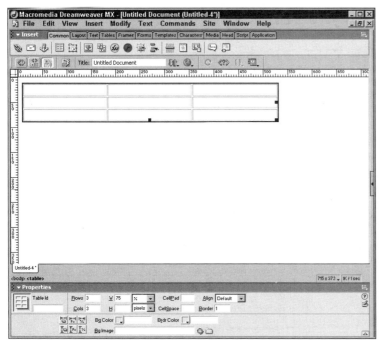

Figure 207-2: Table as a grid that can house any text or graphics you want to place within its cells

tips

- Cell spacing is helpful if you nest tables. In the nested table (the one inside a larger table) create a small amount of cell spacing and apply a background color to the main table. The color shows through the nested table's spacing, creating a nice border whose width equals the spacing. Of course, you need to apply a background color to the nested table's cells so you won't see the main table's background color through them.

- The Insert Table button is fourth from the left, and looks like a small grid. You can also choose Insert ➪ Table or press Ctrl+Alt+T.

- If you create a table and realize you need four rows instead of three, just click in the rightmost cell in the last row and press Tab to insert a whole new row.

cross-reference

- Creating a table in HTML is also covered in Part 6.

Task 208

Modifying an Existing Table

You can easily resize tables, change the background color, and adjust cell padding and spacing. You can also nest a table inside another one for further structural control over the placement of text, graphics, and graphical use of colored backgrounds and borders.

note

- You can enter a name for the table in the Table ID text box. This helps you spot references to the table in HTML code easily.

1. To access tools for changing the appearance and placement of your table, point to any edge of the table. When your mouse turns into a four-headed arrow (see Figure 208-1), click it.

Four-headed arrow

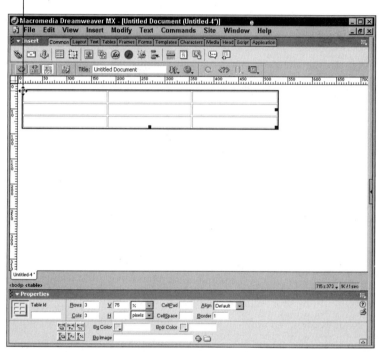

Figure 208-1: The mouse pointer as a four-headed arrow to indicate that table editing is possible

2. In the Properties inspector, change the number of cells in your table by changing values in the Rows and Cols fields.

3. Alter the W (width) and H (height) fields to change the size of the table itself.

caution

- While it's easy to resize a table by dragging its borders, it's not advisable to do this from a coding standpoint. When you drag a cell's walls to make it bigger or smaller, code is created that can conflict the attributes set through the Properties inspector. To adjust a cell's width and height, click inside a cell and use the W and H fields in the Cell section of the Properties inspector to specify a cell size.

4. Use the array of six buttons (see Figure 208-2) to make changes to the table's size and relationship to the page — using the first two buttons, you can clear the row heights and column widths to size the table to its contents, ignoring any previously-set dimensions.

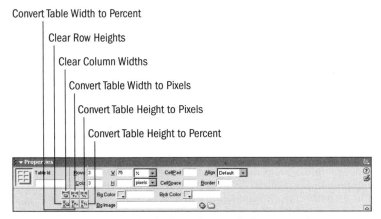

Convert Table Width to Percent
Clear Row Heights
Clear Column Widths
Convert Table Width to Pixels
Convert Table Height to Pixels
Convert Table Height to Percent

Figure 208-2: Tidying your table's dimensions to eliminate wasted space

5. Adjust the CellPad and CellSpace settings (entered in pixels).

6. Choose a new background color (Bg Color) for the table or apply a background image (Bg Image) to the table.

7. Apply a border (set the pixel depth in the Border field) and choose a color (Brdr Color).

8. Align your table relative to the page using the Align list box. Your choices are Left, Center, or Right, or Default.

tips

- If you simply click in one of the table's cells, the Properties inspector offers the standard text-formatting tools. You can, however, adjust the background ("Bg") color of the selected cell and align text and graphics within the cell containing the cursor.

- The % and Pixels options (to the right of W and H) allow you to choose how table dimensions are interpreted. If you choose %, the W or H setting is considered a percentage of the page (its width or height). If you choose Pixels, you express the table's size in direct measurements.

- The Default alignment option is confusing. "Default" means no align attribute is set but it's really the same as Left because when no alignment attribute is set for virtually any page element, the element lines up on the left side of the page.

cross-reference

- Learn about FrontPage's tools for customizing a table through its Table Properties dialog box. This is covered in Part 16.

Creating Forms

Forms allow visitors to interact with your Web page through form objects: text boxes, drop lists, radio buttons, and check boxes. Using these form objects, you can gather information for an online database. Creating a form requires first inserting one and then populating it with form objects. You can use a table to control form object placement as long as the table is within the form itself.

1. To insert a form on your page, click in Design view to place your cursor where the form should appear. Select Insert ➪ Form to open a box with a red dashed border.

2. As desired, insert a table into the form box.

3. Begin populating the form with form objects. To insert a form object, choose Insert ➪ Form Objects.

4. Continue adding objects to your form. For each one, use the Properties inspector to establish the object's settings. Figure 209-1 shows the Properties inspector options for a List/Menu.

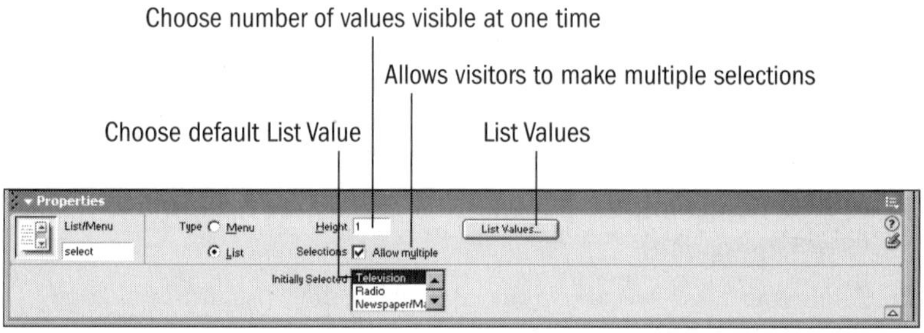

Choose number of values visible at one time

Allows visitors to make multiple selections

Choose default List Value   List Values

Figure 209-1: Customize individual form objects to help visitors make appropriate selections in a form.

5. When you complete the form, click its border to select the entire form. The Properties inspector changes to offer tools for establishing how the form itself works (see Figure 209-2).

Figure 209-2: Add code to run the form with which visitors interact.

6. In the Properties inspector, click the folder icon at the end of the Action text box to establish a pathname for the form processing script.

7. Choose POST or GET as the method for your form.

8. Establish the target method for your form: _blank, _self, _parent, or _top.

9. Choose an Enctype setting.

tips

- Using a table helps give your form structure. You can place different form objects in table cells, giving you greater control over the form's layout. Remove all cell borders so that the form doesn't resemble a straight-out table, from the visitor's perspective.

- When you click the List Values button, you see a box with plus and minus signs (for adding and deleting list items) and a place to type the items in your list. When you create a list, click OK to return to the form and see your list in the Initially Selected box in the Properties inspector.

- To make it easy to spot HTML code references to this form, give it a name in the Form Name text box.

cross-reference

- See Part 7 to read more about forms built in HTML.

Task 210

Working with Frames

Frames aren't always popular with Web designers or the Web-surfing public for a variety of reasons. However, frames do present a flexible structural environment for building a Web page (a *frameset* when a group of frames are built inside it) and they do give the designer some interesting tools for displaying several Web pages within one visual field.

1. To create a frameset, choose File ⇨ New. In the New Document dialog box click Framesets in the Category list (see Figure 210-1).

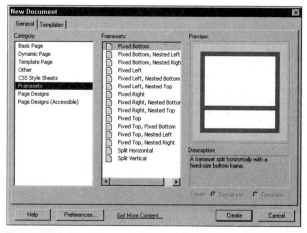

Figure 210-1: The Framesets list providing several arrangement options

2. To see what each of the listed framesets looks like in terms of the frames it creates, click on each one and observe the result in the Preview area.

3. Click Create after you find a frameset that appears to provide the arrangement you need for your page. A new page appears, with frames in place (see Figure 210-2).

4. Use the Properties inspector to set your border preferences.

5. Populate your individual frames by clicking in the desired frame.

6. To set preferences for individual frames (to accommodate the content), press the Alt key and click inside the frame. The Properties inspector changes (see Figure 210-3).

7. If your frame contains another Web page, enter the URL in the Src box. You can click the folder icon to browse to the file as well.

8. Choose whether or not your frame has a scroll bar and whether or not visitors can resize the frame. Continue setting up the remaining frames (see Figure 210-4).

notes

- You can also press Ctrl+N to issue the File ⇨ New command.

- Frames can contain anything – text, graphics, tables, or layers. Enter a source (Src) link for a particular frame so that a particular Web page appears within the frame – for example, a Google search window or an Amazon.com page.

- Search engines are often unable to index frames pages because the pages themselves contain no searchable text; the content comes from elsewhere. If you rely on visitors to find your site by searching Google or Yahoo, structure your pages with tables instead. That way description and keyword attributes will help search engines list your site.

caution

- If your Src page has its own links, be careful how you set up the target for those links. Use "_blank" so that the linked pages open up in new windows, leaving your page (and the active frame) open in the original browser.

Frame border

Walls indicate individual frames   "Untitled Frameset" in title bar

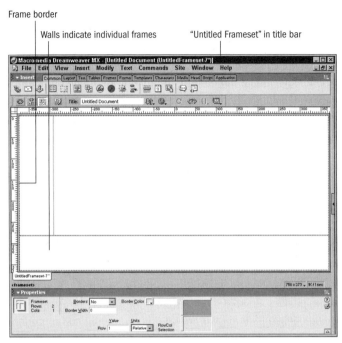

Figure 210-2: Frameset settings in the Properties inspector

Create internal margins   Toggle scrollbar on or off

Src box   No Resize   Turn borders on or off

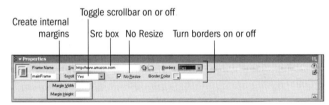

Figure 210-3: Customizing the frame to meet the needs of the page inside it

Figure 210-4: A frameset filled with original content (left) and links to other sites (right and bottom) that the browser fills within the frame borders

Working with Layers

nlike frames and tables, layers float above a Web page; they're not a fixed part of the page. Unless you fill a layer with a background color or image, you can see through them. You can put anything you want in a layer, however: text, graphics, tables, and multimedia. Some older browsers (prior to version 4.0) don't display layers, so use them with care. Only put information in layers if you know your visitors use current versions of Internet Explorer, Netscape, and other browsers.

1. To start the process of creating a layer, click in Design view where you want the upper-left corner of the layer to be.

2. Choose Insert ⇨ Layer. A layer appears on the page (see Figure 211-1).

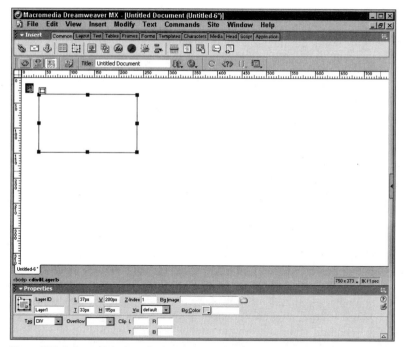

Figure 211-1: Inserting a layer in one step

3. With the layer selected, observe the Properties inspector (see Figure 211-2), which you can use to customize the layer's appearance and placement.

Figure 211-2: Selecting a layer displays the Properties inspector and its layer-related tools

Task 211

4. If you don't like your layer's size and position, adjust them using the L (Left), T (Top), W (width), and H (height) fields.

5. If you have more than one layer occupying any portion of the same space on the page, adjust the z-index (the layer's stacking order) for the active layer.

6. Choose a Vis (visibility) setting: Default, Inherit, Visible, or Hidden.

7. Set any background (Bg) treatments (images or colors) for the layer. Without any background color or image set, the layer is transparent.

8. Use the Tag field to choose the HTML tag that defines the active layer (DIV is the default).

9. Choose how you want content that overflows the layer's dimensions to appear. Your choices in the Overflow field are Visible, Hidden, Scroll, and Auto.

10. After establishing these settings for your layer, fill it with text, graphics, tables, even other layers (called *nested layers*). Figure 211-3 shows a layer with text and graphics, and a scroll bar to let the visitor read it all.

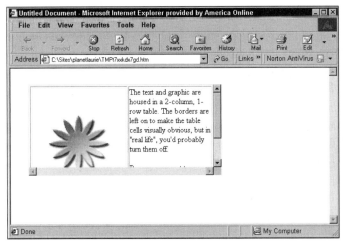

Figure 211-3: Layers give you design freedom, but with potential drawbacks in older browsers

tips

- Give your layer a name in the Layer ID box so you can spot references to it within HTML.

- For the Vis setting, Visible and Hidden are self-explanatory. Default doesn't set a visibility setting; it relies on the browser, which probably goes with Inherit if Default is chosen. Inherit uses the visibility setting of the layer's parent. If you want your layer to be visible at all times, choose Visible.

- To make sure your layer remains the same size no matter how much content appears in it, choose Scroll from the Overflow field. If your layer's content exceeds its size, horizontal or vertical scroll bar(s) allow visitors to read all the content.

- If your layer includes content, be sure to give the layer a background color. This prevents text from becoming illegible if it sits on top of another page or a busy background image.

cross-reference

- Learn how to build layers in HTML (see Tasks 99–101).

Creating Style Sheets

Cascading Style Sheets allow you to bundle several formats into one easily applied tool. Viewed and created through the CSS Styles palette, you can create them for sitewide or single-document use. Build them based on existing content's formatting or from scratch.

note

- If the style sheet is only useful for the active Web page, click the This Document Only option.

1. In the Design panel, click the CSS Styles tab. If the Design panel is not visible, choose Window ➪ CSS Styles to display the panel.

2. Click the New CSS Style button (the document icon with the plus sign) at the bottom of the Design panel (see Figure 212-1).

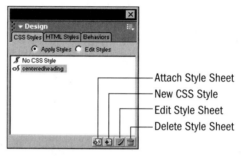

— Attach Style Sheet
— New CSS Style
— Edit Style Sheet
— Delete Style Sheet

Figure 212-1: The CSS Styles tab in the Design panel

3. In the New CSS Style dialog box, use the Name box to name your new style sheet.

4. Accept the default Make Custom Style setting in the Type area.

5. Determine the Define In location — typically, the same as the style name (entered in the Name box), with the .css extension.

6. Click OK to open the Save Style Sheet File As dialog box (see Figure 212-2).

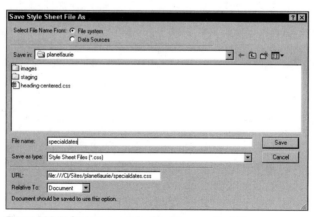

Figure 212-2: Saving your style sheet in your site folder

Task 212

7. Click Save to save the CSS file.

8. In the CSS Style Definition dialog box (see Figure 212-3), establish the formatting that the style sheet applies.

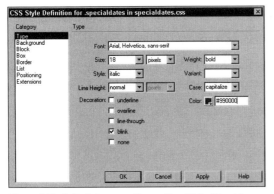

Figure 212-3: Defining your Cascading Style Sheet in one or more categories

9. When your style sheet formats are established, click the OK button to close the CSS Style Definition dialog box.

10. To use your style sheet, select content in the Web page and then click the CSS name in the CSS Styles tab on the Design panel. Figure 212-4 shows a CSS applied to text in a Web page.

Font color and size applied by CSS   Design panel

Figure 212-4: Formatting applied easily with a CSS in the Design panel

tips

- Use a name that indicates when and why you'd use the style — something like "specialdate" for a style that is applied to dates of various events. Start your style name with a period to make it stand out as a CSS style within your HTML document. The only requirement is that the name start with a letter and contain no spaces or punctuation.

- Setting up your style sheet's effects requires making a Category selection and then using the Type options on the right side of the dialog box (which vary by category). If you want to set up formatting from more than one category, use the Apply button to apply the settings so far and then choose a new category and set the formats for that.

- To edit a style sheet, select it from the CSS Style tab and click the Edit Style Sheet button at the bottom of the Design panel. The same dialog box options from the CSS Style Definition dialog box appear, making it simple to change things.

cross-reference

- Learn more about Cascading Style Sheets in Appendix D, available on www.wiley.com/compbooks/10simplestepsorless.

Task 213

Using Behaviors

By generating JavaScript code in HTML documents, Dreamweaver behaviors allow you to create ways for visitors to interact with your Web page. Typical uses include something that happens when a mouse pointer hovers over or clicks on a graphic, providing more options for interactive outcomes than a simple rollover or Flash button does.

1. To access the Behaviors tab, activate the Design panel. If the panel is not visible, choose Windows ➪ Behaviors to display it. Select the Behaviors tab (see Figure 213-1).

Figure 213-1: The Behaviors tab in the Design panel

2. In your Web page select the graphic or other component that you want to associate with the behavior.

3. Click the plus-sign button in the Behaviors tab to display a list of behaviors you can associate with the selected page element (see Figure 213-2).

4. Depending on the behavior you cho0se, you may have to select a file — an image to swap, a sound to play, and so on.

5. Click OK to confirm that the sound, image, or other file is associated with the event.

6. Back in the Behaviors tab, click the drop triangle on the behavior you've added. It lists the events that can trigger the selected behavior (see Figure 213-3).

7. To add to or reduce the list of events to match the browsers your visitors are most likely to use, choose Show Events For from the events list and make a selection from the submenu.

8. Repeat Steps 2 through 7 for any elements in your page you'd like to make more interactive for visitors.

Figure 213-2: Choosing the behavior you want to occur

Figure 213-3: Choosing a way for visitors to interact with the Web page

tips

- Press Shift+F3 to display the Behaviors tab in the Design panel.

- When an image or other page object is selected, only those behaviors associated with it will appear in the Behaviors tab. If you associate more than one behavior with a particular object, you can change the behavior's order by selecting an established event/behavior and clicking the up and down triangles in the Behaviors tab.

cross-reference

- To learn a little more about JavaScript, read Part 10.

Using the Preload Images Behavior

The Preload Images behavior loads images into the visitor's browser cache. Once the images are loaded, the browser loads the rest of the page and the entire document appears at once. This provides a more uniform experience for the visitor, so they don't have to watch the site construct itself in front of their eyes.

notes

- This step assures you that the JavaScript code the behavior wrote works with not only current browsers but previous ones as well. Of course, selecting really old browsers limits the effects you can use.

- If you don't click the plus button before attempting to enter another image, the image you last chose will be replaced by the next image you choose.

1. Attach the Preload Images behavior to the body section of your document by selecting the `<body>` tag on the tag selector in the lower-left corner of the document window (see Figure 214-1).

Figure 214-1: Selecting the `<body>` tag in the document window's tag selector

2. Open the Behaviors panel by selecting Windows ⇨ Behaviors from the menu bar.

3. Click the Behaviors panel's plus button and choose Show Events For ⇨ 4.0 and Later Browsers.

4. Click the Behaviors panel's plus button a second time and choose Actions ⇨ Preload Images. This opens the Preload Images dialog box (see Figure 214-2).

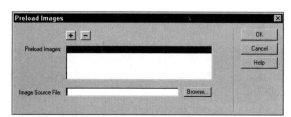

Figure 214-2: The Preload Images dialog box

5. Click Browse to locate an image file to preload or else enter an image's pathname in the Image Source File field.

6. Click the plus button at the top of the dialog box to add the image from the Image Source File field to the Preload Images list. This clears the Image Source File field so you can select another image.

7. Repeat Steps 5 and 6 for each image you want to preload for this document.

8. To remove an image from the Preload Images list, select the image in the list and click the minus button.

9. When you've selected all the images you want to preload, click OK to close the dialog box.

cross-reference

- See Part 10 to learn more about how to write this kind of JavaScript yourself.

Using the Open Browser Window Behavior

The Open Browser Window behavior opens a pop-up browser window that goes to a URL you specify. You can specify all sorts of properties for this window, such as dimensions, window name, resizability, and appearance of menus, tools, and scroll bars, and so on.

1. Select the element to which you want to attach a pop-up window.

2. Open the Behaviors panel by choosing Windows ⇨ Behaviors from the main menu bar.

3. Click the Behaviors panel's plus button and choose Show Events For ⇨ 4.0 and Later Browsers.

4. Click the plus button again and choose Open Browser Window from the submenu. This opens the Open Browser Window dialog box (see Figure 215-1).

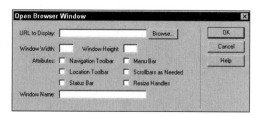

Figure 215-1: The Open Browser Window dialog box

5. Click the Browse button to locate the file you want opened in the new window.

6. Use the Window Width and Window Height fields to set the dimensions for the new window.

7. Set any of the following options by marking the corresponding check box:

   • **Navigation Toolbar:** The row of standard browser buttons (Back, Forward, Home, etc.)

   • **Location Toolbar:** The window's address field

   • **Status Bar:** The window's status bar, where messages like remaining load times and link URLs appear

notes

• If you want a window to open when the document you're working on opens, select the `<body>` tag and use an `onLoad` behavior. If you want a pop-up window triggered by a link, select the link text or image and use an `onClick` behavior.

• If you specify no attributes for the window, it opens with the same dimensions and attributes as the window that launched it. Specifying any attribute for the window automatically turns off all other attributes that are not explicitly turned on.

- **Menu Bar:** The standard menu bar (File, Edit, View, Go, etc).

- **Scrollbars as Needed:** Scroll bars, which appear if content extends beyond the viewable area

- **Resize Handles:** Window that users can resize either by dragging the lower right corner of the window or by clicking the maximize button (Windows) or size box (Macintosh) in the upper right corner

- **Window Name:** Name of the new window object, which allows you to target it with links or manipulate it with JavaScript

8. Click OK to close the Open Browser Window dialog box.

9. Choose the event handler you want to trigger the behavior. Figure 215-2 shows a pop-up window triggered by a hyperlink.

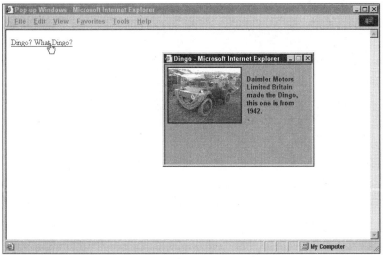

Figure 215-2: A simple pop-up window (right) triggered by clicking on a link (top left)

cross-reference

- Dreamweaver behaviors can also validate the entries visitors place in form fields (see Task 216).

Using the Validate Form Behavior

The Validate Form behavior makes sure your visitors have entered the right kind of data into specified text fields. If the visitor enters any bad data (data of the wrong type for a field's specifications), the JavaScript in this behavior prevents the form from being submitted to the server.

notes

▪ Selecting Anything without also choosing Required has no effect.

▪ The Anything option is the default value for a required field. It only makes sure that content is indeed entered into the field by the visitor.

1. Attach the Validate Form behavior to the `<form>` tag of your document by selecting it with the tag selector in the lower left corner of the document window (see Figure 216-1).

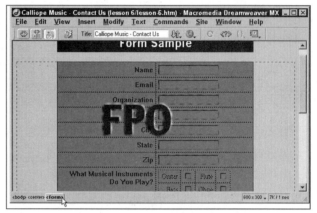

Figure 216-1: Selecting the <form> tag in the document window

2. Open the Behaviors panel by choosing Window ⇨ Behaviors from the menu bar.

3. Click the Behaviors panel's plus button and choose Show Events For ⇨ 4.0 and Later Browsers.

4. Click the Behaviors panel's plus button again and choose Validate Form from the submenu. This opens the Validate Form dialog box (see Figure 216-2). Each text field in the form appears in the Named Fields list box.

Figure 216-2: The Validate Form dialog box, showing all fields in the form

5. Select a text field from the Named Fields list.

6. Click the Required check box if the field must be filled in by the visitor.

7. Choose one of the following Accept options:

   - **Anything:** For a required field accepting basic text content, like names or street addresses

   - **E-mail Address:** To check that the field contains the @ symbol

   - **Number:** To check that the field contains only numbers

   - **Number From:** To check that the field contains a number in a specific range, which you enter in the fields to the right

8. Repeat Steps 5 through 7 for each field you validate.

9. Click OK to close the Validate Form dialog box.

cross–reference

- Behaviors make use of JavaScript. To learn more about JavaScript, see Part 10.

Task **216**

Using the Set Text for Status Bar Behavior

Every browser has a status bar. It typically runs along the bottom of the browser window and displays what the browser is currently doing. For example, when you run your mouse over a link, the URL the link points to appears. When you click a link, the status of the download appears too — typically the phrase, "Downloading http://...". The Set Text of Status Bar behavior writes a message to the status bar in response to some action taken by the site visitor.

1. Select the element you want the to trigger the status bar message.

2. Open the Behaviors panel by choosing Windows ⇨ Behaviors from the menu bar.

3. Click the Behaviors panel's plus button and choose Show Events For ⇨ 4.0 and Later Browsers (see Figure 217-1).

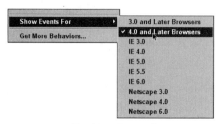

Figure 217-1: The Show Events For submenu

4. Click the plus button again and choose Set Text ⇨ Set Text of Status Bar from the submenu. This opens the Set Text for Status Bar dialog box (see Figure 217-2).

Figure 217-2: The Set Text for Status Bar dialog box

5. Type your message in the Message field.

6. Click OK to close the Set Text for Status Bar dialog box.

7. Choose the event handler you want to trigger the behavior.

cross-reference

▪ One of the most time-saving tools in Dreamweaver is the Assets panel (see Task 218).

Working with Assets

The Assets panel provides a list of the weapons in your Web design arsenal — images, colors, sounds, movies, URLs, templates — that you can use in Web pages. Any of these items you add to pages are automatically added to your Assets list. You can also add items from the Assets panel or Favorites folder to your Web page quickly and easily — it's just a matter of drag and drop.

notes

• Press F11 to display the Assets panel.

• Colors are stored whenever you apply them to anything — text, table cells, borders — but only apply directly to text using the drag-and-drop method. If you want to use an asset color for anything else, click the Properties inspector color field for the element you want to color and then take the eyedropper up to the Assets panel to grab the color you want to use.

1. Before you can use your Assets, you have to display them. Choose Window ➪ Assets, or click the Assets tab in the Files panel.

2. For a page that already has some images and other elements inserted, the Assets panel will already have some items in it you can use. To view them for each of the categories (see Figure 218-1), click the buttons on the right side of the tab.

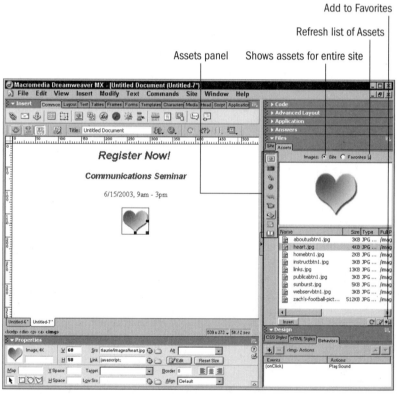

Add to Favorites

Refresh list of Assets

Assets panel   Shows assets for entire site

Figure 218-1: Assets stored in nine categories (right side)

3. To use an asset, click the category it belongs in and drag it from the Assets panel onto the page (see Figure 218-2).

4. To move an asset to the Favorites folder, simply click on it and click the Add to Favorites button in the lower right corner of the Assets panel. Figure 218-3 shows the current Favorites folder for a particular site.

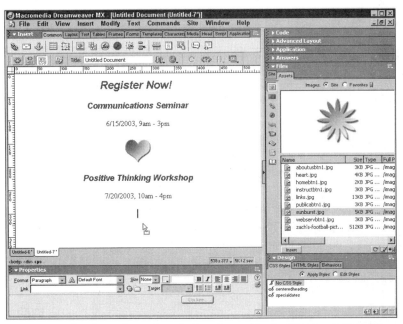

Figure 218-2: Reusing an image from the Assets panel by dragging it onto the page

Create a folder   Edit Favorites   Remove from Favorites

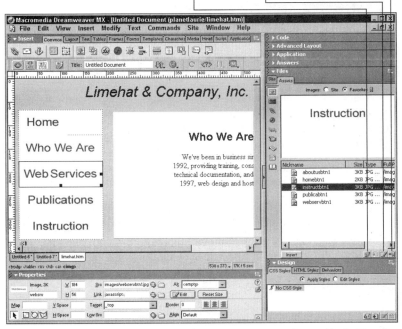

Figure 218-3: Your most-used images, colors, and other page elements in the Favorites folder for easy access

5. To take an asset out of the Favorites folder, select it and then click the Remove From Favorites button.

Task 219

Setting Up a Remote Host

When it's finally time to upload your site to a Web server, you need to pre-pare for it first. After you tell Dreamweaver how you will connect to your Web server, you establish login and security settings for the connection.

1. Choose Site ⇨ Edit Sites. The Site Definition dialog box (Basic tab) appears (see Figure 219-1). If you already see the Advanced tab, go to Step 2.

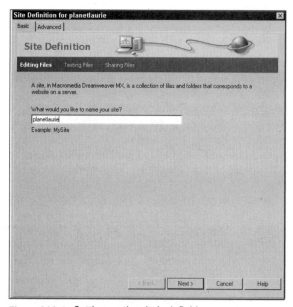

Figure 219-1: Setting up the site's definition

2. Click the Advanced tab in the Site Definition dialog box and select the Remote Info category. The Web server information appears on the right (see Figure 219-2).

3. Choose your access method.

4. In the FTP Host box, type the physical location of your FTP server — an IP address or something like ftp.*domain*.com.

5. If there's a particular directory within the FTP server you need to connect to, enter it in the Host Directory box.

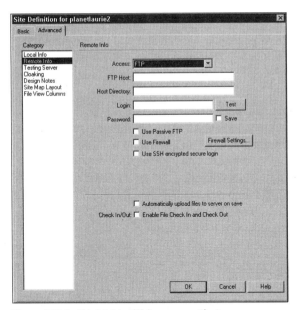

Figure 219-2: Establishing Web server settings

6. Type your login name — typically a user ID or username — and enter your password.

7. Check any of the three additional options — Use Passive FTP, Use Firewall, or Use SSH Encrypted Secure Login.

8. If you want your edited files to be automatically uploaded whenever you save them, click the Automatically Upload Files to Server on Save option.

9. If you work in a group and want to make sure two people can't work on the same file at the same time, click the Enable File Check In and Check Out option.

10. Click OK to save your remote server settings.

tips

- Using FTP is easiest if you're not physically connected to your Web server on a network. The other options in the Access list assume some sort of connection other than dial-up or broadband connection to a remote server provided by a Web hosting company.

- Your password appears as asterisks ("***") so that if people stand nearby, they can't see your password. Click the Save check box only if you don't want to enter your password every time you log on.

- If you're not sure which option(s) to select, check with your Web host's technical support staff. They can tell you whatever you need to know about logging in and successfully transferring your files.

cross-references

- Check In and Check Out is covered in Task 221.

- Check Part 16 for information on how FrontPage handles uploading pages to the server.

Downloading and Uploading Files

Once you set up a remote folder, you're ready to upload your files to the Web server. You can also move files in the other direction, from the Web server to your local drive — either to back up what's on the server or to replace local files with what's stored remotely on the server. Uploading and downloading are referred to, respectively, as *put* and *get*.

1. Before using Get or Put, you must activate the Files panel and click the Site tab. To display the Files panel, choose Window ⇨ Site.

2. To put your files on the remote server (or into a local or network folder), click the right-most drop list (to the right of the Site drop list) and choose Local View (if it's not selected already). Then select the folder/s or file/s you want to upload (see Figure 220-1)

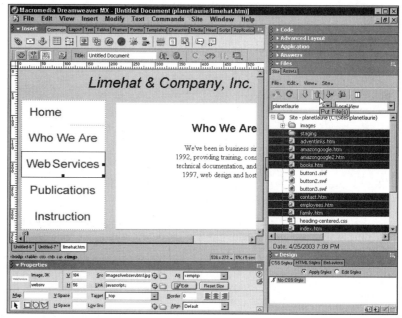

Figure 220-1: Selected files in a folder for uploading

3. Click the Put button (with the blue upward arrow), and then choose Remote View from the right-hand drop-down list.

4. Click the Refresh button to see your remote server or local/network file and the uploaded files there (see Figure 220-2).

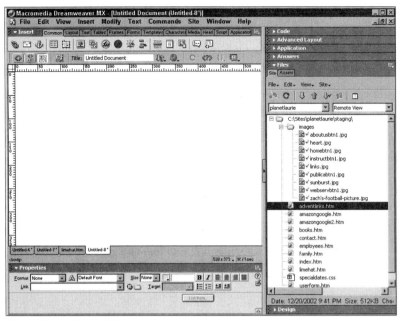

Figure 220-2: Viewing files on the remote server

5. To get, or download, files from a remote server or another local/network folder, select the content you want to download.

6. Click the Get button (with the green downward arrow).

7. When your Get/Put session is complete, click the Disconnect from Remote Host button.

tips

- Another way to display the Site tab of the Files panel is to press F8.

- You may see a prompt after clicking the Put button, asking if you want to "include dependent files." If you're uploading a page that includes images or anything other than HTML code, click Yes to send the image and other files as well. On the other hand, if you're part of a Web design team and don't know if you're about to upload the latest versions of files others may be editing, click No.

- Always disconnect if you leave your desk, do other work where you might bump the keyboard or mouse, or are away from your computer for a while. Disconnecting prevents accidental puts or gets, and keeps others from using your computer to upload or download files you may not want them to access.

cross-reference

- Appendix F covers the process of uploading files to your host's Web server. Check it out online at www.wiley.com/compbooks/10simplestepsorless.

Using Check In/Check Out

When two or more people edit pages in a particular site, it makes sense to use Dreamweaver's Check In and Check Out feature. Much like taking books out of a library, the Check In and Check Out system ensures that if one person checks out a file, no one else can work on it at the same time (they can view it, however). Check In and Check Out makes the process of multiple designers uploading files to the Web server more orderly.

note

- As soon as you turn on Check In and Check Out, fields appear in the dialog box allowing you to enter your identifying information.

1. To use Check In and Check Out, first turn Check In and Check Out on. Select Site ⇨ Edit Sites.

2. The Edit Sites dialog box opens (see Figure 221-1). Select the site you want to edit.

Figure 221-1: Choosing the site to control with Check In and Check Out

3. Double-click the site you want to edit, or select it and click the Edit button.

4. In the Site Definition dialog box, click the Advanced tab if it isn't already selected.

5. Click the Remote Info category (see Figure 221-2).

6. Next to Check In/Out, click both the Enable File Check In and Check Out option and the Check Out Files When Opening option.

7. Type your name in the Check Out Name text box and also enter an e-mail address in the Email Address text box. Click OK to close the dialog box.

caution

- If you don't check out the dependent files as well, you can end up with an HTML document but no access to the images and other elements included in the page.

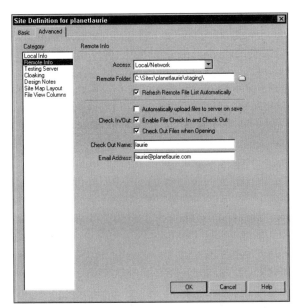

Figure 221-2: Accessing advanced settings in the Site Definition dialog box

8. To use Check In and Check Out, go to the Site tab of the Files panel and select the file(s) you wish to edit or upload (put) to the Web server.

9. Click the Check Out Files button (the green downward arrow with the check mark). Depending on your situation make your selection in the Dependent Files dialog box.

10. When you finish editing the file, select it in the site list and click the Check In button (the blue upward arrow with the padlock next to it). Again, depending on your situation, make your selection in the Dependent Files dialog box.

tip

■ Be considerate of the other members of your team and make efficient use of Check In and Check Out. Don't forget to check files back in after you've edited or uploaded them — otherwise, coworkers will be unable to access a file overnight, over a weekend, or even for a crucial hour during the day.

cross-reference

■ Dreamweaver is the only application we're covering in this book that offers any controls for file sharing. If you're working alone and don't have file sharing concerns, check out our HomeSite coverage in Part 14 for more information on opening existing HTML files for editing.

Part 16: Working with FrontPage

Task 222

Setting Up a Web Site

Microsoft FrontPage is a Web design tool that uses a WYSIWYG interface to allow you to design your pages and sites graphically. You can also get a good look at the code, too, and preview your work in a browser window to check your progress as you design. FrontPage is famous for its themes, the preset styles that control the buttons, background, and overall look of sites designed with the product. This speeds and simplifies the design process, but also creates sites that are immediately identified as "FrontPage sites," which isn't usually a good thing. You can also design from scratch, avoiding the potential pitfalls of a site with graphics that thousands of other FrontPage designers will have also used. When beginning the design process in FrontPage, it's best to set up a site, and to do so following a set of prescribed steps. It's also important to realize that a Web site is more than a collection of pages. It's a cohesive, logical structure that incorporates pages, graphics, and links into a functioning system. The need to build a functioning Web site locally is key to uploading the site to a remote server and having all the pages and their components appear and function properly.

1. With FrontPage launched, choose File ➪ New. This opens the New task pane (see Figure 222-1).

Figure 222-1: The New task pane gives you options for starting a new page or site.

2. Click the More Web Site Templates link in the middle of the task pane to access the Web Site Templates dialog box.

3. Double-click the Empty Web Site icon to create a new site (see Figure 222-2).

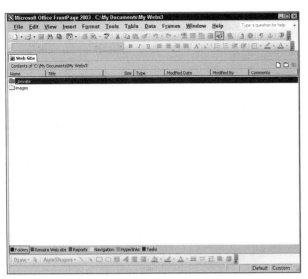

Figure 222-2: View a list of existing sites (if any) and your new site's starting folder structure, which includes an images folder.

4. Click the Navigation button at the bottom of the window to access tools for a hierarchical view of the pages in your site. Figure 222-3 shows the resulting view and tools.

New page button

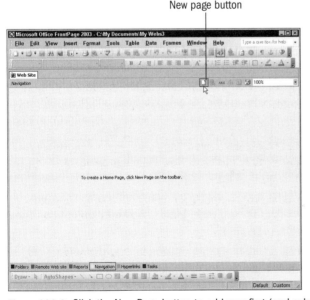

Figure 222-3: Click the New Page button to add your first (and subsequent) page.

tip

- Empty Web Site is a good choice if your site will not include a prescribed group of pages, such as the standard "About Us" or "Contact Us" pages (although you can still add such pages to your site). It gives you total freedom to build the pages you need in the order you want to create and connect them.

cross-reference

- Part 15's coverage of Dreamweaver contains instructions for building a Web site utilizing yet another graphical web design environment.

Task 223

Creating and Rearranging Blank Web Pages

After creating a blank Web site, you're ready to insert pages — starting with the home page and creating a tiered, hierarchical structure of subpages that branch off of it. Using the Navigation view of your new site, it's easy to insert pages and access additional site-building tools.

1. In Navigation view, click the New Page button. If this creates your home page, click on the Home Page icon that appears (shown in Figure 223-1).

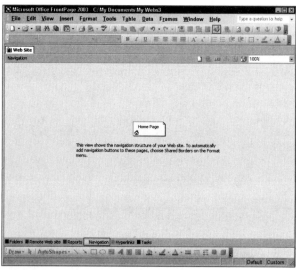

Figure 223-1: The Home Page is the first page you create and also the top-most page of the site.

2. With the Home Page icon selected, indicating that the next page should be a subpage to it, click the New Page button again. A subpage icon appears (see Figure 223-2).

3. To create a third level of pages, click one of the existing subpage icons and then click the New Page button. A third tier appears, along with an icon for its first page.

4. To rearrange pages and tiers of pages, simply drag them with your mouse. You may find yourself wanting to rearrange them for any number of reasons – to establish the connections between pages that FrontPage will later use to create navigation tools based on your page hierarchy, or to help you view your site more logically, grouping your pages logically. Whatever your reason for rearranging your existing pages, you can drag them within the same tier or between tiers (see Figure 223-3).

caution

- Watch the lines that appear as you drag your pages around. The line shows which page your moved page will be attached to and what relationship will be forged: a subpage or equal page on the same tier.

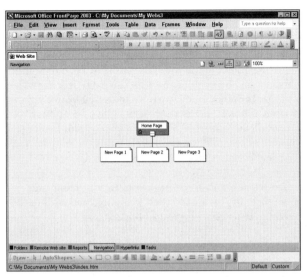

Figure 223-2: Each time you click the New Page button, another subpage appears.

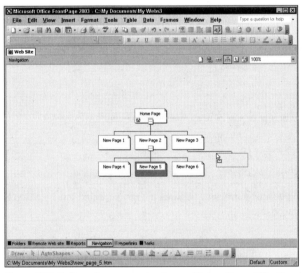

Figure 223-3: Dragging a page to change its location within the site hierarchy

tip

▪ The small minus sign that appears in page icons that have subpages indicates that those subpages are visible within Navigation view. Click the minus back to a plus sign to hide those subpages from view.

cross-reference

▪ Dreamweaver provides a similar tool for adding pages to a site. Read about the specifics of setting up pages in Part 15, tasks 189 and 190, and throughout Part 15, where page-building techniques are discussed.

Naming and Saving Pages

A fter adding pages to a blank Web site and rearranging them to meet your needs, you should name and save the pages. In so doing, you're determining the page names that appear on any page banners, in the page title bars when the pages are viewed through a browser, and the page names that you'll refer to as you edit the site over time. Choose names that make it clear what the page does. Don't limit yourself to using all lowercase letters, underscores in lieu of spaces ("about_us"), or abbreviated names ("page3a"). Pick names that make it easy for you to select the right file when it comes time to edit it later.

notes

• The page names that FrontPage assigns are based on the page's location in the site's hierarchy. Even after you rearrange them (as we did in Task 223), the generic names don't change. It doesn't matter if a "Top Page" became a second-level page, stemming from another top page.

• What do I mean by "Web server-friendly"? Most Web servers prefer filenames in all-lowercase letters, without an excess of punctuation (avoid slashes, question marks, periods, and ampersands), and without any spaces unless you want to create the illusion of a space with the underscore character. If you adhere to these basic guidelines, you should have no problem uploading and accessing your files.

1. In Navigation view, click once on the page you want to name and save. The selected page in Navigation view is highlighted, and its name appears in a white box (see Figure 224-1).

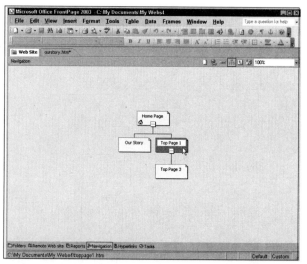

Figure 224-1: The generic name applied when a page is created (such as "Top Page 1") is easily replaced later

2. Right-click the page icon and choose Rename from the menu that appears (see Figure 224-2). The name you give the page will appear in the navigation view of the site, as well as on the page title bar when viewed through a browser.

3. Once you select Rename, the existing (generic) name is highlighted, which you can type over. The name you type here will also appear in any page banner, so feel free to use spaces, proper capitalization, and so forth (see Figure 224-3).

4. Continue to name the rest of your pages, at least those whose function you're sure about.

5. To save your pages with useful filenames, double-click the page icon to see the Page view of the page and then choose File ⇨ Save As. The Save As dialog box appears (see Figure 224-4).

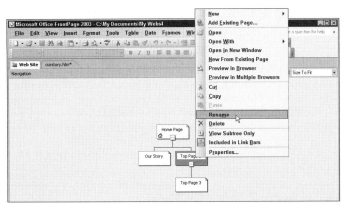

Figure 224-2: The shortcut menu offers a series of page-specific commands, including Rename.

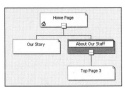

Figure 224-3: Entering the display name for the page in question

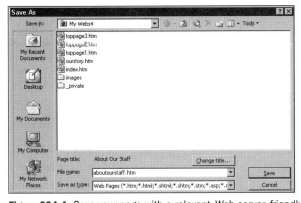

Figure 224-4: Save your page with a relevant, Web server–friendly name.

6. Type a name for your file in the File Name field and be sure to add the extension, especially if you have a preference for .htm versus .html.

7. Click Save to confirm the name, and repeat Steps 5 and 6 for the rest of your pages that you want to save.

tip

• You can rename pages as many times as you want — to fix spelling errors or typos, or simply because you decide you want a different name to appear in the page banner.

cross-reference

• Most WYSIWYG Web design applications have similar procedures for similar tasks. Find out about Dreamweaver's file naming and techniques in Part 15, Task 190.

Viewing and Changing Page Properties

At any point in the process of building a Web site it's good to view the proper-ties of your pages – the page title, the background image, link colors, and so on – so you can make changes before you get too far in the design process.

1. In Navigation view, double-click the page whose properties you want to view and potentially change. This takes you to the Page view.

2. Choose Format ➪ Properties. This opens the Page Properties dialog box (see Figure 225-1).

note

- The remaining tabs (Advanced, Custom, Language, Workgroup) con-tain options for customizing the way scripting languages and protocols apply to your page. The Workgroup tab gives you options for attributing a page and the work done on it to an expense or activity category.

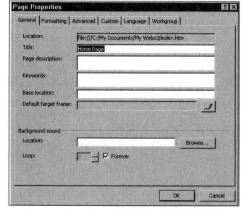

Figure 225-1: Six tabs of page property options in the Page Properties dialog box

3. On the General tab type a title for your page, as desired. Keep the title short, but clear. Remember that it will appear on a visitor's title bar, and there may be other text on that bar – their brower name, for example, which may truncate longer titles.

4. On the Formatting tab designate a background image for the page. When you click the Background Picture option, you can use the Browse button to select a graphic to serve as a background.

caution

- If you use a theme for your Web site (see Task 226), choosing a background image or color is really a moot point because the theme will override it.

5. Still on the Formatting tab, choose a background color for your page. You can click the color drop list (set to Automatic by default) to view a palette of Web-safe colors (see Figure 225-2).

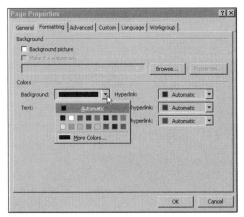

Figure 225-2: A group of 16 basic, Web-safe colors in the color palette

6. You can also set text and hyperlink colors from the same Web-safe color palette. Why change the defaults for text and hyperlinks? For text, you may want to use a color that's more visible or legible on your chosen background color. For hyperlinks, you may want your link text to stand out on your background or to not clash with other colors in your page. It's generally an aesthetic decision, and/or one based on legibility.

7. Repeat Steps 1 through 6 for any other pages in your site that you want to customize. Revert to Navigation view to access another page using the View menu.

tip

- If the graphic you want to use for a background is not designed to fade out behind your page content, click the Make it a Watermark option to create that effect automatically. Remember, the background image you choose should be one that doesn't compete visually with your text or graphics, and that loads quickly.

cross-reference

- Dreamweaver offers a Page Properties dialog box through which many of the same settings can be made for an individual Web page (see Part 15, Task 190).

Applying Themes

Besides applying individual background images and colors, text colors, and link colors to individual pages in your site, you can apply a theme so that all your pages look the same — only the page content will vary.

1. In either Navigation or Page view, choose Format ➪ Theme. This opens the Theme task pane (see Figure 226-1).

Figure 226-1: Choosing a theme by viewing its thumbnail image

2. Scroll through the themes. If you (or anyone else who uses your computer) have created a page or site before, the most recently used themes will appear first, followed by those that were installed with FrontPage. If you've never used the application before, the Theme task pane will start with the installed themes.

3. When you find a theme you want to apply to your site, point to the thumbnail for that theme with your mouse and make a selection from the pop-up menu (see Figure 226-2).

4. Choose Apply As Default Theme from the menu.

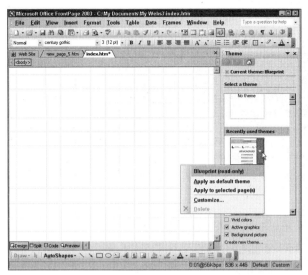

Figure 226-2: Options for applying a theme

5. To see your selected theme on individual pages, work in Page view and see the background image in place (see Figure 226-3).

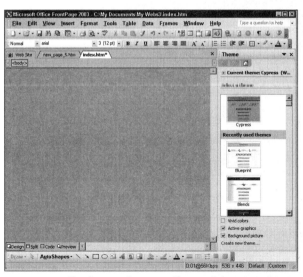

Figure 226-3: The Cypress theme applies a subtle green pattern to the page background.

tip
- A prompt appears to tell you that any existing formatting (set through the Page Properties dialog box — see Task 225) will be replaced if you proceed.

cross-reference
- Task 9 covers applying a background image to a Web page in HTML.

Task 227

Creating a New Theme

FrontPage offers a seemingly endless series of themes (visible in the task pane). You might think there are enough to fit most Web sites. Problem is, most FrontPage designers like working with a small selection of them, which makes many Web sites shout "Made with FrontPage!" when you visit them because of their familiar background, navigation bar, page banner, and so on. To break away from the crowd and make your pages look more unique, create your own theme.

1. Choose Format ➪ Theme to open the Theme task pane. At the bottom of the task pane click Create a New Theme to open the Customize Theme window (see Figure 227-1).

Figure 227-1: The Customize Theme dialog box lets you build a new theme from scratch, piece by piece

2. Using the three buttons under the question, "What would you like to modify?", choose Colors, Graphics, and Text settings for your custom theme.

3. When you click the Colors button, the Color Scheme, Color Wheel, and Custom tabs appear at the top of the dialog box (see Figure 227-2). Pick a grouping of complementary colors that work well together.

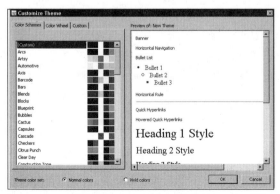

Figure 227-2: Picking from swatches that show sets of five complementary colors, most including black and/or white

4. If none of the groups of colors appeals to you, click the Color Wheel tab and view the color wheel (see Figure 227-3). Drag your mouse around the color wheel and watch the displayed scheme change to reflect the complementary and opposite colors for the spot on the wheel your mouse points to. Drag the Brightness slider as desired to make these colors lighter or darker.

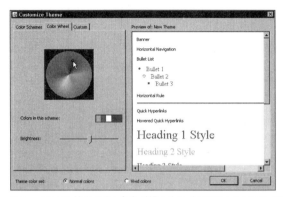

Figure 227-3: Using the Color Wheel to develop your own group of complementary colors

5. To set up your page colors one at a time, go to the Custom tab and select an item. With that item selected, choose a color. Continue selecting items until you've applied a color to each one that your page might contain.

6. Click OK to apply your color changes. This returns you to the original Customize Theme dialog box where you can use the Graphics and Text buttons to customize the remaining aspects of your theme.

7. Click the Graphics button to display a series of options for applying graphics to different page elements. Select an item from the field at the top of the window and click the Browse button to find an image to use for the selected Item.

8. After clicking OK to return to the Customize Theme dialog box, click the Text button to open a version of the window that offers fonts for each page element (see Item list again) that could be in text form — body text, headings, and so forth.

9. Click OK to apply your text changes and return once again to the original Customize Theme dialog box.

10. Click the Save button to give your new theme a name in the Save Theme dialog box. Click OK to confirm it.

tips

■ When you select a graphic for your background image, choose one that doesn't compete visually with any page content. Choose a small file size to decrease the time it takes the overall page to download for visitors with slower connections.

■ When you name your theme, pick one that describes either the look and feel (or "tone") of the theme to help you remember its purpose and help others understand why it's an effective choice. It can be explicit, as in "Sage Green Page with Black Text," or more abstract, as in "Business Khaki."

cross-reference

■ Use Cascading Style Sheets to establish page backgrounds, graphic elements, and text colors (see Part 9).

Task 228

Creating and Using Templates

To add to the pool of web page templates that can be applied to individual new pages (when you use the File ⇨ New command and resulting New task pane), you can save an existing Web page as a template. This allows you to reuse a page's properties — background colors and images, text colors, fonts, even graphics and text — in subsequent pages you create for the site. Templates help speed the development process by providing ready-made pages with the basics already in place, and unlike Themes, include page content — text, images, information, anything you choose to have on the page when you save it as a template.

1. After you've designed a page containing the elements — text, graphics, and formatting — you want to save for later use, choose File ⇨ Save As.

2. In the Save As dialog box, click the Save As Type drop-down list and choose FrontPage Template (*.tem) from the list (see Figure 228-1).

Figure 228-1: Saving a page as a FrontPage template

3. Pick a template name that describes its purpose or design. Enter it in the File Name text box.

4. Click Save to complete the process.

5. The Save As Template dialog box appears (see Figure 228-2). Enter the requested information — page title, page name, and if desired, a description.

Figure 228-2: A little more information is required before your template is saved and ready for use

6. The Save Embedded Files dialog box appears, listing any files used in the page you just saved. Click OK to confirm.

7. To use a template, choose File ⇨ New and click More Page Templates in the New task pane. In the Page Templates dialog box, double-click the icon of the template you just made to create a new page based on that template.

Task 229

Inserting and Formatting Text

Text is the backbone of any Web page. It shares information, provides instructions, and compels the reader to take some action or purchase something. FrontPage makes it easy to type text onto a page and format it for maximum effectiveness.

1. In Page view click to position your cursor.

2. Type your text.

3. If you have existing text from another application — such as Microsoft Word or a text editor — copy it to the Clipboard and then choose Edit ⇨ Paste in FrontPage to paste it into your page.

4. Before you format any text, select the text you want to format.

5. Use the Formatting toolbar (shown in Figure 229-1) to apply a different font, font size, or to apply bold, italic, or underline styles to the text.

Figure 229-1: If you're familiar with Microsoft Word, you'll recognize the formatting tools in FrontPage immediately

6. If your text is a heading, use the Style drop-down list to apply the appropriate level of heading to the text (see Figure 229-2) so it stands out.

note

▪ Any formatting from the copied text will be lost when you paste it into the Web page. The default font from the page or theme applies to copied text until you reformat it.

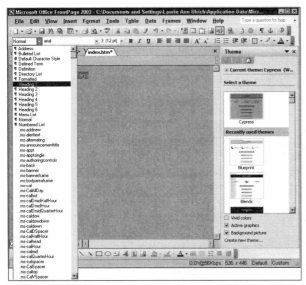

Figure 229-2: Applying heading styles to text

7. If you need to rearrange your text, use the "drag and drop" method: Select the text with your mouse and then drag it to another location on the same page. (This mimics the same feature in Microsoft Word.)

tips

- If you have already applied a theme to a Web page, the default body text font from that theme will be applied to the text as you type it.

- When you set a heading style to your text, heading tags such as `<h1>...</h1>` are applied to the text in HTML. You can see the code by clicking the Code button at the lower left of the Page view window.

- Turn any text into a link by selecting it and clicking the Insert Hyperlink button on the Standard toolbar. This opens the Insert Hyperlink dialog box, where you enter a URL or file path for the link.

cross-reference

- Heading tags in HTML code are covered in Task 11.

Proofing and Improving Web Page Text

It's bad enough to find a spelling error or typo in a printed document that everyone knows you wrote. It's worse when a mistake appears in something the entire world can see. Proof your pages before you publish them on the Web! With FrontPage you can spell-check your pages for text errors and use a thesaurus to help you select the best word (*le mot juste*, as they say in literary circles) when you're in doubt. Use the thesaurus to find substitutes for overused words too (such as "nice" or "effective") or to help define them for you.

1. In Page view choose Tools ➪ Spelling to open the Spelling dialog box (see Figure 230-1).

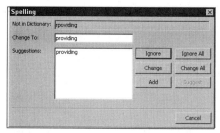

Figure 230-1: Viewing the words that FrontPage finds on your page that don't match the internal main or custom dictionaries

2. For each word that FrontPage cannot match with either the main or custom dictionary, check out the list in the Suggestions box. The topmost one appears in the Change To field.

3. Decide how to handle things. If it's a name or some terminology you know is spelled correctly, click the Add button. If you want to pick one of the suggestions, select it and click the Change button. If you know the word is correct but you don't want to add it to the custom dictionary, click Ignore or Ignore All (for times when the word appears more than once).

notes

- How does spell-checking work? When you open the Spelling dialog box, FrontPage automatically scans the page and compares each word with the internal main dictionary (a word list installed with FrontPage or Microsoft Office) as well as with the custom dictionary each user creates. If the word isn't found in either list, FrontPage displays it in the Not in Dictionary field.

- If no suggestions appear, that means FrontPage is unable to find any words similar to your allegedly misspelled word. To remedy this, find the right spelling on your own (the dictionary on your shelf, an online reference, or an articulate friend) and type the correction in the Change To field directly.

4. As you resolve each spelling error, the next one appears in the Not in Dictionary field. Repeat Steps 2 and 3 for each error that FrontPage finds.

5. To find the best word to substitute for an overused or undesirable word on your page, or to define a word you're not sure of, select the word in question (it must be typed already in the Web page) and choose Tools ➪ Thesaurus to open the Thesaurus dialog box (see Figure 230-2).

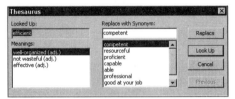

Figure 230-2: Looking up a word to make sure you're using it correctly or finding an alternative to overused words, such as "efficient"

6. If there is more than one meaning for the word — perhaps it's a noun or adjective — choose the role the word plays in the context of your page and view the list of synonyms in the Replace with Synonym list.

7. Select a new word and click Replace. If you're in the dialog box just to check a word's meaning by viewing it's synonyms, you can click Cancel now to close the Thesaurus. If you're in the dialog box to find an alternative word, select one.

tips

- Click Change All after choosing the correct word to change all instances of the same misspelling.

- Use the Look Up button to find synonyms of words in the Replace list. Select a word and click Look Up. All words that mean the same thing will appear in the list. This is handy for really delving into the meaning of a word you're not sure of.

cross-reference

- You can spell-check in HomeSite, too (see Task 171).

Inserting Clip Art and Pictures

Pictures impart meaning and information more efficiently than words — when they're used well. FrontPage makes it easy to convey a message or provide instructions through graphics, saving the designer a lot of typing (and the visitor a lot of reading) through the use of photographs and clip-art images.

1. In Page view click your cursor where you want the image to appear.

2. Choose Insert ➪ Picture to open the submenu (see Figure 231-1).

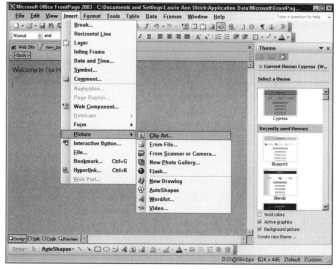

Figure 231-1: Inserting stored photos, clip art, or scanned and digitally-captured images

3. To insert a piece of Microsoft Office clip art, choose Clip Art to open the Clip Art task pane (see Figure 231-2).

4. Type a keyword (or more than one) in the Search For text box and click Go.

5. When you find the image you want to use, right-click it and choose Insert from the shortcut menu.

Figure 231-2: Searching for clip art by keyword

6. To insert a stored photo or other image, choose Insert ➪ Picture and then select From File in the submenu.

7. The Picture dialog box (see Figure 231-3) allows you to navigate to the folder where your image is stored and select it from that location.

Figure 231-3: Picking the picture you want to insert into your Web page

tips

- Resize clip art by dragging its corner and side handles. If this distorts it or reduces the image quality, return it to the default size and use a third-party application to resize the image. Then reinsert the edited image.

- Turn any graphic into a link by selecting it and then clicking the Insert Hyperlink button on the standard toolbar. In the Insert Hyperlink dialog box, enter a URL or path to a file that the selected graphic should link to. Edit a hyperlink by right-clicking it (whether text or a graphic) and choosing Edit Hyperlink from the shortcut menu.

cross-reference

- The HTML tags that insert an image are discussed in Task 29.

Adding Alternative Text to Images

So-called "alternative text" helps people whose browsers don't show graphics or load them slowly. Words appear instead of graphics; they also pop up when you mouse over an image that does appear. You can make this text instructive ("Click here to see our list of phone numbers") or informative ("We had a great time at our recent retreat in the Adirondacks!"). Whatever motivates you to use alternative text, it gives you a chance to say more about your images and other page content than the space on the page may allow.

1. In Page view, click on the graphic to which you'd like to apply alternative text. This selects the picture. Handles appear around it so you know you selected the right image.

2. Right-click the image and choose Picture Properties from the shortcut menu (see Figure 232-1).

Figure 232-1: Associating alternative text with the selected graphic

3. Click the General tab in the Picture Properties dialog box (see Figure 232-2).

4. Move to the Text field in the Alternative Representations section of the dialog box and click the Text check box. This turns on the alternative text feature.

5. Type your alternative text in the Text field. Use proper spelling, capitalization, and spacing.

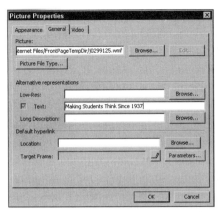

Figure 232-2: The Alternative Representations section allows you to type text to describe a graphic within your Web page

6. Click OK to apply the text to the selected image.

7. Preview your page and test the alternative text. As you can see in Figure 232-3, the text appears in a little pop-up box (much like the tool tip or screen tip you see when pointing to buttons within a software interface). It should appear as soon as you mouse over the graphic that uses alternative text. If you test your pages in various browsers, you may have different results — some browsers don't support Alt text, and others may display it differently than your default browser.

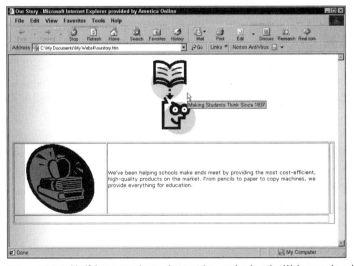

Figure 232-3: Verifying your alternative text by previewing the Web page in a browser

tip

- The Long Description field allows you to use substantially more text than you'd want to enter into that relatively short Text field. Click the Browse button to find the text, wherever it may reside — in a document (.doc, from Word) or in any text file.

cross-reference

- See Task 29 for information on inserting alternative text in HTML code.

Drawing and Formatting Shapes and Lines

Your graphical options don't end with clip art and photos. FrontPage allows you to draw shapes and lines using the Drawing toolbar found in all Microsoft Office applications. Apply colored fills and outlines to your shapes and use various options for creating dotted and dashed lines, with or without arrowheads.

notes

- The palette displayed offers colors that match any theme that's currently applied to your Web pages. You can also access a full palette of hundreds of Web-safe colors.

- Resize a shape or line by selecting it and then dragging the handles — side or corner handles on shapes, endpoint handles on lines and arrows — to make the shape bigger or smaller, or the line/arrow longer or shorter. Change the angle of a line by dragging one of the endpoints up or down.

1. Display the Drawing toolbar by right-clicking the currently displayed toolbar and choosing Drawing from the submenu.

2. Using the Drawing toolbar, click the AutoShapes button and choose a shape category (see Figure 233-1).

Figure 233-1: Choosing from five shape categories

3. From the shape category, such as Block Arrows, select a shape to draw (see Figure 233-2).

4. Move your mouse to the spot where you want to draw and then click and drag to draw the selected shape.

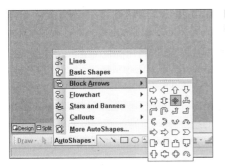

Figure 233-2: From within a category, choose the shape you want to draw

5. Change the fill color or outline color of your drawn shape using the Fill Color and Line Color buttons on the Drawing toolbar.

6. To draw a line or arrow, click the Line or Arrow tool and draw a straight line/arrow in any direction.

7. To change the style of the line or arrow, click the line or arrow you drew (handles appear at both ends of the line/arrow), and use the Line Style or Arrow Style buttons to choose a thickness, apply dots and dashes, or choose from a variety of arrowheads. Figure 233-3 shows the Arrow Style option.

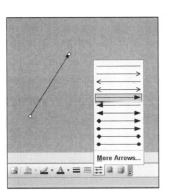

Figure 233-3: Customizing your arrow or line

tips

- Drag diagonally away from the starting point — the farther you drag, the bigger the shape is. By controlling the angle of the drag, you can control the proportions of the image — the relative width and height.

- Constrain the angle of the line (or arrow) to 45-degree angles by holding down the Shift key as you draw the line.

cross-reference

- You can achieve the look of colored rectangles with table cells that have colored backgrounds (see Task 48).

Adding Flash Content to Web Pages

Moving pictures catch the eye and capture the attention of your site's visitors. To add movies in the form of Macromedia Flash files, all you need to do is insert the object and preview the page in a browser to see the movie play as it would online. It couldn't be easier.

1. In Page view click the Design button to make sure you're in that view.

2. Click to position your cursor where the Flash content should appear on the page.

3. Choose Insert ➪ Picture ➪ Flash (see Figure 234-1).

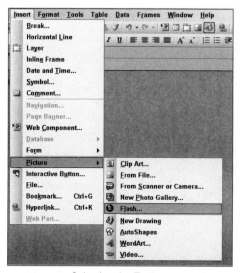

Figure 234-1: Selecting the Flash command

4. Using the Select Flash File dialog box (see Figure 234-2), navigate to the file you wish to insert.

5. When you find the file you want to insert, double-click it or select the filename and click the Insert button.

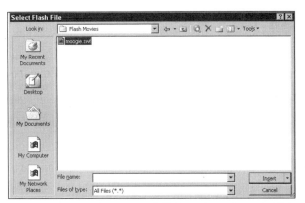

Figure 234-2: Look for the right SWF file to insert into your Web page

6. With the Flash object on your Web page, click the Preview button to see the page in a browser window. View the Flash movie to make sure it works properly (see Figure 234-3).

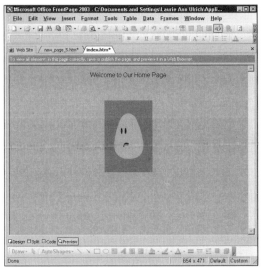

Figure 234-3: Watching the Flash movie run in a browser window through Preview mode

tip

- Why be in Page view? If you're in Code view, it's more difficult to choose the spot where the movie should appear. FrontPage is designed to be used in a graphical way — working with its WYSIWYG features more so than the tools that show and allow you to edit HTML code.

cross-reference

- Inserting multimedia in HTML is covered in Part 4.

Creating WordArt Images

Because FrontPage is part of the Microsoft Office suite, you get the benefit of some of the features in other Office components, such as WordArt. Adding WordArt on a Web page does add a lot of FrontPage-specific code to your otherwise HTML, but for sites that are viewed primarily through Microsoft Internet Explorer, the ability to easily create graphic text can be a creative, convenient addition to your Web page.

1. In Page view, be sure your Drawing toolbar is displayed by choosing View ➪ Toolbars ➪ Drawing.

2. Click to position your cursor where the WordArt will go.

3. Click the WordArt button on the Drawing toolbar. The WordArt Gallery opens (see Figure 235-1).

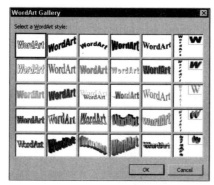

Figure 235-1: Pick from 30 different WordArt styles

4. Double-click the style you want to work with, or select it and click OK. The Edit WordArt Text dialog box opens (see Figure 235-2).

Figure 235-2: Replacing the sample text with your own

5. Type the text you want to render in the selected WordArt style. After you type your text, click OK.

6. When your WordArt object appears on the page (see Figure 235-3), drag it to reposition it or resize it by dragging its handles.

Figure 235-3: Using your mouse to position and resize your WordArt object

Task 235

tip
- Keep your WordArt's current aspect ratio (proportions) by holding down the Shift key while you drag a corner handle. Be sure to release the mouse before you release the Shift key to maintain the proportions.

cross-reference
- Sizing graphic objects in HTML is discussed in Part 3.

Task 236

Adding Navigation Bars

Based on the theme you apply to your Web page (or the entire site), you can add navigation bars to help visitors move through your site, navigate from the home page to the subpages and back again. You can also add buttons and other types of links for navigating to external pages or sites, but that's covered in the next task – for now, we'll be creating navigation tools for moving around within our own site.

note

- When you add a link bar to subpages, be sure to include a Home Page link by clicking that option in the Link Bar Properties dialog box.

1. In Page view of the home page, click to position your cursor where you want the navigation bar to appear.

2. Choose Insert ➪ Navigation to open the Insert Web Component dialog box (see Figure 236-1).

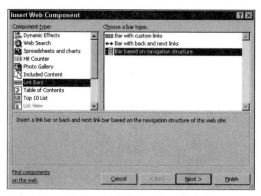

Figure 236-1: A list of all Web components, from counters to search boxes

3. If it's not already selected, choose Link Bars from the list of component types.

4. On the right side of the dialog box click Bar Based on Navigation Structure.

5. Click Next.

6. In the Choose a Bar Style version of the Insert Web Component dialog box, click Next to confirm that the link bar you're creating should adhere to the current theme.

caution

- Ignore the displayed theme in the Choose a Bar Style box. It won't look like your current theme and will only confuse you.

7. In the next box, click to choose either vertical or horizontal orientation for your link bar (see Figure 236-2).

8. Click Finish. The Link Bar Properties dialog box opens (see Figure 236-3), allowing you to choose which pages to include in the link bar you're creating.

9. Click OK to create the finished navigation bar (see Figure 236-4).

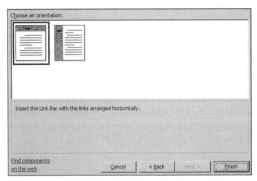

Figure 236-2: Choosing the direction (up and down or across) that your link bar should run on the page

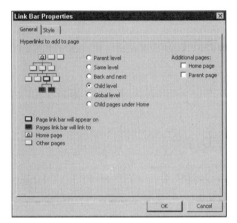

Figure 236-3: Establishing your link bar properties

tips

- Start with your site's home page and then repeat the following steps for each page in your site.

- Let FrontPage do as much work for you as possible. By basing the link bar on your site's structure, links between pages are set up automatically. When you rearrange pages later in Navigation view, the links will update automatically.

- When adding a link bar to the home page, select Child Level from the list of hyperlinks to add, but do not click the Home Page option on the right.

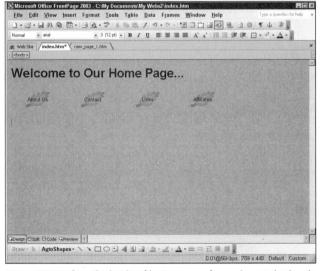

Figure 236-4: A vertical strip of buttons, one for each page in the site, appears on the home page.

cross-reference

- When creating navigational tools in HTML, you have to insert a series of text or image links. Read about how to do this in Part 5.

Task 237

Inserting and Aligning Page Banners

A page banner is really just a page title, and is normally the same text that appears on a browser's title bar while the page in question is displayed. The graphic page banner is more visually dynamic than the title bar, however, and people are more likely to notice it. While the term "banner" reminds people of advertising banners — which, of course, you can also create with this feature, for our purposes, you will simply insert a banner to inform visitors what the name of the page is.

1. In Page view, click the Design button to make sure you can see the entire Web page.

2. Click to place your cursor at the top of the page, on the left side.

3. Choose Insert ➪ Page Banner to open the Page Banner Properties dialog box (see Figure 237-1).

Figure 237-1: Confirming your page banner properties

4. Choose whether the banner will be a picture or text, and type the text that should appear in the banner itself.

5. Click OK. The banner appears on the page (see Figure 237-2).

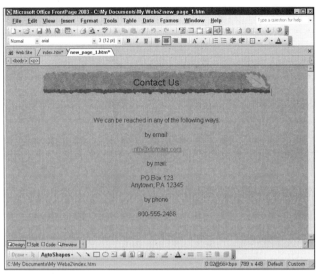

Figure 237-2: A picture banner across the top of the page

6. To change the alignment of your banner, click on the banner to select it, and then use the Alignment buttons (Left, Center, or Right) on the Formatting toolbar.

7. If you change your page theme, the page banner's design will change, too. To see how various themes will affect your banner, choose Format ⟿ Theme, and view the task pane. You can click on individual themes and see how they'll look on your page or pages.

tips

- A picture banner incorporates graphics from your selected theme, such as patterns from your background image, graphics from the buttons, and navigation tools that are part of the theme's defaults. A text banner is just that — text — that adheres to the theme's font and font color only.

- Keep the alignment of elements consistent throughout the Web site. If most of your text and graphical content is left-aligned, you may want your banner to be left-aligned as well. On the other hand, if you have a centered navigation bar across the top of the page and then put a banner above it, the banner should probably be centered as well.

cross-reference

- You can create a page banner in HTML, using `<font>` tag attributes to control the size, font, and color of text across the top of a page (see Part 2).

Creating Interactive Buttons

The term "interactive" means that when your visitor performs an action, something happens. FrontPage allows you to insert interactive buttons that perform a number of tasks — from linking to another Web site to playing a song. These buttons come in a variety of preset styles, and you can customize the text that appears on the button face.

1. Working in Page view, click to position your cursor where you want the new interactive button to appear.

2. Choose Insert ⇨ Interactive Button to open the Interactive Buttons dialog box (see Figure 238-1).

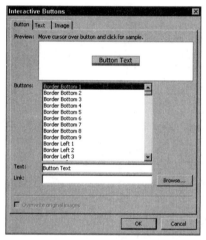

Figure 238-1: Choose a button style and type your button face text

3. After the dialog box appears, scroll through the Buttons list and choose the button you'd like to use. As you click on individual items in the list, a preview appears at the top of the dialog box.

4. Type the text into the Text box that should appear on the button face. The preview updates to show your text on the selected button.

5. To establish the file, page, or site to which the button links, click in the Link box and type the path or URL, or click the Browse button to locate the file, page, or site manually.

6. Click the Text tab in the Interactive Buttons dialog box (see Figure 238-2) to make any required adjustments to the font, size, and color of the text in your button.

7. Click the Image tab (see Figure 238-3) to increase the button width and height.

8. When your button's appearance in the Preview box is as you want it, click OK to create the button. Figure 238-4 shows a series of interactive buttons.

caution

- If you create a series of interactive buttons that appear in a group, make them all the same size. Otherwise, they'll look like a "crazy quilt." If you increase the size of one button to accommodate extra text, size the other buttons equally, even if they don't require it.

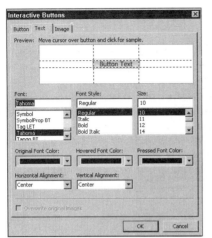

Figure 238-2: Changing the text attributes of your interactive button

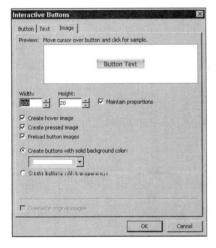

Figure 238-3: Making your button bigger or smaller

cross-reference

* Dreamweaver gives you the ability to create Flash buttons, which look and act very much like FrontPage interactive buttons (see Task 201).

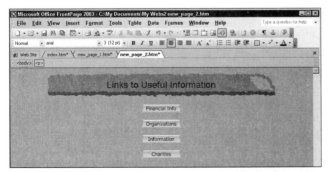

Figure 238-4: A group of similarly-styled interactive buttons to build a central navigation area for your site

Task 239

Changing Page Backgrounds and Colors

After you apply a theme to a site or use a template that determines the colors and backgrounds in your Web pages, you can still change your mind after the fact. Either apply a new theme, which updates all your themed pages to the new one, or reopen the Page Properties dialog box and make your desired changes. Through the Page Properties dialog box, you can change your background image, choose a solid color for your page background, and even set the color of your text links.

1. If you applied a theme and want to change it, choose Format ➪ Theme to open the Theme task pane (see Figure 239-1).

note

- Theme elements cannot be changed from within the Page Properties dialog box.

Figure 239-1: Viewing the current theme and selecting an alternative one

caution

- When you change themes, all the theme-based banners, link bars, and elements change as well. This can cause problems if the new theme's graphical elements don't go as well with your content. To see if your intended theme will cause problems, click once on the thumbnail to preview the theme on the page that currently appears in Page view. This doesn't change the site's theme yet; you can still try different themes on for size until you find one to apply to the site.

2. When you find the theme you want to use in place of the one that's already in use, right-click it and choose Apply As Default Theme from the shortcut menu.

3. To change your manually-applied background image and text/link colors on individual pages, where no theme was applied, go to the first page you want to change and choose File ⇨ Properties to open the Page Properties dialog box (see Figure 239-2).

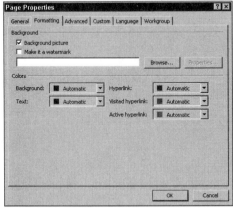

Figure 239-2: Viewing your page's background and color settings

4. On the Formatting tab, change your page's background by choosing a new or different background image, or by selecting a solid color for the background.

5. Adjust text and link colors by making selections in the color fields on the Formatting tab.

tip

- Use the General tab to change the page's name or enter new keywords and description text. Your entries here will create the content of your `keyword` and `description` meta tags.

cross-reference

- Establishing a page background in HTML is covered in Task 9.

Creating Bulleted and Numbered Lists

Lists help arrange instructions, features, and ideas on the page. In HTML these lists are referred to as ordered and unordered lists, but FrontPage refers to them (as it does throughout Microsoft Office) as numbered and bulleted lists.

1. Switch to Page view of the desired page.

2. Click to position your cursor where the first line of the list begins.

3. Type the first line of your bulleted or numbered list and press Enter when you're ready to go down to the next item in the list.

4. Continue typing the items in your list and press Enter between each line. Before applying a bulleted or numbered style, your list looks like that in Figure 240-1.

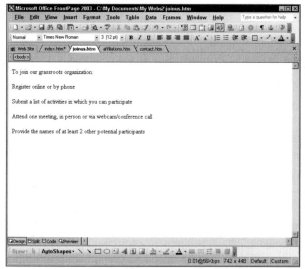

Figure 240-1: A list appearing like a series of short paragraphs before numbers or bullets are applied

5. Select the items in your list, from beginning to end (or vice-versa). Be certain to select all of the text in all of the paragraphs.

6. If there will be a hierarchy within your list — higher and lower-level bullets, for example, or an outline combining both numbers and letters, use the Tab key when typing your text — the use of the tab key reduces the eventual rank of the item in your list, and the more tabs, the lower in rank the text will be. First-level bullets or numbers should not be tabbed at all, and for each rank beneath that, use one tab per level down from the top.

7. To create a bulleted list, click the Bullets button on the Formatting toolbar. Bullets appear in front of each item in your list.

8. To create a numbered list, click the Numbering button on the Formatting toolbar. Numbers appear in sequence in front of each item in your list, and by default, you get Arabic numerals (1, 2, 3. . .).

9. To change to different bullets or numbers, select some or all of the items in the list and choose Format ⇨ Bullets and Numbering. In the List Properties dialog box (see Figure 240-2), use the Picture Bullets, Numbers, or Other tabs to choose different characters to precede your list items.

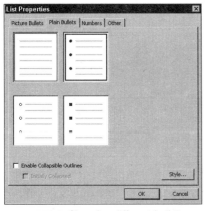

Figure 240-2: Choosing different bullets or numbers for a list

Task **240**

tips

- If the bulleted or numbered item is a long sentence or a paragraph, let word-wrapping control the flow of the text from one line to another. Do not press Enter unless you're ready to start a new bulleted or numbered item.

- The appearance of the bullets is dictated by the theme you have in place. If you use a blank Web page with no theme, the bullets will be generic black dots (similar to a Word document based on the Normal template).

cross-reference

- Creating ordered and unordered lists in HTML is covered in Part 2.

Applying Borders to Text

You can apply a top, bottom, left, and/or right border to any text, whether it's a single word — such as a heading or section title — or a paragraph. Placing a border around text helps draw attention to itself. Like many of FrontPage's formatting commands, the Borders and Shading feature should be familiar to you if you use Word a lot.

1. To apply a border to text — a single word or block of text (a paragraph) — first select the text.

2. Choose Format ➪ Borders and Shading to open the Borders and Shading dialog box (see Figure 241-1).

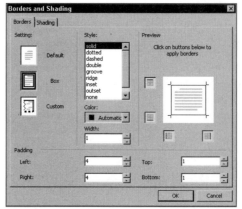

Figure 241-1: Applying formatting in the Borders and Shading dialog box

3. If it's not already on top, click the Borders tab to view those tools.

4. Choose one of the three Setting options: Default, Box, or Custom.

5. Choose a style for your border.

6. In the Preview area, click the border buttons (top, bottom, left, and right) to turn on the four possible sides of your border. You can click one, two, three, or all four sides.

7. Choose a color for your border by clicking the Color drop-down list and making a selection from the palette (see Figure 241-2). Colors that work best with the current theme appear first in the Color palette.

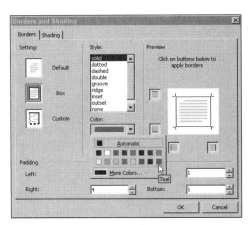

Figure 241-2: Picking colors for borders

8. Set the width (in pixels) for your border. The default is 3.

9. Establish the padding — the distance between the border and the text it encompasses.

10. Click OK to apply the border (see Figure 241-3).

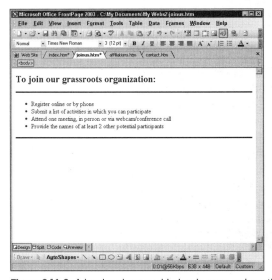

Figure 241-3: A border above and below is more unique than a border on all sides

tip

- Zero is the default padding for all four border sides. Setting higher padding levels improves text legibility because the text won't run right into the border. A padding of 3 or 4 yields a reasonable amount of space and legibility.

cross-reference

- Borders help separate sections in forms and define cells within tables (see Part 7).

Applying Shading to Text or Blank Lines

Shading blank areas of your page, or a block of text, helps guide visitors' eyes to areas you want to emphasize.

1. To apply shading to text — a single word or a block of text (a paragraph) — first select the text.

2. Choose Format ⇨ Borders and Shading to open the Borders and Shading dialog box (see Figure 242-1).

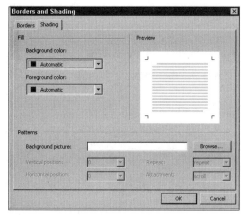

Figure 242-1: Applying formatting using either tab in the Borders and Shading dialog box

3. If it's not already on top, click the Shading tab to view those tools.

4. Click the Background Color drop-down list. A palette appears (see Figure 242-2), displaying colors that go with the current theme, plus other Web-safe colors.

5. Choose a foreground color from an identical palette.

6. If you prefer to use a background image for shading, click the Browse button across from the Background Picture text box.

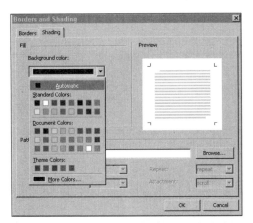

Figure 242-2: Choosing a color for your shaded area

7. Navigate to the image file you want to use as a background pattern for the shaded area.

8. Click OK to apply your shading (see Figure 242-3).

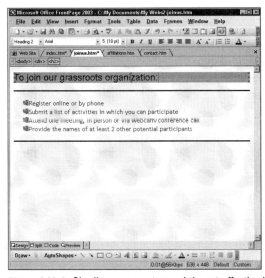

Figure 242-3: Shading can create a subtle, yet effective block of color on the page

tips

- To apply a bar of shading to a blank line, just click on that line. It's the equivalent of selecting text to apply shading.

- If the image is a small one, repeat (tile) it within the shading area. Use the Horizontal and Vertical position settings, as well as the Repeat setting, to establish the tiling behavior of your background image.

cross-reference

- Using hexadecimal values in HTML to apply colors to backgrounds, borders, and text is covered in Part 9.

Inserting Tables

Tables may be one of the most powerful design features you can employ in a Web page — and FrontPage makes creating and customizing tables so easy, you'll find yourself using them all the time to control the placement of text and images.

note

- Use the Borders and Shading command discussed in the previous task to apply borders and shading to individual cells, single rows or columns, or to an entire table. Just select the portion of the table you want to border or shade and then choose Format ⇨ Borders and Shading.

1. In Page view, click to place your cursor where the new table should appear.

2. Determine ahead of time the number of rows and columns for your table. You can do this in any number of ways, as described in Steps 3 and 4.

3. Click the Insert Table button on the toolbar and drag through the resulting grid (see Figure 243-1) to indicate the dimensions of the table.

Figure 243-1: Dragging through the grid in the Insert Table tool

4. You can also choose Table ⇨ Insert ⇨ Table to open the Insert Table dialog box (see Figure 243-2).

5. Click OK to insert the prescribed table (see Figure 243-3).

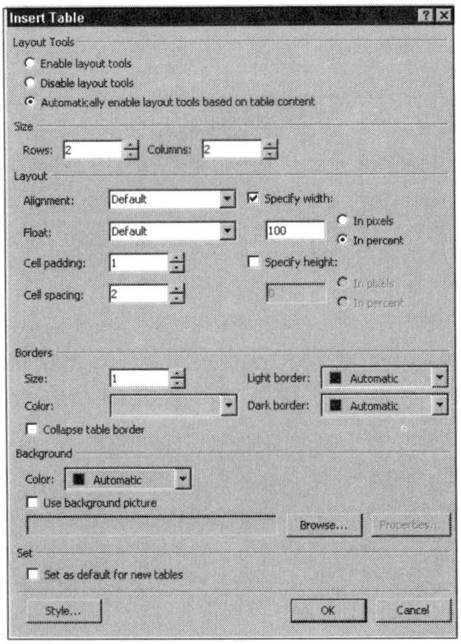

Figure 243-2: Setting table dimensions and attributes more precisely

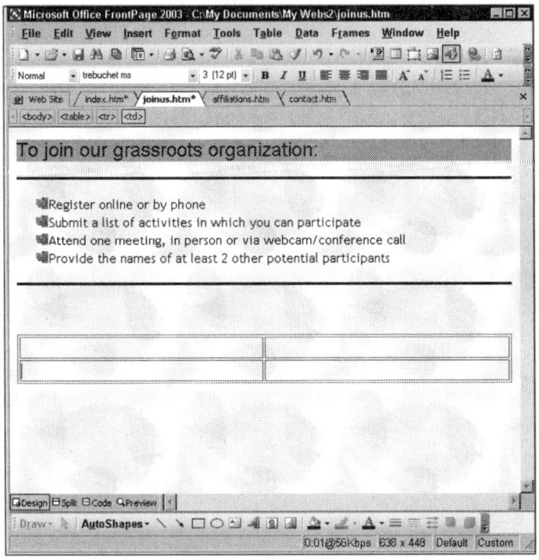

Figure 243-3: A table ready to house text, images, or simply blocks of color based on cell background colors

tip

- Using the Insert Table dialog box allows you to perform several table-planning tasks in one place. Set table dimensions; establish cell alignment, spacing, and padding; and choose border options. You can also apply a background to your table.

cross-reference

- Learn to insert a table with Dreamweaver (see Task 207).

Adding and Deleting Table Rows, Columns, and Cells

Once you build a table, you can always make changes later. Insert new rows or delete existing ones, and add or delete columns.

1. In Page view, select the column (see Figure 244-1) or row you want to delete, or click next to where a new column or row should appear. Look for a small black arrow just outside a column or row and then click to select it.

Figure 244-1: Selecting a table column

2. To delete the selected row or column, choose Table ⇨ Delete ⇨ Rows, or Columns (depending on what you're doing). The selected row or column disappears.

3. To insert a new column or row next to the selected table content, choose Table ⇨ Insert ⇨ Rows, or Columns (depending on what you're doing). The Insert Rows or Columns dialog box opens (see Figure 244-2).

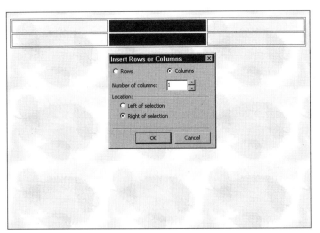

Figure 244-2: Selecting how many new rows or columns to add, and where they should appear

4. To insert a lone cell within a table, first click in the cell that should be to the left of the new one.

5. Choose Table ➪ Insert ➪ Cell. A single cell appears to the right of the selected cell (see Figure 244-3).

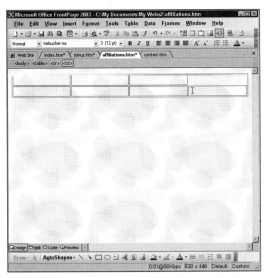

Figure 244-3: Adding a single cell to a block of cells

tip

- Use this technique to build a single-cell table (where there was no table at all before). Just click where you want the cell to appear on the page and choose Table ➪ Insert ➪ Cell. Resize the cell and adjust its border and background settings by choosing Table ➪ Properties ➪ Cell.

cross-reference

- You can build a single cell in Dreamweaver, too (see Part 15).

Splitting and Merging Table Cells

I t's easy to change the dimensions of a table after you've created it. You can break existing cells into more cells or merge two or more cells into a single large cell. Splitting or merging cells makes it possible to build tables that accommodate your content as you want to present it, with the layout you had in mind. By using the Split Cells and Merge Cells commands, you achieve a greater degree of flexibility than can sometimes be achieved by adding whole rows and columns.

1. To split a single cell into multiple cells, start by clicking in the cell you want to split.

2. Choose Table ⇨ Split Cells to open the Split Cells dialog box (see Figure 245-1).

Figure 245-1: Making two or more cells from a single cell

Task **245**

3. In the Split Cells dialog box, enter the number of columns or rows you want to create from the cell.

4. Click OK. The cell splits (see Figure 245-2).

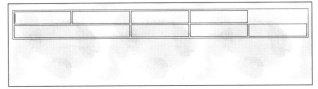

Figure 245-2: Splitting a single cell into three cells

5. To merge two or more cells into one, start by selecting the cells — they must be adjoining cells, either side by side, above or below each other, or in a block.

6. Choose Table ➪ Merge Cells. The cells merge into one. This can be useful for creating a single cell to house a table's title, to create a big cell for a lot of text, or to make room for a large image without changing the entire table's layout.

tip

- Merge all cells in the top row of a table to create a handy place for the table's title.

cross-reference

- Controlling table dimensions in HTML, including cell merging and splitting, is covered in Part 6.

Resizing and Reformatting Table Cells

FrontPage makes it easy to change any aspect of a cell's appearance, size, and position.

1. To resize a table cell in Page view, point to a side border on the cell in question and look for your mouse to change to a two-headed arrow (see Figure 246-1).

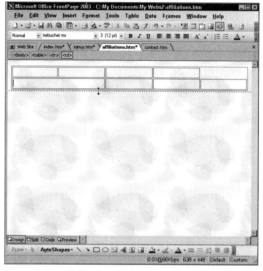

Figure 246-1: A two-headed resizing arrow appears when you mouse over a cell's border

2. Click and drag to resize the cell. Drag outward to make the cell larger, or inward to make it smaller. Unlike Dreamweaver, which allows you to resize table cells vertically as well as horizontally (see Task 208), FrontPage sticks to the pixel height set when the table was created; you cannot drag to make a cell taller or shorter.

3. To make fine adjustments over and above (or instead of) the changes you can make manually with the mouse, click in the cell you want to resize and choose Table ➪ Table Properties.

4. From the submenu, choose Cell to open the Cell Properties dialog box (see Figure 246-2).

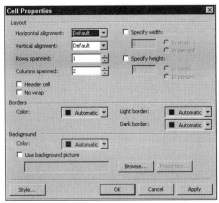

Figure 246-2: Adjusting the size, fill, border, and alignment of any selected cell with the Cell Properties dialog box

5. Using the Cell Properties dialog box, enter new numbers in the Specify Height and Specify Width fields.

tips

- Open the Cell Properties dialog box by right-clicking the cell and choosing Cell Properties from the short-cut menu.

- The Rows Spanned and Columns Spanned fields don't explain themselves very accurately to anyone not completely familiar with table construction in HTML. The concept of *spanning* other parts of the table comes from the `colspan` attribute in HTML (see Task 45). What happens when you use these options is the same as when you use Table ➪ Merge Cells and Table ➪ Split Cells. If your selected cell is changed to span two columns, it appears like two merged cells above or below the cells that remain in two columns. If you span two or more rows, the single cell overlaps the number of cells (vertically) that you specified in the field.

cross-reference

- Adjusting cell height and width in HTML is a matter of entering new values for table properties (see Part 6).

Populating a Table with Graphics and Text

Inserting a picture or text in a table is a little more complicated than doing so on a simple Web page. You have to choose which cell contains the picture or text and inform FrontPage how to align the content (horizontally and vertically). You can also format the text to fit within the table if the table's dimensions are dictated by the page design or some other constraint.

1. To insert a graphic inside a table cell, click within the cell to select it (see Figure 247-1).

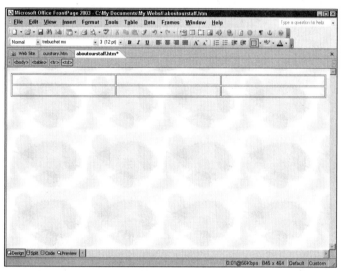

Figure 247-1: Populating your table by clicking in the first cell to receive content

2. Choose Insert ⇨ Picture ⇨ Clip Art, or From File — whichever is appropriate for the image you want to insert.

3. Once the image appears in the cell, manipulate its placement by using the Formatting toolbar (see the relevant tools in Figure 247-2).

Center alignment

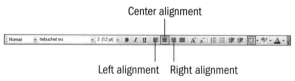

Left alignment   Right alignment

Figure 247-2: Applying horizontal alignment from the formatting toolbar by clicking the Left, Center, or Right alignment buttons

To access more tools for controlling cell content, right-click the cell and choose Cell Properties (see Figure 247-3).

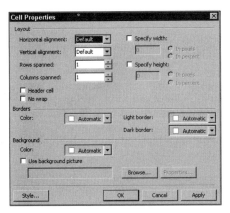

Figure 247-3: Specifying horizontal and vertical alignment for the cell's content in the Cell Properties dialog box

tip

- Merge cells before typing text into them. Alternatively, use the Cell Properties dialog box and enter a number of columns for your text to span.

4. To add and format text in a table cell, click inside the cell and simply start typing. You can also use the Paste command (Edit ⇨ Paste or Ctrl+V) to copy text from elsewhere — a Microsoft Word document or another Web page — and see it fill the cell (see Figure 247-4). The cell's dimensions control word-wrapping within the cell.

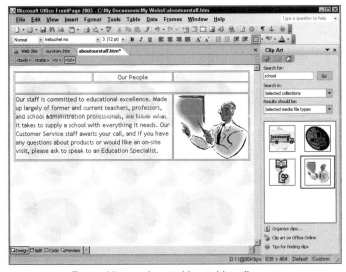

Figure 247-4: Text and images inserted into table cells

cross-reference

- Fine-tune your tables in HTML (see Part 6).

5. Continue typing in cells, using the cell resizing techniques discussed in Task 246 to make the cells the right width for the overall page and table design, as well as to accommodate your text. The size of the cell when you start typing dictates the width of any paragraph you type (see Figure 247-4).

6. After typing in any particular cell, reopen the Cell Properties dialog box (by right-clicking the cell, not the text) and make sure No Wrap is turned off (it's off by default) so that your table cells don't widen to accommodate your text. They'll lengthen but you may not want them to widen, which could throw off the overall table layout.

Creating Frames

Frames are Web pages within a frameset. Once you add frames to a Web page, that page goes from being a simple Web page to being a home (frameset) to one or more frames that are pages unto themselves. Through FrontPage's frame-creation and customization tools you can determine where frames appear, how big they are, how to display their content, and whether or not visitors can resize them in the browser.

1. Choose File ➪ New to open the New task pane.

2. In the New task pane select More Page Templates.

3. In the Page Templates dialog box, click the Frames Pages tab to see a series of frame constructs you can apply to the new page.

4. Click once on each of the Frames Pages icons. Each one displays a different preview, which shows you the arrangement of frames within that template.

5. Double-click the Frames Page template you want to use and see the frames created on a new page (see Figure 248-1).

note

- Clicking Set Initial Page brings up the Insert Hyperlink dialog box, which allows you to choose a Web page (by entering a URL) or an existing HTML file stored locally on your server. Either option displays the page within that frame. Clicking New Page inserts a blank Web page within the frame. Use FrontPage to populate that page with text and graphics.

caution

- Frames pages are usually ignored by search engines. This makes using frames slightly risky if you rely on visitors coming to your site from Yahoo or Google.

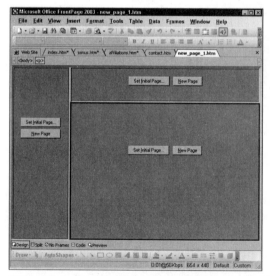

Figure 248-1: Creating frames automatically from a template instead of one at a time by hand

6. Click the appropriate button (Set Initial Page or New Page) in each frame.

7. Resize the frames as needed by pointing to their borders and dragging with your mouse.

8. To customize an individual frame, right-click it and select the Frame Properties button to open the Frame Properties dialog box (shown in Figure 248-2).

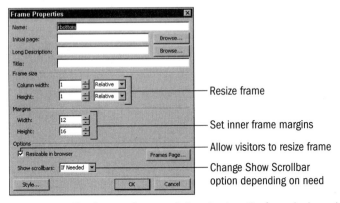

— Resize frame

— Set inner frame margins

— Allow visitors to resize frame

— Change Show Scrollbar option depending on need

Figure 248-2: Naming your frame and choosing how the frame looks and functions for the user

9. Once the frames are set up as you want them, proceed to add content to them, inserting text and graphics as desired (see Figure 248-3).

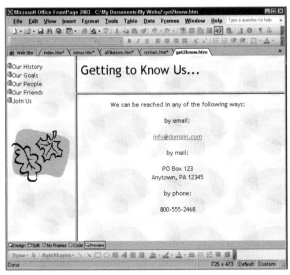

Figure 248-3: Each frame contains original content you inserted or displays an existing page from another site

tips

■ Add what's called an inline frame to an existing page. Choose Insert ➪ Inline Frame and click New Page (one of the two buttons that appears inside this new "box" on your page). This creates a frame within your page, rather than turning your entire page into a frames page or frameset.

■ If you chose New Page as the content for a given frame, right-click the frame and choose Page Properties from the short-cut menu to format the page (within the frame) as you would any other Web page. You can even use the Format ➪ Theme command on an individual frame and apply a separate theme to that frame only

cross-reference

■ Learn how to format frames in HTML in Part 8.

Adding Layers

Layers are like frames that float above the Web page, and by virtue of the fact that they're not part of a rigid frameset, you have greater flexibility in their placement, size, and relationship to other content on the page. You can size and format them easily, and they can contain anything you want: images, text, tables, even other layers. Some older versions of browsers don't display them, however, so use them judiciously if you know your audience is likely to view your site with older computers, older operating systems, and older browsers.

1. In Page view, click to position your cursor where the layer should appear.

2. Choose Insert ➪ Layer. A layer appears on the page (see Figure 249-1).

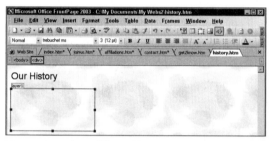

Figure 249-1: A small box with a numbered Layer tab appears on the page

3. Move the layer, as needed, with your mouse. Point to the layer and when your mouse turns to a four-headed arrow, drag to reposition the layer.

4. If desired, resize the layer by clicking on it to display its handles (see Figure 249-2) and drag from any handle to increase or decrease it.

5. To build layer content, click inside the layer and use FrontPage's tools to insert and format text, and to insert graphics (see Figure 249-3).

6. Right-click the layer and choose Page Properties to open the Page Properties dialog box. Here you make adjustments to the layer's background, font colors, and font sizes and adjust internal margins.

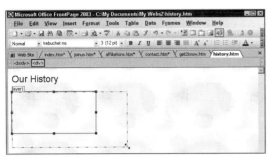

Figure 249-2: Using the mouse to resize a layer — larger or smaller, taller or shorter, wider or narrower

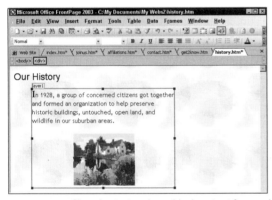

Figure 249-3: Choosing text and graphical content for your layer that matches the look and feel of the rest of your page

7. Right-click the layer and choose Layer Properties to display the Layers task pane (see Figure 249-4).

Figure 249-4: Changing the layer border and shading settings, and turning layer visibility on and off

tip

- Apply behaviors to a layer by clicking the Behaviors link at the bottom of the Layers task pane. This allows you to assign events to visitors' interaction with your layers — such as clicking on a layer or pointing to it. A strong knowledge of JavaScript (see Part 10) is recommended here so you can interpret the code that's created by choosing events and applying them to layers.

cross-reference

- Create layers with Dreamweaver in Task 211.

Building Page Bookmarks

If your page has lots of text on it — say, a long article or a series of questions and answers (as in an FAQ) — you may find it helpful to create bookmarks. These are areas of the page that you can scroll to quickly by clicking links to them. Bookmarks are easy to set up and use, and can be a big help to visitors attempting to navigate a complex or text-heavy document.

1. In Page view (in Design mode), select a word, usually the first word in a section that you want to bookmark, by double-clicking the word.

2. Choose Insert ➪ Bookmark to open the Bookmark dialog box (see Figure 250-1).

Figure 250-1: The Bookmark dialog box

3. Type a name for the bookmark or just use the word that appears automatically in the Bookmark Name text box. Click OK. The dialog box closes and a dashed line appears under the selected word (see Figure 250-2).

4. Continue bookmarking other words in your document, repeating Steps 1 through 3 for each one.

5. To create the links that take visitors to the bookmarked text, type or select existing triggers, such as those shown in Figure 250-3.

6. Select the words/phrases in your table of contents, one at a time, and click the Insert Hyperlink button for each one.

7. In the Insert Hyperlink dialog box, click the Bookmark button.

8. In the Select Place in Document dialog box, select the bookmark by name (see Figure 250-4) that you want to use as your link for the selected text. Click OK here and then again in the Insert Hyperlink dialog box. Your link is created.

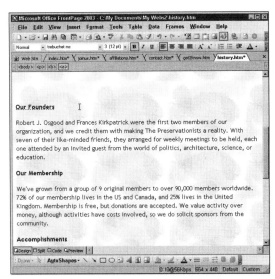

Figure 250-2: A dashed underline indicating a bookmarked word

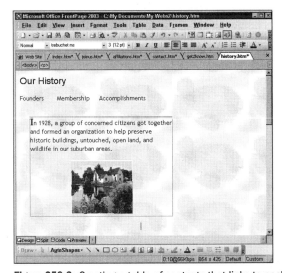

Figure 250-3: Creating a table of contents that links to each bookmark

Figure 250-4: Choosing your bookmark to complete the hyperlink setup

tips

- A vertical or horizontal list of text links is the simplest form your bookmark triggers can take. Short phrases or single words work best, as long as it's clear what the links take visitors to. Make it work like an index or table of contents.

- After creating bookmarks, test them. Click each one to make sure it takes you to the right spot on the page.

cross-reference

- Check out Tasks 193, 204, and 213 in Part 15 to find out more about how Dreamweaver deals with links.

Setting Up Keywords and Page Description Text

The <meta> tags that appear at the top of your document (in Code view) contain, among other things, keywords and descriptive text that search engines use to help visitors find your site. FrontPage makes it easy to build these tags outside of Code view.

1. Open or display the page for which you want to set up keywords and a description.

2. Choose File ➪ Page Properties to open the Page Properties dialog box.

3. Click the General tab, if it's not already chosen (see Figure 251-1).

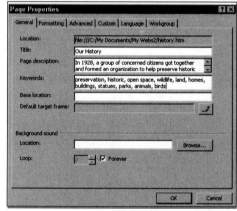

Figure 251-1: Entering keywords and description text in the Page Properties dialog box

4. Enter a short description of your page in the Page Description text box.

5. Enter your keywords in the Keywords text box. Use words that people might type into a search engine to find your site.

6. Verify that your page title (what appears in the browser's title bar) is accurate.

7. Click OK to close the dialog box and build the `<meta>` tag code (see Figure 251-2).

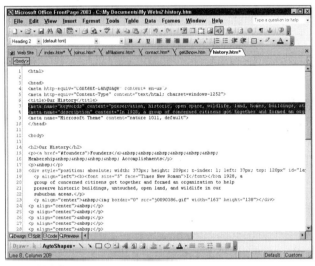

Figure 251-2: Generating <meta> tag code the easy way

tips

- Keep your description to fewer than 250 characters.

- Separate keywords with commas and avoid repeating words. If your site offers organic foods, some relevant keywords might be "healthy, organic, food, vegetables, fruit, produce, pesticides, pollution, safe." Also include the name of your business, any specific product names (phrases are OK), and any lingo that's peculiar to your industry or area of interest.

cross-reference

- Read more about <meta> tags in Part 1.

Publishing a FrontPage Web Site

Getting your Web publishing achievement "out there" for the Web-surfing public to see and enjoy requires publishing your site to the Web. Uploading your FrontPage-created pages to a Web server requires the presence of FrontPage server extensions on both your computer (where you installed FrontPage for design purposes) and on the Web host's server. Check with your Web host to make sure they support FrontPage server extensions. If they don't, either request that they do or find another host. You need them in order for your FrontPage-designed pages, with all their FrontPage-specific code, to appear and function properly in the browser.

notes

* Have your server access information ready before you start the publishing process. Gathering this information ahead of time (and making sure it's accurate) will save you much time and aggravation. You won't have to stop halfway through or find out later that you don't have the right password to connect to the server.

* Clicking Yes saves all your pages locally first and then uploads the latest versions. Clicking No uploads the versions of your pages prior to saving changes in any open files.

* Choosing Yes when you have unsaved pages opens the Save As dialog box for each unsaved page. You have to save each page first before you can return to uploading the pages to the Web server.

1. Choose File ⇨ Publish Site to open the Remote Web Site Properties dialog box (see Figure 252-1).

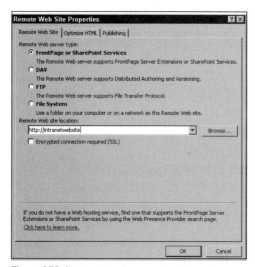

Figure 252-1: Choosing the type of Web server you are publishing to

2. Choose the remote Web server type that matches your Web server and click OK. A two-sided window appears (see Figure 252-2), showing the pages and folders on your local site as well as the remote site.

3. Click the Publish Web Site button in the lower-right corner.

4. If a prompt asks whether or not to upload modified pages, click Yes or No depending on your situation.

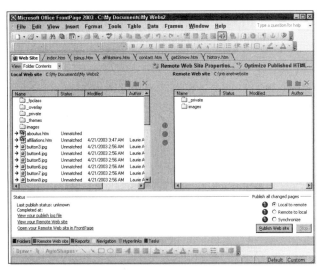

Figure 252-2: Seeing the Web pages and folders on both the local site (on your computer) and the remote site (the Web server)

5. Observe the Status area of the window (see Figure 252-3). When the uploading finishes, you'll see what was uploaded and when.

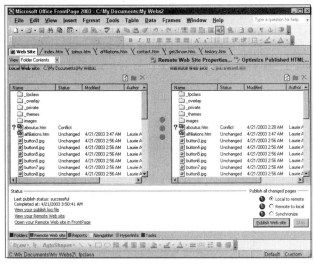

Figure 252-3: All folders and pages that make your site run locally should now be on the remote server so that the site runs on the Web.

tips

- Before publishing your site to the Web, preview it locally in your browser. Choose File ➪ Preview in Browser and repeat this process for at least three or four of the browsers listed in the submenu, including Internet Explorer and Netscape in several of their common versions.

- Depending on which server type you select, a dialog box appears asking for information regarding the Web server itself: physical location, name, and any information required for you to access it — such as your login ID and password.

cross-reference

- Appendix F covers many issues and techniques involved in publishing a site to the Web. Read it online at www.wiley .com/compbooks/ 10simplestepsorless.

Index

Symbols

/ (forward slash), directories, 89
<!- and -> comment tags
    HomeSite, 356–357
    introduction, 109
< (less than) symbol in tags, 2
> (greater than) symbol in tags, 2

A

`<a>` tags
    document location, 93
    `href` attribute, 86
    links, 86–87
absolute pathnames, 88
absolute positions, 214–215
absolute scale, fonts, 30
`accesskey` attribute, form
    controls, 138–139
Add a Project Folder dialog box
    (HomeSite), 349
Add All Subfolders option
    (HomeSite), File Types drop-
    down list, 346
addresses (e-mail), hiding from
    spammers, 230–231
`align` attribute
    heading tags, 24–25
    paragraphs, 27
    tables, 102–103
alignment
    banners in FrontPage, 505
    CSS and, 27
    headings, 24
    horizontal rules (HomeSite), 370
    images, 64–65
    images in BBEdit, 309
    images in Dreamweaver MX,
        426–427
    inline frames, 158–159
    line spacing and, 184–185
    table elements, 102–103
    tables in BBEdit, 310
    text (CSS), 190–191
    vertical (CSS), 184–185
alphabetical ordered lists, 48
`alt` attribute
    BBEdit, 308
    `<img>` tag, 62

alternative text (FrontPage),
    494–495
7am news ticker, 242–243
Amazon.com associates, 246–247
Anchor dialog box (BBEdit), 305
anchor tags, links, 86–87
anchors, named in links, 92–93
`<applet>` tags, applet embedding,
    82–83
applets (Java)
    downloading, 82
    embedding, 82–83
Arabic numeral lists, 48
`arc` attribute, `<img>` tags, 63
arguments (JavaScript),
    definition, 226
Assets panel (Dreamweaver MX),
    464–465
associates with Amazon.com,
    246–247
asterisk, Document Selector
    filenames, 274
attributes
    `accesskey`, 138–139
    `align`, 102–103
    BBEdit list items, 307
    `bgcolor`, 18–19
    `border`, 98–99
    `bordercolor`, 98–99
    `cellpadding`, 98–99
    `cellspacing`, 98–99
    `checked` (check boxes), 122
    `checked` (radio buttons), 124
    `class`, 168–169
    `cols`, 146–147
    `colspan`, 100–101
    displaying in BBEdit, 303
    equal sign in values, 3
    `face`, 28
    `frameborder`, 148
    `height`, 104–105
    `href`, 86–87
    `href`, `mailto:` and, 90
    `hspace`, `<img>` tags and, 64
    inserting with HomeSite,
        356–357
    `leftmargin`, 44
    `marginheight`, 150–151
    `marginwidth`, 150–151

`maxlength` in password fields,
    118–119
`maxlength` in text fields, 116
`name`, check boxes and, 123
`name`, pop-up lists and, 126–127
`name`, property/value pair and, 8
`name`, radio buttons and, 124
`name`, value pairs and, 116
`order`, 229
previewing, HomeSite Browse
    tab, 356–357
as properties, 3
property/value pair, 8
quotation marks in values, 3
`rel`, 167
`rows`, 146–147
`rowspan`, 100–101
scrolling, 151
`selected`, in pop-up lists,
    126–127
`size`, in password fields, 118–119
`size`, in text fields, 116
`start`, 50–51
`tabindex`, 138–139
tags, 3
`target`, 154–155
`topmargin`, 44
`type`, check boxes and, 122–123
`type`, radio buttons and, 124
`type`, text fields and, 116
`valign`, 103
`value`, check boxes and,
    122–123
`value`, password fields and,
    118–119
`value`, pop-up lists and,
    126–127
`value`, radio buttons and, 124
`width`, 104–105
`wrap`, 120
audio files. *See also* sound
    delaying play, 76
    downloading, 77
    embedding, 76–77
    .mid, 76
    .mp3 format, 76
    .ra format, 76
    .wav format, 76